Life in a Jar

THE IRENA SENDLER PROJECT

Life in a Jar

The Irena Sendler Project

by Jack Mayer

Based on the True Story of Irena Sendler,
a Holocaust Hero, and the Kansas Teens
Who "Rescued the Rescuer"

LONG TRAIL PRESS
MIDDLEBURY, VERMONT

Life in a Jar: The Irena Sendler Project
Second Edition, March 2011
(First Edition published June 2010)

Text copyright © 2011 by Jack Mayer
Author photo by Chip Mayer
Design by Winslow Colwell/WColwell Design

Published in the United States by Long Trail Press
PO Box 1227
Middlebury, VT 05753
www.longtrailpress.com

The text of this publication was set in Quadraat.

ISBN 978-0-9841113-1-2

Library of Congress Control Number: 2010903215

TABLE OF CONTENTS

AUTHOR'S NOTE

Life in a Jar: The Irena Sendler Project is a work of creative non-fiction based on these primary and secondary sources:

- Interviews with Irena Sendler, other rescuers, child survivors, and Polish academics, as well as the educator responsible for this project, Norm Conard, and his remarkable students, Megan (Stewart) Felt, Elizabeth Cambers-Hutton, Sabrina Coons-Murphy, Jessica Shelton-Ripper, and other students involved in *Life in a Jar.*

- *Matka Dzieci Holocaustu: Historia Ireny Sendlerowej*, (Muza SA, Warsaw, 2004), a book of Irena Sendler's life by Anna Mieszkowska and Janina Zgrzembska with Irena Sendler.

- Articles written by Irena Sendler.

- References to Irena Sendler's history in scholarly works about the Warsaw ghetto.

An extensive research bibliography is appended.

★   ★   ★   ★   ★   ★   ★   ★   ★   ★

Imagined dialogue is based on research and interviews. In Part II, dealing with wartime Poland, I have given names to several individuals who played a role in this history but were not named. Prof. Pikatowski, "Pika": Irena Sendler's secondary school teacher is never named, however the events of Irena's childhood and experiences at the University of Warsaw are all true. Schmuel, the Jewish ghetto policeman: Irena never names the Jewish policeman who helped her. Adam, the Jewish ghetto fighter and "brother" of Eva Rechtman: To my knowledge, Eva Rechtman did not have a brother who was a ghetto fighter, but Irena did work closely with the Jewish underground. Some German officials' names are fictional, though their stories are true. In Parts I and III, some characters are given fictitious names: Mr. Kayhart, social studies teacher at Uniontown High School, and several students.

For the Unsung Heroes

"Sometimes our light goes out, but is blown again
into instant flame by an encounter with another human being.
Each of us owes the deepest thanks to those
who have rekindled this inner light."

- ALBERT SCHWEITZER

The Warsaw Ghetto
November 16, 1940 – May 16, 1943

THE WARSAW GHETTO

 = Main Gates to the ghetto

= Area of ghetto remaining after liquidation
of ghetto, September 1942

PART ONE

Kansas, September 1999 – February 2000

CHAPTER 1

A Chip on Her Shoulder

Kansas, 1999

Liz pressed her forehead against the jet window, staring hard at the sun just pricking the ocean's black edge. The night had been interminable, a restless vigilance droning with the jet engine hum. The plane banked gently right, the horizon tilted left, a weird sensation. She wished the boundless boredom of the flight would resume, instead of tilting and dropping into something unknowable, something strange, something bold. When this all began, when she read that first tantalizing paragraph about Irena Sendler in U.S. *News & World Report* eighteen months ago, who but a crazy person could ever have imagined Liz Cambers sitting at this window, on this 747, flying across an ocean, to Europe, to Poland, to Warsaw.

What seemed unthinkable when she was fourteen, an extra-curricular National History Day project, certainly not something she would volunteer for, was now as real and consequential as the tilted sunrise. Though grandparents, teachers, friends, and relatives could not hide their astonishment, no one was more bewildered than Liz. It was just as inconceivable that Liz would be traveling with her classmate, Megan Stewart, as different from her as moonlight from sunlight, with whom she shared only a graduation year. Across the aisle, Megan's dark head tipped in sleep, her thick hair disarrayed across her face. Liz had no doubt that if she could time travel forward and read Megan's yearbook caption, under her confident moon face, she would see a long list of credits, clubs, and accomplishments ending with, "Valedictorian, Class of 2003. Most Likely to Succeed." And under Liz's awkward yearbook smile? – the generic, yet ominous salutation for losers – "Good Luck!"

Turning back to the window, Liz finger-brushed her short blond hair and, against her will, thought of that troublesome new word in her vocabulary – *legacy*. She was startled to discover that a word could weigh so much.

Legacy. Their Social Studies teacher and National History Day advisor, Mr. Conard, had said Irena Sendler's legacy was in their hands. What had begun a year and a half earlier as a simple National History Day (NHD) project had taken on a life of its own as *The Irena Sendler Project*. They had presented *Life in a Jar* at State History Day (Abilene, Kansas) and National History Day (College Park, Maryland) events. But it didn't end there, as every other NHD project ended. They had already performed *Life in a Jar* for the Jewish Foundation for the Righteous in New York City, for the Kansas Board of Education, and for several synagogues in Kansas City.

Life in a Jar – a simple, some would say naïve, play – depicted Irena Sendler knocking on Jewish doors, asking mothers in the Warsaw ghetto to give up their babies and children to save them. Uncovering Sendler's lost story felt compelling to Liz, frightening and curious, something horrible from which she could not look away. Mothers giving up their children.

For Liz, the word *legacy* carried a very different meaning – more personal, less heroic. Liz's mother had given up a child – she had given up Liz when she was five. Liz stared hard at the brightening horizon and worried about her personal legacy, a curse carrying the weight of genetic inevitability, passed from mother to daughter like an incurable disease.

She felt the engine thrum ease off and her ears clogged with the pressure of descent. The sun lit the ocean sufficiently for Liz to make out the wake of a ship. She loosened her seat belt, reclined in this unfriendly seat, and felt "the grumps" take down her pensive mood. She closed the window shade, which only emphasized how she was jammed into this flying tin can, how she could not escape these thoughts that made her heart beat fast and hard. Even with her eyes closed she stared into memories that would not let go.

★   ★   ★   ★   ★   ★   ★   ★   ★   ★

It happened when Liz was five, one evening during dinner in the run-down kitchen of a West Kansas farmhouse where prairie winds blew dust and cold through clapboard walls. Liz and her mother had lived in too many places to count. At least at the farm Liz had her own room. The farm was owned and operated by two aging brothers. She remembered yet another argument between her mother and her mother's current boyfriend. Liz was at the table trying to chew a tough chunk of meat – one that the boyfriend, (maybe his name was Reggie?) insisted she swallow. Liz thought it was just normal misery to hear her mother fighting – now she knew it was the drugs and the booze. But this was the last fight. Her mother bolted from the table, knocked over her chair, and crashed out the screen door. Moments later Liz heard the cranking of a tired, old engine that suddenly roared to life. She slid off her chair and ran to the door just in time to see her mother in Reggie's old Buick, tires spinning, spitting dirt as if pursued by the devil himself. It was the last time Liz saw her. She never said good-bye. Liz watched her mother's dust cloud fleeing over the rolling hills until it was finally indistinguishable from the horizon.

She remembered that moment as clearly as a photograph, but everything else about that time blurred – muddied memory whose stain she could neither define nor erase. A friendly social worker took her into state's custody and determined that her father was unfit to care for her, but her father's father, Grandpa Bill, and his wife, Phyllis, were "willing to give it a try," and they adopted Liz. It wasn't easy; they were one generation removed from parenting. Still, they tried their best, but the damage had been done.

As she grew older, Liz kept her blond hair bobbed short, so there would be no mistaking her for the long-haired blond woman in the two Polaroids she kept in a shoe box in the bottom of her closet, a box she never opened. Over the years she heard repeated fragments of family conversation – words like "drugs and prostitution" – slips of the tongue, which gradually evolved into the story of her mother's tragedy. But what made her feel marked was something much deeper. She thought that Grandpa Bill must have been coached by the psychologists or the social workers. Every chance he got, he repeated his practiced answer to her oft-repeated question, "It's not that she didn't love you, honey, she just couldn't take care of you. It wasn't your fault."

Though Liz's father lived nearby, he rarely visited, and the few times he did Liz thought he was afraid of her and always seemed anxious to leave, as if she carried some contamination or disease. He sent her a birthday and Christmas card every year, though last year her birthday card was two weeks late. There were counselors and social workers who talked and talked and talked at her about being abandoned, about her anger, her confusion, her shame, her grief. Mostly she listened to each therapist for the required 50 minutes and left bloated with roiling, nameless feelings that ruled her.

⋆　⋆　⋆　⋆　⋆　⋆　⋆　⋆　⋆　⋆

Grandpa Bill was a big man, over six feet and stout, but solid, with brown tinted sunglasses and a big head. He usually wore a baseball cap that advertised "The Fort" from his work driving a tour bus around historic Fort Scott. Grandpa Bill, Grandma Phyllis, and Liz lived in a modest house in Mapleton, a farming community of less than a hundred in Southeastern Kansas.

Liz was a handful at home and sure to the predictions of the therapists, she had problems in school. She couldn't sit still, didn't pay attention, refused to do anything she didn't want to, and was often in fights. In one way or another, every year's teacher observed that Liz had an attitude. She had a tendency to swear, which Grandpa Bill reminded her was not very Methodist-like. There were school counselors who tried to break through to Liz, and others who gave up on her. In 6th grade, with Liz sitting in the same room, the counselor told Grandpa Bill that her anger wasn't surprising, given her history. Big Bill looked at Liz and sighed – a sigh that said to her, "I love you, but I'm tired."

Driving home he had asked rhetorically, why was she so difficult? After a few minutes Liz answered with her own question. "Why did she leave me?"

"I guess in the long run it doesn't make a heck o'difference," he said. "You were only five, honey, and your Mom and Dad had lots of problems. Your Dad still does. And God only knows where your Mom is, if she's alive."

Liz could see it did make a "heck o'difference" to Grandpa Bill, how he turned away all choked up. And it sure as hell made a "heck o'difference" to Liz, but she never cried about it; she hid all her questions in a dark, quiet spot, where they festered.

One thing Liz did exceptionally well was play the alto saxophone – first chair in the Uniontown football and concert band. She hated rap and hip-hop, loved jazz and the blues, and she knew Duke Ellington, John Coltrane, and Charlie Parker, musical taste that set her apart from her bandmates, which suited her just fine. When Liz had a bad day, and she had lots of them, she retreated to her room, pulled down the window shades and took out her sax. She stood in front of the full length mirror behind her door, put on her sunglasses, turned her reading lamp on high and aimed it into her face – close enough to feel its heat – a spotlight in a smoky Kansas City jazz bar. And Liz wailed.

★   ★   ★   ★   ★   ★   ★   ★   ★   ★

High school did not begin auspiciously for Liz Cambers. Distress came on her first day when she learned that this year she was again assigned to Mr. Kayhart's Social Studies class. Last year at a parent-teacher conference, Mr. Kayhart told Grandpa Bill, "Liz has a chip on her shoulder the size of Kansas."

Most teachers had problems with Liz, but they at least put on a façade of understanding or tried to reach past her defiant carapace. But not Mr. Kayhart. As far as Liz was concerned, he was one of the most disturbing teachers she ever had – one she could neither ignore, nor make peace with. Grandpa Bill said they just had "bad chemistry" and Liz should learn to "buck up." But Liz didn't often do as she was told, and on the second day of classes she pleaded with Mr. Conard to transfer into his 4th period Creative Social Studies class.

"It's Mr. C. and my class is hard work," he said. "Can you do it, Elizabeth?"

"It's Liz. I don't like Elizabeth. And, yeah, I can do the work." Technically it wasn't a lie, but she crossed her fingers behind her back. "And besides, if I have to spend another year with Mr. Kayhart, I will freak out. I'll explode." She figured he'd say no; he must have heard all eight years of stories from other teachers, and he wouldn't want a troublemaker like Liz in his class.

He looked Liz in the eye, discomforting her, and then nodded, more in contemplation than assent. "Liz," he finally said. "My class is not just another class. It's called Creative Social Studies for a good reason. I expect a lot from every student. It's voluntary, but I urge everyone to consider a National History Day project. There's after-school work and research. It's a commitment. Are you up for that?"

How corny, Liz thought. Every teacher must think his class was the most important in the whole world. "Oh, yeah. No problem."

To everyone's satisfaction the change was made that day, and Liz settled into the back row of Room 104. The classroom was larger than most in Uniontown High School, airy and expansive, with murals on the walls and kids always hanging around, talking about history projects. A windowless, soundproof video room in the back was equipped with three VCRs, a camcorder, film and slide projectors, screens, and an array of videotapes of past National History Day projects – over 40 of them. Plaques from competition winners covered the classroom's Wall of Fame.

On that first day Mr. C. talked about National History Day and some of the diversity and tolerance projects that students in his class had created. One of the most dramatic was a project in which the students arranged for the reunion of Elizabeth Eckford, one of the "Little Rock Nine," the nine African-American students who integrated Little Rock High School in 1957, with Ken Reinhardt, one of the few whites at the school to befriend them. His mission as an educator, he expounded, was to teach respect and understanding of all people, regardless of race, religion, or creed, through unsung heroes projects, documentaries and exhibits, and project-based learning. By 1999, after 11 years teaching at Uniontown, his students had produced over 40 National History Day projects, many of which dealt with the civil rights struggle, the Depression, issues of respect for diversity and tolerance, and multiculturalism.

"My expectation," he continued, "is for these history projects to make a difference in your lives, teach you research skills, and encourage you to collaborate, using primary resources. My hope is that you'll understand

6

the power of one person to make a difference in history – and that one person can be you."

Liz slouched in the back row, unable and unwilling to take his words seriously, mystified by the class motto that hung over the blackboard:

"Who changes one person, changes the world whole."
– The Jewish Talmud

CHAPTER 2

Picking Rock

Kansas, 1999

It was Thursday, September 23rd (a date whose coincidence would later haunt the project) when National History Day 2000 came up in class. Mr. C. seemed to look right at Liz when he said, "The theme this year is 'Turning Points in History.' You never know where this can go." He pointed to the Wall of Fame. "Half a million kids across the country participate. Kids like you, from little 'ole Uniontown High, have won District, State, even National championships." He read aloud the names of those few with gold leaf National certificates. "National History Day is like varsity basketball of the mind. Maybe someday you'll be on that wall."

Not likely, Liz thought, her head tipped against the back wall, eyes closed.

The students broke up into small groups, each with a NHD file. Liz picked one labeled "NHD – *Ideas* – 1995." She thumbed through it without much interest or attention until she turned to an article torn from a magazine she didn't know, *U.S. News and World Report*, March 21, 1994, *The Other Schindlers*. A few paragraphs had been circled in red magic marker:

POLAND: IRENA SENDLER, SOCIAL WORKER

She gave nearly 2,500 children new identities, and buried their real names for safekeeping.

When Hitler built the Warsaw Ghetto in 1940 and herded 500,000 Polish Jews behind its walls to await liquidation, most Polish gentiles turned their backs or applauded. Not Irena Sendler. A Warsaw social worker, Sendler wangled a permit to enter the teeming ghetto and check for signs of typhus, something the Nazis feared would spread beyond the ghetto.

Shocked by what she saw, Sendler joined ZEGOTA, a tiny underground cell dedicated to helping Jews, and took on the code name "Jolanta." The deportations had already begun, and although it was impossible to save adults, Sendler began smuggling children out in an ambulance. "Can you guarantee they will live?" Sendler recalls the distraught parents asking. But she could only guarantee they would die if they stayed. "In my dreams," she says, "I still hear the cries when they left their parents."

Sendler successfully smuggled almost 2,500 Jewish children to safety and gave them temporary new identities. To remember who was who, she wrote the real names on sheets of paper, burying them in bottles in her garden. Finding Christians to hide them was not easy: "There weren't many Poles who wanted to help Jews, [even] children." But Sendler organized a network of families and convents ready to give sanctuary. "I would write, 'I have clothing for the convent'; a nun would come and pick up children."

Liz read the short piece a few times then brought it to the front desk. "Mr. C.? Is this lady, like, famous?"

He read the page and shrugged. "No, Liz, she's not famous. I never heard of her. Maybe it's a typo – you know – not 2,500 kids – but 250. You could check it out."

"She's, like, an unknown person?" Liz pursed her lips. "It's a little sketchy."

"That's the point, Liz," he said. "Unsung heroes. Anyone can change the world, even you. Why don't you sleep on it. Tell me tomorrow."

She didn't just "sleep on it;" she carried Irena Sendler's story with her all day. Intrusive images of Irena Sendler, code named Jolanta, asking a mother for her baby, disturbed her long bus ride home, hijacked notes when she practiced her saxophone, and subverted Geometry proofs. How did she convince a mother to give up her child? And when the mother and child cried and cried at the last moment, what did she feel? Liz imagined Irena Sendler carrying a baby under her coat to a waiting ambulance where she gently hid it among bandages. What if the baby cried? Didn't the Nazis search cars going in and out? What if she had been caught? In her imaginings there was always a ferocious Nazi guard at the gate to the ghetto. Liz wondered if her own mother had cried when she fled, wondered if she even considered five-year-old Liz waiting at the screen door for her to return. In foster care those first nine months, Liz cried and raged, but her reservoir of grief inexorably froze into resentment. Her mother didn't weep for Liz; she would not weep for her mother, or for herself.

During dinner that night she was quiet, and Grandpa asked if she was feeling all right. It was long after midnight when she finally fell asleep.

The next day, Liz waited after class until only Mr. C. remained. "I guess I'll check out this Irena Sendler lady," she said. "But I don't know where to begin."

"Good, Liz. This won't be easy. I suggest you team up with two or three other kids and work on it as a performance piece – sort of like *Schindler's List*."

"Who?"

He pointed to Schindler's name in the article's title. "*Schindler's List*. It's the true story of a man who saved more than 1,000 Jews from death in World War II. That's why I think it's a typo. Everybody knows Schindler. Nobody knows..." He took the page from her hand.

"Irena Sendler," Liz said.

"See, Liz. You're an expert already. You know more than I do."

He suggested she team up with Megan Stewart, a bright and eager freshman who had also signed up for National History Day. Uniontown High School was small, the freshman class had only 29 students, and, for better or worse, everybody was known in one way or another. Megan Stewart was everything Liz was not. Liz had a long face, one she judged harshly in the mirror, whereas Megan's bright, ruddy-cheeked round face naturally radiated a smile even when she was serious. Liz's short blond hair, straight and fine as silk fluttered in the lightest breeze; Megan's thick dark curls, meticulously brushed, hung on her shoulders dignified and opulent as velvet drapes. In the cafeteria Liz noticed Megan said a private grace before eating.

Though Megan Stewart didn't conform to any of the convenient and conventional boxes most kids fit into, everybody seemed to like her. Liz was certain the same was not true of herself; in fact, she was pretty sure that people like Megan avoided people like her. She anticipated her polite refusal, her no thank you, or I'll wait until next year, or I think I'd rather do another project, or anybody but you Liz. And, Liz wondered – why was she doing this? What was so compelling as to cause her to do something so unexpected, so *not* Liz Cambers? And maybe now was the right time to stop. But to her amazement, when she asked Megan if she wanted to work on *The Irena Sendler Project*, she said, "Yeah. I think that would be good. I hope I can do it. I've got so many other things going on already – cheer-leading, the Fellowship of Christian Athletes, band, golf. And I just joined the Kansas Association of Youth."

Liz felt a curious relief listening to Megan's yearbook list of activities; she'd be too busy to take charge of the project. Already Liz felt a kind of protective jealousy. Still, she was glad for Megan's interest, for although she felt totally inadequate by comparison, there was no denying the magic of Megan's attractive force, her energy, her competence, her luster. And, above all, Liz feared that if she did this alone she would fail miserably.

"Can we talk at Activity period today?" Liz asked.

"Sure. Activity period."

Later that afternoon, when they were alone in Room 104, Liz felt awkward and unsure again. Working collaboratively was neither something she did, nor something she aspired to, and she didn't have a clue how to begin.

Megan carefully set down her bulging backpack. "You live in Mapleton?"

"Yeah. And you're, like, in Bronson, right?"

"Bronson it is," Megan said. "I guess compared to you I come from the big city."

Liz tried to laugh, but it came out all nervous and stupid. She gave Megan *The Other Schindlers* article. "This is all I know," Liz shrugged, "but if it's true, it's pretty amazing. Could be a typo – you know, 250 kids instead of 2,500."

Liz watched Megan's face, watched her smile wither and disappear as she read the few paragraphs once, twice, and then looked up at Liz, furrows across her forehead.

"Wow." Megan nodded thoughtfully. "That's amazing – if it's true."
Still studying Liz, she said, "They say this History Day stuff is hard work.
I hear you have to come in extra and stay late."

Liz thought Megan looked at her in a queer way, checking her out,
testing her to see if she was for real, if she was reliable. "Yeah," Liz said.
"I heard that, too."

★   ★   ★   ★   ★   ★   ★   ★   ★   ★

Now that Megan had agreed, Liz had second thoughts. She felt strong
urges to abandon this Irena Sendler thing before it got too big and complicated. It was a spooky feeling – she had no trouble saying "no" to
anything else she didn't want to do – but this was different. It haunted
her, especially at night when her imagination all too easily produced the
moment when Irena Sendler knocked on a door and a Jewish mother
gave up her child – or sometimes it was a baby – to this woman she didn't
know, in order to save her. There was something singularly unnerving
about stirring up this history.

It was also difficult to stir up actual information. A web search yielded
only one hit, the Jewish Foundation for the Righteous, the JFR, an organization that helped to support non-Jewish people who rescued Jews during
the Holocaust.

During 4th period, she wondered when she should tell Mr. C. that she
wouldn't be doing NHD this year. As she gathered her books together to
leave, the original article, The Other Schindlers, fell out of a folder. Curiosity
got the better of her and instead of quitting, Liz asked Mr. C. about the
movie, Schindler's List

"It's a great movie, Liz, but it's R-rated. I can't recommend it to you."

"Is Irena Sendler in the movie?"

"No. But if you knew the story of Schindler's List you'd get a feel for what
this Irena Sendler project is all about."

Liz thought, why go through all this trouble? She started for the door.

"Liz?" He held up the JFR print-out she had left behind. "Call them,
Liz. Do it now, before you forget. Here's a phone pass."

Half an hour later she sat in the front office staring at the telephone, gathering her courage to call New York City. She asked herself again, why am I doing this? As she pushed each phone button she took a deep breath, steadied her finger, and something inside urged her on. These people in New York City – they were probably way too busy to talk to a dumb ninth grader from Kansas who wasn't really sure what happened in the "Warsaw ghetto," or even what a ghetto was for that matter, except that it was in Poland, somewhere in Europe, and it was World War Two.

Central Kansas City was called a ghetto – a dangerous place to walk at night; there were drugs and gangs and murders and a lot of poor Black people. Not a single Black person lived in the Uniontown school district, and, as far as she knew, there had never been a kid of any other color except white in the high school. Kansas City also had a lot of Jewish people, but she was pretty sure there had never been a Jewish kid in Uniontown High School either. Warsaw and Kansas City were other worlds – Jews and Blacks were other people – and until now she didn't think much about it.

"Hello. Hello. I... I'm... This is Liz... Elizabeth... Elizabeth Cambers, from Kansas. In America. I need some help with a school assignment."

Silence on the phone, then the operator said, "Just a moment. I'll connect you with Ms. Stahl's assistant."

Voice mail. What a relief! Liz let out the air she had been holding and waited for the beep. "This is Elizabeth Cambers. I'm a freshman in high school in Uniontown. I mean... in Kansas. I read a story in the U.S. News and World Report magazine about a woman who saved 2,500 kids. Her name was Irena Sendler..." She looked at her notes again. "Her code name was Jolanta – in the Warsaw ghetto. Please call me at 620-720-4090. Good-by. Oh, I mean thank you."

Liz sat back in the teachers' lounge and felt the sweat under her arms. It was so much easier to be an angry slacker who just got by. And anyway, this was never going to work.

The next day the front office secretary came into Liz's Geometry class and motioned for her to come into the hall. The secretary reassured her that this time she was not in trouble. It was a phone call – from New York City. Liz took the call in the front office under the secretary's scrutiny.

"Hello? Yes, this is Elizabeth – I mean, Liz."

"I'm Stanlee Stahl's assistant from The Jewish Foundation for the

Righteous. You called about Irena Sendler?"

"Yeah. The lady who rescued all those Jewish kids."

"How can I help you?"

Liz grabbed a piece of scrap paper from the garbage and a pencil in need of sharpening. "Yeah. I, like, I just wanted to know if it was true. Like, did she really rescue 2,500 kids or is that a mistake?"

"Mistake? No, no. It's true. She helped smuggle more than 2,500 Jewish children out of the Warsaw ghetto and saved their lives. It's an amazing story. She's recognized by *Yad Vashem*. Do you know what *Yad Vashem* is?"

"No, ma'am, I surely do not."

"It's a Holocaust memorial in Israel. *Yad Vashem* is Hebrew for 'Memory of a Name.' They recognize righteous Gentiles – non-Jews who risked their lives to rescue Jews during World War II – during the Holocaust. This woman you're looking for – this Irena Sendler is one of those heroes. In 1965 Irena Sendler was recognized by *Yad Vashem* as 'Righteous Among the Nations.' An olive tree was planted in Israel in her honor in 1983."

"So it's, like, really true? And why did she do that – I mean rescue all those kids?"

"The children would have been killed along with their parents. Almost everyone in the Warsaw ghetto was killed by the Nazis during the war. This woman...." Liz heard the rustle of papers during a long pause. "She convinced parents to give up their children so she could smuggle them out of the ghetto and place them in foster homes and convents. Are you studying the Holocaust in school?"

"Sort of. It's a history project. Could you send me some stuff about her?"

"We could send you material about other rescuers as well."

"Yeah, that would be great. But I really need the stuff on Irena Sendler."

After Liz hung up, a storm of questions came to her, questions she wished she had asked the New York City lady. How could someone so courageous, so good, not be known? How did she actually get the kids out? How dangerous was it? What if she was caught? When did she die? Why did she do it? Then even more disturbing questions – questions the New York City lady could not have answered. What must it have felt like for the kids? For their parents? If Liz had been in Warsaw would she have had Irena Sendler's courage? Would she have given up her child? One thing Liz knew with certainty; Irena Sendler's heroism was as remarkable as her own mother's cowardice was unforgivable.

$$\star \quad \star \quad \star \quad \star \quad \star \quad \star \quad \star \quad \star \quad \star \quad \star$$

A few days later a package from The Jewish Foundation for the Righteous arrived describing the exploits of many Holocaust rescuers, including a brief article about Irena Sendler's heroism, with more specific stories of babies smuggled out of the ghetto in carpenters' boxes, coffins, and ambulances, of children led to safety through a courthouse, through a church, through a hole in the wall. There was also a list of Holocaust survivors in the Kansas City area willing to speak with students and tell their stories. Liz gave the article to Megan before Geometry, and, though she knew she shouldn't, Megan read it surreptitiously on her lap during class. She didn't raise her hand once, and as she was leaving, her teacher asked if she was feeling ill.

Megan thought she'd just skim the material Liz gave her but found herself compelled by each detail that morphed in her imagination into a dramatic scene for their NHD project. She couldn't help thinking that her mother, Debra Stewart, was similar in many ways to Irena Sendler, not in deeds, but in character, both unassuming and humble women who did so much good with tireless energy and humility. They even looked a bit alike based on the one photograph they had of 29-year-old Irena in wartime Warsaw.

Megan couldn't stop thinking about the project, but she also found herself preoccupied with the strange bond forming between herself and Liz, almost against her will, as if something larger than either of them was at work, something disturbingly out of her control. There was no rhyme or reason for it – they couldn't be more different – and Liz had a reputation; she could be difficult. Megan's pastor at the Assembly of God Church would counsel, "What would Jesus do?" or sermonize to the Youth Group about "the finger of God pushing you to follow His path, however strange or unlikely – however incomprehensible."

In spite of her concerns about working with Liz, Megan felt something compelling about her as well. Everyone knew how Liz had been raised by her grandparents, and Megan felt a sisterly respect for what Liz had overcome. She couldn't imagine life without her own mother. There but for the grace of God, Megan thought, and that helped as well.

She tried to model herself on her mother, a slender farmwife, a rural woman with urban poise, who kept the farm's books, did the shopping, cooking, and cleaning, and attended to her responsibilities at the Assembly of God Church. Megan felt the glow of satisfaction and reassurance when the ladies of the church told her mother, "Megan is the apple of your eye," and "the acorn does not fall far from the tree."

She kept her room in the same impeccable order as her mother kept the farmhouse, bed made each day, her desk orderly and cleared, shoes paired, clothes lined up neatly in her closet. Grownups agreed that she was a "good kid" – she didn't hang out or waste time. Though she was frequently late and always bemoaned how much she had to do, her life was full and it didn't bother her too much that she had little extra time to be with friends.

NHD was not the only new preoccupation in Megan's life – nor was it the most emotionally intense. A few weeks earlier, she had met Kenny, and her life, usually a challenging but predictable whirlwind, suddenly felt more like a Kansas tornado. In the first week of school, during band tryouts, Kenny Felt, a junior who played trumpet, golf, and basketball, talked with her after school for over half an hour. Megan was embarrassed, but she told her mother they made "goo-goo eyes at each other." She'd never felt like this before, and suddenly Heaven didn't seem so unknowable. Kenny asked her out on a first date just a few hours before Liz approached her about *The Irena Sendler Project*.

Every weekend Megan put on her field clothes and did farm chores with her taciturn father, Mark, and her 10-year-old brother, Travis, equally shy (or, as her father said, "reserved") like so many Kansas men. Autumn, after the last hay cut, after the wheat was harvested and the fields were plowed, was rock season. It seemed to Megan that their farm produced more rocks than crops, and one of her chores was to drive the beat-up Toyota pickup into the fields and "pick rock." The first stones fell with sharp, metallic distinction onto the truck bed – clanging, disturbing – but as the pile grew and the Toyota sagged on its springs, the sound became a dull, repetitive, soothing balm.

She calculated that at an average of 500 rocks per load, two to three loads on a good day, she had picked more than 100,000 rocks out of the fields in her life. Unlike other farm chores, "picking rock" was strangely relaxing, though her muscles ached in the evening. Rocks didn't talk back, rocks didn't need you to be on time, rocks were predictable, and there was no standard of excellence when it came to picking them, as there was with everything else Megan did. "Picking rock" was a good time to put things in perspective, to try to keep the busy-ness of her life organized. It was a good time to think about Jesus and her family; it was a good time to pray. Menial labor, her pastor had sermonized, was a humble time to meditate on her relationship with Jesus and God. "Make something of the gift of your life," he encouraged the Youth Group. But, truth be told, in the heat of Indian summer it was Kenny who occupied the largest portion of her thoughts, and when she wasn't thinking of Kenny, she wondered about Irena Sendler.

Megan spent her study-hall period in the library reading and rereading Irena Sendler's story. At times she felt the hair on her arms raise, as if ghosts drifted by. This tiny woman – she was supposedly less than five feet tall – this dead hero, exerted a power over her and maybe Liz too – a force from the grave.

She met up with Liz coming out of Room 104, and they joined the tidal surge of students between classes. Her mind raced, and she spoke quickly, mindful of the short time. "This lady, this Irena Sendler, was tiny and she was so organized. She had this whole network of rescuers. She kept all the kids' names written down and hidden from the Nazis in glass jars. And she buried the jars under an apple tree. She fooled the Nazis every day by sneaking in and out of the ghetto. She had a code name, 'Jolanta' (Megan pronounced it with a hard J). How cool is that?"

"Yeah," Liz said. "It's pretty cool. Listen, I've been thinking that one scene in the play should definitely be when she tries to get parents to give up their kids and..."

"This is awesome," Megan went on as if Liz hadn't said a thing. "We could have a scene in the ghetto where a German soldier threatens her and she keeps on rescuing kids. And a scene with a foster family that takes in a kid. I wonder when she died?"

"What about my idea?"

"Yeah. It's good. It's good," Megan said, but she was thinking of two or three other scenes at once. "Hey, you know Sabrina Coons?"

"The new kid? Yeah. She's in my 4th period Social Studies. Why?"

"Mr. C. stopped me in the hall yesterday. She signed up for History Day and he thought she should join our group. She's a junior – just moved here from somewhere – Oklahoma, I think. Her Dad's, like, in the army or something. I met her and she seems really nice. A little geeky and quiet, but nice. I think she's real smart. I told her to meet us tomorrow after school."

"Wait a minute," Liz protested. "I didn't say I wanted her in my group. It's my project, you know. I found it first."

Megan sighed. "I thought we were in this together." (What would Jesus do?)

"Yeah, I guess. But I wish someone had asked me."

"OK. I'm asking you." (There but for the grace of God.)

Liz started to walk away.

"Tomorrow after school?" Megan called after her.

"Yeah. Whatever."

★ ★ ★ ★ ★ ★ ★ ★ ★

That night Liz asked Grandpa Bill about the Warsaw ghetto and the war, and he said he was just a kid, but he remembered horrible stories from the grownups. He said it was an awful time and "this business with the Jews, that was the worst of it. People just went crazy."

She told him about Irena Sendler's story being like *Schindler's List* and asked him if he would allow her to watch it, even though it was R-rated. He thought about it and said, "If it's for a school project, I guess so." Would he watch with her? "No," he said. "I don't like those kinds of movies."

Liz's first surprise was that the movie was in black and white, immediately old, curiously authentic, completely out of the ordinary. At the end, when the people Oskar Schindler rescued and their children walked past his grave to leave a reverential stone on his headstone, Liz found herself weeping – something she didn't do.

CHAPTER 3

The Irena Sendler Project
Kansas, 1999

Liz and Megan were due to meet in Room 104 after school, their first with Sabrina, the new girl. The meeting had been rescheduled because of Sabrina's three-day absence. She came in late, a head taller than Megan or Liz, mumbling a bashful apology. Megan was unsure whether she was unable or unwilling to make eye contact. Sabrina's black-rimmed glasses – Megan couldn't decide if they were very cool or just cheap and geeky – cut a chord across her almond face. Her shoulders drooped under a hooded blue sweatshirt zippered up, ready to leave. Ungainly, she dropped her lanky body onto the seat of a student desk next to Megan and rooted about her backpack. She found her project journal, then sat completely still, her Bic pen poised over a blank page, the kinetic opposite of Liz. Her face was pale and impassive, frozen as if she waited for the open lens of an old-fashioned box camera. She's scared, Megan thought. Probably wants people to look right through her.

Megan and Sabrina both lived in Bronson, Kansas, a town of only a few hundred souls. Though Sabrina had only just moved in, everyone knew that she was a military kid and that she had a dark-skinned sister in the 7th grade. Megan sized her up as the "artsy" type – jeans and scuffed tennis shoes, neither fashionably new nor grungy in a cool way – geeky, like her glasses. When she saw Sabrina in the cafeteria, Megan was sorely tempted to try to make her feel at home or at least accepted. Pastor Williamson at her Sunday School often preached compassion for the stranger. Here was an opportunity to live her creed, but she couldn't muster her courage.

"Were you sick or something?" Megan asked.

"Mom was sick, but she's OK now." Sabrina smiled in a way that

Megan knew meant she was not OK and did not want to talk about it. "I had to help out with the house and the kids."

"Did you read the stuff I gave you?" Liz asked brusquely.

Sabrina nodded. "Yeah. It's pretty amazing. Are the numbers right? I mean, magazines make mistakes."

"We checked it out," Liz said. "It's true."

Sabrina had said there were six of them, and technically it was true, though only her Mom and younger sister, Sarah, currently lived together in Bronson. Her four older siblings and her father were still in Oklahoma. As a military family they had moved frequently – three new schools in four years – but the move to Uniontown High School was particularly stressful. From an early age, Sabrina had learned that if she kept a low profile, didn't share personal information, and smiled as if everything was all right, then people assumed it was, and they didn't ask questions. But those were big schools – at Uniontown, with only 120 students in six grades, it was impossible to disappear. Sabrina suspected that by now the gossip mill had informed everyone that her family was poor and that she had a "colored" sister. She had learned enough about Bourbon County to know that being poor was no big deal – being "colored" was.

She wouldn't have volunteered for a NHD project if Mr. C. had not specifically asked her to help two freshmen who were onto something amazing but needed an older team member. She suspected that he was being part teacher, part social worker – probably felt badly for her, maybe pitied her, which bothered her even more.

After three weeks she still got lost in the corridors, another familiar humiliation. Under the best of circumstances Sabrina didn't make friends easily, friends she would all too soon leave behind. By now, she'd figured out some basics about the world and her place in it. She had to endure two more years of high school and everything that came with it, and she would just have to suck it up and deal. Sabrina Coons believed as an article of faith that if she was self-sufficient and invisible, she would be invulnerable.

She let herself be convinced to join the NHD project. Her mother, Lorinda Coons, encouraged and prodded her – said it would help her college application. Sabrina felt most secure, and most needed, at home with the business of helping her Mom and her sister, already a handful at thirteen. Sabrina was the youngest of her parents' five biological children and three years older than Sarah, who they had adopted when her father was stationed in the Marshall Islands. Though they lived in the same town, Sabrina hardly recognized Megan, but that was not too surprising. Megan's family owned the Stewart Farm, Sabrina lived in town; Megan was Assembly of God, Sabrina Mormon. And in any case Sabrina wasn't really looking for a friend. She had already found a job, which left little time to spare, at a small eatery in Bronson, *The Chicken Shack*, and saved her wages to help with the bills at home.

"What do you think, Sabrina?" Megan asked.

Sabrina nodded. "I wonder why she did this rescue business."

"Maybe it wasn't that dangerous," Liz said.

Sabrina didn't want to tell Liz she was wrong; she didn't want to stir things up, but she already knew something about the Holocaust. "I think that if the Nazis had caught her they would have killed her." She said it quietly, looking down again at the blank page on her desk. "I read that Poland was the worst. The Nazis tried to kill every Jew. I also read that the Nazis killed Poles who helped Jews – people like Irena." Now she looked up. "Would you do what she did?"

"We'll never know exactly why she did it," Megan said, "but it's way beyond just `cause it was the right thing to do. I think most everybody would say it was the right thing. But she did something. She stood up for what she believed in. She saw injustice and she did something to make it right."

"But if she was caught, her whole family would have been killed," Sabrina said quietly, but firmly. "Would you still do it if your whole family could be killed?"

Sabrina had thought about this before. Ever since reading *The Diary of Anne Frank* in 6th grade, she had been intrigued by the Holocaust, a curious, bewildering, and grim attraction. She had already answered the question for herself; she would not risk her life to save a stranger. Maybe to save her sister, or some other relative, but not a stranger. Once, when Sabrina was 12, a boy called Sarah "nigger," and Sabrina had jumped on his back and ended up with a bloody lip and a loose tooth. What baffled Sabrina was that Irena Sendler had saved complete strangers.

She wondered why the Jews stayed – why they didn't flee the Nazis. Was there no place to hide? Or more likely, they just couldn't bring themselves to leave their homes – to leave everything and run away. Maybe they knew what Sabrina knew about uprooting and going someplace strange where no one knew you, no one cared about you, a place where nothing was predictable, where it was normal for your world to turn upside down from one day to the next.

"I hope I'd have Irena's courage," Megan said. "But I really don't know. I don't suppose anybody really knows until the moment you have to make that choice. I just hope that I would be able to take a stand and do the right thing."

Liz opened her project notebook and cleared her throat to interrupt. "I was reading how, like, only one percent of regular non-Jewish Polish people did anything to help Jews. I don't know what I'd do. The right thing, I hope, but the odds are against it. I think I'd be too scared."

"I don't think I could," Sabrina said. "Not for strangers. I'd be too afraid. I really want to know why she did it."

Megan's response to Sabrina's question concealed a crack of uncertainty, as if Sabrina had thrown sand into the grinding wheel of Megan's purposeful, sometimes frenetic life – church, sports, band, clubs, homework, farm chores. In that moment, Megan worried that had she walked in Irena's shoes she might be too frightened, as Liz had suggested – a deeply unsettling thought.

Megan deflected the conversation. "I wonder if Irena has family left in Poland. Maybe they could tell us more about her. Or people she rescued who were old enough to remember. I'll bet some of them were babies and don't even know they were rescued."

Mr. C. walked into his classroom. "How's it going, ladies?"

Megan's smile grew large again and her confidence returned. "Really good. We have lots of ideas."

"Sabrina?"

Megan thought she looked uncomfortable. "There's not much to go on."

"Liz?"

"Yeah. We got, like, tons of stuff on the Holocaust. Too much. But

Irena – I mean Irena Sendler – hardly anything."

"Next week is the research trip to Kansas City," he said. "You're all going, right?" He looked hopefully at each girl. "The Midwest Center for Holocaust Education has lightning fast internet. You'll find something, guaranteed."

Liz hefted her backpack onto her desk. "I don't know. Someone told me you just, like, sit around in a library and stuff."

"I'm going." Sabrina closed her journal. "I'm really curious."

"I have a conflict," Megan said. "Cheerleading."

"Priorities, Megan." He sounded irritated.

"I know, I know," Megan said. "But Coach Riley said..."

"Your choice, Megan," he said. "Can't please everyone. Liz?"

"I guess."

"Yes or no, Liz," he said.

"Yeah, I guess." She was tempted anew to just give it up right then and there and that would be the end of it. No big deal. Then she remembered *Schindler's List* and something turned inside her. "I watched that movie – *Schindler's List*. It's a scary movie. There are some scenes – I don't know. It's an amazing story. But I got to thinking, Irena Sendler's story is even more amazing." She felt as if she had just proclaimed "Yes" to Mr. C., to Megan and Sabrina, to the project – to herself.

Mr. C. picked up his cracked leather briefcase. "You know, I've seen a lot of History Day projects. But this one feels..." He was uniquely at a loss for words. "It feels – I don't know – alive. Like it has an intelligence of its own – a life force. Every once in a while history is like that – like grabbing hold of a tiger by the tail." He nodded as if this was a revelation for himself as well. "Good night, ladies." He closed the door and left them with the custodian and the football team in the shuttered school.

Megan shuffled loose-leaf pages, and Sabrina thought she looked troubled or guilty. Liz seemed about to say something, but Megan spoke first. "Couple days ago I started to write the play."

"You what?" Liz burst out. "How could you do that? We hardly know anything about Irena!"

"Well, we have to start somewhere, with something. We can change it. I'm a firm believer in..."

"And besides, what do you know about writing plays? This dinky school doesn't even have a drama teacher. And the only stage is in the friggin' gym."

"Well, we have to start somewhere." Megan lost her smile. "We can't just talk about it. Any one of us can write a play – all we need is a really good story, and this could be one of those really good stories. I think it is."

"Or not." Liz hefted her backpack onto her shoulders.

Sabrina interrupted. "It'll be good for us to go to Kansas City – find out more about this lady. Then we can write the play – together." Sabrina surprised herself. Maybe she felt empowered to mediate by virtue of being two years older, or maybe this project was just too important to fail because of petty squabbling. As she left school, Sabrina thought the only "tiger by the tail" was Liz and Megan. Conflicts, demands, personalities, deadlines, pressures. She would have preferred working alone, and she certainly did not want to be a referee between these two. But she also knew intuitively that there were some places in her heart she should not go alone, and though the Holocaust compelled powerful feelings, it also approached a fragile and wounded place inside her. If she chose to swim in these waters, she would need help.

Despite those powerful feelings, or maybe because of them, Sabrina felt less emotionally involved in the project than Megan or Liz, and she was glad for it. Liz was reactive to and possessive of *The Irena Sendler Project* – a level of intensity that made Sabrina nervous. Megan, intense in her own way – zealous, searching, perplexed – wore her heart on her sleeve. Megan cried without shame when they looked at pictures of the ghetto. Sabrina couldn't cry for the Jews of Warsaw – she didn't know them. Their tragedy was only history, and history was chock-a-block full of tragedy, best kept at arm's length. The safest strategy was to treat National History Day like the National Science Fair. You do the project, you compete, you lose, you move on. Afterwards you don't think about it anymore.

★ ★ ★ ★ ★ ★ ★ ★ ★

When they met again a few days later, Megan announced, "Deadline for the script is Thanksgiving. Only eight weeks." Though habitually late,

Megan became the timekeeper of *The Irena Sendler Project*. Her motivation was to move it along so it wouldn't consume such a large proportion of her crazy schedule. "Too many pokers in the fire," her mother said over and over, to which Megan replied, "Just like you, Mom." Liz and Sabrina saw each other every day in 4th period class, whereas Megan had to make special time. At times she considered backing out, especially when she and Liz quarreled, but her mother would remind her that she was no quitter.

Sabrina was right, of course; they needed to know more about Irena before going ahead. In spite of Sabrina's social awkwardness, Megan felt her raw intelligence. If Sabrina weren't two years older, if Megan weren't so busy, and if it weren't for Kenny, maybe they'd have become better friends.

"I think we should set a deadline," Megan said. "Like only one or two more weeks of research – you know, books and folders and stuff. OK?"

"It's a lot of stuff." Liz sounded defeated.

Sabrina said, "Maybe we should each take one book or video then trade and talk about what we learned and what might be good in the play. I don't mind staying after school. Liz?"

"Yeah. That's cool. I don't mind, I guess."

Megan looked at her watch and gathered her books, feeling pulled in a million directions. There was still time to attend at least half of cheerleading; they were starting to cut her from new formations.

"Sabrina, is your Dad, like, unemployed?" Liz asked direct questions.

Sabrina averted her eyes again, and Megan wondered what secrets she held fast. "He was in the military," Sabrina said coolly. "He's looking for a good job. It's not easy."

CHAPTER 4

Research
Kansas, 1999

Ever since she could speak, Megan told her mother everything that went on in her life, and these last few weeks most of her excitement was about *The Irena Sendler Project*. Debra Stewart was almost as stirred up as her daughter, and when Megan mentioned how affected Liz had been by *Schindler's List*, she rented the movie from the video store.

Her mother knocked on Megan's door and let herself in. She held up the video. "I think we should watch this together," she said. "Maybe tonight – before you go on your research trip tomorrow."

Megan put aside her English assignment. No R-rated film had ever been brought into the Stewart home, and Megan wondered if her mother had not made a mistake. "Are you sure, Mom?" Megan pointed to the rating.

"Just this once, I think we should give it a try. We can always turn it off if..."

After her father went to bed at 8:30, as he did every night, the house was quiet except for the radio playing softly in the living room where her mother knitted a winter toque for her younger brother Travis. Megan turned off the radio and inserted the video cassette. She curled up on the couch beside her mother as the movie began. Before long Debra Stewart laid aside her knitting. Travis stood watching from the door to the living room for an hour before he joined them on the couch. Megan worried that her 11-year-old brother shouldn't watch this, but her mother said nothing, which amounted to tacit approval.

For three hours Megan could not take her eyes off the screen, though at several scenes she wanted to. By the end it was all a teary-eyed blur as the "Schindler Jews" and their children solemnly passed by his grave in Israel and placed a commemorative stone on his headstone. Megan and her mother had emptied the box of Kleenex; Travis cleared his throat and swallowed his tears. It was way past everyone's bedtime.

As the video rewound, Megan felt the implications of *Schindler's List* growing weightier, dramatizing a horror so complete, yet recent enough that people were still alive who had miraculously lived through it. Could the Holocaust happen again? It wasn't that long ago, and maybe this time it would be Christians like herself, instead of Jews. She ejected the video, which felt warm and alive. Her mother and Travis had already gone to bed without saying goodnight.

Until Megan saw *Schindler's List*, Irena Sendler's amazing rescue story was just that – a story to which she applied the same academic focus she dedicated to other school activities. Words worked well to insulate her from feeling the impact of the Holocaust, but this movie, these images had chilled her to the heart – a boundary had been breached, and Megan could no longer hold the Holocaust at a safe distance. She had learned enough history to accept that the human chronicle was one of greed, enslavement, and murder – the very sins Jesus came into this world to redeem. But as *Schindler's List* so painfully demonstrated, in spite of one flawed hero's efforts, without a miracle, mankind had a long road ahead before arriving at Redemption.

She needed to get to sleep – it was so late – but her imagination was agitated. She finally dozed off, though it seemed only a few moments later her alarm startled her awake at five AM. In the pre-dawn darkness she reluctantly left her bed and stumbled downstairs to breakfast with her father, who left his bed every day at five.

During the three-hour ride to Kansas City with Liz and Sabrina and a few other History Day students, Megan tried to repress the video images, restrict her thoughts to Kenny, to the church social on Wednesday evening, to "picking rocks."

★   ★   ★   ★   ★   ★   ★   ★   ★

At the Midwest Center for Holocaust Education in Kansas City each of the girls sat in front of a monitor and easily found web site after web site devoted to the Holocaust and the Warsaw ghetto. Megan scrolled through a site about rescuers, reading through fresh tears one story after another, many reminiscent of *Schindler's List*. Though her tears were for what had happened to these poor people, she couldn't help wondering about all the thousands – the millions of others to whom this happened, whose stories would never be told. And what if she had been one of those people? What if this had happened to her and her family, and she cried to think of saying good-bye to her life.

She felt a soft touch on her shoulder and startled. It was Mr. C., kneeling beside her chair asking if she was OK. She sat back and wiped her eyes with a wet handkerchief. "I'm OK – really I am." She took a deep hitching breath. "I cry easily; it's just the way I am. These stories are so horrible – so sad."

"It was a horrible and sad time," he said. "It's like wading into a sewer. But people like Oskar Schindler and Irena Sendler – they are the people we all wish we could be – ordinary people who made a big difference. And so can you. Anything you do to repair the world is heroic."

Megan clicked onto the next web page. "Here's another one – Elzbieta Ficowska." She struggled with the name she would come to know so well and read out loud, her voice thick with emotion. "She was rescued from the Warsaw ghetto as a six-month-old baby, smuggled out in a carpenter's box. Her whole family was killed in Treblinka." Megan scrolled further down and caught her breath. "Oh, my goodness. It's her! Liz! Sabrina!" She backed away from the screen, her tear-shined eyes wide. "It's her! It's Irena. This baby – Elzbieta – she was rescued by Irena Sendler." Megan wiped hard at her eyes.

Liz and Sabrina huddled behind Megan, reading Elzbieta's account of her miraculous rescue.

"You know," Sabrina said. "I was thinking. What makes Irena's story different is how much she cared who each kid was. You know, how she buried their names in a bottle under the apple tree so they would know who they were and that they were Jewish. That's important. That should be in our play."

"That's it!" Megan looked from Liz to Sabrina. "The names. She kept their families' names alive. The worst thing is to lose your name. Then your whole family dies. No one remembers you. It's like you never existed."

Sabrina pulled her chair close to Megan's. "It could be the title of our play – *Names in a Bottle.*"

Liz knelt on the carpeted floor. "How about *Life in a Bottle*?"

"No, sounds like an alcoholic," Sabrina said.

"*Names under a Tree?*"

"*Names in the ground?*"

"*Names in a Jar?*"

"*Life in a Jar?*"

"That's it!" Sabrina sat back hard. "*Life in a Jar.* The kids' names in a jar were, like, the only guarantee for their parents."

"And that helped them give up their kids," Liz said. "They thought they'd get their kids back again – like, after the war."

"Or maybe," Sabrina said, "because Irena cared about their names – who they were."

"Shhhh!" A gray-haired woman across the room hushed them.

"*Life in a Jar?*" Megan nodded her head and said it again to herself. "Yeah, that's good."

Their heads almost touched, and Sabrina whispered, "I can't even imagine what it must have been like to give up their kids."

Megan felt embarrassed for Sabrina who probably didn't know Liz's story. She said, "It's always hard," and she hoped it was true for Liz's mother as well.

"I wonder about my sister Sarah," Sabrina said. "We adopted her when she was a baby. Her Mom was only fourteen – and poor. Her family wouldn't let her come home until she got rid of Sarah. Lots of times Sarah asks me if her real Mom loved her. I say that her mother couldn't take care of her; I say she loved her so much that she gave her up. But I don't really know."

* * * * * * * * * *

The girls made several more research trips to libraries, including the Kansas State Historical Society, the Kansas Heritage Center, the Eisenhower Center, and the Midwest Center for Holocaust Education. Their specific online search for Irena Sendler had turned up only one web site, a mention of her recognition in 1965 in Israel by *Yad Vashem* as "Righteous Among the Nations," and a tree planted in her honor in Israel in 1983. They consulted dozens of books, National Archives microfilms and articles, including government studies on the Holocaust and medical treatises on typhus and typhoid fever. They talked by phone with World War II veterans and Holocaust survivors in the Kansas City area, watched documentary films, and wrote letter after letter asking people named in scholarly sources about Irena Sendler. Some had heard of her wartime heroism, some had even been saved by her network, but none knew her fate.

Using the search term "ZEGOTA," the resistance organization Irena worked with, the three girls found references that mentioned Irena as head of the Children's Division, but there were few details. They were surprised to learn that neither Irena's heroism nor ZEGOTA were celebrated or even recognized by the Communist Polish state. An internet database of cemetery records revealed nothing. All through October, two and three afternoons a week, and mornings from 6:30 until classes began at 8:15, the three young women met, answered e-mails from Holocaust survivors, shared research findings and script ideas. By now they had acquired books about rescuers and a thick folder of web print-outs.

Since the Jewish Foundation for the Righteous had been helpful before, they sent another e-mail seeking contact information for Irena Sendler. After a few days they were excited to receive a short e-mail:

> *Irena Sendler's son Adam Zgrzebski lives in Warsaw. I'm sure when he learns what you're doing he'd be happy to answer your questions. Here is his address:*

They immediately wrote Irena's son a letter, hoping he would find a translator, or maybe he spoke English. Meanwhile the research continued, and the script evolved through trial and error, arguments, and compromise. Megan thought the play should open with the German invasion of Poland. Liz wanted to get right to the story – start with a mother giving up her child. Megan thought there should be more information about the ghetto, about hunger, disease, and rationing, about the brutality of the Nazis, about ZEGOTA, about Irena's code name, *Jolanta*. The script veered off on tangents. At one particularly contentious meeting Sabrina reminded them of the theme, "Turning Points in History," and the duration, "ten minutes."

They agreed on a large backdrop – a stage flat – then went back and forth about what to paint on it – a single scene, the apple tree, or multiple images – and finally settled on a triptych of an apartment block in the ghetto, a woman leading a child by the hand through an archway, and the apple tree under which the jars were buried. Across the top of the stage flat they wrote "TIKKUN OLAM" (To Repair the World) and the same words in Hebrew on the bottom.

Since Megan and Liz played multiple roles, costumes were important. Sabrina wore a white shirt and black pants to be neutral as the narrator. Liz as Irena wore a dress and head scarf that came from the costume closet on the "stage" in the gym. Megan's Mrs. Rosner's dress came from her mother's closet – a suit she wore in the `70's and `80's, whose color and style were reminiscent of the `30's. A man in Fort Scott let them borrow the German helmet and SS uniform he had acquired. It was so large that it hung on Megan and the sleeves extended beyond her fingers.

They tried various strategies to transition from one scene to another with as few props as possible; what seemed so simple when they brainstormed in the classroom became a tangle of details on the stage. What worked the best was to think of the stage as divided in two, one side for ghetto scenes in front of the stage flat, the other for Irena's apartment, just outside the ghetto, which they represented with only a table and chair with a jar and the lists. Mrs. Rosner carried a battered old suitcase and a doll wrapped in a baby blanket.

By early November, according to their checklist, it was time to finalize the script. On a Wednesday afternoon they sat together in Room 104 at the computer.

"I'll be the typist," Sabrina said, her fingers poised on the keyboard. "I think we need to work on the Mrs. Rosner scene. It's the most important in the play. It has to be right."

"I agree," Megan said. "Mrs. Rosner wouldn't just give up her kids. She'd probably say no at first. Maybe she thought..."

"What's to think about?" Liz flushed. "They all knew they would die in that concentration camp – Treblinka. Otherwise, they never would have given up their kids."

"Maybe they thought there was a chance," Megan said. "Maybe they hoped for a miracle."

"They were being killed." Liz shouted, then clutched her forehead and closed her eyes.

"Are you OK?" Megan asked.

Liz nodded but kept her eyes closed. "A headache."

"I'm just trying to be logical," Megan said.

"Logical?" Liz glared anew at Megan, then looked to Sabrina for help.

"Turning Points in History," Megan said. "Not soap opera in Poland."

"Soap operas are impossible. This really happened."

Sabrina made a T with her hands. "Time out! I think it must have seemed impossible to them. If it was me, it would feel impossible to think that I could be killed."

"There were all sorts of rumors," Megan said. "I think people would hang onto any straw of hope. So maybe Mrs. Rosner would hope for the best. I mean you have to believe in something, not your own death, not your children's deaths, not your whole family. They had to think..."

"You're both right," Sabrina said. "It would have been hard. I think Mrs. Rosner would have refused at first, but in the end she would have realized that there was no hope. She'd have seen that there was no other choice – she had to do the unthinkable – she had to give up her kids to save them. I think that's how we should write the scene."

Liz held her head. "Whatever!"

Two hours later they had a final draft.

★   ★   ★   ★   ★   ★   ★   ★   ★   ★

Who would play Irena at NHD? The question hung unasked and unanswered.

After the script was finalized, tensions dissipated, arguments ended, and Megan commented to Liz about how "up" she seemed and how pleased she was that they were working so well together. Though Liz was glad to hear Megan say that, she still worried that Megan wanted to play Irena, something Liz desperately needed to do for herself. She had an urgent but very private reason for needing to be Irena – something she could not share with anyone. Her secret fantasy, one she could almost not allow herself, was that word would somehow get to her mother, if she was alive, about this amazing project her Lizzie was in charge of, and she'd come and see her as Irena in the play. In her feverish imaginings, Liz saw her mother sneak into the District competition. She'd find Liz afterwards and beg for her forgiveness, but Liz would turn away, glad for her suffering.

* * * * * * * * * *

By mid-November the leaves had yellowed, the orange-brown fields awaited the last plowing before snowfall, and it was time to choose roles – the Narrator, Irena, and one person would play three roles – Mrs. Rosner, the fictional mother being asked by Irena Sendler to give up her children, Marie, Irena's co-conspirator, and a Nazi soldier. In their research they had come across a family named Rosner from the Warsaw ghetto. They imagined a dramatic encounter constructed from the testimony of survivors, stitched together as a composite, a fiction illuminating the truth.

They all agreed that Sabrina had the perfect Narrator's voice, calm and authoritative.

Megan and Liz, both of whom wanted to play Irena, took turns reading her lines on the tiny stage at one end of the gym. Sabrina sat on a folding chair on the free throw line, listening to one girl, then the other.

Megan played Irena for pathos and gentle persistence, her voice choked with genuine emotion. Liz embodied a fierce Irena, a firebrand ready to stand up to anyone for her principles.

Irena: *Shhhhh! Watch what you say aloud about the Underground. We are members of this Polish clan-*

destine organization. Secrecy is vital. Remember my code name. It is Jolanta. You must not forget, and I'll remember yours. We are in a river of rage; each must jump in to save others. This will all end someday

Sabrina was quiet for a moment, then said, "I think, Megan, you should be Mrs. Rosner. You're more... I don't know... emotional. I'm thinking Mrs. Rosner would have cried and Irena must have been one tough cookie."

Megan's instinct was to avoid conflict, and she didn't want to injure Liz any more than she already was, though she would have preferred to play Irena herself. But in her heart, she knew that Sabrina's assessment was correct. "OK," she said. "I don't really care."

★   ★   ★   ★   ★   ★   ★   ★   ★   ★

The morning radio news reporter noted that it was the 36th anniversary of President Kennedy's assassination, November 22, 1999, and Megan asked her mother if she remembered that day.

Debra Stewart walked around the breakfast table serving fried eggs from a black fry pan. "I was just a little girl," she said, "but I remember it was the first time I ever saw my mother cry."

Over the scraping of the spatula Megan heard familiar reporters reading the farm weather forecast, then the commodities report from the Chicago Mercantile Exchange. "How would you feel," she asked her mother, "if you had to give me away and you thought maybe you were losing me forever?"

Her mother set the fry pan in the sink and covered her eyes with one hand. Soybean futures and pork bellies rattled from the radio. Her father pushed back from the table and excused himself.

Debra Stewart turned on the water, and the hot pan hissed.

"Mom? You didn't answer my question."

Megan wasn't sure if what she heard was the running water or the scrub brush, until her mother turned around and, for the first time in

Megan's life, she saw tears running down her mother's cheeks.

She dried her eyes with a hand towel. "Megan. Travis. I have to tell you something. I was at the hospital yesterday. I found a lump in my breast and Doc sent me for a mammogram." The water still ran behind her. "It's cancer."

CHAPTER 5

Millennium

Kansas, December 1999 – January 2000

Megan told no one except Kenny and swore him to secrecy, praying that would suffice to keep her world from shaking apart. Outside of her home there were no tears, and only a careful observer would have noticed that the blush was off Megan's cheeks, her hallmark smile slight and unnatural. During rare quiet moments at home, when she was alone with her mother, when no one talked about high school football, the price of wheat or corn, or the church social next week, Megan talked about her most recent research, about orphans, concentration camps, and Nazi brutalities – realities worse than her own, which was cold comfort.

Debra Stewart called the school nurse to ask that she keep an eye on Megan – and tell no one of her cancer except Mr. Conard. She kept up the work of the house and the farm right up to her surgery, two days before Christmas. The evening before surgery, she sat on Megan's bed and reminded her that until she was back on her feet Megan was the woman of the house. It was her responsibility to prepare breakfast for her father and brother, even on those days when she had to leave by 6:15 to drive to school for a rehearsal. Dinner was to be on the table by 6 PM so her father could watch TV in the evening and be in bed by 8:30.

Though the word cancer was rarely uttered on the Stewart farm, Megan's pastor was not reticent about the "spiritual and corporeal battle that Debra Stewart would wage against this cancer" – a struggle for healing that would summon the faith and support of the entire community. Megan's household responsibilities were eased by the coordinated bounty of casseroles and dinners often accompanied by whole families who came to visit and pray with the Stewarts.

Just before Christmas vacation, at an after-school rehearsal, Mr. C. said to Megan privately, "Your mother wanted me to know about the cancer. Are you able to continue the project? Everyone will understand if you can't."

As she was explaining, "Oh, really I'm fine. Mom will be fine. Of course I'll continue the project," she began to weep. "I'm sorry. I'm OK – really I am." It was one thing to weep about the Warsaw ghetto and the children, something she did frequently and without shame, quite another to weep for herself, which felt self-indulgent, unnecessary, weak.

Christmas break couldn't have been more timely. Before they left school for vacation, Megan circled the next History Day deadline in her NHD journal – "Scripts Memorized – after X-mas break."

★　★　★　★　★　★　★　★　★

On December 23, 1999, in a Kansas City hospital, Debra Stewart had a cancerous lump removed from her breast. The surgery went well and she was discharged on Christmas Eve, but during the two-hour ride home she began vomiting and there was nothing Megan or her father could do to help her except pray. When they finally drove into the farm's driveway, Megan went directly to her mother's closet for a fresh nightgown. There, on the closet floor, she saw a cardboard box filled with Christmas presents, wrapped and labeled in her mother's handwriting. She picked one out and read the festive tag: *"To Megan, with boundless love, your Mom and Dad."*

Megan fell to her knees, still holding the wrapped gift, her stomach aching, tears streaming down her face, her one prayer pouring out as if her own life depended on its fulfillment. "Please, dear Jesus, let Mom be completely healed."

★　★　★　★　★　★　★　★　★

Although there were six Coons children, only Sabrina and her younger sister Sarah celebrated their first Christmas in Kansas with their mother, Lorinda. The other four were still with their father in Oklahoma. There were only a few gifts under a small artificial tree decorated with tinsel. Later on Christmas Eve, they went to the Methodist church for midnight service, where Sarah fell asleep in Sabrina's lap. A spotlight illuminated the crèche on the altar, Baby Jesus without a home, lying in straw on a cold night, and it made her think of her own family wandering from place to place, nowhere really home. Nobody saw her eyes well up, and she stopped her tears before they could betray her. The pastor's voice droned, and Sabrina felt the chill of her loneliness.

First holidays in a new town were particularly difficult for Sabrina – first birthday, first Mother's Day, first Christmas, even more so this year because money was tight. Though she worked as many evening hours as possible at *The Chicken Shack*, it was never enough. She worked Christmas Eve until they closed early, and she would have stayed longer if the owner had asked. Her mother joked that Sabrina would make a fine banker; she was focused, quick with numbers, and squirreled away every penny.

★ ★ ★ ★ ★ ★ ★ ★ ★ ★

Every night before dinner, Liz and her grandparents bowed their heads as Grandma Phyllis said grace. "Bless us, Lord, and these Thy gifts, which we are about to receive, from Thy bounty, through Jesus Christ, Amen."

It was all she had saved from her Catholic upbringing. When dinner guests asked about the Catholic prayer, she said, "After my divorce the church threw me out. Only thing I kept was grace."

Liz attended the Fulton United Methodist Church in Fulton, Kansas every Sunday with Grandma Phyllis. There was no youth group to distract or attract her, and Liz's mind wandered during the sermon. Except at Christmas, Grandpa Bill didn't come along, though he said, "I do pray during hard times, especially about you, Liz."

For Liz, Christmas was "The Slam-bang, All-you-can-eat, All-American Family Holiday Get-Together." Every year the routine was the same starting with Christmas Eve service at Fulton United, then to her great-grandmother's for Christmas Eve dinner, followed by several days of family visits where gifts were exchanged, food was eaten, and football was discussed. Until this year it was always the anticipation of Christmas that kept Liz up late on Christmas Eve, but this year she tossed and turned because of *Schindler's List*, because of black-and-white photographs and documentaries of the ghetto and children, dead in the street, or worse yet, on the verge of death, their emaciated hands reaching out for bread. She gave up on sleep and picked up Mary Berg's *Warsaw Ghetto Diary*, the journal of a Jewish teenager in the ghetto, and opened to her entry for Christmas Eve, December 24, 1941:

> *Today everyone on the "Aryan" side is wearing his Sunday best. I even fancy that I can smell the odor of good food. It is Christmas Eve. One half a year ago there were rumors that by Christmas the war would be over and that on November 11th – Armistice Day – the Allied troops would march into Warsaw. True, there are foreign troops in Warsaw; whole battalions of them are marching in the street in green uniforms, but they are enemy troops who terrorize the population.*

After reading this Liz couldn't help but whisper a prayer. "Thank you, God, that I'm not in the Warsaw ghetto. Thank you for this warm bed. Thank you for Grandma and Grandpa shuffling around in the living room." She thought it wouldn't hurt to pray for the soul of this lady, Irena Sendler, as well – pray that whatever happened to her, she died peacefully.

$\star$ $\star$ $\star$ $\star$ $\star$ $\star$ $\star$ $\star$ $\star$ $\star$

After her mother's surgery, when school resumed in January, Megan missed two after-school rehearsals to complete her chores and catch up on homework. When she returned, though she had memorized her lines, she didn't have much energy. She could feel how flat and unemotional her Mrs. Rosner was – her grief mechanical and unconvincing. At one early morning script run-through she fell asleep. Sabrina asked if she was feeling sick.

"Yeah – maybe a touch of the flu that's going around."

The next day, as they were about to leave from rehearsal, Megan asked Liz and Sabrina to wait; she had something to tell them. She had thought about this for weeks, rehearsed how she would say it, often when she couldn't sleep, and finally just blurted out, "My Mom has breast cancer."

Hearing her own words startled her, but she went on. "She's doing OK and I'm doing OK. It was just a shock, you know, at first. But I'm back to my old self again. She starts chemo at the end of January."

Liz asked, "Is it, like, a bad cancer?"

Megan hated for anyone to feel sorry for her. "I'd rather not talk about it. I just thought you should know." And she left.

★ ★ ★ ★ ★ ★ ★ ★ ★ ★

Their research became much more efficient when Uniontown's high speed internet connection was upgraded after Christmas break, and they found more primary sources, even survivors' web sites with personal memoirs of how they were rescued. One afternoon when Megan and Liz were alone in the classroom after school, Megan suddenly began weeping at the computer screen. Liz thought she must be reading another tragic story from the ghetto, until she came closer and read the screen:

"Five Year Survival Curves – Primary Breast Cancer."

Liz dropped to her knees beside Megan and draped her arm across her shoulders.

Megan's head fell against Liz's, and in a hoarse whisper she said, "I don't think I can do this."

Megan turned off the computer, and the screen darkened. Liz said, "I'm sorry to tell you something I've known for a long time, Megan. The world is a crappy place."

Megan fussed with her backpack. "It's late. I have to get home to cook dinner."

Liz worried that Megan would drop out of the project, but it wasn't Megan she needed to worry about. Two days later, Liz was caught with alcohol in school and suspended. *The Irena Sendler Project* came to an abrupt halt.

CHAPTER 6

Opening Night

Kansas, January 2000

The whole mess with the alcohol wasn't really Liz's fault – it was just a prank, and she didn't even drink any of it. Grandpa kept an old bottle of Jack Daniels on the kitchen counter, way back behind the cookbooks, the label turned to the wall. The bottle had been there for so long it had dust on it. She knew Wayne was a troublemaker, and she should have said no, but he'd kept at her, bugging her about it since before Thanksgiving. That particular day maybe Liz was pissed off at Grandpa for God knows what, or she'd had another weird dream about her mother. Things just got raw during the holidays.

It was Wednesday evening, the night Grandma Phyllis played piano for the church choir practice. Liz slipped the bottle out from behind the cookbooks and poured some into her "*Jump Rope for Life*" sports bottle, added an equal amount of Pepsi and stuck it into her backpack. The whiskey smelled pungent, and the little bit of it on her fingers tasted like something no one should drink. The next day, crouched in the backseat of the bus, Wayne drank it all down. By the time the yellow bus pulled into Uniontown High's driveway, Wayne was plastered, talking too loudly, too slowly, over-pronouncing his words, stumbling in the lobby directly in front of the main office. In his first period science class he was loud and disruptive, and when he got up to go to the bathroom, Mr. Spencer said he had to wait.

Wayne laughed. "There ain't no way I'm gonna wait. In fact, I'm gonna piss on this here desk."

The police were called, and Wayne immediately ratted out Liz. The guidance counselor searched her locker where he smelled liquor in her water bottle. He summoned her from class, then kept her standing in his office and looked at her as if to say "Why am I not surprised?"

"You're suspended for the rest of the week," he finally said. "Your grandfather's on his way in to pick you up, and he's really mad."

Liz waited for Grandpa Bill in the office, shivering every few minutes, the unyielding *tap, tap, tap* of the clock above her head a mechanical torture device. She had messed up – again – and there would be hell to pay at home, but worse yet, she was pretty sure *The Irena Sendler Project* was dead. She had let down so many people – Grandpa and Grandma, Mr. C., Sabrina, Megan – Megan who had every reason to quit but hadn't. The weight of failure felt familiar, inevitable, the curse that everything good in her life inexorably fell apart as if failure was preordained. But the disappointment of falling from grace with *The Irena Sendler Project*, when she was so near to success, felt so much more bitter.

Liz returned to school the following Monday, after four miserable days grounded in her room. As she entered Room 104, conversation hushed. She felt twenty pair of eyes on her. She fully expected to be cut from the project and had been sick with anticipation all weekend. Mr. C. asked her to stay after class, closed the door and pointed to a chair. "Sit down." His cheeks glowed red, and he paced before her. "I can't believe you did this. You damaged not only yourself, but Megan and Sabrina. It's a very hurtful thing you did, and you should be dropped from the project."

Liz's heart ached. "Yes, sir."

"It's only a month to District. How could you do this? What were you thinking?"

They were the same questions Grandpa Bill had asked. "I wasn't thinking. It was a big fat mistake – and I'm really sorry." A rare tear formed at the corner of one eye, a familiar panic in her heart. "Listen, Mr. C., I know how stupid this sounds, but I am truly sorry and I will never mess up again. I swear." She paused to catch her breath, to relieve the choking sensation. "I have to do this project. It's really important. Don't drop me. Please, don't drop me. I will be the best little girl you could ever hope for. Please, don't drop me."

She was begging for mercy, drowning. Mr. C. paced some more, and Liz stewed in fear and self-loathing. Finally, he pulled a chair noisily and sat across from her. He stared hard into her eyes, measuring her. "I talked with Megan and Sabrina. We made this decision together. Megan said, 'hate the sin, not the sinner,' and Sabrina said, 'what's the big deal – no one died.' They want you to stay in the project." He waited a moment staring at her so intently that she had to look down. "Liz, I believe in you, but there won't be another chance after this."

Liz slowly understood – couldn't believe what she was hearing – then smiled and fussed with her backpack. She felt no need to hide two tears. "Thank you, Mr. C. – you won't be sorry. No, sir. You won't be sorry."

★   ★   ★   ★   ★   ★   ★   ★   ★   ★

District National History Day competition was still more than a month away when Debra Stewart had recovered sufficiently from surgery to resume her duties at home, on the farm, and at church. Though her chemotherapy would start in less than a month, with its threats of more debilitation, Megan's mother seemed buoyed by her renewed energy, a restored capacity to accomplish more than seemed possible to Megan. "Today is a good day," she often told her daughter. "I'm going to live it 110%."

Megan felt as if God had given her and her family a green light, a thumbs up, and her relief made her feel as if she too could live 110%. Her authentic smile returned, as did the blush of her cheeks, with exuberance like new growth after a fire, enriched by the ashes. She plunged into *Life in a Jar*, searched the internet for more documents from the National Archives and Records Administration, read *The Diary of Anne Frank*, *The Warsaw Ghetto: a Diary by Mary Berg*, and Dawid Sierakowiak's *Life in Lodz*, about another Polish ghetto. She studied William Shirer's *Berlin Diary* and tried to understand how normal people could go so crazy so quickly. And she read this from a diary of ghetto life:

> "We packed our suitcases, what do you take? Here's a house we lived in. My grandparents lived in this house; my great-grandparents lived in this house. There were things in that house over 150 years which belonged to the family. You're allowed to take one little suitcase. What do you take?"

Megan read the entry to Liz and Sabrina at their next rehearsal. "When I first read that I wondered, what would I take – what would be most important? They had ten or fifteen minutes to pack one small valise. How could you decide what to take?"

★ ★ ★ ★ ★ ★ ★ ★ ★ ★

Every year during the January thaw, the eye of winter's tempest, a tantalizing hint of spring visited with temperatures often climbing into the 60's. Most of the snow melted, and for a few days it was warm enough to "pick rock." Full of renewed energy and eager for a physical release, Megan drove the pickup to the north wheat field, her *Life in a Jar* script on the cracked passenger seat. She stood still for a moment, inhaling the odor of loam and decay, grateful for the warm wind from Oklahoma at her back, the rustle of leaves in the trees bordering this pasture – strange weather – gray clouds scudding northeast. She had read once – she couldn't remember where – that the dead were not really underground in their graves. Only their bones rested in their coffins. The spirits of the dead were in the wind, in rushing water, in sunset and moonrise, in the smell of the earth. She dropped rocks into the pickup bed and repeated her lines as Mrs. Rosner, the Jewish mother in the Warsaw ghetto. The wind sucked up her words, the rocks beating a deliberate and fitful percussion. She felt Mrs. Rosner's journey through grief as she first refused to give up her baby to Irena Sendler, argued with her husband, saw the inevitability of their imminent deaths, and reconsidered, then said her final good-bye. Megan wailed Mrs. Rosner's sorrow with real tears, and each time the words felt more and more substantial, until she could almost feel a mother's grief.

As she did several times every day, she prayed for her own mother, at first her usual whispered plea to Jesus for healing, then louder as each rock banged into the half-full truck bed, rocks she could barely see for her tears. When she drove the heavily laden truck home, her father joked that it must be a good year for rocks.

★ ★ ★ ★ ★ ★ ★ ★ ★ ★

Four more weeks. Megan's checklist announced: "*Refine Presentation.*"

In the gymnasium, Liz, Megan, and Sabrina sat on the stage reading over their scripts, while the boys' basketball team finished practice, sneakers squeaking, balls bouncing, slamming backboards. Coach blew his whistle, screamed at his players, and suddenly it was over. In less than a minute the gym magically emptied, and Mr. C. sat alone on a folding chair on the free throw line, his arms crossed over his chest waiting for Sabrina to begin.

Narrator: *Poland had millions of Jews. They were made to take whatever they could carry into the most run-down section of town. Over 400 ghettos were established by the Germans. The Nazis persecuted more than just the Jews: political enemies, communists, the handicapped and more. They forced over 400,000 into 16 square blocks of the Warsaw ghetto.*

"Louder, Sabrina! More conviction."

Irena: *Mrs. Rosner, may I speak with you in private? Your children, they need to be taken out of here. They will die in here or be deported to Treblinka – a death camp.*

"No, Liz. Too edgy. More compassion. You're not mad; you're scared. Megan, loosen up and be sure not to move when Irena or the Narrator are speaking. It's distracting."

They ran through the play again.

"Girls, this is awful," Mr. C. said. "Do it again."

A few days later Megan talked with the Agricultural Shop teacher who agreed to let two students assemble a metal prop – black wrought iron bars welded to form a crude and menacing gate with white metal letters – **WARSAW GHETTO** – over the archway to balance the painted stage flat. With only two weeks remaining, they practiced three mornings a week before classes and every weekday after school.

Megan rarely talked about her mother, and when Liz or Sabrina asked, she said she was fine. But she dreaded her Mom's first chemo, only a week away, and once again her faith clashed with her fear. Focusing on *Life in a Jar* was at least a sanctuary.

They kept up their research and e-mail communications with survivors and continued to make small changes to the script. After the alcohol incident Liz was more subdued, more compliant, less inclined to argue. Sabrina was steady, as always. She found a brief reference to Irena's capture and torture by the Gestapo in October of 1943, and they added another scene to the play.

Three weeks before History Day, on a Thursday, Debra Stewart began chemotherapy, and Megan couldn't dispel the dread that everything might fall apart. Megan's father figured that the best way to deal with his wife's chemotherapy was to keep to his routine, "like clockwork and one day at a time," to "buck up" as best he could, and he told Megan she ought to do the same with her extra chores – preparing meals, laundry, vacuuming, making up beds, cleaning dishes, picking up – to keep it routine. No complaints. Her father's logic was seductive, if, in retrospect, circular. Everything will be OK, everything will stay the same, if she just kept everything the same – mealtime, bedtime, chore time, school time. And Megan rose to her responsibility, kept up with all her schoolwork and extra chores, and fell into bed exhausted each night. As they often did on Saturdays, Mark and Travis Stewart drove to the Sale Barn to buy and sell cattle and visit with other farmers. It would be an all-day affair, and Megan was to stay home with her mother, catch up on schoolwork, and have dinner on the table at the usual time, 6 o'clock, when they were due home.

But this was the first Saturday since starting chemo, and Debra Stewart was not doing well. As the day wore on she had more and more difficulty swallowing even sips of water. She sat in her blue lounge chair, pale and exhausted, too tired to move, holding a washcloth to her mouth to absorb the saliva she couldn't swallow. By late afternoon she began to vomit into a yellow bucket, and, by the time twilight was darkening, her eyes had sunk into the shadows as well. She swayed dizzily each time she stood, and Megan had to steady her and walk beside her. She sponged her mother's forehead and watched her wilt like a desiccating flower. As the hours crept by she felt increasingly anxious and impatient for her father and Travis to return home. It was getting dark, and Megan's confidence had completely failed her. "Do I have to take you to the ER?"

"No, honey," Debra Stewart said, her tongue sticking in her mouth. "I'll be fine. They said this could happen."

"Not this bad, Mom. I'm scared."

Megan prayed for the cancer to be just a bad dream, for time itself to reverse, for the blush in her mother's cheek, for the sparkle in her eyes. Her father's pickup skidded to a stop in their farmyard, disturbing her meditation. Megan felt her tension suddenly release, and she held the front door open expectantly.

As soon as her father saw Debra's pallor, his head jerked as if something snapped inside. "Get your mother's coat, Megan!" It was an order. "We're going to the hospital."

Debra could be stubborn in her own way. "I'll be fine, Mark. Megan, honey, get your father his dinner."

They drove her to the local hospital ER, where she was urgently rehydrated with two IVs wide open and deemed sick enough to transfer by ambulance to Kansas City. By midnight, when she was stable and finally asleep, the oncologist said it was good they had brought her in. Without IV fluids she would not have survived the night.

Her mother remained in the hospital for five days, during which Megan continued her punishing pace of chores and schoolwork, helped Travis with his homework, and drove with her father to the hospital in Kansas City. By the third day, she could barely rouse herself from bed in the morning, and nodded asleep in Geometry class. The next night, after dinner, her father settled into his recliner as usual to watch television. Megan stormed into the living room, grabbed the remote, and muted the TV.

"Daddy, I can't do it anymore!" She was furious. "You sit there like nothing is happening. I'm scared, too, you know."

He looked at her in the strangest way.

"I need your help," she said through her tears. Travis stood up from the sofa, his brow furrowed and confused. "You too, Travis," she said.

Mark Stewart was a man of few words, but he used them now. "I didn't plan for your mother to be sick, honey. God works in mysterious ways and he wants us to take care of her now. That's our most important job. Other things may have to go by the wayside."

Megan's heart sank. Her greatest fear, the anxiety that her father would pull her out of National History Day, was about to be realized, and in that moment she knew she would not surrender *The Irena Sendler Project* without a fight. "It's *our* job, not just my job. History Day is in two weeks. I made a commitment to Liz and Sabrina. You always taught me to keep my word and I will not quit. You have to help. I can't do it alone, Daddy. Do it for Mom – do it for me. Please."

Travis started up the stairs, as if this didn't involve him, then stopped and came back down. "She's right, Dad. Megan's project is, like, really a big deal. I can do laundry. I can do dishes and clean house. Mom wants us all to help."

Her father picked up the TV remote, and Megan knew that if the volume returned to normal she had lost the battle. But he clicked the TV off and lumbered to his feet, steadying his sore back. "I'll wash," he said. "You dry."

* * * * * * * * * *

Debra Stewart's fellow church members brought food, fellowship, and prayer, Grandpa Bill came by to help Mark and Travis stack cord wood and put up hay, and Grandma Phyllis brought over a meatloaf and an apple pie a few nights later. She helped with house chores and encouraged Megan to "keep right on a-goin' with that history project." Liz felt insufficient and wished there was something uniquely helpful, something substantial she could do for Megan – not cooking or cleaning, but something only Liz could provide. She couldn't soothe Megan's pain, but she could let her know that she understood, that she was sorry, that she knew what it felt like to worry about your Mom.

One thing Liz could do uniquely and with pride was play her saxophone. Liz had been thinking about a musical accompaniment for *Life in a Jar* and had come upon the perfect song – Eugene Bozza's *Aria*, a saxophone solo in a minor key that gave dignity to suffering. After all was said and done, after all the raging, all the sorrow, all the counseling, the one thing Liz wanted for Megan, for herself – maybe what everyone wanted and needed – was dignity in their suffering.

To acclimate the three girls to NHD stage conditions, Mr. C. had them rehearse in Room 104 every day at lunchtime where students and teachers stopped to watch through the open door. He also wanted as many people as possible to see this amazing story; this was a story to share. Something curious began to happen as people paused to watch – conversations ceased, first out of curiosity, which quickly morphed into the reverential silence of church. Every adult, man or woman, and many of the teens who watched Mrs. Rosner give up her children to Irena, had either to accommodate or conceal their tears.

★ ★ ★ ★ ★ ★ ★ ★ ★ ★

It was a cold evening in late January when they gave their first public performance, a dress rehearsal of sorts, on the small stage in the gym. Megan wasn't sure her Mom would be well enough to attend. Since cancer had become a member of her family, nothing was sure anymore, but as they were setting up, she saw the golden flash of Debra Stewart's "chemo outfit" – a bright yellow jumpsuit and yellow sports cap. Debra and Mark sat with Liz's grandparents in the first row of folding chairs. Behind them sat Sabrina's mother and sister. Most of the seats were empty, but a few community people came – a local nurse, the banker, the librarian, a minister, and other History Day parents.

Mr. C. thanked the audience for coming out on a cold night and thought they would be warmed by what they were about to see. He introduced the students and The Irena Sendler Project with a few words about "the power of one person to change the world." The stage, partially blocked by the visiting team's basket, had neither curtain nor theater lights, and when the three bare bulbs went out, it was completely dark until a candle was lit on stage. Liz, dressed as young Irena, stood stage left looking off stage.

Young Irena: *Father, are you awake?*

Father:	(offstage) *Irena, don't come in my room, stay down the hall.*
Young Irena:	*Will the typhus go away? Will you be all right?*
Father:	*No, I'm afraid it won't go away, but you and your mother need to go to another house, and don't get close to me, Irena.* (Pause) *Irena, remember all the things I have taught you.*
Young Irena:	*Yes, Father.* (Voice trembles)
Father:	*Remember that we have stayed in this Polish town to help the poor, to help the Jewish people sick with this epidemic. Remember what I have always told you. If you see someone drowning, you must try to rescue them. Will you remember that?*
Young Irena:	*Yes, I will always remember that, and I will also remember what you say about people all being the same, regardless of race or religion. I will not forget your words – ever.* (Blows out candle – lights come on)
Young Irena:	*And now we present,* Life in a Jar.

The welded **WARSAW GHETTO** gate stood stage right. Stage center – the wood flat painted in three panels. Stage left – a battered trunk, its lid open behind a small table with a glass jar.

During her narration, Sabrina's voice choked with emotion and anxiety, a surprise to Liz, for Sabrina had always been rock-steady, her emotions buried. Already sweating, Liz changed into the full-length dress of grown-up Irena. Her breath was short as she explained ZEGOTA and her mission to save children. The elderly librarian at the end of the third row dried her eyes. Megan came onstage as Mrs. Rosner.

Mrs. Rosner: *I've talked with my husband. You must take our children. It breaks our hearts, but you must take them. We will all die. (Long hesitation) There is no hope in the ghetto, people are shot every day without reason, no reason is ever given; they looked the wrong way, they walked too slowly, they were in the wrong place. How horrible.*

Irena: *We are in a river of rage. Each must jump in to save others. This will all end someday.*

Liz looked into Megan's eyes and begged her to give up her children. Her voice, which began with Irena Sendler's surety and feistiness, slowed and thickened into a tear-choked and halting delivery. She had to breathe deeply to keep her voice from cracking, to regain her composure. She heard sniffling in the audience.

Mrs. Rosner: *Is this the time?*

Irena: *Yes. I will take your children. If I am caught, I will tell the guards they have typhus and I must get them to the hospital.*

Mrs. Rosner: *Take them now, for we cannot bear to think about this any longer. We have them ready to go. Hannah, this nice lady will take you and Baby Isek to someplace where you will feel much better. We will see you sometime soon.*

Irena: *Hannah, take my hand. Say good-bye to Mama and Papa.*

Mrs. Rosner gave Irena her Baby Isek, a doll wrapped in ghetto rags, and the invisible hand of Hannah. Megan and Liz finished their lines and Sabrina ended the play.

After the war, the communists branded the ZEGOTA members as fascists. Irena's story would not be known by the world. Except for a tree planted in her honor in Israel, for nearly 60 years her story was buried, forgotten, until three Kansas students brought it back into the light.

Darkness.

One by one, three bare bulbs came back on. Except for the recording of Liz playing the saxophone, the gymnasium was silent. Liz seemed confused, at loose ends with what to do in the awkward silence. Sabrina looked down shyly, her hair curtaining her face. Megan fussed with the jar.

After what seemed to Megan like a long time, one person started to clap, then another, and in a moment the small audience was on its feet, applauding until the girls could take a few deep breaths and dry their eyes. They bowed awkwardly, without coordination. Megan saw her mother with tears in her eyes; her father, on one side, eased her to her feet, ever so gently, and Grandpa Bill helped her on the other. Big Bill's face looked permanently cracked by a huge smile, tears glistening on his cheeks, and Megan began to weep all over again.

The first time Liz shed tears was just a few weeks earlier, watching Schindler's List – a tear-jerker, she told herself, the exception that proved the rule that Liz did not cry. But here she was again, only this time her tears flowed independent of her will, and she wondered what had changed?

★　★　★　★　★　★　★　★　★　★

The second Saturday in February, District History Day, jammed into the school's Suburban van with stage props, they drove down Highway 69, fifty miles south of Uniontown to Columbus High School in Columbus, Kansas. Though it was not a long drive, Liz couldn't find a comfortable position in the backseat, part of the **WARSAW GHETTO** prop poking her over the seat back. Megan asked to stop the car several times to use the bathroom. Once at the high school, which bustled with parents, kids,

History Day judges, and the local TV station, they found their assigned classroom, where they fussed with their costumes and reviewed last-minute script changes, then proceeded to the auditorium where they watched other performances, ready to set up quickly when their turn came.

They performed flawlessly, and afterwards, still in costume, they answered questions from the three-judge panel. The first judge peered at them over his half spectacles. "What else was going on in history during this time period?"

Megan and Liz looked nervously at each other. Liz's mind went blank.

"It was during World War II," Sabrina said. "The United States was at war with Germany, Italy and... and Japan. The war didn't end until 1945 and in 1942 and 1943, when Irena Sendler was rescuing Jews, the Germans were winning the war. It was the same time that Jewish children, like Anne Frank, were being hidden all over the world to save their lives."

Thank goodness for Sabrina! Liz took a deep breath and marveled again that a smart kid like Sabrina, level-headed, sweet, unafraid, would want a loser like Liz to be part of her life.

"What happened to this woman, Irena Sendler?" another judge asked.

Megan said, "We don't know. We think she must be dead. She was arrested and tortured in this awful prison, Pawiak. Maybe she died there – we just don't know. She'd be, like, 90 years old today. We don't know many people in their 90's – and after what she went through..."

"We searched Polish cemetery records," Liz was glad to contribute something concrete. "We sent letters to her son, Adam, who lives in Warsaw. But he never wrote back. We're still looking. We're not done with her story. We're going to find her resting place and find out how she died."

The judges had only to confer briefly before awarding *Life in a Jar* First Prize in the Performance category. As if a spring had been released, the three girls leapt into each other's arms, Liz jumping like the cheerleader she never was, Megan smiling broadly at the first good thing to happen in a long time. Sabrina, more subdued, held onto the other two, and when she jumped her feet didn't quite leave the ground. Grandpa Bill was just a step behind Grandma Phyllis, who bounded down the aisle, took Liz into her arms, and spun her around like a proud mother.

The Irena Sendler Project was going to State.

CHAPTER 7

Where is Irena Buried?

Kansas, February, 2000

Kansas in February is desolate and windswept, ice freezing onto the faces of beef cattle unlucky enough to be away from a windbreak of trees. Mud freezes solid on the back roads, and rural schools like Uniontown High School have frequent weather closings. The holidays are over; those depressed by meager light are irritable if not deep in melancholy. Megan struggled to keep up her spirits.

The Monday after District History Day, the Fort Scott Tribune featured this story:

> Twenty-one Uniontown High School students won awards and recognition at National History Day in Columbus. One of the winning projects, Life in a Jar, has already been the subject of local media stories. Liz Cambers, Sabrina Coons, and Megan Stewart placed first in their category with a dramatic presentation about Irena Sendler, a forgotten Holocaust hero who rescued 2,500 Jewish children from certain death in the Warsaw ghetto during World War II. They will present this moving drama for the public next Thursday evening at the Uniontown Methodist Church in Uniontown.

★ ★ ★ ★ ★ ★ ★ ★ ★

After District History Day the girls continued to refine the script with renewed optimism and purpose. Liz and Megan still butted heads over lines or scenes or practice schedules, but with less intensity.

The day of their performance at the Methodist Church in town the three girls prepared after school. Megan sewed a purposely distressed hem on Mrs. Rosner's dress. Sabrina checked for e-mails and Liz rummaged through her backpack.

"Nothing from Poland?" Megan asked, knowing the answer. Each day without a response from Irena's son Adam in Poland was a fresh disappointment

"Nothing," Sabrina said without looking up from the computer. She turned to face them, and Megan thought she was about to say something, then swallowed it, and said, instead, to Liz, "It's a wonder you can find anything in there."

"That's what my Grandma says, but believe it or not, I usually find what I'm looking for."

"I guess you have your own kind of organization – Liz's System." Sabrina returned to the screen and scrolled through a new web site. "With this Warsaw ghetto stuff we all need a system. You can't stay with any one story or picture for too long. It gets too close – it makes me too sad or mad or something. They're all so terrible."

Megan asked if Sabrina's mother was coming that night, and Sabrina looked back at Megan and then Liz, her lips pursed with anxiety. "My Mom is sick," she said tentatively. "She takes lots of medicine. She has diabetes – the bad kind. I think she got it when I was in 1st grade, but I'm not sure." Sabrina paused, and Megan thought she contemplated whether or not to continue. "Couple years ago she crashed her car. It was a bad accident and it took her a long time to get better. She still has problems. She takes insulin shots twice a day and checks her blood all the time. I don't usually tell people stuff like this, so don't go spreadin' it around. I just think you ought to know, that's all."

★　★　★　★　★　★　★　★　★　★

It began to snow that afternoon, and by the time of their first public performance the roads were treacherous and the Methodist Church sanctuary barely half full. There was no need for Megan to reserve two seats in the front row for her mother and father, but she did anyway, though she doubted her mother would be there. Debra Stewart had begun another round of chemotherapy, and she was sick and weak again.

None of them had any expectations for that evening's presentation. Mr. C. welcomed the small audience and explained how the project was "conceived and carried out by three courageous and dedicated young women." He praised their thorough research and dedication to this project about respect for others and one woman's extraordinary courage. There would be a question and answer period afterwards.

Megan had three roles – Irena's co-conspirator Marie, a German soldier, and Mrs. Rosner, the Jewish woman Irena "talked out of her children" just before she and her husband were deported to their deaths at Treblinka. She peeked through the curtain and recognized mostly local folks, some older people, a few kids from school. There was Sabrina's mother, her sister Sarah, Grandpa Bill and Grandma Phyllis. Sabrina came onstage as the Narrator in a new costume, a 1939 overcoat. She waited for the rustling and stirring in the sanctuary to cease.

Narrator: *We are about to begin a journey, one that will not be easy. We must walk lightly, for we are dealing with fragile and precious memories. Irena Sendler was a Polish Catholic social worker, a small woman, less than five feet tall...*

Megan entered as Mrs. Rosner, a dark kerchief tied over her head, carrying a battered old suitcase, leading an imaginary child by the hand.

Mrs. Rosner: (Recorded sounds of panic, people screaming in the background.) *Hurry Isek, hurry Hanna, don't look at them, don't look at the German officers. Solomon, keep the children moving.*

After the first scene Megan hastily changed into the over-large German soldier's uniform, then changed again to become Marie, one of Irena's network of social workers who helped smuggle children out of the ghetto.

Irena:	*Marie, I want to go down to the Warsaw ghetto and see what is going on.*
Marie:	*That would be very dangerous. What if the Germans think you are Jewish, and why would they let you in?*
Irena:	*I have my papers. I'm a child welfare worker, a Polish Christian. That can be proved. And I'll... I'll say I'm a nurse looking at conditions. Besides, the Germans have given me permission to visit the ghetto, to check on diseases.*
Marie:	(Smiling) *I can see you as a social worker, or maybe a member of ZEGOTA!!* (Smiles again.)
Irena:	(Angry) *Don't say that. Don't you even believe for one minute that I am a member of ZEGOTA, even if you know it, don't ever say it!* (Loudly)
Marie:	*I'm sorry, you are right. But you are Jolanta. I know your code name and others may know it also. Be careful in the Warsaw ghetto.*

There was rustling in the audience, and in the darkness Megan saw her mother's yellow "chemo" coveralls and hat – and the dark hulk of her father easing her into the reserved seat. She caught Megan's eye and smiled.

On stage, Marie and Irena walked through the welded metal **WARSAW GHETTO** gate. Behind the stage flat, Sabrina played a tape recording of chaos and panic, the sounds of Jews being packed into the ghetto, fading into Liz's mournful saxophone solo, Eugene Bozza's *Aria*.

Megan:	(As 14-year-old Megan Stewart) *During the long night of the Holocaust, among the few points of*

light were the men and women who risked their
lives to save others.

Sabrina: These people were a turning point in one of his-
          tory's greatest turning points, the Holocaust.

Liz: (Still dressed as Irena, but clearly now she is
          Liz.) In 1965 Irena Sendler was named one of
          the Righteous Among the Nations. No one knows
          when she died or where she is buried. Her cour-
          age, the courage of one small woman with a big
          heart, showed the courage and commitment which
          changed the world.

Mr. C. dried his eyes and marveled yet again at the uncommon power
of this simple and innocent drama; like slicing an onion, no matter how
often he'd seen it and read the script, he welled up every time.

★   ★   ★   ★   ★   ★   ★   ★   ★   ★

Though Kansas History Day was still three months away, Megan
announced a demanding rehearsal schedule.

"Three days a week in March. Four days a week in April, then every day
the last week. I think the script needs a lot of work."

"And the stage flat needs to be repainted," said Sabrina.

At the used clothing store in Fort Scott, Megan bought a 1930's dress
and blouse for Mrs. Rosner, a size too large, to emphasize her starvation
in the ghetto.

Their research continued, and though Megan found it distressing, she
felt compelled to read everything she could about the Warsaw ghetto. The
photographs disturbed her the most – black-and-white images of starving
children and orphans staring at her through the mystery of time and the
harsh freezing of a painful moment. No doubt all of these children had
died shortly after these photos were taken. They were not the abstraction
called "The Holocaust," not an imagined reconstruction in words; they

were specific children, so real that she felt she could enter their photographs, or they could step out of their hell. Their skeletal faces beseeched her, their bony hands reached out to her for bread.

★   ★   ★   ★   ★   ★   ★   ★   ★   ★

After more weeks of fruitless searching for information about Irena Sendler, Liz complained to Mr. C., "Why is this so hard? I mean, she's a hero – she did amazing things. Why isn't she in every history book? Why don't Poles know her?"

"I'm wondering the same thing, Liz," he said.

"They could at least put flowers on her grave once a year, but no one even knows where that is. When we find her grave, I'm sending money to someone in Poland to put flowers on it, at least on her birthday."

Street scene with beggar children, Warsaw Ghetto. Everyone over 9 years old wears the Star of David armband on their right sleeve. *(Heinrich Jost photo, courtesy of the Emanuel Ringelblum Jewish Historical Institute, Warsaw, Poland)*

The Wall. Autumn 1940. Eleven miles long, 10 feet high, topped with shards of broken glass. *(Courtesy of the State Archives of the Capital City, Warsaw)*

November, 1940. Jews line up to move into the ghetto. They are permitted to take only what they can carry on their backs. *(Courtesy of the Emanuel Ringelblum Jewish Historical Institute, Warsaw, Poland)*

Chlodna Street divides the Large Ghetto (pop. 300,000) from the Little Ghetto (pop. 100,000). The wooden footbridge allows Jews to cross over the Aryan thoroughfare where they see "normal" existence in the occupied city. *(Courtesy of The Archive of Documentary and Film Studio, Poland)*

Four Jewish beggar children caught by an SS officer. The boy in front has bulging pants stuffed with root vegetables collected on the Aryan side. *(Courtesy of The Archive of Documentary and Film Studio, Poland)*

The beggars empty their clothing of food they had hoped to smuggle into the ghetto. They will be taken to Gensia Prison in the ghetto, where they will likely die of starvation and infectious disease. *(Courtesy of The Archive of Documentary and Film Studio, Poland)*

A common ghetto street scene. Starving children with stick-thin legs, some orphans, some with their mothers. (*Courtesy of the Emanuel Ringelblum Jewish Historical Institute, Warsaw, Poland*)

Jews rounded up during the liquidation of the ghetto (July 22 – Sept. 21, 1942) are marched to the train-loading platform (*Umschlagplatz*) at the northern end of the ghetto. They are escorted to the death trains by Jewish policemen. A German SS officer stands at the head of the column. (*Courtesy of the Emanuel Ringelblum Jewish Historical Institute, Warsaw, Poland*)

Umschlagplatz. A small field beside the train-loading area where up to 10,000 Jews wait without food or drink for up to 20 hours before being loaded into cattle cars for transport to Treblinka. (*Courtesy of the Emanuel Ringelblum Jewish Historical Institute, Warsaw, Poland*)

Jews are loaded into cattle cars destined for murder at Treblinka. During the liquidation of the ghetto, between 2,000 and 13,500 people are taken each day. (*Courtesy of the Emanuel Ringelblum Jewish Historical Institute, Warsaw, Poland*)

April 1943. An Easter Fair at Krasinski Square beside the ghetto on the first day of the Jewish Uprising. The child on the swing looks into the ghetto with each arc and hears gunfire coming from across the wall. *(Photograph by Jan Lissowski, courtesy of the Emanuel Ringelblum Jewish Historical Institute, Warsaw, Poland)*

1945. The Germans completely destroyed the area of the Warsaw ghetto, leaving only a damaged church, St. Augustine's Catholic Church on Nowolipki Street. *(Reproduction of images found on p. 45 of the book – Six Year Plan for the Reconstruction of Warsaw [Szescioletni Plan Odbudowy Warszawy], by Boleslaw Bierut, Warsaw, 1959)*

PART TWO

Warsaw, September 1939 – January 1944

CHAPTER 8

Invasion
Warsaw, September 1939

September 1, 1939 – Irena was shaken from sleep at dawn by explosions that rattled her bed, the walls, the entire building. A water glass vibrated to the edge of her nightstand, and she seized it just before it fell. Air raid sirens cacophonized an ominous and untuned choir. Irena's mother, Janina, often up before the sun, rapped hard on Irena's door, something she never did.

"Irena! Dress quickly! The shelter!"

Irena's pulse sprinted from sleep to pounding in just a few seconds, though it came as no surprise that the war had finally begun. Through her bedroom door she heard Radio Warsaw report several hours of fighting on the German frontier and an air raid on Warsaw. Outside their flat, urgent footfalls thundered down the stairs, and Irena and her mother followed their neighbors to the basement air raid shelter. Irena thought of her husband Mietek, a lieutenant on the frontier, and prayed he would not try to be a hero.

She had known Mietek from childhood, ice skated with him in Piotrków, but the marriage was difficult. Though they retained affection for each other, they had lived apart for years. Mietek had returned to Warsaw for Irena's university graduation this past June, handsome in his uniform, a Classics scholar poised to stop a German invasion. They were cordial with each other and used the occasion to come to an agreement about their future. He would continue teaching Classics in Poznan, she her social work in Warsaw and caring for her mother. There would be no miraculous reconciliation, just a sad realization that they did not have the same dreams. The only miracle was Irena's graduation. After six years of disciplinary suspension, Irena had been reinstated and allowed to complete her thesis. Her mother's dream was fulfilled – her only child had secured an advanced degree.

An hour later the all-clear sounded, and, along with their neighbors, many still in their night clothes, Irena and her mother trudged back upstairs. She dressed for work, took her gas mask, and joined the sparse but confused rush hour of Warsovians trying to live normally on the first day of war.

On the street she saw a column of smoke rising a few blocks away. Trams ran on schedule, as if nothing out of the ordinary had happened, though everyone inside the tram car carried a black rubber gas mask. An unusual camaraderie prevailed. Irena spoke freely with strangers whom she recognized from her daily commute, exchanging rumors, reassurance, companionship, and perhaps courage. She studied her fellow passengers and wondered how many would survive the war.

At her Social Welfare office Irena's desk was piled high with claims and files. As she opened the first file on her desk the sirens began again, and hundreds of people who worked in the building crowded into the basement bomb shelter. Rumor had it that these shelters could protect against all but a direct hit. Above the shelter, explosions rattled the foundation. The other Irena – Irena Schultz – sat beside her on the hard bench, her eyes closed, lips praying or singing, Irena wasn't sure.

Irena Schultz had been Irena's supervisor back in 1932, when she was first hired to be a social worker. Now they routinely altered documents and engaged in other welfare fraud for the benefit of their Jewish clients. They were referred to as "the two Irenas."

Irena Schultz had an ironic sense of humor when it came to working the social welfare system for the benefit of their clients. But she also had the discipline and intelligence of a general, and a photographic memory. She knew about each fraudulent welfare transaction, each petty larceny of public funds, where each co-conspirator was located. She knew whom to trust and how to trust them.

Another bomb detonated dangerously close to their building. Sitting across from the two Irenas, Jaga Piotrowska, secretary to Social Welfare director Jan Dobraczynski, who sat beside her, made a move to link her arm with Dobraczynski's, but she pulled back at the last moment.

Another bone rattling concussion, close enough to shake dust loose from the ceiling. The lights flickered; someone screamed. Irena felt the hairs on her arm.

Irena Schultz crossed the room to sit on the other side of Jan Dobraczynski. Only in the shelter did Irena realize just how big a man he was. He'd had to duck his head to come through the door, and was unable to stand fully erect in the cellar itself. Everything about Jan Dobraczynski was big and tight. The mass of his muscles pulled his shoulders and head forward; his thick dark hair was slicked back precisely. Until recently, he rarely left his office and did not smile. When he stood, his arms hung gracelessly at his side, as if his creator had attached them as an afterthought. That all began to change six months ago, when Jaga Piotrowska had become his administrative assistant and Dobraczynski began to thaw. There were all manner of rumors and innuendoes.

Like opposites that attract, Irena was intrigued by Jaga's bohemian worldliness, and Jaga seemed naturally fond of Irena. She was a head taller, and Irena thought she could be on the cover of a fashion magazine. Jaga frequented artists' cafés and nightclubs like the *Romanishes Café*, which gave her many unusual stories to share with Irena. Even for work she dressed as if she were going to a nightclub – bright red nail polish and lipstick, her nut-brown hair stylishly short, a provocative smile. Jaga whispered to Dobraczynski and fitted a cheap Bulgarian cigarette into her shiny black cigarette holder. She blew out the smoke with her head tilted up, accentuating the curve of her long neck. Jaga's eyeglasses had heavy black frames that she had painted with colorful squiggles and dots. She created her own avant-garde clothing, and today she wore a collage of velvets, burgundies and greens, triangles and circles stitched together to fashion a novel dress.

In the dim shelter light Irena watched the silhouette of Dobraczynski's angular features, a finely chiseled chin, sharp nose, and square jaw, his dark hair slicked back from a sharp widow's peak. Irena Schultz whispered with Dobraczynski and scribbled notes.

Suddenly another rattling blast, the closest yet, and they all cried out as if they were on a demonic roller coaster. Irena hated the thought of dying this way, buried under tons of rubble, rotting, maybe never found, or, worse yet, entombed alive but unable to move.

Irena Schultz returned to her place beside Irena on the bench. His expression inscrutable, Dobraczynski picked up his novel, *Crime and Punishment.*

"What did you two talk about?" Irena whispered.

She shrugged. "Work. Details." She tried to smile. "I know you think ill of him, Irena, but he's a changed man."

A rivulet of sweat ran down Irena's chest. "I wish he were more tolerant."

"As a matter of fact, we talked about the Jews," Irena Schultz said. "How their needs will be much greater now, with the war. He feels sorry for them."

Irena could not let the statement stand. "Jews can't eat pity."

Irena Schultz fussed with her gas mask. "Jan Dobraczynski is a complicated man. Jaga says we should trust him."

"You didn't tell him about our..."

"No. No, of course not. But I think soon enough we'll have to."

There was a lull in the bombardment – the bomb blasts few and far away. Irena sat back against the wall and closed her eyes. She remembered her harrowing first encounter with Irena Schultz in 1935, three years after she had been hired.

That day had begun with an overnight snowfall, which had transformed Warsaw into a fairy-tale city. Irena knew that by midday the virginal snow would be soiled and the magic would melt into slush. Her week had already been frustrating as she struggled to understand the government's new welfare restrictions imposed on Jews and Gypsies. When she arrived at her office, Irena's assistant reported that Irena Schultz, her supervisor from the central office at Zlota #74, had called. She would visit that day to "review some files." After three years working as a social worker, she still had never met the infamous and aloof Irena Schultz. Judging from the precise handwriting of her memos, her attention to detail and careful accounting, Irena envisaged her phantom boss as a bureaucratic functionary, a stern older woman who liked to put young girls in their place.

But that was not who arrived later that day. She noticed her immediately – a tall, dignified woman a few years older than Irena, with strong shoulders, wearing a fashionable but functional gray suit and carrying a man's briefcase. She walked with the confidence of an actress – shoulders squared, chest forward, her head tipped up in a way that suggested either affectation or pluck. When the supervisor was just two desks away, Irena saw that she kept her short blond hair fixed flat with black hair pins that added severity. Her blue-eyed stare held steady on Irena.

She held out her hand to shake like a man. "I'm Miss Schultz – from the main office." Her voice was husky. "I have some questions." She discretely looked about her to establish their zone of privacy, then sat in the chair next to Irena's desk and pulled several files from her leather briefcase. She leaned forward, her head close, and spoke just above a whisper. "There are mistakes."

Irena recognized each file – Piszczek, Goldblatt, Stern. Her heart triphammered. She knew exactly why Miss Schultz had come. In an instant she saw herself being fired, wondered how quickly she would lose her apartment. There wouldn't be enough money for her mother's heart medicine and food. And, of course, this was a criminal offense; Irena would go to prison.

Irena Schultz opened the Piszczek file. "There are mistakes," she said again, and Irena braced herself.

After Marshal Pilsudski's death earlier that year, government policies had veered sharply to the right, and Dmowski's National Democratic movement gained popularity and power. New welfare rules, especially restrictive for Jews, caused great suffering to most of Irena's clients. All that was required for the Piszczek family to continue their relief eligibility were two minor "alterations" of the record. Trivial changes, nothing serious. The Piszczeks' apartment, more of a hovel, was listed as "three people sharing two rooms," but anyone could see it was only one room crudely divided with a wooden partition by a miserly landlord. So Irena changed the listing to "one room." Their three-year-old daughter Sara was too old to receive benefits, so Irena altered her birthday by six months – only half a year – that was all. She rationalized her criminality by reminding herself of something her father, a proud Socialist, had taught her – that compassion and the law were sometimes at odds, in which case decency trumped the rules. Her clients were the Piszczeks, not anti-Semitic legislators. Her father had given his poor Jewish patients in Otwock free medicine that he pilfered from the sanitarium. Was this not similar? Minor violations for a greater good.

Her supervisor pointed to one line in the document. "The child – Sara Piszczek – her birth date is wrong on both documents."

"How careless of me. A clerical error. There are so many forms."

Irena Schultz said nothing as another worker passed by, then pointed to Irena's "error" with the tip of a sharp pencil and quietly said, "You changed the entire birth date – day, month, year. I immediately became suspicious. You know it's illegal to assign benefits for people who are not entitled. Did Mr. Piszczek bribe you?"

Irena sat up sharply, shocked by the accusation, and in hushed tones replied, "No money, no bribes. I did it so their daughter Sara could eat. I did it for Sara. She's only three." She stared pleadingly into Irena Schultz's sky blue eyes. "She's starving."

Their eyes remained locked. Irena Schultz finally looked down and circled the larcenous birth date. "Next time, only change the year. That's an honest, careless mistake and even someone as careful as I might not notice."

Their friendship and conspiracy grew from that first meeting. In the autumn of 1938, another wave of refugees suddenly appeared in Warsaw, and the two Irenas devised strategies for obtaining welfare benefits for those among the poorest who were no longer eligible. It became a macabre game; the government enacted discriminatory rules, and the two Irenas found clever ways to circumvent them. They became bolder and more adept. They knew which food warehouse workers were sympathetic to their cause; they knew the trusted social workers in other offices, where to get forged identity cards and documents. Their cabal bonded them into a peculiar but vigorous friendship. Periodically, Irena Schultz would lament how out of character this deceitful behavior was for her, how in ordinary times she was a stickler for the rules.

The two Irenas looked a sight together. Irena Schultz, blond and tall for a woman, towered over Irena, dark-haired and red-cheeked. During the last months of peace they worked 12-hour days. Two or three times a day, including Saturday and Sunday, they carried dry food, money, and medicine into the Jewish district. Irena Schultz had obtained a forged warehouse pass and a letter signed by Jan Dobraczynski, newly appointed Director of Social Welfare in Warsaw. He had been made to think he was signing a letter about janitors' salaries.

By the summer of 1939 virtually every Jewish child in Warsaw was destitute. The two Irenas devised more elaborate untraceable strategies to overcome new restrictions. They worked closely with Ewa Rechtman, a former social worker in Irena's office who had been fired because she was Jewish. Ewa and Irena had both been hired in 1932, the first social work employment for each of them, and they became friends. Ewa had unusual Semitic features, a round face, olive skin and fair hair, her nose generous though not peculiarly large, and kindhearted hazel eyes set wide apart, exotic. One couldn't help but notice Ewa Rechtman in a crowd, her long legs and slim waist turned men's heads. Her natural expression was to smile.

In their Social Welfare office, Ewa was known as "that amazing Jewish girl who can get anything done." "She's got a photographic memory," her colleagues marveled. "She is always happy. Sometimes I don't think she's real."

Ewa had been fired during the winter of 1938-1939, when the Polish government had decreed that all Jewish Welfare workers employed by the state were to be terminated.

"Don't make a fuss about this," Ewa had said on her last day of work. "I'll be fine. It's just the way it is now. It wasn't Dobraczynski. He had no choice. Here, read this." She showed Irena a handwritten note on formal stationary from Dobraczynski:

Dear Miss Rechtman,

I apologize for the poor judgment and arbitrary cruelty of my superiors in terminating your employment. I condemn their opinions and their decision. During the six years of your employment you have demonstrated the most extraordinary skill and devotion. I had no recourse but to let you go; however, I would happily recommend you for any position you might apply for.

My deepest regret,
Jan Dobraczynski

$\star \quad \star \quad \star \quad \star \quad \star \quad \star \quad \star \quad \star \quad \star \quad \star$

After the all-clear sounded, Dobraczynski, his head bent forward, called for everyone's attention. "Please. Please, everyone. There's something I must say." Conversations stopped. "Everyone, please go home," he said. "No need for paperwork or house visits today or over the weekend. We'll see what Monday brings."

Irena thought he was finished, but he closed his eyes, took a deep breath and began in a rich baritone to sing the Polish national anthem, *Danbrowski Mazurka*.

"Poland has not yet perished..."

Jaga's bold soprano voice joined him, followed shortly by Irena Schultz's gravelly alto and other voices, more and less melodic, until the shelter resonated with Poland's anthem. Heretofore, Irena had felt no affinity for *Danbrowski Mazurka*; she considered herself an internationalist, not a patriot. But on this day she sang with ardor and feeling, proud, bristling, wistful, stouthearted. Irena Schultz sang with her eyes closed, two tears rolling down her cheeks.

The two Irenas left the office together, their black gas masks dangling beside their purses, into an altered Warsaw, its air fouled by the many columns of black smoke that rose over the city. Electricity had been lost, immobilizing trams like insects in amber. Dazed like their fellow Warsovians, they began to walk home, through Saxony Garden, absurdly lush with summer foliage and flowers, past their tram stop on Leszno Street. Ambulance and fire sirens performed an eerie polyphony. A block past the gardens they came upon something Irena had never seen before, a shocking thing, smoldering ruins that yesterday had been a three-story building with shops on the ground floor. The fire wagons were just leaving; they were urgently needed elsewhere. Civil defense workers clambered over the rubble pile digging for survivors, but it didn't seem likely that anyone could have lived through the blast. Some corpses had already been laid out on the street, awaiting the morgue wagon.

A detached, hazy silence settled over Marszalkowska Street – smoke, debris, a dead horse and its overturned wagon, no evidence of the driver. The two Irenas didn't speak as they turned onto Zelazna Street. At the corner of Zelazna and Zlota another house had been reduced to smoldering rubble. Suddenly, there was sparking of overhead wires, a humming, a grinding and squealing as trams came to life. Electric pumps in the Water Works started up again, and water pressure in fire hoses suddenly returned to normal. It was as if Warsaw revived from a heart attack. People ventured out of shelters, an automobile zig-zagged around debris, and horse drawn *droshky* and pedi-cabs resumed their commerce. A fire truck raced by, its siren piercing.

Tram #25 came to a stop, and Irena Schultz moved to board, but first she hugged Irena tightly to her chest, something she had never done before.

That evening Irena and her mother heard on Radio Warsaw that 41 German bombers had taken part in the first raids, two had been shot down, and more than 100 Warsaw civilians had been killed. No word on conditions on the frontier, but the German assault was described as massive and swift.

Two days later Irena saw a line of men too old and too young for military service, shovels balanced like rifles on their shoulders, marching without discipline toward the river. Wall posters exhorted everyone to defend the homeland; Mayor Stefan Starzynski pleaded for citizens to dig defensive trenches against the Germans. Shovels against Hitler's Panzers.

"ABLE-BODIED MEN!
LEAVE THE CITY!
CROSS THE VISTULA!
REGROUP FOR A DEFENSIVE LINE."

The ragged legion of boys and old men marching with their shovels disquieted Irena. When she returned to her flat the telephone was ring-

75

ing. It was Stefan, the history instructor whom Irena had met at the University of Warsaw. Irena thought he had romantic feelings toward her – and if she was honest, she felt the same way toward him. But she was still married to Mietek, so she and Stefan settled for frequent late-night discussions about Socialism, minorities, and avant-garde poets.

"I'm leaving the city," he said on the telephone. "It seems I am to regroup." Then he laughed, and Irena heard the politically cynical Stefan, the enigmatic man she was so attracted to. "I just find it rather odd. How can one regroup, when one has never grouped?"

"Must you make a joke of everything?" Irena said. The line was silent, and she wondered if they'd been disconnected or if she'd been too harsh. "Stefan? Are you going to fight?"

"I can't refuse." He sounded vulnerable. "People will think me a coward. I suppose my shame is more potent than either my cynicism or my terror."

"It's not shame," Irena said. "You're a Pole. It's integrity." The telephone connection crackled and faded, and then he was back. "Call me when you can," she said. "Be careful. Don't be a hero." The same wish she had given to Mietek.

"Not likely." There was another awkward silence as if he had something else to say.

Irena's face flushed. She thought of Mietek and all she could say was, "Be careful, Stefan."

That afternoon, Radio Warsaw announced that Britain and France had declared war on Germany. By early evening spontaneous demonstrations erupted in the street, as if waving Polish, British, and French flags could blow the German bombers off course or make them crash into each other. Irena's mother sat up close to the radio savoring the first good news in three days, and Irena was glad to see her smile again.

Their optimism was painfully brief. Early on Tuesday morning, September 5th, a police officer, a Polish Blue, pounded on the door to Irena's flat. Eyes wide with panic and authority, he barged in and ordered them to leave immediately. His blue cape was askew and it made him look slightly ridiculous, like a cartoon.

"German troops, armored vehicles, tanks," he said, out of breath, "near the outskirts of the city. Trenches are being dug. A barricade must be erected on this street." He pointed to Irena's furniture, her beloved books and bookcases. "All of it – everything that can be moved – onto the barricade. Immediately!"

Irena began to explain why that was impossible, but the officer jerked out his police baton and smashed it against the wall, cracking the plaster. "You cannot refuse my order!" Spittle sprayed from his lips. "Martial law has been declared! Ludwiki Street is closed. Everyone must leave."

Under the officer's supervision the tenants of Ludwiki #6 emptied their apartments of everything he thought should be on the barricade. He ordered them to form a human chain to pass down mattresses, tables, and chairs. Irena was most distressed to see her books, once so dignified in her bookcase, now flotsam and jetsam strewn over a crude barrier erected to stop a German tank.

Luckily for Irena, her Aunt Kazimiera Karbowska lived nearby, and she graciously took in Janina. Irena defied the Polish Blue's order and remained in her empty Ludwiki Street apartment. She spent her first night alone in a vortex of worry. The entire city was blacked out, her street deserted, her building's hollowness huge and echoing. She tossed and turned on her mattress on the floor, trying not to look at the gap where her books had been. Her mind jumped like a monkey from Stefan to Mietek, to her mother's heart, to worrying about a direct hit on her bomb shelter. Her only reassurance and companion was Radio Warsaw, a pianist, Wladyslaw Szpilman, playing Chopin.

Irena worried about Mietek. Reports from the front were grim, and the first official casualty lists were posted. Every family had someone in uniform, and every family held its breath each time another wall poster went up. Irena searched for his name, fearing the worst.

Air raids hammered the city day and night, and by the end of the first week people spoke of a siege. Electricity was a thing of the past, water pressure low again, and fires burned unabated. Wall posters ordered residents not to bathe. *Robotnik*, Warsaw's daily newspaper, still managed to publish every day, an inspiration to Irena, and daily wall posters appeared with news and announcements. Except for essential services – fire, water, police, and social welfare – commerce ceased.

The German advance was so swift that by the end of the first week rumors put German artillery, the fearsome "88s," less than 20 miles away. That same day the first artillery shells hit Warsaw – a new terror. At least with bombing raids there was time to take shelter. Artillery gave only seconds of warning: a brief whistling sound, a moment of silence, a brilliant flash, then the blast.

Despite the threat of bombardment, Irena walked every day to her Social Welfare office, which offered a sense of purpose, or at least distraction – completing forms, writing reports, telephoning clients and landlords. Fewer than half of the other social workers showed up, further aggravating the crisis of need that had mushroomed before the war began and now was a catastrophe. She looked around her and wondered what kept the others at their desks. Was it courage, denial, or some other kind of optimism? Or was it mere loyalty, an institutional habit?

Irena had risen in the welfare hierarchy to become a senior administrator with a small office of her own. By the end of that first devastating week of war, as if the challenges of a bombardment weren't daunting enough, refugees from the fighting began to trickle, then stream, into Warsaw. Jan Dobraczynski and his assistant, Jaga, came into Irena's office together and closed the door. He remained standing, his arms crossed over his chest, his expression enigmatic. Irena still wasn't sure she could trust Dobraczynski. Jaga, noticeably shorter today without her heels, fitted a cigarette into her black cigarette holder.

Dobraczynski had recently given Irena the added responsibility of assisting refugees from *Wielkopolska*, Greater Poland, the western regions through which the German army had rolled. Now, standing in her office, he said, "I'm afraid I've given you too many new families, mostly Jews. Jaga can help you. Assigning benefits – it will be tricky. We need more liaisons with CENTOS and TOZ. Your connections there will be important."

Irena thought he was trying to sound hopeful, as if this was a reasonable request, but she could see in his eyes that he knew differently.

"Jaga will fill you in on the details. I have another meeting." He almost smiled and left.

Jaga put a folder on Irena's desk labeled **BOROWSKI**. It looked like all the others, but inside were five blank birth certificates, at least as many baptismal certificates and marriage licenses, and a package of registration forms. "They're for Irena Schultz, Jadwiga Deneka, and you. Jan – I mean Pan Dobraczynski calls what you do 'creative social work.'" Jaga winked. "I can get more."

Irena felt light-headed for a moment, exposed. "Jaga. I don't understand."

"I'm sure you know what to do with these. Nothing more need be said."

Irena was now sure that Dobraczynski was a friend as well.

★　★　★　★　★　★　★　★　★　★

Warsaw had too few homeless shelters, and Warsovians fleeing bomb-damaged homes already filled those, leaving little room for the refugees from the countryside, driven to Warsaw by the German Blitzkrieg. Thousands of refugees, most of them lice-infested, malnourished, sick, and in desperate need of emergency shelter and food, mistakenly thought Warsaw was a safe place. Irena managed to identify a trusted social worker in each of the ten district Social Welfare offices, each worker willing to alter documents or provide fraudulent ones, the way she and Irena Schultz had been doing for the previous few years. She referred to them as her liaisons, nine women and one man, all of whom created their own networks of Poles willing to temporarily house refugees, mostly Jews, until they could be placed more permanently. Only Irena and Irena Schultz knew the identities of these angels – her "Emergency Care Service."

But the challenge was overwhelming, and Irena saw more and more refugees begging on the streets, whole families dressed in rags, crying out in Yiddish, "Haks Rakhmunes!" (Have mercy!)

One day at the height of the bombardment in mid-September, Irena forged Dobraczynski's signature for emergency food vouchers and several hundred zloty for three large Polish refugee families. It was an impetuous act, born of frustration and urgency – one she could rationalize any number of ways: They had no food. Winter was only a few months away. The food warehouses were still well stocked. Social Welfare funds sat idle in state accounts.

To her surprise, Irena found the forgery relatively simple. She had the artistic ability, and after a few days of practice she was able to reproduce his signature easily. She went to the food warehouse herself. Normally there would have been rigorous accounting of every transaction, but the warehouse clerk, a terrified young man, was so anxious about the bombing that he quickly filled the forged orders and returned to his shelter.

The heaviest bombardment rained down on Warsaw during the final two days of the month-long siege, September 25th and 26th. Buildings near Irena's house were destroyed; hundreds died each day. Irena slept in the basement shelter, fearful each night that it might become her tomb should the building sustain a direct hit. On the last day she went upstairs to her empty apartment to change clothing. She looked at her reflection and could scarcely recognize the girl in the mirror, eyes dark under heavy lids, her lips still naturally red but turned down, her hair hanging in greasy ringlets.

Mercifully, the next day Warsaw surrendered. Irena walked out onto the silent street, the air rotten with smoke and the stench of decomposing bodies and garbage, an olfactory fugue from hell. She walked from her office on Zlota Street to Stawki Street and back, then to Franciszkanska Street, where she succeeded in placing two more families in temporary shelter. In every household children were sick, hungry, and dirty. She looked into the eyes of the children on the street, the families huddled together wondering where their next meal would come from, where they could shelter when night came and the weather turned cold.

At twilight, as she walked home through her ravaged city, the sky furnace-red, Irena thought that someday an historian would write about this time and would tell it all wrong, because nothing written or explained logically could ever capture what Warsaw endured in September 1939.

★   ★   ★   ★   ★   ★   ★   ★   ★   ★

Irena's friend Ewa now worked with CENTOS, one of several Jewish self-help charities funded by the Joint Distribution Committee, which tried to feed the poor at least one meal a day in field kitchens — soup and black bread. Very soon even that would come to seem like a feast. Irena funneled misappropriated general funds, food, and medicine through Ewa at CENTOS.

Ewa's natural optimism and persistent smile had always been a relief for Irena, an oasis of hope. "Thanks be to God," Ewa said again and again. "Everything will turn out all right. I think everything happens for a reason, though we may not understand it. Over time, things get better." But as conditions became more desperate, especially for the Jews, Irena found Ewa's cheerfulness maddening and wondered, what was the limit of her acceptance?

A few days before Warsaw surrendered, Irena had gone to see Ewa. She hurried down Karmelicka Street, one of the busiest in the Jewish District before the war, now virtually deserted. There had already been two air raids that day. She walked quickly, carrying two canvas bags filled with lint bandages from the warehouse. Stitched into the seam of one bag was 1,200 zloty.

As Irena entered CENTOS headquarters she was overwhelmed by the cacophony of Yiddish, Polish, and Hebrew, by the foul odor of musk, urine, and sweat, too many frantic people jammed into too small a space. Refugee families jockeyed for room, children cried while their parents argued. These people had been homeless for weeks, many had walked hundreds of miles to reach Warsaw, hoping for a bath and some food. They found neither.

Irena maneuvered through the crowd to Ewa Rechtman's office; the door was ajar, and Ewa was on the telephone – it still worked most of the time. When she saw Irena, her smile grew wide, and she waved her inside.

"135 kilos... 420 zloty," she said into the phone. "That's all I can offer. Don't bother! You're not the only thief in Warsaw. I'll try someone else." She slammed down the phone. "Jackass!" Even angry and frustrated, Ewa smiled.

They hugged each other. "Thanks be to God you're all right. Your house? Your mother?"

"All fine," Irena said. She noticed Ewa still wore makeup. "And you? Your parents? Your brother?"

Ewa nodded. "So far, God willing. We had a scare a few days ago. Adam was almost killed. He had just left a building on Ostrowska Street when it was hit by a shell. Ten people died. He helped dig out survivors. I'm afraid for him. He was angry before; now he's enraged."

"What was he doing there?"

"I sent him to deliver food and money to a paralyzed woman. She died. If he had been killed..."

An assistant interrupted with a form to sign. When she left, Ewa's smile vanished. "I heard a disturbing rumor today."

"There's no shortage of rumors," Irena said. "Mostly untrue."

"This one is true." Ewa's eyes welled up; she cleared her throat and carefully dabbed at the corners of her eyes to preserve her mascara. "What I heard was that the General Staff and President Moscicki fled to Romania yesterday."

"Are you surprised?" Irena said.

"I didn't think this could happen." She found a compact in her handbag and reapplied her face powder. "It's unsettling. But I'm all right now," she said. "Really. It's just that I haven't slept much." Ewa looked through the two canvas sacks of lint bandages. "Can I ask where they came from?"

Irena shook her head. "Better not. And here's 1,200 zloty."

By the time she left CENTOS to return to her office, new posters were going up on walls and kiosks announcing the "tactical relocation" of the Polish government to Romania.

For the first time Irena saw retreating Polish soldiers on the street, weary and dejected, those improbable few who had survived and eluded capture at the front. They were mostly unshaven and loud – some clearly drunk – their uniforms soiled, their boots mud-caked. Some still carried rifles slung carelessly over their shoulders. Gas masks dangled from their belts.

One grizzled soldier – it was hard to tell if he was old or not – leaned against a lamppost. Irena noticed him because he wore Mietek's unit insignia. "Excuse me," she said. He straightened up, but not to attention. "My husband, Mietek Sendler. Do you know what happened to him?"

The soldier asked for a cigarette, and she gave him one. Her hand trembled as she held the lighter Mietek had given her last October on her Naming Day.

"We were overrun," he said, a faraway look in his eyes, the terror returning. "There was no end to them. Bombers, tanks, artillery, ten of their infantry for every one of ours. I saw a Polish officer on a white horse charge a tank with his sword."

Irena wondered how much of his account was meant to keep her from thinking him a coward. "Mietek Sendler," she said again. "Lieutenant Sendler?"

He furrowed his brow, then nodded. "Yes. Sendler. He was one of the good ones."

Irena's blood ran cold.

"He wasn't afraid."

"Is he..."

"Dead? I don't know. The last I saw him he was alive. Like I said, Ma'am. He was a damn good officer and a damn good Pole. We didn't have a chance. Might I trouble you for another cigarette, Ma'am – for later?"

CHAPTER 9

Bread Lines

Warsaw, October 1939 – January 1940

Not a single explosion overnight. Except for the chattering of swallows and cooing of pigeons, who seemed unfazed by the smoke, a preternatural silence blanketed Warsaw. Irena slept more than twelve hours, longer than she had ever slept in her life, a profound sleep in which gigantic dreams slipped from her grasp like gas balloons.

Now that Poland had been defeated, Stefan returned to Warsaw. He came to Irena's apartment and insisted she not walk alone to her office. The streets were as quiet and deserted as a Sunday morning, everything gray and black, no sirens, no trams, no traffic. The destruction was appalling. Rubbish, ash, and glass crunched underfoot. Irena knew that thousands of decomposing bodies baked in the rubble along with a stew of garbage and sewage. Smoke from burning buildings, profane incense, partially disguised the putrefaction.

She and Stefan hardly spoke as they walked through this ashen landscape. Though it was a warm day, a woman in a red wool coat appeared at the entrance to her courtyard on Leszno Street, bringing color back to the world.

Today Irena would make home visits for the first time in over two weeks. It felt like a small restoration of normalcy – a repair of September's catastrophe. The German bombing had selectively targeted the Jewish district, and, compared to other parts of Warsaw, that area had suffered twice as many destroyed buildings, some still smoldering. At the corner of Zelazna and Grzybowska, two men cut gray meat from a dead horse. Two other men stood by, guarding the butchers with long cudgels.

"Valuable meat," Stefan said.

For an odious moment the horsemeat looked enticing, but Irena said, "It might be tainted."

"It might not be tainted. Starving people will eat almost anything."

Warsaw was completely cut off. Radio Warsaw had been bombed off the air, *Robotnik* had stopped publication two weeks earlier, and now there were not even wall posters. Wireless radios still received propaganda from Radio Berlin and Radio Moscow, trumpeting the German and Soviet "liberation" of Poland. Occasionally a BBC or Paris station was tunable. Each reported a different war.

Irena's mother was glad to leave Aunt Kazimiera's apartment and return home, though she looked more sickly and had a persistent cough. When she slept at all, Janina required three pillows. She ate only one meal a day, and that only because Irena insisted. One night Irena found her sitting at their small kitchen table with a candle, looking through the family album of photographs from a happier time – pictures of Irena's father and aunts and uncles in Otwock.

Irena felt she had intruded on a private moment, but just then Janina looked up at her. She had been crying. "Irena, you should be asleep."

"What are you looking at?"

"Old pictures – just to pass the time."

Irena sat next to her and saw a familiar photograph taken before she was born. Four adults, perhaps on a picnic, sat on the ground, expressionless, except for Irena's father, a handsome man with a fine mustache, who wore a peaked cap and a wry smile. He lay across Janina's lap at a jaunty angle, flanked by his sister, Irena's Aunt Kazimiera, and Grandmother Konstancja.

Janina's speech came in short, wheezing phrases, her lungs bubbling. "Sometimes I wish I was with him. I miss him; I want to tell him everything. Your father was a good man. He would have been so proud of you." She turned the page. "I just want to die peacefully."

Irena hated to hear her mother talk like that, something she did more and more often. On the next page was a photograph of Irena on her 5th Naming Day holding her new kitten, which was a blur of ghostly motion. Irena said, "That picture always made you laugh."

"You always loved animals, especially cats. You were a spitfire and so was that cat of yours."

★　★　★　★　★　★　★　★　★　★

The next day Mayor Starzynski surrendered Warsaw to a Wehrmacht officer who wasted no time posting decrees.

DECREE: SEPTEMBER 28, 1939

All Poles are guaranteed their rights as citizens under the care of the German Reich. Jews will be guaranteed their rights including property and security.

DECREE: SEPTEMBER 29, 1939

All Jewish businesses must be transferred to German "trustees" who must not retain Jewish employees. Pension rights for Jews are revoked. Jewish "administrators" who run apartment buildings owned by Jews are removed from their posts. Jewish landlords are deprived of their properties. New enterprise licenses can only be issued to those who can prove pure "Aryan" extraction. Jewish peddlers may only appear on streets populated by Jews.

DECREE: SEPTEMBER 30, 1939

A complete census is to be taken immediately.

The Wehrmacht arrived, and immediately the streets of Warsaw teemed with the green uniformed occupying army – soldiers, military trucks, and equipment. Some Poles watched the German goose-stepping parades, and on October 5th Hitler himself came to Warsaw to celebrate his victory, but by and large civilians avoided the invaders, or watched warily through curtained windows. Stores remained closed, and trams stood idle in the Muranowski Square depot just blocks from the railroad freight platforms, *Umschlagplatz*, where trainloads of troops and cattle cars filled with war material arrived daily.

The first official act of the German administration was one of kind-

86

ness; the army doled out warm soup and black bread. German armored cars drove slowly through the streets, announcing the distribution, and long lines began to form. A German airplane circled overhead, and Stefan said it was probably photographing the defeated Poles for the archives of the Thousand Year Reich.

In that first awkward meeting of conqueror and victim, Poles sized up their occupiers. Stefan accompanied Irena every day, trying to avoid eye contact with the Wehrmacht soldiers, whose boots slapped Warsaw cobblestones in unison.

"I was expecting supermen," Stefan said. "But really, take away their boots and their uniforms and they're no different than us."

"They hate us," Irena said. "They look at us and see animals."

As they walked down Sienna Street toward Irena's office they passed a soup line – hundreds of Poles with cups and tins – a line that seemed orderly until a sudden disturbance erupted near the Wehrmacht wagon. A Pole further back in the line pointed ahead of him and repeated in German, "Ein Jude!"

Two German soldiers, SS Special Operations – Einsatzgruppen – not Wehrmacht – responded to the disruption. One of the SS men pulled the bearded Jew and his wife from the line and taunted them in German.

"Keep walking," Stefan said and pushed Irena forward with his hand on her back.

"But, Stefan. That man..."

"They're Jews."

A pistol shot cut Stefan short. Irena tried to turn around, but Stefan's arm urged her on. "Don't look! Keep walking."

There were no words between them. Irena was angry with Stefan, but more so with herself. Ever since she was a young girl, Irena had followed her parents' injunction to stand up for those treated unjustly. One episode stood out in her memory, when she was no more than thirteen, when her adherence to her parents' philosophy had ended in bloodshed. Irena had come to the aid of the only Jewish girl in her class – Rachela, a shy, withdrawn girl with dark, stringy hair, who wore the same peasant shoes every day.

She had a clear memory of a warm spring day, the kind of day when nothing should go wrong. Irena witnessed Rachela being attacked by two strong girls in the park beside their school. Without thinking, she dropped her lunch sack and leaped onto the bigger girl's back, punching blindly at her head. The other girl pulled Irena onto the ground, where the two girls pummeled her. She tried to take a breath but nothing came; her vision grew dark, and she lost consciousness.

Suddenly, there was sunlight again, and she looked up at the face of her history teacher, Professor Pikatowski, "Pika" to her classmates, a right-wing admirer of Roman Dmowski. Pika had no patience for Irena's socialist ideas and he said so often in class, to Irena's humiliation, but she never backed down, never apologized for her views. Now he hauled Irena to her feet, his fat fingers digging into her arms. "This will not go unpunished, young lady."

After school that day, Irena waited in the hallway until her language teacher, a young woman, new to the school, still fresh and nervous, motioned for Irena to come into the classroom and closed the door. "Why were you fighting?"

Irena explained about Rachela, about her poverty, and about the epithets, the beating. There had been a wrong, and it needed to be righted. The teacher interrupted her, and Irena prepared to receive her punishment.

"You did the right thing," the teacher said, then patted her on the back and held the door for her to leave. Irena was stupefied: she was rescued instead of punished.

After this incident, some students became openly hostile to Irena, calling her "Jew slave" and "Rachela's secret sister." Other students shunned her. When she felt discouraged, she remembered her father and could almost hear his voice reminding her, "There are two kinds of people in this world, good and bad. It doesn't matter if they are rich or poor, what religion or race. What matters is if they are good or bad."

Irena was in serious trouble again during her last year of high school, after she had already been accepted to the Law Faculty of Warsaw University, a rarity for a woman. Once again the difficulty involved her history teacher, 'Pika,' who harangued his students about minorities – Hungarians, Gypsies, Jews, Ukrainians – "taking over Poland, like a cancer." In her last year, Irena wrote a paper about minorities entitled

"Repairing Poland." Her thesis postulated that growing political chaos and the splintering of parties, accompanied by inflation, led to the scapegoating of minorities by the nationalist right, instigating fear and xenophobia. If this course was not corrected, she warned, Poland would follow an inexorable path to instability, *coup d'etat*, and, ultimately, self-destruction. Her hero, Marshal Jozef Pilsudski, leader of the revolutionary Socialist movement, emphasized the importance of an ethnically diverse Poland. Irena's villain, Roman Dmowski, spokesperson for the Nationalist movement and the National Democratic Party, advocated a centralized, unitary state dominated by ethnic Poles. Germans and Jews were to be excluded; other non-Polish minorities were to be assimilated and "turned into Poles or deported."

In the course of her research, Irena read everything she could about anti-Semitism in Poland. She was bewildered by the conflicting reasons given for loathing the Jews, often by the same parties or groups, running the gamut from hating Jews because they spoke Yiddish, dressed peculiarly, and were so different from Poles, to hating Jews because they were so like the Poles, well-dressed, well-spoken, and even thought of themselves as Poles before Jews. As bankers and capitalists, Jews were responsible for Poland's economic woes, and as Bolshevik Communists and dangerous anarchists, Jews threatened the status quo.

In her paper, Irena pointed out that one-third of Poland's population was non-Polish, and ten percent was Jewish. Anti-Semitism, she wrote, had no place in Poland, and General Pilsudski himself acknowledged the sacrifice of Jewish soldiers in the Great War and the Polish-Soviet War. Dmowski's nationalists, supported by the intolerance and blatant anti-Semitism of some political and religious leaders, took full advantage of the surge in nationalist pride that accompanied victory in the Polish-Soviet war. Irena railed against the most recent manifestation of intolerance, the proposed *numerus clausus*, a direct quota system for university admissions meant to exclude minorities in general, and Jews in particular.

Irena ended the paper saying that "she would live to see the day when there would be no more colonies and no more state boundaries." She wrote eloquently of her dream of a peaceful world governed by love and respect.

A few days later 'Pika' slammed the paper down before her with a big red "F" on the front. She was to see the Headmaster.

Headmaster Pan Wyszinski ordered Irena to stand straight and unmoving before his desk while he read her paper. He made notes in the margins with a red pencil. Finally, he turned back to the first page and crossed out Pikatowski's "F." He sighed deeply, considered for a moment, then replaced it with a "B+."

"You are a headstrong girl," he said, peering over the top of thick spectacles. "The world doesn't like headstrong girls and would just as soon squash you like a bug! That said, I see you are also an eloquent and persuasive writer. But!" He let the admonition hang. "You are stating a political theory," he said, "and not a very popular one. You clearly demonstrate that you have learned your history well. But heed my warning, young lady. Many academics at Warsaw University share Professor Pikatowski's political views. Step out of line and you will get into serious trouble."

Soon enough, she did.

In the early '30s, when Irena was a student, the University of Warsaw was a hotbed of anger and agitation, from the left and the right. Hitler had inspired anti-Semitic legislators in the Polish parliament to adopt the *numerus clausus* quota limiting the number of Jewish students. Terrible articles appeared in newspapers and magazines about Jews, Gypsies, and foreigners. Jews were singled out first for intellectual assault, cloaked in academic finesse and scientific reason. Before long that façade was abandoned in favor of fists and batons. The student radicals – some of them wearing brown shirts in homage to the Nazis – belonged to the Camp for a Greater Poland (OWP). On one occasion they threw a Jewish girl through a second story window. Though she was seriously injured the University did nothing. On another occasion, in front of a crowd of witnesses, a gang of OWP students dragged two Jewish girls by the hair down a university stairway.

In an effort to keep the peace, the university decreed that Jews should sit on separate benches in lecture halls – the so-called 'ghetto bench' or 'Jewish bench.' Credit books for grades were clearly marked 'ARYAN' or 'JEW.' Irena began to cross out the word 'ARYAN' from the front of her credit book. One day, frustration and anger overwhelmed her, and, on an impulse, as she walked into a crowded lecture hall, Irena turned left instead of right and sat in the front row of the 'Jewish bench.' There was immediate buzzing and murmuring. The professor waited at the lectern glowering at her, then cleared his throat and demanded an explanation.

"Today I am a Jew," Irena said defiantly.

The next day Irena was summoned to the Dean's office. Professor Wieczorkiewicz had her stand in the hallway for two hours before calling her in, then required her to remain standing before his desk as he looked through her file.

He did not look up. "I see you are an intelligent girl – but not a very sensible one." He was a tall man, and when he stood, he towered over Irena. "You have dishonored the law and the University by defacing your credit book and by willfully sitting on the 'Jewish bench.' I hereby suspend you from the University."

Irena had known she might face this severe consequence, but an internal urgency had forced her to act. As she explained to her mother when she came home that evening, "I had to do it. It was a need of my heart."

Irena's parents were both activists, members of the Polish Socialist Party, the PPS, as was Irena. Her mother had courted imprisonment as an underground teacher of Polish history and literature for *Macierz Polska*, an illegal organization during the Russian occupation. Her grandfather and great-grandfather had been patriots for Polish independence. Social justice was a family tradition.

"I can't help being afraid for my little girl," Janina said to her head-strong daughter. "But I understand. You're like your father that way."

★   ★   ★   ★   ★   ★   ★   ★   ★   ★

Stefan pushed her firmly along, away from the disturbance on the bread line, towards Irena's office. "It's like it was at University," she said. "The fascists – the 'Jewish Bench.'"

"You're right," Stefan said. "You were such a little spitfire back then, ready to take on every fascist."

"I can't be a bystander," Irena protested.

"Then it meant a disciplinary suspension, now it means a bullet in your head." Stefan was agitated. "I worry about you."

"That's sweet." They continued in silence.

When they arrived at her office, both of them breathing hard, Irena stepped away from Stefan's arm. "I'll come get you at five o'clock," he said.

She avoided his gaze. "Yes... that would be lovely," she said, and hurried up the stairs. At the entrance to her Social Welfare office, she almost collided with a small man with nervous eyes who was waiting for her.

"Pani Sendler, we have a very big problem." He spoke too quickly. "I'm Elihu Giterman, Chairman of the Nowolipki Street #20 House Committee. The Germans forced us out at gunpoint. Numbers 12, 14, 16, 18, and 20. Here, I wrote it all down for you. No warning – they simply ordered us out. Hundreds of families. We've no place to go – no food. Something must be done!"

Irena brought Elihu Giterman into Dobraczynski's office, and he rattled off his story again. "I'm very sorry, Mr. Giterman," Dobraczynski said from his chair. "I'm not in a position to tell the Germans what they can and cannot do."

"Can't you talk to them? You're a Christian – they'll listen to you."

"Take it up with the *Judenrat* – it's just a few blocks away – Grzybowska #26."

"The new *Kehilla*? What can they do?"

"I don't know. Everything is different now, Pan Giterman. As of yesterday, the *Judenrat* is the Jewish authority. They answer to the Germans. Czerniakow is head of the council. He has connections; he has clout with the Germans. I don't."

Giterman gnawed his lower lip, his breath short and quick. "You're the goddam Welfare office! It's your job."

Dobraczynski rose to his full height, dwarfing his petitioner. "Pan Giterman! The Germans make the rules now. You'd better get used to it. Your only recourse is with the *Judenrat* or a shelter. Good day."

Irena recognized that Dobraczynski was correct, though unduly harsh. She shared his frustration and maybe his anxiety as well, with how quickly conditions in Warsaw had deteriorated. And there was little any of them could do about it.

CHAPTER 10

Decrees

Warsaw, October 1939 – January 1940

DECREE: OCTOBER 4, 1939

A dusk to dawn curfew is established for all. Violators will be shot.

$\star \quad \star \quad \star \quad \star \quad \star \quad \star \quad \star \quad \star \quad \star \quad \star$

A week after the Polish surrender there was still no electricity, no radio, no newspaper. Irena had to reconstruct the world out of rumor and daily propaganda sheets plastered on walls and kiosk pillars. She searched for Mietek on every posted list of the dead and wounded, an incomplete accounting to be sure, that allowed some to grieve, the rest to wonder, and everybody to pray.

In spite of their difficulties, she felt warmly toward Mietck, the boy she had grown up with, the boy who ice-skated with her in Piotrków's public park. They went to Warsaw University together, where he was a gifted classics scholar, where they courted and married in 1931. Not long after their marriage Irena was suspended from the University for the 'Jewish Bench' incident. Although she had completed everything except her thesis, she had to give up her studies and find work. In September 1932, she was hired by the Department of Assistance to Mother and Child, part of the Citizens' Committee of Social Work in Warsaw, conducting interviews with people seeking food, money, shelter, and clothing. She learned how the system functioned and malfunctioned and how to fix it for her clients, how to bend the rules.

Ironically, their marriage's demise began as a stroke of good fortune for Mietek. He was offered a teaching position in Poznan – one he could not refuse for his academic career. He assumed Irena would go with him, finish her studies in Poznan, or be content to raise a family. But Irena insisted on staying in Warsaw. She vowed to reverse her university suspension and graduate, and she decided to dedicate her career to social work, a career to which she felt well suited.

In the end, Mietek went to Poznan. He wanted a wife; Irena wanted to change the world. Mietek's name did not appear on that day's wall poster.

A few days earlier, a rudimentary postal service was re-established, and when Irena came home that evening, she found a letter with Mietek's distinctive handwriting. She held the unopened envelope and wept grateful tears.

The letter was addressed to Irena and his family – a terse missive with more information than emotion. He was alive, a prisoner of war at *Oflag IIC Woldenberg*. Mietek instructed Irena to forward this letter to his parents immediately. Dutifully, she sent his letter on to Piotrków.

★ ★ ★ ★ ★ ★ ★ ★ ★ ★

DECREE: OCTOBER 12, 1939
Jewish emigration from the General Gouvernement is strictly forbidden.

DECREE: OCTOBER 12, 1939
Jewish deposits and bank accounts are frozen. It is illegal to pay a Jew more than 500 zloty. Banks are forbidden to pay out more than 250 zloty to a Jew. It is forbidden for Jewish families to hold more than 2,000 zloty in cash.

DECREE: OCTOBER 18, 1939
Social Welfare benefits or services may not be awarded to any Jew.

DECREE:
As of October 26, 1939, Jews resident in the General Gouvernement are obliged to work. With this aim in mind, Jews will be concentrated in forced labor teams.

★ ★ ★ ★ ★ ★ ★ ★ ★ ★

Garbage went uncollected, and the city smelled worse each day. After visiting a family in the Jewish district on Prosta Street, Irena walked two blocks to the Rechtman's third-floor apartment on Sienna Street, where Ewa lived as an observant Jew with her parents and her brother, Adam. Irena had a gift for her friend.

Before the war, Irena had envied Ewa her good looks, her easy nature, and her warm and loving family. But though Ewa was beautiful, she had what forgers of illegitimate documents called "bad looks" – too Semitic – the shape of her eyes too oriental, her nose too prominent. It would be difficult for her to "pass" as a Pole.

Irena knocked at Ewa's flat. Her brother, Adam, opened the door. He was completely unlike his sister, his body compact, dark-haired, with fierce brown eyes.

He shook Irena's hand with a strong grip. "I'm Adam."

Irena thought his smile flirtatious. "I'm Irena Send…"

"Oh yes. I've heard all about you. You're shorter than I would have guessed. Ewa talks as if you are gigantic."

"Adam!" Ewa came into the room and pushed him away. He retreated to the kitchen where he exchanged harsh words with his mother and then slammed the door behind him.

"Adam makes Mother quite sad," Ewa said. "I tell her, he's just angry, young, and male. He has a lot of confusion inside."

"How are all of you doing?" Irena asked.

"We'll be all right. God willing, the worst is over. I don't think the Germans will stay more than a month. England and France are in the war, maybe America. I have to believe, Irena, that it will be all right."

Irena wanted to shake her, but said, "We should pray for the best but prepare for the worst."

"Amen." Then, as if she reported nothing more consequential than the weather, Ewa said, "Adam was picked up by German soldiers a few days ago." Her smile disappeared. "It was a random sweep for forced labor. He had to collect bricks from the rubble for ten hours. I was sick with worry. Finally, just before curfew, he came home exhausted, covered with brick dust. It made him look pink. He said one of the Germans made him dance a jig in the middle of the street. Traffic stopped – there was a crowd.

People laughed at him. I think the humiliation hurt him the most. Adam has a short temper anyway. I worry he'll do something rash. He said he would kill them. He means it. I see it in his eyes."

"He should be careful," Irena said.

"He'll get used to the Germans. We'll all get used to the Germans."

Was that really the best they could hope for? Curfew was approaching. Irena gave Ewa her 'gift,' several thousand Zloty in a plain envelope. "It's for your supervisor, Adolf Berman – from our Social Welfare budget in Warsaw. I'm sure he'll use it well."

★   ★   ★   ★   ★   ★   ★   ★   ★   ★

The first barbed wire fences appeared in October, enclosing some of the main Jewish streets. The entire Jewish district was decreed a "Quarantine Area." Signs appeared overnight:

ATTENTION: EPIDEMIC AREA – ENTRY FORBIDDEN

Despite the Germans' obsessive fear of contagion and disease, especially typhus, they had created in the Jewish district the ideal conditions for pestilence. Irena called it Warsaw's Four Horsemen of the Apocalypse – overcrowding, poor sanitation, rodents, and malnutrition. Refugees from Germany were forced into one overcrowded part of town, into crowded shelters, cold and hungry, their children crying, or lethargic, beyond tears.

Irena accompanied Jan Dobraczynski to a special meeting with the head of the German Epidemic Control Authority, Dr. Kurt Schrempf, a short, fat, balding man who strained the seams of his Wehrmacht uniform. A little swastika flag stood on his desk and behind him hung a royal-red, wall-sized swastika banner. Through a translator, Schrempf told them that he was a scientist, not a soldier.

"There are certain inescapable truths about infectious disease," he lectured. "Poor people, ignorant people, dirty, lice-infested, rejected and starving parasites, still fight for their miserable lives. Jews in particular carry and spread typhus. They put the entire city of Warsaw at risk. It would be inhumane not to quarantine them." He squinted at Dobraczynski as if he could look into his soul. "It's the right thing to do, don't you agree?"

Dobraczynski, his breathing still regular, did not look up from his notes. Irena wanted to believe his restraint an act of resistance, and quickly attended her own notepad as she fumed inside; Schrempf's idiocy would cost lives – but maybe that was the point. But another, more encouraging idea occurred to her; she might actually use the Germans' phobia about typhus and TB to the advantage of her clients. In the meantime, this imbecile was responsible for public health in Warsaw. She looked into his piggy eyes and said to herself, "You will not prevail." Her pencil lead snapped.

★　★　★　★　★　★　★　★　★　★

Still no electricity, and candles were scarce. Carbide lamps, which looked like sealed soup cans filled with solid carbide, became the standard light source. Water was poured into the cans through a tube, and the resultant reaction released carbide gas, which burned with a humming blue flame that did not flicker and gave off a distinctive, harsh odor.

Water pressure was low, and for many Warsovians, hand pumps on the street were their only source of water. Most homes in the Jewish district lacked a flush toilet. Garbage continued to accumulate.

Soon after the first German units arrived, they began distributing a propaganda newspaper, the two-page *Nowy Kurier Warszawski*, the New Warsaw Gazette. Now the German decrees could be printed in the daily newspaper.

DECREE: OCTOBER 20, 1939

All radios must be surrendered to the authorities immediately. Possession of a radio receiver is punishable by imprisonment. Possession of a radio transmitter is punishable by death.

When Irena arrived home that evening she found Janina packing up their radio.

"Don't, Mother!" Irena said. "Tonight, after everyone is asleep, I'll hide it in the attic, covered with the old comforters. If it's found we can always plead ignorance. Tell no one."

"For God's sake, Irena! Everyone in the building knows we have a radio. They come in to listen all the time. Why not just call up the Germans and explain that you're terribly sorry, you can't give up your radio. I'm sure they'll understand."

"Mother! Sarcasm is unnecessary. I have a very strong feeling that someday a radio might be valuable. If any of the neighbors ask, say we've given it up."

Janina relented, and in the middle of the night Irena climbed the unstable ladder into a crawl space too small for a man to stand in and covered the radio with blankets.

* * * * * * * * * *

DECREE: OCTOBER 23, 1939
It is strictly forbidden for Jews to deal in textile goods (manufactures) and processed hides (leather) and any sort of manufacturing that involves these materials.

* * * * * * * * * *

The *Nowy Kurier Warszawski* printed stories every day about the sinful and criminal ways of the Jews, their filth and propensity for disease, their violation of the norms of behavior. On Monday, October 23, 1939, the newspaper headline read:

"JEWISH CENSUS"

The following Saturday every Jew was to be counted and listed with address and date of birth. The official decree followed:

DECREE: OCTOBER 25, 1939
There will be a mandatory census of Jewish inhabitants of Warsaw on Saturday, October 28th. The Judenrat, under the leadership of engineer Czerniakow, is required to carry out the census.

With the fighting over, the roads were safe to travel again, and the children of Warsaw had their first milk in over a month. Commerce resumed and spawned a chain of gossip about a new underground movement – partisans. Stefan explained that he was beginning to attend meetings of a fledgling underground group of Polish socialists from the PPS, the Polish Socialist Party that he and Irena both belonged to.

After nearly two months of occupation, Stefan still came to Irena's office most days to escort her home. "I'm worried for your safety," he explained. "A male escort still counts for something."

Cafés, restaurants, and nightclubs opened again, though the mood inside them was hardly celebratory. On one of the last warm days of November, when one could still sit at a sidewalk table, she and Stefan stopped for a coffee after work. A German lorry with a score of SS soldiers in the back rumbled along Okopowa Street, the late afternoon sun reflecting off the twin lightning bolts on their lapels.

Before the war, Stefan and Irena argued about the relative merits of his cynicism versus her principled optimism. He hadn't changed his mind; he still mocked organizations for their interminable meetings and arguments. "A lot of talking. Something Jews and Socialists do all the time," he said.

"I suppose it's all right to mock Socialists," Irena said, "because you are one, but you shouldn't make fun of Jews."

Stefan took his just-issued *Kennkarte* from his breast pocket, a product of the recent census, and opened it for Irena to see. It was stamped 'JUDE.' He sat back and smiled, enjoying Irena's confusion. "So, I guess I can mock the Jews."

Irena didn't know what to say. Of course, it didn't matter, she told herself, but how could she have known him for so long and not known this? She glanced around to make sure their conversation was secure. "Stefan – is this a secret?"

"I was Jewish. My father and mother became Evangelicals when I was a young boy. I don't remember very much about it. But the Germans seem to know all the details and consider me a Jew. I'm a chameleon, changing from Jew to Evangelical and now to Jew again. I'm thinking of changing yet again. Maybe next time I'll be a Catholic."

"Stefan! Be serious. How can you make a joke of this?"

He pulled his chair up close and leaned forward to Irena, their heads almost touching. "I met a new artist," he said. "He works for the PPS. He makes the most realistic documents – *Kennkarte*, work certificates, residence certificates, baptismal and marriage certificates. Anything you want. He's very good. He has a certain sympathy for Jews. Very reasonably priced."

She drank her coffee and looked into Stefan's eyes. "I'm interested," she said. "Who is this artist?"

Stefan wrote a name and telephone exchange on a scrap of paper and pushed it across the table.

"Money is hard to come by, Stefan. We're producing our own documents. Maybe not as perfect as your PPS artist, but good enough for now."

"Be careful," he said earnestly. "Whoever denounces you will be well rewarded with zloty and bacon. Tempting."

"Don't be silly, Stefan. I'm a nobody to the Germans."

"That's what they all say, until they're caught – or hungry enough – or tortured."

"Why do you trust those socialists you were with today?" Irena asked. "Maybe one of them would like the Gestapo's bacon. One never knows."

"Jews won't do it for bacon. Not yet, anyway. Do you know Ringelblum?" Stefan asked. "A Jew. He calls himself a social historian. Quite a remarkable fellow, actually. He works for the 'Joint' – the Joint Distribution Committee. Near as I can tell, he never sleeps. I went to a meeting he convened with representatives of all the Jewish political parties. Quite a mélange."

Now it was Irena who was impatient with bureaucracy. "Talk is cheap, Stefan. Meetings are cheap. Real help – food, documents, housing, medicine – costs a lot of money."

"According to Ringelblum, the Joint will get us money."

"Us? Stefan. You just said 'us.'"

"The Germans consider me a Jew. It's my heritage – for thousands of years. I suppose they're right."

* * * * * * * * * *

DECREE: NOVEMBER 23, 1939

All Jews and Jewesses staying in the General Gouvernement ten years of age and over are obliged to wear a four-inch armband in white with a blue Star of Zion on the right sleeve of their inner and outer clothing, as of 1 December 1939. These armbands are to be secured and also provided with the relevant sign, by the Jews and Jewesses themselves. (1) Transgressions will be punished with imprisonment. (2) Judgment will be passed by the special courts.

DECREE: NOVEMBER 30, 1939

Every Jewish shop must display a large Star of Zion at the entrance.

After December 1st, with the decree of armbands, it was as if the Jews of Warsaw had suddenly become a different species. Irena saw Jews excluded from shops and thrown off moving trams. Once she watched a Polish youth who, as he passed a white-armbanded family of Jews, threw his fist into the face of the father, who had no recourse but to bleed on his knees while his children cried.

Until he had forged papers and an Aryan identity, Stefan was compelled to wear the Star of David armband, and when Irena was with him she felt conspicuous, in danger. Among Aryan Poles, the blue on white Star of David quickly became known as the "badge of shame."

Stefan's mother, living with relatives in the Praga suburb of Warsaw, simply refused to wear the armband, saying that at her age it didn't matter. In any case, she was certain that the Germans had no record of her, since she had never worked a day in her life, had no worker's identity card, and had not registered for the census. "They can shoot me," she snorted. "I don't give a damn."

Shortly after the edict of the armbands, the *Nowy Kurier Warszawski* printed an interview with Dr. Ludwig Fischer, the governor of the Warsaw District. "One purpose of the armbands," Dr. Fischer explained, "was to tell from a distance whether a woman flirting with a German was a Jewess – to prevent him from being beguiled by the seductive wiles of Jewish women into sinning against the purity of the race."

★ ★ ★ ★ ★ ★ ★ ★ ★ ★

In the first week of December, 1939, a spate of decrees were issued:

DECREE:

Anyone, Pole or Jew, found selling or buying bread at prices higher than the pre-war price is liable to be executed.

DECREE:

Jews are forbidden to enter the central post office on Warecki St.

DECREE:

Every loan and mortgage establishment owned by Jews must appoint an Aryan commissioner.

DECREE:

All Jewish schools are closed.

DECREE:

The Judenrat and Chairman Czerniakow have sole responsibility for Jewish hospital care, which may not be given by an Aryan or Aryan institution or hospital to any Jew.

DECREE: DECEMBER 19, 1939

Jewish lawyers are forbidden to engage in the practice of law.

DECREE: DECEMBER 22, 1939

Prayer in synagogues is forbidden.

DECREE: DECEMBER 27, 1939

The discovery of secret radios is punishable by death.

★ ★ ★ ★ ★ ★ ★ ★ ★ ★

Food rationing began in December. Irena and her mother received ration cards divided into small colored squares, each marked with types and quantities of food. As Poles they had to register at a Polish grocery licensed to sell food near their building. Jews received ration cards of a different color stamped with a Star of David and could only use them in Jewish groceries.

Germans received 2,613 calories a day, Jews only 184; the only way Jews could stay alive was to buy black market or stolen food at five to ten times pre-war prices.

What could not be banished by decree was the Polish imagination. Rumors became more and more fantastic: The German army was demoralized, on the brink of collapse! German officers deserted their units and fled to the Russian lines! Hitler was dead!

It was December, and the rumors felt like the gifts of Swiety Mikolaj, St. Nicholas, who left presents for good children under their pillows or next to their beds every December 5th.

Ewa told Irena that the Jewish holiday of Chanukah also began that year on December 5th. Each evening she and her family (not Adam, she was sad to say) lit another candle to commemorate a great miracle. "I still expect a miracle," Ewa said. "Great things come at the most unlikely times."

Irena didn't have the heart to disagree.

"The Chanukah candles are lights in the darkness," Ewa said. "Like the miracle of the Maccabees."

Irena didn't know the story of the Maccabees, but she felt sorry for Ewa in this modern time, when miracles no longer occurred.

CHAPTER 11

Occupation
Warsaw, January – October 1940

German concerns about typhus were well-founded. The first cases appeared in January, just three months after the start of the occupation, and the incidence increased week to week, almost exclusively in the Jewish district, where most of Irena's clients lived. Every day when she returned from work, her mother searched her clothes for lice and crushed any she found. Though Irena knew it unlikely, she worried that her mother would contract this same disease that had killed her father, perhaps from a louse that Irena would bring home. In 1917, when Irena was seven years old, her father contracted typhus from treating sick and impoverished Jews. For this to be the cause of her mother's death would be an unthinkable cruelty.

As if fate conspired with the Germans, the winter of 1939-1940 brought historic cold to Poland. Coal was scarce and expensive. Irena, like most Poles, became accustomed to seeing every breath, even when indoors, and usually wore her wool coat in the homes of the poor. Janina suffered a chest infection with a high fever, and it was days before Irena could find a doctor to attend her. The harried physician, who had had only two hours of sleep the night before, told Irena he had not seen so much illness since the 1918 Spanish Flu pandemic.

As Irena waited outside her mother's bedroom for the doctor to finish his examination, she recalled being seven years old, standing in the hallway outside her father's bedroom as his colleagues from St. Spirit Hospital in Warsaw examined him. They trooped out of the sickroom with long faces, murmuring to each other, ignoring Irena – tiny, invisible, expectant. Her mother followed them out and closed the door. She would only say, "Your father is ill – nothing too serious – and he's sending us to Warsaw, just until the epidemic passes Otwock." One of her father's colleagues, Dr. Siennicki, had offered his house; he lived alone in a mansion. Irena's mother reassured her it would only be for a few days, but they packed five large valises to take with them. Her mother told her not to worry, then instructed her to say goodbye to her father. Dr. Siennicki said to stay well back from the bed. He shook a long finger at her. "No touching! No kissing!"

It was dark in her father's bedroom, except for the candle lantern Irena carried. Seared in memory, she could still hear the coarse bubbling of her father's breathing. Irena held her light up high to see his face, alone in the bed, his eyes partly open as if half asleep. She thought maybe the candlelight turned his face yellow. There were red spots on his arms. Irena didn't care what the doctor said; she would kiss him.

From lips that barely moved, he commanded, "Don't, Irena! I love you, but you must leave – with your mother. Be my big girl and take care of her."

Words stuck to his tongue, but he was determined. "Irena. Always remember what I've taught you. People are all the same – there are only good people or bad people."

"I'll remember, Father." She stood at the foot of his bed, her eyes wide, the candlelight flickering.

"Always remember, my darling Irena. If you see someone drowning, you must rescue him, even if you cannot swim."

She'd heard both of these injunctions many times before, but until now, she never asked the one question that always bothered her. "If I can't swim, won't both of us drown?"

"You must do something," he said. "You cannot watch him drown."

Five days later her father died of typhus.

And now, twenty-five years later, the sword of typhus hung again over their heads. Irena paced in her small flat, sick in her stomach at the thought of losing another parent to this disease. Irena wondered how she could go on, how she could bear the grief of being an orphan. The doctor folded up his stethoscope and sat next to the coal stove with Irena. "It's not typhus," he said. "It's her heart disease. There's so much fluid in her lungs that even a small illness becomes serious."

Irena dabbed at her tears. "Will she recover?"

"From this – yes, probably. But her heart disease will only worsen. I'm afraid she hasn't long to live." He could hardly keep his eyes open. He drank half a cup of tea, and left.

After she closed the door, Irena sat by the stove and considered the doctor's grim prognosis. She wept as quietly as she could; she did not want her mother to be afraid.

★ ★ ★ ★ ★ ★ ★ ★ ★ ★

DECREE: JANUARY 20, 1940

As a public health measure, to stem the Jewish epidemic of typhus, all synagogues, yeshivas, study houses, and ritual baths are closed. Public prayer is forbidden.

DECREE: JANUARY 22, 1940

Every Jewish male from 12 to 60 years of age must register with the Judenrat as a candidate for forced labor. The registration must be effected within the ten days from February 1ˢᵗ to February 10ᵗʰ.

DECREE: JANUARY 23, 1940

All Jewish welfare in Warsaw and occupied Poland will be consolidated into a single central Jewish welfare body, the Jewish Social Self-Help (JSS).

★ ★ ★ ★ ★ ★ ★ ★ ★ ★

New decrees were issued almost daily – a new restriction, another indignity, a slow tightening of the occupation vice, now six months old. Some of Warsaw's bomb-damaged streets had been repaired, and, once again, pedicabs, *droshky*, and automobiles filled Leszno and Zelazna Streets. Partially destroyed buildings remained as memorials of Poland's defeat. Trams screeched from Leszno Street onto Karmelicka, both main thoroughfares as crowded as before the war. It might just as well have been 1938, were it not for the stench of rot and the fact that most pedestrians wore white armbands on their right arms. Jewish men walked with their heads down, wearing rumpled suits, now one or two sizes too large, purchased before the rationing. Women no longer wore hats, preferring plain kerchiefs and old clothes. Any evidence of opulence invited seizure by the green-uniformed Wehrmacht or, worse, the black leather-coated Gestapo agents eager to satisfy their lust for plunder.

On a day in late January, Irena waited for Ewa at the wind-whipped, bitter cold intersection of Leszno and Zelazna. They had agreed to meet at midday, when pedestrian and vehicular traffic was heavy. In Irena's canvas bag, beneath a skein of yarn and knitting needles, she carried the forged *Kennkarte* identity cards, baptismal certificates, and ration cards of three dead Poles. Father Stimecki, from the Catholic Church in the Wawer suburb, had supplied the names, birthdates, addresses, and other necessary information about the three, who had died in the fighting, but whose deaths he had not yet entered into parish records. This and the priest's other acts of resistance, allowed the two Irenas to register Jews with Polish identities, thereby assigning them full welfare benefits and Aryan ration cards.

Irena felt particularly vulnerable carrying these documents, and avoided CENTOS headquarters and other Jewish self-help offices, where Gestapo agents often searched bags and folders. To be apprehended with these documents meant interrogation at Szucha #25, Gestapo Headquarters, and death in notorious Pawiak Prison.

After waiting more than half an hour, Irena began to worry; Ewa was always punctual. Behind her, on the wall of a tenement, a red street poster listed the names of those executed the day before. Irena walked up and down Leszno, fearing the worst; it was hazardous to loiter.

In the middle of the block someone suddenly thrust an arm at her. She jumped, collided with several disgruntled people, then saw it was a white-armbanded beggar, who had accosted her with his cap and had already moved on to the next person.

"*Haks Rakhmunes! A shtikel broit?*" (Have Mercy! A piece of bread?)

He wasn't the only one in search of a piece of bread. Irena knew that virtually every person on that cold Wednesday in January sought black market bread or coal, or perhaps was on his way to sell hidden diamonds for forged documents like the ones she herself carried. All of them, Aryan and Jew, bumping, pushing, grumbling, involved in one criminal activity or another.

As Irena approached the intersection, a Wehrmacht paddy wagon suddenly swerved to the curb, and its doors flew open. Every pedestrian turned and began to flee – like a school of fish suddenly spooked. Three burly SS men jumped from its back and waded into the stampeding crowd, swinging black batons over their heads, grabbing at white-banded arms. Three men were seized and stuffed into the wagon, which continued down Zelazna like a shark. The entire drama took no more than a minute, and when it was over, the crowds re-formed, once more orderly, opposing schools of fish.

Another hand grabbed at her elbow, a fierce grip. Irena jumped, and her breath caught. Ewa held her too tightly and walked too quickly. "You look a fright," Irena said. "What is it?"

Ewa pulled Irena down Leszno Street, past the courthouse. They linked arms and Irena felt how thin Ewa had already become. Irena stopped her when they reached the Femina Theater and pulled her through the doors. In the incandescent lobby Irena saw that Ewa's face had been washed clean of powder, her blond hair carelessly brushed.

"I'm so nervous all the time," Ewa said. "Sometimes I just can't stand it." She began to cry, and Irena was glad to be off the street. Ewa quickly composed herself.

"I'm sorry, Irena. You know I'm not like this." Though Ewa didn't smoke, she asked for a cigarette.

"What happened today?" Irena asked again. "You're never late."

"I was on my way here. I was seized by two Germans. They said I was to help clean an apartment. They took me into the washroom of a house taken over by the Germans and ordered me to clean a latrine that was filthy with, you know... feces. I asked what I should use to clean. He said with my blouse, and ordered me to take it off. I thought they were going to rape me. I did as I was told. After I finished and went to put on my coat, he grabbed me by the arm again and wrapped my filthy blouse about my face. Then he pushed me out into the street. I had to go home to wash and change."

*   *   *   *   *   *   *   *   *   *

DECREE: FEBRUARY 18, 1940

The Jewish Council (Judenrat) is ordered to register every Jew and Convert from the Jewish race, between the ages of 13 and 59.

Irena's encounter with Ewa left her more disturbed and discouraged than she expected. Everyone had heard accounts of assault, even murder, perpetrated against unlucky and unknown Jews in Warsaw. But Ewa – her best friend Ewa – had suffered directly from the occupier's excess. Her mother's declining health weighed heavily as well, but there was little she could do beyond seeking black market digitalis. And always, she heard her father's injunction about saving drowning people. To keep despair at bay, Irena conjured new strategies around German welfare restrictions and starvation rations, thoughts that inspired a peculiar sensation, something akin to satisfaction. It felt like her small way of fighting back.

In mid-February, Irena took another gamble. She invited Irena Schultz, Jan Dobraczynski, and Jaga Piotrowska to spend an evening at her flat to talk about "work issues that I don't feel comfortable discussing in the office." She also invited Ewa, whom she hadn't seen in a few weeks, not since her assault. February 15th also happened to be Irena's 30th birthday. She didn't mention it, but Jaga knew and told Dobraczynski and Irena Schultz.

Ewa arrived first. When she took off her coat, the stigma of her armband disappeared.

Irena put extra coal in the stove, but could still see her breath condense. Ewa had lost more weight. The muscles of her neck stood out like ropes. She looked older, her exotic eyes sagging and underhung with loose flesh; her soft, round face broken up by angles, her golden hair brittle.

Ewa must have seen Irena's shock. "It's all right, Irena. I know I look a sight. Please don't worry about me. I would be very unhappy if you worried. One day at a time. God willing, everything will be all right."

It is a Polish custom to always bring flowers when visiting, but it was February under a brutal occupation and their gifts were more utilitarian. Jan Dobraczynski and Jaga, who arrived together, each brought a birthday gift, a lump of coal wrapped in butcher paper and tied with a red ribbon. "A black pearl," Jaga joked. "It's the gift to give this year." Under her drab winter coat Jaga wore a plain skirt but stitched with a strange geometric pattern one could only appreciate up close. Dobraczynski sat in a straight-back wooden chair, his body rigid, stiff like his starched white shirt. He loosened his tie.

Irena introduced Ewa to Dobraczynski and Jaga. "Ewa is not only my good friend, but the heart and soul of CENTOS, and the beloved leader of a Youth Circle on Sienna Street."

Dobraczynski blushed when he shook Ewa's hand. "We know each other," he said.

Irena remembered his letter to Ewa after she and every other Jewish social worker had been fired.

"I still keep the note you wrote me," Ewa said, and looked straight at him. "I know there are decent Poles such as you. In any case, everything is for the best. I'm glad to be at CENTOS. It's where I belong. And it's such an inspiration to work with the young people in my building's Youth Circle. I hope you can meet them one day. They're full of hope and ideals and plans. They're quite extraordinary. They help take care of orphans and refugee children. Humanitarians, in spite of Hitler."

Irena Schultz finally arrived, half an hour late, out of breath, strands of her short blond hair out of place. "Identity checks," she explained. She adjusted her black hair pins so they were parallel again. "SS officers stopped my tram. They checked papers. Found a Jew without an armband. He was taken off the tram, and they made us watch as they beat him. When he was unconscious, they threw him into the back of a Gestapo wagon and let us go on. I thought I would be sick."

Irena Schultz and Ewa hadn't seen each other for several months, and as they embraced, Irena saw the horrified moment when Irena Schultz felt Ewa's bones.

By combining ration cards they scraped together a modest dinner of soup, bread, butter, eggs, and vegetables. Irena had told Ewa not to bring any food; her rations as a Jew were meager enough. Though the menu was spare, the conversation was opulent, regularly returning to recipes and memorable meals. Janina was especially pleased to have young people for company.

After dinner Irena said they had work-related matters to discuss, and she suggested that her mother excuse herself and listen to her phonograph in her bedroom. She knew Janina would soon be asleep.

Irena served black tea and sugar after dinner, a rare luxury. She tried to give Ewa the rest of her sugar ration to take home, but she refused. Irena pushed further. "Give it to your young people," she said. "They deserve some sweetness in their lives."

Ewa relented. "Thanks be to God for friends like you."

"I saw Adam just a few days ago," Irena said. "I was making a home visit."

"He's fallen in with a rough crowd," Ewa said.

"He helped me with some documents and registering a refugee family for aid. Because he's your brother, I feel I can trust him."

Irena Schultz said to Ewa, "Dealing with the smugglers – it must be hard."

Ewa nodded, her smile wry and whimsical. "Yes, of course. Most of us deal with smugglers. Actually, I'm told that I am quite clever at it – bargaining and such. I'm completely surprised and a little bit proud."

"Bravo, Ewa," Jaga said and fitted another cigarette into her black cigarette holder. "You are the sweetest, most innocent criminal I have ever met."

Janina's phonograph played a Chopin Prelude from the other room. Irena cleared her throat and began. "I know I've been short-tempered with some of you lately, and I apologize. We've all been under tremendous pressure. I've had ideas – very clear ideas of how we can help our Jewish clients." She looked around the room. "But they're not legal."

Irena Schultz and Jaga nodded. Ewa's brow creased, and her smile vanished. Dobraczynski sat stone-faced. Irena continued. "In ten of our Welfare districts I know at least one sympathetic worker who is willing to help in some way – distribute false papers, ration cards, food, clothing, medicine, even money."

Ewa began scribbling in the notepad she always carried. Irena laid her hand across the paper. "Don't, Ewa. There can be no record of this conversation."

"My mind goes too fast," Ewa said. "I get too many ideas. Like butterflies – I have to catch them and pin them to the page."

"How lyrical," Irena said. "But don't worry. I have a clear vision of what to do. I hope you'll help me, because I can't do it alone. There are risks – large risks. If you don't want anything to do with this, now is a good time to say goodnight." Dobraczynski squirmed in his chair, looked to Jaga, but made no move to leave. "We all know someone, who knows someone else," Irena continued. "My friend Stefan, that nice young man who often walks me home, is part of what he calls 'a nascent underground.' Money could be made available from our government-in-exile. Ewa, you know people involved with the Joint Distribution Committee. Pan Dobraczynski, you know people in the ministry. Everybody knows somebody."

"This is a dangerous conversation, Irena," Dobraczynski said. His breath fogged in the cold, yet he wiped sweat from his forehead.

"I hope we can trust each other," Irena said. "The loyalty of thieves. We all already commit little acts of forgery and falsification. But it's not enough. We have to be more creative – more coordinated. We have to think bigger."

"And what do you propose?" Dobraczynski said.

"A network. At least one worker in each district office."

"That's who, not what."

"Typhus." Irena looked around the room to see the impact of her words. "You know how the Germans are obsessively afraid of contamination and epidemics. I'm suggesting we use their fears against them. I have a friend at Czyste Hospital who says that TB is spreading. There are more cases of dysentery. As horrible as it sounds, typhus becomes an opportunity."

In part, her father's memory had inspired her to use the dread disease to her advantage. It felt like a rebalancing of scales, making meaning out of a death she would forever mourn.

"I don't follow," Dobraczynski said.

"Let me give you an example. What are our most critical needs right now?"

"Housing and food," he said, and everybody agreed.

"All right. Here's a ploy that won't cost us very much at all. We have housing allowances for Aryan Poles. Now, suppose we have a Jewish family – the Prelutzkis. They're recorded in the Jewish census. In spite of their need they get no assistance. But what if their name, as recorded in the Aryan census, is Sipowicz and their address is in an Aryan neighborhood? I can easily obtain welfare benefits, money and food for the non-existent Sipowicz family and give their aid and rations to the Prelutzki family."

"And when the Gestapo come looking for Mr. Sipowicz?"

"In the Sipowicz file is a report from the Epidemic Control and Sanitation Unit at Zakladow Sanitarium confirming household TB in Mr. Sipowicz's wife and brother-in-law. No German will visit. For 100 zloty the landlord corroborates our story."

There was an unnatural silence, and Irena wondered if she had gone too far. Every person around the table seemed immersed in his or her own thoughts. Jaga lit another cigarette. Ewa dabbed a napkin at the corners of her mouth.

"The warehouses are full," Irena continued. "It's shockingly simple to get food and clothing with even poorly forged letters."

Jaga broke the silence. "The Hygiene Wagon," she said. "We can smuggle food in the wagon."

Dobraczynski played the role of devil's advocate, finding fault with each strategy, and when they came up with plausible solutions he offered another attack on the logic of Irena's plan. He was brilliant in his thinking, and Irena understood how he had risen so high in the bureaucracy.

"There is risk," Irena conceded. "Desperate times – desperate measures."

It was well past curfew, and their conversation was not exhausted. They would have to spend the night. Dobraczynski telephoned his wife to explain he wouldn't be coming home, and not to worry. Irena could hear the strain in his conversation, and, out of decency, Jaga turned her back and looked out the window.

When he returned, Dobraczynski continued his dissection of Irena's plan to obtain false documents. "Ultimately, the biggest obstacle to quality forgeries is money. The accounting for such expenditures…"

Irena finally could not contain herself. "With all due respect," she said, "we can talk about this until we're blue in the face, but I need to know from each of you if you will help me."

Ewa spoke first, in a soft voice. "You have my complete support – but,

113

I don't have very much to risk, and we Jews have little left to lose."

"I'm with you, Irena," Jaga said and lit another cigarette.

"First I was your supervisor," Irena Schultz said. "Now I'm your accomplice. I trust you know what you're doing."

Everybody looked at Dobraczynski – the main doubter of the evening. He put his hands together in front of his lips, as if praying. His brow furrowed. Slowly, at first almost imperceptibly, he nodded 'yes,' and Jaga impulsively gave him a hug.

Well past midnight Irena lay awake, her mind jumping from one idea to another only to be distracted by yet another. She felt excited, overwhelmed, frightened – like primary colors running together on a palette. She'd need a new list, new priorities; she'd have to delegate responsibility. Her only balm was the regular breathing of her co-conspirators sleeping under down comforters around the coal stove.

★　★　★　★　★　★　★　★　★　★

The spring of 1940 brought relief from the harsh winter, but in every other way it was a season of disaster. Norway, Holland, and Belgium fell to the Germans in May. The British army retreated in defeat at Dunkirk in June, and a week later, on June 14th, columns of Wehrmacht troops goose-stepped down the Champs-Elysées under hundreds of swastika flags and banners. German wall posters in Warsaw trumpeted their victories.

On pain of death, every Jew and Convert had to report to the Judenrat for slave labor assignment. Each laborer worked more than 12 hours, most often hauling bricks for the Jewish masons building a wall around and through the Jewish District. It was backbreaking labor, and some died of beatings or dehydration. Rumors of a closed ghetto multiplied. Most other Polish cities with a Jewish district already had a closed ghetto, including Piotrków, Radomsko, Czestochowa, Lodz, Lublin, Kovno, and others.

As a wealthy member of the Polish Socialist Party, the PPS, Stefan was able to buy an Aryan identity – a *Kennkarte*, a new residence, baptismal and birth certificates – and disappear. Under his new name he lived in a run-down apartment at Markowski #15 in the Praga District, with two university colleagues. The apartment had been vacated by a Jewish family that could no longer afford to pay the Aryan landlord. In contrast to most Warsovians, Stefan looked remarkably fit, his hair still fashionably long, hanging over his collar, a peasant's cap tilted at a jaunty angle, his wire-rimmed glasses perfectly balanced. When he smiled, Irena marveled at the perfection of his teeth. Stefan's forged papers freed him of the armband, and he once more visited Irena on most days, either at the office or at her flat; it was unpredictable.

Underground newspapers began to appear at the beginning of 1940, and by the first anniversary of the occupation, in October 1940, fifty different publications, printed in Polish, Yiddish, and Hebrew surreptitiously made their way from hand to hand. More than once Gestapo agents inspected the mimeograph machine at Irena's office for evidence of illegal use, which would have drawn a death sentence.

"I never thought I'd be a newsboy," Stefan said in the spring of 1940 when he gave Irena the first illicit printing of the *Biuletyn*, a four-page newspaper that he had wrapped around his lower legs and pulled his stockings over. Irena passed her copy to Irena Schultz, who passed it to Jaga and then to Jadwiga Deneka, and so on.

Through Stefan, Irena came to know the various cafés in the Jewish District, the marketplace of the underground, places to make a deal, to hear news or gossip. Each café had its own reputation. The *Nowoczesna Café* on Nowolipki Street was known for the best entertainment, the most flavorful food, and the most reliable information. Even the Germans patronized it. In contrast, the *Sztuka Café*, on Leszno Street attracted what was left of the middle class, those who came for black market deals, underground connections, and bootleg vodka. Smugglers considered the *Sztuka* their office, some even made appointments. Warsaw's intelligentsia patronized the *Sienna Street Café*.

By March, the German authorities had erected wooden quarantine fences with gates on Krochmalna Street and seven others to discourage the mixing of Jews and Aryans. German wall posters and newspapers continued to rail against the Jews as carriers of typhus and other infectious diseases. The typhus epidemic continued unabated, and Jews suffered disproportionately because of their malnutrition. By April more than 500 new cases were reported each month.

Dr. Majkowski, the director of the Zakladow Sanitarium's Sanitary Epidemiological Station, called Irena on the first day of May. "I must see you in my office tomorrow morning," he said. "It's quite urgent." There was something both ominous and conspiratorial in his tone.

Dr. Juliusz Majkowski locked the door to his office. He was an older, distinguished gentleman, bald and bearded, with drooping shoulders. The skin of his neck and face sagged, suggesting he had once been stout. He returned to his desk and looked hard at her through spectacles that magnified his eyes. "Do you know Krochmalna #35?" he asked.

"Yes, of course. I have clients there."

"One died last week." He opened a file on his blotter. "Nachum Smolensk – 18 years old. Apartment 33, third floor."

Irena was sorry to hear this, but it was hardly unusual for a Jew to die, certainly nothing necessitating a locked door.

"It was typhus."

"I'm sorry to hear of it." Irena was still suspicious.

"So this young man died, and now it is a disaster for all who live on his block – not just his building, but his entire block. The new quarantine laws – they're quite draconian – and, I think, barbaric. Of course the Germans leave it to the Jewish Council to fulfill their dictate."

He went on to describe the new quarantine regulations and what would happen at Krochmalna #35 in a few days. The Jewish Police, the SP (*Sluzba Porzadkowa*), hired by the Jewish Council (the *Judenrat*) would herd the Jewish residents through the streets to the Leszno #109 bath house, where they would undergo delousing and showering. Everyone, men and women, would have their heads shaved. While the residents were in the bath house, Polish disinfection brigades would go through the tenements wearing masks and burning sulfur in sealed rooms to disinfect bundles of clothing, bedding, and pillows. The sulfur gas had to permeate the bundles to kill the lice, a process thought to take a whole day. Creosote and Lysol would be sprayed everywhere else. It was understood that disinfection brigades stole valuables left lying around. From past experience with quarantines, bribes were expected – 50 zloty for every room exempted from disinfection. For 2,000 zloty an entire building could be exempted, but not this time.

While the sulfur gas did its killing, families could not return to their flats. There were often delays at the bath house, no place to sleep, no food. Once delousing was certified, the SP would herd everyone back to their tenement, the gates would be chained and locked, and all residents would be placed under quarantine – preventive detention – for 21 days. Nothing and no one could come in or out. No food, no garbage, no mail – complete isolation.

"In the next few days," he continued, "there will be what the Germans call an *Aktion*, quarantining Krochmalna Street from Ciepla to Walicow. Twenty thousand people. The biggest quarantine yet. The first under the new decrees"

"How do you know this?"

"I have friends – expensive friends. I understand you too have expensive friends."

He said it in a way that made her uncomfortable. "I'm not sure what you mean."

He drummed his fingers on the desk. "Twenty thousand people are going to be quarantined without food for three weeks unless something is done. I thought you might be helpful. Dobraczynski speaks highly of you. He says you have thought about this already in some detail. He says you can do the impossible."

She felt herself blush. Now she felt sure of Dobraczynski's allegiance. "We do what we can."

"I can issue Epidemic Control Unit identity passes for you and..." He looked through the file. "Yes – you and the other Irena, Irena Schultz. With these you will be admitted into the tenements. I suspect the Germans will avoid the area. Hopefully, you'll only have to deal with Polish Blues, and they will already have been well paid."

Irena had anticipated this moment, prepared for it. She knew exactly how to mobilize her network of social workers for this project. Ideas and strategies percolated through her mind, problems, risks, but she knew very quickly what she would do. She began calling each social worker and identified herself as *Jolanta*, then told them "to prepare Procedure #5 – Krochmalna. More to follow."

Procedure #5 meant something was about to happen that would

require immediate and concerted action with regard to food. It alerted her network to secure burlap bags full of grains, flour, and root vegetables and to procure as many false documents as possible with Polish instead of Jewish names.

The next day Irena walked up Krochmalna Street, from one tenement to another, speaking with the chairman of each House Committee, warning of the impending "disinfection *Aktion*." At the same time, the Social Welfare Hygiene Wagon, driven by Antoni Danbrowski, began to deliver sacks of grain and root vegetables concealed under foul smelling dressings, bandages, and sheets. Taking care not to be seen by SP or Polish Blues, teens from the Youth Circles quickly hid the burlap sacks in cellars and attics. Irena arranged for Jews who thought they were wanted by the German authorities to receive new identity cards, and she secured temporary housing away from Krochmalna Street until the *Aktion* was over.

By now there were at least 30 known cases of typhus on Krochmalna Street, and the German *Aktion* could come at any time. On the fourth day of the alert, May 7th, a warm spring day, dreary and silent, just as she left #35, Irena heard the dreaded wail of sirens and police whistles. People began to run every which way on Krochmalna Street, known for its criminal class as well as its observant Jews. German troops had sealed the street and were closing in from each end, a contingent of Polish Blues in between. Orders bellowed through loudspeakers on Wehrmacht trucks.

"*Alle Juden raus!* All Jews out! Delousing! Anyone not out in 15 minutes will be shot."

Irena jumped at a sudden burst of automatic rifle fire from down the block. The German officer in charge dispatched the Polish Blues, who went into each tenement pounding on doors and emptying apartments. Boots rattled staircases; tin whistles echoed in hallways; police batons crashed on doors and walls. Men and women spewed onto the street and were herded together in the middle of each block under the Germans' guns. More gunfire. A woman cried out in agony. The German soldiers fingered their rifles nervously. A Polish Blue grabbed Irena's coat and dragged her into the middle of the street. "Move, Jewess. Into the middle! Where's your armband?"

Irena was furious to be handled so roughly, but then she saw that the gendarme was a young boy, frightened, probably from the countryside, lucky to have a job at all. Most likely, he had no use for the Jews before the war; now he was paid to mistreat them.

"I'm not a Jew. I have a pass," Irena said. "Epidemic Control. Public Health." She showed him Dr. Majkowski's pass. The boy seemed glad to let her go. Moments later she saw him swing his baton wildly at a confused old woman trying to return to her tenement. She collapsed in the street, blood pouring from her scalp. Automatically, Irena ran up to her, thinking to at least stop her bleeding, when she was grabbed by a soldier and dragged before the German officer in charge. He wore a supercilious expression and scrutinized Irena's eyes, her breasts, her legs, then held out his leather-gloved hand for her papers. She tried not to look afraid.

"You need my permission to go to her aid," he sneered, then examined her pass. "I'm sure this is forged," he said. "And I'm sure you're doing something illegal, but I haven't time to deal with you." He spit at her feet. "That woman is not suffering from an infectious disease. You may not assist her. Now get out of here."

As she walked away, Irena felt the burgeoning vigor of her anger far outweigh her fear, and that in and of itself was a welcome revelation.

★ ★ ★ ★ ★ ★ ★ ★ ★ ★

DECREE: SEPTEMBER 28, 1940

Jews may not ride in trams with Aryans. Jews may only ride in cars marked "For Jews." A Jewish car will be added to every third tram.

DECREE: OCTOBER 4, 1940

All Aryan maids working for Jews must register with the German authority.

DECREE: OCTOBER 10, 1940

Jews must step aside and make way before every German, both soldier and civil servant in uniform, until the German leaves the sidewalk. Caps and hats of any kind must be removed in deference to and respect for the uniform.

CHAPTER 12

The Warsaw Ghetto
Warsaw, October 1940 – January 1941

DECREE: WARSAW – OCTOBER 12, 1940

All Jews living outside the predominantly Jewish district must prepare to leave their homes and move to the designated Jewish area. Only such belongings as can be moved by hand or cart can be taken. Everything else is to be left behind. Movement of Poles out of the Jewish area and the movement of all Jews into the Jewish area must be completed by the end of October. By order of Ludwig Fischer, Governor of Warsaw.

★   ★   ★   ★   ★   ★   ★   ★   ★   ★

After more than a year of occupation, Warsovians had recreated a peculiar sense of normality – a fragile homeostasis – which for most constituted relief, if not happiness. Black market connections were established, and Warsovians learned how to circumvent starvation rations. Irena thought it remarkable what humans could accommodate, what they could bear. But fragile was the operative word, and the sealing of the ghetto threw everything into turmoil again.

As Irena made her home visits in the Jewish district, German trucks with powerful loudspeakers drove through the teeming streets warning Jews and Poles of the approaching deadline for "sealing off the Jewish District." It was not by accident that the Germans chose Yom Kippur, the holiest day of the Jewish year, to decree the Warsaw ghetto. On Yom Kippur the Torah commands Jews to fast and pray for 24 hours – a day of confession, atonement, and redemption. But there was no rest for the bricklayers, who were brutally compelled to complete the eleven-mile wall that would define the ghetto. Many of the Jewish workers who fasted, fainted or died while laying bricks. Their bodies were pushed to the side of the work site where the morgue wagon came every day.

★ ★ ★ ★ ★ ★ ★ ★ ★ ★

DECREE: WARSAW – OCTOBER 28, 1940
The time for evacuating apartments has been extended from November 1ˢᵗ to November 15ᵗʰ.

DECREE: WARSAW – NOVEMBER 10, 1940
All buildings in the Jewish section are to be turned over to the Judenrat for control. No Aryan managers may remain.

DECREE: WARSAW – NOVEMBER 12, 1940
Any Jew who wishes to ride the Jewish Tram must pay a monthly tax of 5 zloty in addition to the fare. Any Jew without a permit must pay four times the normal fare.

DECREE: WARSAW – NOVEMBER 15, 1940
The Jewish District is sealed.

★ ★ ★ ★ ★ ★ ★ ★ ★ ★

In the German propaganda press, and in official pronouncements of the German occupation authority, the word "ghetto" was never used. Jews were to be "sealed" or "sequestered" within the Jewish District. Among other proffered reasons, it was a sanitary necessity – a preventive quarantine.

The day before the final deadline for closing what Poles and Jews called the ghetto, Irena witnessed a mournful parade of Jews, with only the belongings they could carry or pile onto hand carts, marching over the bridges across the Vistula, from the slums of Praga, to their new flats in a walled city within a city. Children carried pillowcases stuffed with clothing, bed sheets, and for some, a favorite doll or toy. It was not a cold day, but they wore all their coats, jackets, dresses, and pants and thus, though starving, they looked stout and overweight.

Irena's network expanded. She secured "grants" from the PPS (Home Army parachute drops from the London government-in-exile), forgeries (especially from Janina Bukolska's Miodowa #11 office), couriers (mostly young women, Jewish and Aryan), safe houses, food, and medicine from warehouses.

On November 15th the last bricks were cemented into the wall that now completely encircled 400,000 Jews. Though Jews couldn't leave, the Germans routinely entered the ghetto and ransacked houses for furniture and other valuables, a plunder that only came to an end with the resurgence of typhus in the ghetto.

Still more Jewish refugees arrived, confused, hungry and dirty from weeks of travel, often by foot. They asked directions in Yiddish, German, Czech, or Romanian and were directed to the ghetto, where they became beggars, many living on the street.

★   ★   ★   ★   ★   ★   ★   ★   ★   ★

DECREE: WARSAW

Social Workers are forbidden the right to enter the Jewish District for any reason. Social Welfare benefits for Jews are forbidden.

Twenty-two gates punctuated the wall and regulated access to the ghetto. At least once a day, the two Irenas showed their Epidemic Control passes and entered the ghetto dressed in nurse's uniforms – white nurse's caps with a red cross. The first few crossings were frightening to Irena, until she realized that her papers were indisputable, signed by Dr. Majkowski himself. To allay suspicion they made it a practice to enter and leave the ghetto through different gates. As she grew more confident, Irena brought more contraband in with her. She was so thin and small that she could enter wearing five layers of clothing and leave four behind for her clients. Money and forged documents were easy enough to conceal, sewn into clothing, layered into the false bottoms of her canvas nurse's bag stuffed with soiled dressings, which the Germans were none too eager to search.

Each time Irena entered the ghetto she felt herself moving into another world – from the Aryan boulevards, still noisy with trams, automobiles, trucks, *droshky*, and the jingling bells of pedi-cabs, to the ominous silence of the ghetto, where motor vehicles were banned. Different rules of physics applied in the ghetto – the atmosphere thicker, gravity more ponderous. Every person wore a white armband of exact specifications, and Irena quickly learned that it was best to wear the Jewish armband herself in the ghetto as a way of becoming invisible. Reminiscent of her university days, wearing the armband also felt like a measure of solidarity.

Every resident of Warsaw quickly learned the spectrum of colors identified with each occupation and police force. Wehrmacht wore green, SS blue-gray, Ukrainians yellow, Polish Gendarmes blue, and the SP black and white.

With the closing of the ghetto and strict rationing, black market smuggling became more hazardous, more expensive, and more necessary. Every Jew depended on the black market, which spawned an underground army of smugglers and criminals. The foot soldiers of this army were young Jewish boys and girls, small, agile, fast, and fearless. They found ways to sneak under and through the new wall, to beg for food on the Aryan side and bring it back under their clothing. They were chased and arrested by the Jewish Police (SP) who, upon opening the children's oversized coats, often dumped out turnips, carrots, and potatoes. The thieves were handled roughly and thrown into Gensia Prison.

Other ghetto children became "snatchers," lurking outside food stores or bakeries to grab what they could from customers leaving. More than once Irena watched a snatcher with stolen bread set upon by other beggar children, knocking him down and battling over whatever was left. They crammed their mouths as they struggled, and when the battle was over they calmly helped each other to their feet.

Housing in the ghetto was impossible. It became normal for seven or eight people to live in each room of a flat. The ghetto sidewalks were so crowded that discrete human rivers flowed in opposite directions. The only permitted motor vehicles were trams marked with a large Star of David. Within the ghetto there was no park, no patch of green, no field where children could enjoy the natural world, and rubble piles became playgrounds. Wherever the sun shone on a street, homeless families and beggars gathered for warmth, monotonously pleading for a piece of bread, for a place to live, or for nothing more than mercy. Women holding babies competed with orphans, jostling each other for a spot in the warm rays.

Each day as Irena went into the ghetto she made note of the beggars and came to be familiar with some of the more colorful ones. A handsome young man, painfully thin, played the violin badly on the same corner every day. On Leszno Street, across from the famous Femina Theater, a synagogue choir, 15 to 20 congregants, begged by singing melancholic Hebrew prayers and hymns under the direction of their white-haired cantor, who conducted in a frayed great coat and a black skullcap. An orthodox man's black hat sat upended behind the conductor with a sign that said: Tzedakah (Charity).

Perhaps the most celebrated of the beggars was a man by the name of Rubinsztejn, sometimes referred to as "the king of the beggars," also known as "Alle glajch" (Everyone's equal), which was his oft-repeated refrain. Alle glajch was a natural performer, and he usually gathered a crowd. He dressed in costumes and told jokes that everyone repeated. Irena stopped one day when he appeared on the street wearing a woman's dress. "I don't have a wife," he explained. "So I guess I'll have to be my own wife today; not bad, eh?"

Irena reckoned time in the ghetto by noting the disappearance of those beggars she came to recognize. One family in particular caught her attention – their sole possessions seemed to be two baby strollers. The father pushed three children in one, while the mother pushed three more in another. They sang old Yiddish songs, and their voices were beautiful. Over that first winter, Irena gave them a few coins every day and listened to their singing. After some months she noticed that the mother and father were accompanied by only four children, then three; eventually one stroller disappeared, as did the family's shoes and their coats. Finally, only the father and mother were left. They still managed to sing, but the mother was skeletal and weak, and the father had to push her in the stroller. Then she too was gone, and there was no more singing.

The plight of the beggar children particularly saddened Irena, and she began to daydream, contemplate, and finally plan strategies to save at least some of them. By late December Irena and Irena Schultz entered the ghetto two and three times a day in their nurses' disguises. As often as possible, sometimes once a week, Irena's mission in the ghetto included delivering money and documents to Ewa at CENTOS. One particularly cold day, Irena could see that Ewa had been crying. They embraced, and Ewa could not hold back her tears.

"It gets worse and worse," Ewa sobbed. "Every day more refugees come in. It's so cold, and thousands have no place to live, no heat. There's no soup in the soup kitchens. I'm so tired, but I can't sleep. And I'm afraid – all the time. It never stops."

Irena sat Ewa down in her chair and knelt before her. "Compose yourself, Ewa. Will you walk with me down Leszno Street? You need to get out of here, even just briefly. I have something to show you."

"I don't understand. Where are we going?"

"Just a few blocks – the courthouse, to meet a friend. Maybe you know her. Izabela Kuczkowska – she graduated from the Polish Free University about the same time as you."

Ewa shook her head. "I don't know her."

"You will. She works in another Welfare district office as a specialist in legal appeals and court-related matters. She's one of my liaisons."

"How many are there now?"

"Almost 25 people on the Aryan side I can trust who are willing to help. My biggest heartache is the orphans freezing on the street. I see them every day." She stopped and glanced both ways to ensure privacy. "I've decided to take some of them out of here. I need your help, Ewa."

"Are you crazy?"

"I don't think so. I have foster homes waiting – some temporary, others more permanent. At least they won't die on the street. They'll have food and a warm place to sleep."

"How will you get them out?"

"The courthouse. Come along, I'll show you."

They walked down Leszno, and Irena saw that a new German slogan had been plastered on walls and kiosks. Unlike most wall posters, pretentious with legalistic jargon, this one was simple and to the point:

By the end of the week this newest exhortation would cover walls throughout Warsaw and its suburbs.

Irena stopped when they reached the entrance to the courthouse. "The courthouse is half in the ghetto and half out; Leszno Street entrance in the ghetto, Ogrodowa Street entrance in Aryan Warsaw. There are ways to get past the checkpoints and locked doors. Izabela knows the janitor, Jozef. He has keys to the basement tunnels. Izabela and I are to walk through today, to test it. I'd like you to meet Izabela. If this goes well you'll be hearing from her more often."

Irena had to add, "You know, it wouldn't be that difficult to get you out of the ghetto. I know people..."

Ewa's hand on Irena's arm stopped her words. Ewa laughed. "Can you get me a new nose? Look at me. I have Jew written all over my face. The ghetto may be a prison, or a zoo, but outside this wall I'm a hunted animal. Here, at least I have an identity – I have a mission with my young people – a shred of dignity. My place is on Sienna Street with my Youth Circle. They're wonderful and brave. I have to provide a good example and reassurance. I have to be at least as brave as they are, don't you think? We'll be all right, God willing. This too shall pass. You'll see."

"You're my friend. It saddens me to see you here. I want to help you."

"Save your strength, Irena. It's the beggars and orphans who need your help. I have a place to live – a little heat – a little food. Most important, I have my family. And I have Schmuel."

"That goofy guy with the space between his teeth?" Irena caught herself too late. "I'm sorry, Ewa. My mouth has a mind of its own."

Ewa smiled broadly. "He is a little funny-looking, but very sweet. He joined the Jewish Police – the SP."

Irena's expression must have betrayed her disappointment.

"No, no," said Ewa. "Really it's a good thing. A lot of young professionals have joined. Schmuel wants to marry me." She blushed. "He said he'd look after my family. The SP get extra rations. My parents like Schmuel. He's observant – sometimes he reads from the Torah. Adam is less generous. He says the Judenrat and the SP are collaborators and opportunists. But Schmuel is one of the good ones."

Irena was about to speak again, but Ewa touched her forearm with boney fingers. Softly, she said, "You cannot know what it's like to live inside, Irena. You don't know what it's like to spend all day, every day trying to get black market food. We are all criminals. We all do what we can and what we must. Those who obey the law are dead or dying."

Irena felt shamed. "Forgive me, my dear friend. I would never presume to... I just want to save you from this."

Ewa's smile returned. "Dear friend, this is where I belong. As for Schmuel, you should get to know him. He's quick-witted and generous. He brings us food and special connections with Aryan traders. The Germans trust him, and he knows which ones can be bought."

Irena's interest was aroused. The part of her brain that schemed about such things considered the advantages a person like Schmuel might bring. Ewa was right; one always had to think like a criminal.

"I'd like to meet your beau," Irena said. "Get to know him better. If you're happy with him, then I should be too."

"And I am, Irena. Most of us think it's a good thing to have our own policemen, our own sons and brothers, who can speak Yiddish, who understand what it is to be a Jew. I think Schmuel is right. We're at the mercy of the Germans. We have no choice but to comply. And better a Jewish policeman who doesn't have a gun, than a German or a Polish Blue who was fed anti-Semitism with his mother's milk."

"Do you love him?"

Ewa could not look her in the eye. "He's a very nice boy."

★　★　★　★　★　★　★　★　★　★

A few days later, a bone-chilling January day, Irena stood in the shadow of a ghetto doorway and studied Schmuel from a distance where he stood watch at the Twarda Gate at the intersection of Zelazna, Zlota, and Twarda streets. The SP's uniforms were odd – black blazers in the summer, belted khaki long coats otherwise, white shirts and ties, peaked black caps with a Star of David, shiny high boots and rubber truncheons. On Schmuel's right sleeve, below the mandatory Star of David, was his burgundy SP armband.

Each of the heavily trafficked ghetto gates was manned by two German gendarmes who checked papers, along with two Polish Blues as translators, sometimes a Lithuanian or Ukrainian soldier, and a few Jewish Police.

From across the square, Schmuel seemed gregarious, chatting and laughing with the Polish Blues. What could Ewa possibly see in this pixie-like youth with pouchy cheeks? He was shorter than Ewa and, in spite of the rationing, one of the few Jews or Poles to still have a slightly rounded belly.

There was a sudden scuffing of feet, a scampering from behind the wall, and a boy, no more than five or six, sprinted around the corner through the opening in the gate. As he ran by, Schmuel snagged him by his ragged, oversized coat and yanked him so his little feet wiggled in the air. In an instant Schmuel swung his black truncheon hard against his legs and dropped him to the ground where the boy lay, screaming. Schmuel hit him again, this time across his lower back, then blew his whistle. Another SP appeared from Twarda Street and dragged the boy back into the ghetto.

Irena waited until the gate was busy to approach Schmuel's post. She presented her *Kennkarte* and Epidemic Control Pass to the German gendarme. He hardly took notice and waved her through without examining her bag.

She approached Ewa's beau. "You're Schmuel, aren't you?" Irena said.

"Does it matter?"

"I'm a friend of Ewa's."

Schmuel had full lips like a woman's and a short forehead. Mocha hair curled tightly on his scalp like tiny shrimp. He could not suppress a gap-toothed smile that negated whatever authority his uniform lent. In a tenor voice he said, "What can I do for you?"

"Can we talk privately?"

"Of course." He led Irena into the ghetto, a little way up Twarda Street, where they mingled with hundreds of Jews. "What's your pleasure?" he said.

Irena had to ask. "That boy you just caught. What will happen to him?"

"Gensia Prison, no doubt." He squared his shoulders back and squinted. "And good for him, too. At least he'll have a meal every day and a place to sleep."

Schmuel was either ignorant or lying. Irena knew that Gensia Prison's child inmates, mostly smugglers lucky enough not to have been shot, received starvation rations and slept on straw mats in a cold dormitory. Mortality in Gensia was notoriously high. Orphans who survived to be released went to the Dzielna #39 orphanage, where many children died as well.

Irena tried to put on her bland face. "I have deliveries – sanitary supplies – that I need to move through the gate tomorrow without scrutiny. I wonder what the going rate is."

He smiled. "A one-time delivery?"

"It depends. My friend would like to try it out."

"Everyone needs friends these days. How many parcels? How heavy?"

"Ten parcels – about 50 pounds each – packed in an ambulance."

Irena watched Schmuel mentally calculate. "Because you're a friend of Ewa, and because you're beautiful, a special price – 2,000 zloty, paid to me at the gate. When?"

"Tomorrow." This was not the shy, somewhat clumsy "sweet boy" that Ewa described. Irena saw plainly that the uniform and his truncheon had transformed Schmuel into something else, something Ewa could not see. "How late are you here?" she asked.

"Only until six. After tomorrow it's 3,000 zloty."

"Before six, then," Irena said.

He took off his glove, and they shook hands. His was small and damp.

Though Irena was distressed at the thought of Ewa marrying this man, finding Schmuel was a stroke of good fortune. In this crazy time, he would become part of her network of specific helpers available on short notice – electricians, plumbers, and Antoni Danbrowski, the Social Welfare Department's ambulance driver.

Danbrowski was a warm and funny man, who flirted with all the social workers and secretaries. He was older but still handsome, his dark hair and thick mustache flecked with gray. Before the war he had complained of being overweight. Now he was merely stout, and he actually looked younger.

Irena had asked him to do small things in the past, smuggling small quantities of food and medicine, one or two burlap bags, buried under medical waste rags that smelled of infection and blood. Now she asked if he could be available the next afternoon for "special purposes." "Tomorrow – four o'clock at the warehouse?"

"I just drive the wagon," he said and winked. "I'll make sure it smells especially nasty, just for you."

The next day, Dobraczynski signed Irena's purchase and warehouse order for ten gunny sacks of grain, flour, and root vegetables and gave her 2,000 zloty.

"Be careful," Jaga said from her desk outside Dobraczynski's office.

Irena met Antoni at the warehouse as the last sacks were loaded into the back of his hygiene wagon, the smell of infection more pungent than usual. She settled into the passenger seat and wrapped her scarf tight against the cold. Her knees trembled.

They arrived at the Twarda Gate just before 6 o'clock, a busy time at the crossing, when the guards, hungry and tired at the end of another cold day, would be preoccupied with returning slave laborers.

Antoni drove the wagon to the gate, and Schmuel came right up to the cab. He took their documents and an envelope with twenty 100 zloty notes. Antoni's special motor vehicle entry form bore the forged signature of the German Health Officer, Dr. Wilhelm Hagen, authorizing their emergency entry. Schmuel opened the back and, along with a Polish Blue, made a show of searching the wagon. The German gendarme studied their papers, and Irena's heart beat frantically. Bribes sometimes failed, and smugglers were shot at the moment of apprehension.

On the German's order, Schmuel opened the gate, and Antoni drove slowly up Twarda Street, his ominous engine parting the pedestrian flow. He turned down ever smaller streets then stopped behind a "typhus quarantined" building guarded by several SPs, each of whom had been paid by Ewa to avert his eyes.

Teenagers from Ewa's Youth Circle on Sienna Street suddenly appeared from the shadows and carried the ten bags into the quarantined alleys through a door left unguarded for now.

The next day Irena sewed 10,000 zloty into the lining of her nurse's bag before reentering the ghetto. This time she entered through the dreaded Leszno Gate. A German sentry she had never seen before approached her, a scowl on his face, his rifle in hand. Irena worried she had been betrayed.

"*Achtung!*" the German snarled. "Show me your bag." A Polish Blue translated. The German grabbed her hard by the upper arm and dragged her to the guardhouse. "We will search you," he said in crude Polish, and began to pull off her coat. The other German in the guardhouse laughed.

Irena grabbed at his hand to stop him, and he slapped her face. "How dare you!" he said. "Maybe you have something to hide. These days, nearly everybody does."

She had more than enough money to bribe them, but what a waste. Her terror turned to anger. She recalled something her Grandfather Ksawery had told her about his time in a Russian prison, when he was tortured. "Fear makes you weak; anger makes you strong."

The SS Guard turned her bag upside down and tore at the lining with his knife. Irena watched in horror as 10,000 zloty spilled onto the table. She debated: play the charade through to its conclusion, or admit guilt and offer a large bribe?

She stamped her foot. "I am authorized to bring this money into the ghetto for infection control projects and sanitary improvements." She showed him her pass from Dr. Majkowski.

"We'll just see about that," he said, and picked up the telephone. He called the Zakladow Sanitarium and asked for Dr. Majkowski.

Irena watched the German's face wilt from the earful he received from Dr. Majkowski. Sheepishly, he put his phone back in its cradle. "Dr. Majkowski corroborates your story. You may go." Before releasing her he took 1,000 zloty from the pile of bills. "For my trouble."

Irena tried to walk away straight and strong, but as soon as she turned the corner and was out of his sight she slumped against a tenement wall, unable to contain her tears. For a moment she worried that she would stand out, but a woman crying on the street was hardly unusual.

CHAPTER 13

Shrinking the Ghetto

Warsaw, October – December 1941

DECREE: WARSAW – OCTOBER 5, 1941

Sienna Street, odd numbered buildings will be evacuated according to posted eviction notices. Once notices have been posted, residents of said evacuated blocks will be allowed no more than three days to obtain other housing.

DECREE: WARSAW

The Jewish District post office is forbidden to handle foreign mail. Parcels from neutral countries will no longer be delivered in the Jewish District.

DECREE: WARSAW

All electric streetcar lines in the Jewish District are abolished. Only horse-drawn Kohn-Heller wagons may be used in the Jewish District.

★ ★ ★ ★ ★ ★ ★ ★ ★ ★

Beginning in October 1941, the Germans began to shrink the ghetto. They re-routed the wall, cut off whole sections ("to stop smugglers and prevent the spread of typhus," the wall posters announced, but everyone knew it was just to squeeze the Jews ever harder). The new wall bisected Sienna Street where Ewa lived, so that when she looked out from her Youth Circle's attic window, she could now see over the wall into the free Aryan side, busy with trams, motor vehicles, droshky, and pedi-cabs.

One of the younger boys had said to her, "Now that I can see over the wall, I feel like an animal in the zoo."

He was not far off the mark. On their days off, German soldiers went sight-seeing through the ghetto, taking photographs, sometimes bringing their wives or sweethearts to show them the depths to which the Jew had sunk.

At the height of the first typhus epidemic in April 1940, five hundred new cases were reported each month. This second epidemic began in February of 1941, and by August up to 4,000 new cases a month were reported. Many more went unreported, the effect of dire quarantine consequences for thousands of neighbors. Before typhus, lice were an embarrassment, an inconvenience, something indigenous to the poor. But with typhus in the louse population, lice could be lethal, and everyone in Warsaw feared them. Irena feared contagion in every flat she visited, in the teeming streets, and at CENTOS headquarters. Nowhere was it worse than at the gate to cross Chlodna Street, the Aryan thoroughfare that divided the Large from the Small Ghetto. Jews waiting for this one and only crossing bunched together in ever-growing numbers, sometimes for half an hour, a restive assemblage waiting for the German guards to stop traffic on Chlodna Street and raise the gate to let them cross over. (On January 26, 1942, much to Irena's relief, a wooden footbridge was opened that arched over Chlodna Street to connect the Large to the Small Ghetto, so traffic would no longer be disrupted to let the Jews cross.)

Each evening when Irena came home, her mother insisted she take off her clothing at the door and usually found one or two lice, which she crushed with tweezers. There wasn't much else Janina could still do. She rarely ventured out and then only to the market, after which her lungs would fill up, and she would have to rest for several hours in a chair.

On October 10th the first snow fell overnight, portending the extra hardship of an early winter, and by January bitter winds scoured the ghetto streets. Every night more child beggars died, their frozen bodies stripped of whatever clothing they wore. For decency, they were covered with newspapers weighted with rubble. After a year of entering the ghetto day after day, Irena developed a sense of how close to death a beggar was by the state of his clothes or rags, or if she wore shoes. There was nothing to be done for the dying – they would freeze to death. Irena noticed that for every beggar that died another two took his place. She mused that maybe in this unaccountable time, death was more desirable than life; only the living know what loss is, Irena thought. The dead want for nothing; they don't need shoes.

Though it was the most congested and dangerous street in the ghetto, it was said that you could get anything on Karmelicka Street if you knew the right person. It was also said that if you couldn't make a black market deal on Karmelicka Street then you probably deserved to die of starvation.

As if the daily terrors of the ghetto were not enough, Karmelicka Street harbored its own unique horror – one that visited the street at least twice a day – the Pawiak Prison lorry that transported inmates to or from Gestapo interrogation at Szucha #25. The lorry raced down Karmelicka, striking pedestrians, scattering everyone in terror. Hanging out the truck's cab window like a crazed madman, an SS soldier (they said his name was Schultz) swung a club studded with nails, and he invariably found his mark.

The Gestapo arrested more Poles suspected of aiding Jews. Every Pole's worst nightmare was Gestapo interrogation; and everyone had some secret or another – everyone was a criminal. Who could predict their tolerance to pain and fear of death?

It was impossible to know whom to trust. Those Jews who survived a Gestapo interrogation were marked – always under suspicion of having denounced someone in exchange for their lives. As distasteful as their betrayal was, Irena was not surprised that frightened people might tell the Gestapo where furs and diamonds were hidden, who was dealing in foreign currency. In exchange the Gestapo gave them their freedom and some bacon or sausage, which they ate, though it violated dietary laws. After betraying your neighbor what possible difference could a dietary indiscretion make?

★　★　★　★　★　★　★　★　★　★

DECREE: NOVEMBER 10, 1941

A Jew who will leave, without proper authorization, a city quarter to which he was assigned will be punished by death. The same punishment

*will be applied to who knowingly provides shelter or assists in other ways,
such as offering a bed for a night, upkeep, providing transportation and
the like. No mercy will be shown in the carrying out of such orders.*

By order of district Governor, Ludwig Fischer

★　★　★　★　★　★　★　★　★　★

Just after the ghetto's perimeter was reduced, the German high command announced another mass deportation of German Jews to Poland. In the weeks that followed, this next wave of pitiful refugees made their way to Warsaw, homeless and without ration books. Some said the ghetto now held almost half a million Jews.

At the same time the Germans became more concerned with Jews escaping the ghetto. Wall posters in December, signed by Commissar Auerswald, announced the execution of eight Jews caught leaving the ghetto without permission. Six of them were women attempting to smuggle food for their families.

By the end of 1941, Ewa's three-bedroom apartment on Sienna Street housed 25 people, and not everyone got along. But, when Irena saw Ewa at CENTOS, she didn't complain; on the contrary, her optimism bloomed anew. "Irena! Thanks be to God." Her face brightened; she had a beyond-the-horizon look in her eyes. "The Americans are in the war. And just today I heard that the Russians have stopped the German advance. The tide is finally turning."

"You always see the good in everything, don't you, Ewa?"

"There is an ancient Jewish saying: On the very day the Temple was destroyed, the 9th day of the month of Av, Messiah will be born."

★　★　★　★　★　★　★　★　★　★

DECREE: DECEMBER 25, 1941

*Jews must surrender all furs to the Judenrat between December 26th and
28th. Failure to do so, or discovery of hidden furs, is punishable by death.*

DECREE:

Gas mains to the Jewish District will be turned off. Only coal may be used for heating and cooking.

CHAPTER 14

Beggars and Orphans

Warsaw, January – February 1942

Every Pole in Warsaw, Aryan and Jew, was hungry. Orphans and starving children begged for food on both sides of the wall.

SS-Lieutenant Colonel Dr. Ludwig Hahn barged into Irena's Social Welfare office, followed by his retinue of aides, and demanded to see Jan Dobraczynski. After the two had been alone for a few minutes, everyone could plainly hear through the closed door German epithets and the stomping of Hahn's military boot. The door opened a crack and a pale Dobraczynski motioned for Irena to come inside, where he introduced her as the supervisor of Children's Services for the district. Lieutenant Colonel Hahn grunted at her. He was sitting now, though no less agitated, crossing and re-crossing his legs, smoking one cigarette after another.

"The beggars are a disgrace," he said through his translator. "A shameful reflection on the Reich. I don't care a fig about the Jewish District, but on the Aryan side there are far too many children begging. They are a blight; they are a menace to public health and order. They must be removed, immediately."

"And what shall we do with them?" Dobraczynski asked.

Hahn's eyes grew wide. "Are you stupid? Bathe them, delouse them, make them disappear."

"How do we keep them off the street?"

"Are you not a social worker, Herr Dobraczynski? If you are unable, I will do it my way. Either way, the beggars will be gone."

The next day several Social Welfare trucks roamed Aryan Warsaw picking up as many begging children as could be caught. Irena convinced

Dobraczynski to let her and Irena Schultz supervise the delousing, and they were there as the first truck deposited 25 beggars into the lobby of the bathhouse. Mostly boys, they were five to fifteen years old, shivering from the cold, some too weak to stand. Their faces were skeletal, and tiny clouds puffed out of each child's mouth.

The door to the delousing house flew open with a blast of cold air, and Lieutenant Colonel Hahn marched in. "Have the beggars been bathed yet?" he demanded.

The Polish Blue supervisor snapped to attention. "We were just about to begin, Your Honor."

"Remove their clothes. Now!"

"But, sir, we are still processing them."

"Now, you idiot!"

The Polish Blue ordered the children to disrobe but keep their shoes. Irena knew this was the "drop your pants" test to find circumcised males, and she suspected that at least some of the beggar children were Jewish boys who had escaped through the wall to beg on the Aryan side where people had food. Any Jewish child found outside the ghetto would at best be sent to Gensia Prison, or Lieutenant Colonel Hahn could have the boy shot immediately, or do it himself. Girls received the benefit of the doubt, unless they had Semitic "bad looks."

Irena stepped forward, showing her Epidemic Control pass. "Your Honor, these children are covered with lice. For the safety and hygiene of us all, they must be deloused. It will only take a few moments to bathe and spray them first."

He lit another cigarette. "Be quick! I haven't all day."

The children disrobed in the communal showering area and left their lice infested clothes in a pile. Irena's fears were realized. Two circumcised boys, who looked like brothers, huddled together. They showered quickly with harsh soap, and went into the adjoining delousing room.

Still carrying their worn shoes out of the steaming shower room, Irena took the hands of the two circumcised boys. "Come with me," she whispered, in Polish and then Yiddish. Irena Schultz distracted the Polish Blue guard with flirtatious conversation while Irena and the two boys slipped out the doorway. "Cover yourselves."   She showed them with her hands.

In the hallway a Polish Blue examined Irena's pass and let her and the two boys through. She dressed them from a pile of stiff cotton pants and blouses.

Another Polish Blue guarded a darkened doorway in the rear of the building, one that Irena knew led out the back to the courtyard and its connecting alleyways. She held out 200 zloty, too generous for her to offer, too much for him to refuse. He took the money and let them out.

She led the boys through a courtyard to Ogrodowa Street, where she hailed a *droshky* and ordered it to Lekarska Street #9, Jaga's flat. Irena didn't know where else to go. She had never been to Jaga's house and was ill-prepared for what she saw when the *droshky* arrived. Directly across from Lekarska #9 was an SS barracks, the narrow street congested with armored cars and staff cars, German soldiers coming and going, two guards with submachine guns at the entrance. Irena paid the *droshky* driver, led the boys up Jaga's concrete steps, rang the bell, and prayed.

One deadbolt unlatched, then another, and the door opened a crack. A young girl, maybe ten or twelve years old, with long brown hair that hung in bohemian disarray below her shoulders, Jaga's daughter Hanna, poked her head out and looked up and down the street. Irena pushed the boys into the entryway. "I'm Irena Sendler, a friend of your mother's. Maybe she has spoken about me. You must be Hanna."

Hanna secured both deadbolts behind Irena. "Yes. She talks about you quite a lot."

"These two boys must stay here, at least until your mother comes home. And they must stay hidden – in the attic or the cellar, whatever is best. Where is your telephone?"

Irena felt herself trembling as she called Jaga at the office. She tried to catch a deep breath as the telephone rang and rang, but still she felt winded. She had to return to Leszno #109, as soon as possible, but Jaga had to know about the boys. She was just about to hang up when Jaga answered.

"Jaga," Irena said with profound relief. "Happy Birthday, darling. I'm at your house. I've brought two packages here for you. Make sure they stay in their boxes so they don't go bad. I'll explain later."

By the time Irena returned, the lorry had deposited another 25 beggars, and by the end of the day, 32 Jewish boys without papers were separated from the Aryan beggars. The two Irenas didn't sleep that night or the next, calling contacts and liaisons to arrange for emergency hiding places. When one fell asleep the other gently shook her. Sister Matylda Getter's convent could take some at least for a few days.

The next day Dobraczynski called Irena into his office and pointed for her to sit down. She could tell there was something wrong.

"A German police official came to see me today. He said 32 beggar children are missing from those rounded up. He said if I paid him 2,000 zloty and proved to him that they were returned to the ghetto, the matter would be closed. If not..."

"I know we can find hiding places on the Aryan side, if only..."

"Irena! Listen – don't speak. The children must be returned to the ghetto – immediately. I wish it were otherwise."

Irena held her tongue. There was no alternative – the Germans knew Jewish children were missing, and Dobraczynski was being blackmailed for a full accounting of their disposition.

How could she ever place 32 children in overcrowded and stressed ghetto flats? There was no room and certainly no food. Impulsively, she called Dr. Janusz Korczak at his famous orphanage on Sliska and Sienna Street in the ghetto. She said she had an urgent need to meet with him. He seemed to know who she was – she had briefly visited his orphanage during one of her forays into the ghetto – and agreed.

Everybody in Poland knew Dr. Janusz Korczak. As a child Irena had read his children's novel, *King Matt the First*, and others. During the 1930's Irena and her mother listened to his radio program, the "Old Doctor," in which he was by turns funny and philosophical. Just hearing his voice never failed to make them feel good. At university Irena studied Korczak's theory of children's moral education and read his books *How to Love a Child* and *The Child's Right to Respect*. Korczak introduced the concept of progressive orphanages designed as egalitarian communities, a model he instituted at his ghetto orphanage of 200 children.

Early the following day, just after the curfew lifted, Irena met the "Old Doctor" at his Sienna Street #16 orphanage, which bustled with purpose and happy activity, an anomaly in the ghetto. A frail man with a graying goatee and ears that protruded from his bald head, Korczak walked with a cane, the result of his arrest and beating at the hands of the Gestapo for refusing to wear the Jewish armband. In spite of his discouraging appearance, his eggshell blue eyes transfixed Irena through lopsided spectacles. She expressed her admiration for his work, then told him her dilemma.

He laughed. "You want to *what?*"

Irena explained about the German sweep of beggars from the Aryan streets and the discovery of those who were Jewish. "I know it's insane," Irena said, "to smuggle children *into* the ghetto."

"Why can't they stay where they are? Wouldn't it be better to keep them in hiding on the Aryan side?"

She explained about the pressure Dobraczynski was under to prove the children were returned to the ghetto. "They're all in emergency shelters – temporary – a week or two at most. I was only hoping..."

"We are all only hoping. It's what keeps us alive." He took a pencil from behind his ear, licked its tip and wrote some numbers on a piece of paper. He looked at her in a way that made Irena feel uncomfortable, as if he was about to decline to help her and chastise her as well. "Why are you doing this, Pani Sendler? You could be executed."

"I'm a social worker. It's what I do."

Korczak laughed again. "No, Pani Sendler. I am fairly certain that is not why you do this. I'm asking about your temperament, not your profession. Some people do this as a way of fighting the Germans – revenge, if you will. Is that it for you?"

She explained about her parents and her father's example. "I can't bear the suffering, and no one suffers as much as the Jewish children. It's just the decent thing to do."

Korczak took off his glasses and cleaned the lenses with a soiled handkerchief. He looked at Irena from the exhaustion and clarity of his blue eyes. "The Hebrew *Talmud* and the *Kabbalah* speak of 36 righteous people for whose sake God keeps the world alive, even in the most barbarous of times. None of the 36 knows that they are one of the righteous. As a matter of fact, if someone claims to be one of the righteous they are almost certainly not, for they lack humility. So in our blessed ignorance we are all encouraged to act as if we are one of them. Perhaps you are one."

"I could say the same for you, Dr. Korczak. I understand you had the opportunity to escape Poland, but you chose to stay for your children."

"The Germans hate it when people like me refuse to be intimidated." He looked over his calculations again. "Thirty-two children? Very expensive. And how would you sneak them into the ghetto? I suspect getting them in is almost as dangerous as getting them out."

"I'll find a way," Irena said defiantly. She knew all the reasons he should say no – it would put the whole orphanage in jeopardy, he was overextended, he couldn't afford to feed them.

He closed his eyes and nodded. "I'll have to make inquiries. Maybe it is possible. Call me later today."

Astonishingly, he agreed to take the children the next night. A boy named "Hirsch," an experienced, if young smuggler, told Korczak of a disguised opening in the wall surrounding the Church of the Annunciation, on the Aryan side, on Leszno Street. That night there would only be a sliver of moon. They would begin just after curfew.

Irena called her ten liaisons at the other district offices, assigned each one to pick up three or four children from emergency care units on the Aryan side before the curfew that night, and bring them to the church. The night watchman was paid a generous bribe to look the other way. The ghetto wall detoured to form a cul-de-sac that excluded the church, its small courtyard, and several other buildings. When Irena arrived she discovered that Hirsch was a very small ten-year-old Jewish smuggler, who described himself as "an important friend of Dr. Korczak." When the children were all gathered in the church, Irena sent the liaisons home. She and Hirsch stayed with the children who shivered in the cold sanctuary. They knew to be absolutely quiet.

At the exact start of curfew, Irena gave Hirsch the sign and he led the children single file out the back of the church, through a warren of courtyards and alleys to a place in the wall where the bricks were loose.

Hirsch threw a pebble over the wall, and a moment later another one came back. In the profound silence, Irena heard the scrape of one brick sliding over another, and an opening gradually appeared as if ghosts operated from the ghetto side. Hirsch and Irena pulled out enough bricks to open a child-sized hole. One by one, they pushed the boys through head first. After the last child was through, Irena heard urgent whispering from the black hole.

"Pani Sendler," Korczak whispered. A bony hand came through the wall. Irena took it and he squeezed. "I hope we meet again, under more favorable circumstances."

CHAPTER 15

Dangerous Rescues

Warsaw, February – April 1942

For several days in a row, on the corner of Karmelicka and Leszno Streets, a central intersection she passed every day, Irena recognized a new beggar, a young girl who looked to be no more than five or six, though it was impossible to guess childrens' ages anymore. There was nothing in particular to distinguish her from the multitude of other skeletal children, rags wrapping her bare feet, a faded kerchief covering her head, shivering, whimpering in the cold, shaking a bowl. Her eyes always seemed to find Irena's when she passed. On a crisp February day when Irena and Jaga were together in the ghetto, Irena saw that the girl could barely sit up; she was alone, near death. The other begging orphans on the street seemed to know to keep away from her, as if she were already dead.

Irena cut across the congestion that was Leszno Street and shook the girl's shoulders. She was still warm; she barely opened her eyes, sunken pits, and moaned through parched lips.

Irena returned to Jaga and pulled her into a doorway, out of the pedestrian flow. "I spoke with Sister Matylda Getter a few days ago," Irena said. "She's the Mother Superior at the Franciscan convent. I brought her a forged *Kennkarte* for that Jewish boy they took in. I asked if she would consider taking in other orphans and she said, 'There is always a seat at God's table.' Do you suppose..." She lifted her chin in the direction of the beggar girl.

Jaga looked from Irena to the listless girl. "How would we get her out?"

"The courthouse."

"I don't think she'll survive the night."

"Break off a piece of that," she said, pointing to a chunk of bread in Jaga's canvas sack.

"Irena. This is dangerous. Where can we take her?"

"To Lekarska Street. If she could stay with you for just a day or two, then Sister Getter can take her. You're right, she won't last another night. We'll bring her by the back alley. No one will see us."

Jaga pointed to the wall poster nearby, which reminded Poles and Jews alike of the death penalty for those who would help Jews. The red poster beside it listed the names and ages of those executed the day before.

Irena looked across Leszno; the girl had slumped against the building again. On an impulse, she pushed her way through the crowd of pedestrians and lifted the girl up into her arms. She weighed almost nothing and hardly reacted, though she must have felt Irena's heart pounding against her chest. Through dry and cracked lips, she whimpered, "Mama... Mama..."

Jaga had joined Irena, and together they made their way further down Leszno towards the courthouse. No one gave her a second look. At the entrance to the courthouse Irena sat down against the building in a line of other beggars.

"Find the janitor," she said to Jaga. "Jozef – the one Izabela Kuczkowska contacted. If he's agreeable, come out and give me a signal. Then go out the Leszno gate, get a *droshky*, and wait for us on the Aryan side at the corner of Ogrodowa and Biala. One hour."

"And if I can't find him – or if he's not agreeable?"

Irena turned to the girl in her arms and, in rudimentary Yiddish, asked her name. "Beryl," she whispered.

"Then Beryl will die tonight."

Irena leaned against the concrete courthouse wall, swaying back and forth, singing a Polish lullaby. The line of beggars beseeched, "*Haks-Rakhmunes! Haks-Rakhmunes!*"

Jaga returned a few minutes later and nodded to Irena, then turned up Leszno toward the gate.

Irena carried Beryl into a frantic crowd in the courthouse, a rare mingling of Aryans and Jews, Poles with and without armbands seeking redress or assistance. The dark marble floor was polished to a hard finish, a contrast to the surly mob that scuffed over it. Marble columns supported a vaulted two story ceiling. At the far end of this cavernous space Irena saw the janitor's tall broom handle and then Jozef's distinctive bald head bobbing in a sea of hats and kerchiefs. Holding Beryl tightly with both arms, Irena took a deep breath, dove into the crowd and swam across.

Irena followed Jozef down a back staircase, and the cacophony of the lobby became a distant rumbling. He unlocked a door and they descended another short flight to where his torch illuminated a dark hallway with a faint strip of light at the end. "Down the hall, up the stairs, and out the first door."

Irena put 50 zloty in his hand. He shook his head and did not take it.

"God bless you," Irena said.

"No." He turned off his torch. "God bless you." Then he was gone, and Irena heard the door lock behind her.

Spider webs stuck to her face as she felt her way down the corridor, her gaze fixed on the line of light under a distant door. That door was unlocked; she pushed through, and suddenly they were outside the courthouse in a small vestibule, below ground level, dazzled by sunlight. Beryl slept.

Irena accustomed her eyes to the brilliance, looked carefully to see that no one was watching, then climbed the steps to the ground level where she saw Jaga standing beside a *droshky* on Biala Street.

The *droshky* let them off around the corner from Lekarska Street and its German barracks, at the entrance to the alleyway behind the Lekarska Street houses. At #9 Jaga's daughter Hanna greeted them at the back door. Irena carried Beryl directly up to the second floor and laid her onto a bed where she started to wake, though still disoriented. "*Haks-Rakhmunes!*" she said and fell asleep.

When Irena came downstairs, Jaga was explaining to Hanna, "If anyone is to ask, she's a sick cousin from Poznan. She'll only be here for a day, maybe two."

Irena left through the front door. Across the narrow street a pair of German soldiers guarded the barracks, others lounged on the steps smoking and laughing. Though the wind was still cold, Irena sweated freely and loosened her coat. As she walked away from Lekarska Street she found herself smiling for the first time in many months.

*   *   *   *   *   *   *   *   *   *

After Beryl's successful escape, Irena was emboldened to try again. There was no shortage of dying orphans, and no one missed them when they were gone. She and her liaisons identified more foster parents, and more emergency care units. The rescues through the courthouse were uncomplicated, and by early spring Irena was taking three to four orphans a week out of the ghetto. When placement was difficult or delayed, the convents of the Sisters of the Family of Mary took in a child.

Then, disaster. One of Irena's couriers, Helena, a young girl of 19, was arrested with a four-year-old orphan and inexpertly forged papers. No one knew exactly how it happened, but one version had it that the child began to cry for his mother in Yiddish, and the courier was stopped by a Gestapo agent, who suspected a forged *Kennkarte.* The orphan, malnourished and weak, was sent to Gensia Prison and died a few days later of dysentery. Helena was taken to Pawiak Prison.

Irena was horrified – though death was commonplace, she had never lost someone from her network before. The risks were well known by all of them. How much did Helena know? How careless were the others? How reliable? How loyal? There could be no doubt that the Gestapo would employ every form of trickery and torture to extract information from Helena before they executed her.

Irena contacted her ten liaisons and instructed them to cease all rescues of orphans and either destroy incriminating evidence or hide it so it could never be found. Irena held one piece of evidence that was perhaps the most damning of all, the most fragile, yet the most necessary – lists of rescued orphans' names, matching their original Jewish names with their new Aryan identities. She and Jaga, the only two who knew where the lists were hidden, understood that there were two critical reasons for the lists. First, each hidden child's address ensured delivery of the monthly support stipend, usually about 500 zloty. It wasn't much, enough for bread and black market butter. When the host family was poor, she tried to give more, and better-off families accepted less or nothing at all. The other reason for the lists, and maybe the more urgent, was her concern that the children be able to recover their Jewish names, so that after the war their relatives could reclaim them. If no relatives survived, at least the children would know that they were Jewish.

When Irena explained about the lists, Irena Schultz objected. "It's an unnecessary risk. They're orphans. They don't have any relatives. What if the lists are found?"

Irena shook her head. "Every child deserves a name." She recognized, though, that the lists, if found, would be a death warrant not only for the hidden children but for the families sheltering them. As soon as she learned of Helena's arrest, Irena went to see Jaga at her home.

Irena breezed past Jaga at the door, saying, "We have to hide the lists. Underground – buried – that's the safest. I thought, maybe, in your back-yard."

Jaga looked up to see her Hanna listening from the doorway. "Hanna, go upstairs! Go now."

After she left, Jaga whispered to Irena, "Stay until Hanna is asleep. I don't want her to know anything about this – just in case..."

It was unnecessary for Jaga to finish. If the Gestapo were to apprehend Hanna there was no telling what brutality they would inflict to extract information. It was an article of faith in the underground that one should only know what was essential. One couldn't confess to what one didn't know.

At midnight, Jaga lit a carbide lamp, and she and Irena tiptoed down the wooden stairs to her garden carrying a spade, a large spoon, a kitchen knife, and a glass jar. Beneath Jaga's beloved apple tree they began to dig. The spade proved too noisy, its blade clinking against the cold, hard ground. Irena stabbed at the ground with the knife until the soil was loose enough to be spooned out. Soon the hole was large enough to accommodate the glass milk jar with the lists inside. Irena laid it in the hole with the reverence usually reserved for coffins. They quickly covered it and flattened the soil.

"How often shall we dig it up?" Jaga asked.

Irena looked at the dark sky. "In a month, at the next new moon." She put her hand on the freshly worked earth. Irena said, "Except for the two of us, no one must know of this. If it's discovered, these children will be lost."

Irena worried about Helena, what she was enduring, what she would reveal. She burned several forged identity documents ready to be delivered and waited for the Gestapo. Two days later, Helena's name appeared on a red poster announcing those executed at Pawiak the day before. When she saw it, Irena had to walk away to hide her tears. She felt completely responsible for Helena's capture and death. She should have insisted on any number of precautions, obtained better forgeries, but her zeal to rescue orphans overwhelmed her discretion. All the details of Helena's capture were not known, but almost certainly, the courthouse as an escape and smuggling venue was now compromised. According to Jozef, the locks to the tunnel were changed, and checkpoints beefed up. It would be some time before they could use the courthouse again.

Irena's network went into hibernation; rescues stopped and the Gestapo never came. Irena could only conclude that Helena had given away nothing under torture or that she had taken her own life with a cyanide capsule before the worst of the torture began. Irena resumed her daily visits to the ghetto, smuggling what she could of lard, money, and medicine. But now she felt watched.

A week after Helena's death, the rescues resumed. Through her network Irena learned where the bricks were loose in the wall, which landlords could be bribed to allow orphans to slip through holes where the wall ran through their tenement. A Jewish courier would bring the child to the cellar where she would meet her Aryan counterpart, who then brought the child to an emergency care home. There was no end to people's imagination and daring. One orphan, Aron Stefanek, was thin enough to escape under the coat of a man leaving the ghetto on a work brigade. He slipped his bare feet into the man's boots and held onto his belt; the man's coat, when closed, made the skeletal boy invisible. Others were smuggled out in garbage bags. The morgue wagon provided another escape vehicle. Sedated orphans, who looked half dead already, were placed among the corpses.

And, of course, there was the Hygiene Wagon driven by Antoni Danbrowski, one of the few Polish motor vehicles still allowed into the ghetto. Danbrowski occasionally transported an ill or injured Aryan who worked in the ghetto or, rarer still, a member of the *Judenrat* who had

149

made special arrangements for treatment for himself or his immediate family outside the ghetto.

Irena entered the ghetto up to three times a day to make home visits or to meet with Ewa. At the end of April, she visited Lea Kucyk and her baby Mina, not yet two months old, who was dying of starvation. Since Mina's birth Irena had visited Lea weekly on Ostrowska #14, a street teeming with refugees. She brought what food and money she could up three flights to their crowded apartment. Nursing added stress to Lea's already malnourished body and barely provided enough milk for Mina, who steadily lost weight and cried with a weak mewing. She needed a wet-nurse, as unobtainable as any miracle.

But now Lea had a high fever and a cough so painful that she splinted her chest. Almost certainly pneumonia – she would not survive another day. When Irena unwrapped the baby she had to contain her horror. Mina writhed on the cotton swaddling, a wrinkled infant who seemed to have shrunken more since her last visit. Her head lolled to one side, her mouth dry, her lips cracked with sucking blisters. Aroused – disturbed from the anodyne of her stupor – she squealed miserably.

"Take her!" Lea said. "Please, Pani Sendler, have pity, take her."

"Where is your husband?"

"They took him – a few days ago – for forced labor." She began to sob. "I've been told that I shouldn't expect to see him again." She pulled up her blouse to show Irena her collapsed breasts. "Empty. Take her, Pani Sendler. For the love of God, before we're both dead."

Irena called on Antoni Danbrowski to assist with Mina's rescue – another "special project" for his Hygiene Wagon. Antoni met her at the Welfare office.

"I have a surprise for you, Pani Sendler." He rubbed his hands together with excitement. "In the wagon."

The ambulance idled at the curb, and when Irena opened the passenger door, she gasped and jumped back. There was a large dog sitting on the front seat. "That's my baby, Shepsi," Antoni said. "Please, get in, Pani Sendler." He held open the passenger door and bowed again in his silly way. Shepsi, a large mixed breed, sniffed Irena all over.

"She's saying hello," Antoni said as they drove from the curb.

"Why did you bring your dog? The last thing we need is unwanted attention."

"Don't worry, Shepsi's quite talented and well trained."

As Antoni drove toward the ghetto gate, Irena explained about Lea and Mina. They had no problem entering the ghetto and stopped at Lea Kucyk's tenement.

Though Irena had brought a clean receiving blanket, Lea insisted that Mina be wrapped in her father's white and black Hebrew prayer shawl. Its silk fringes hung down, oddly decorative, as Irena lifted her carefully. She always carried a small vial of the sedative Luminal for young children, but she didn't dare sedate Mina, fearful she would stop breathing. Antoni cleared away boxed bandages, gauze, muslin and cotton, and foul-smelling bloodied sheets, to reveal a small tomb-like opening, in which Irena gently laid the infant. Antoni maneuvered a perforated board over the secret niche, disguised by rags.

As they approached the Gensia gate to leave, Irena heard Mina's feeble but persistent cry from the back. They pulled up to the gate, and her cry intensified. If the guards discovered her, she would likely be smothered and thrown into the trash.

Two Germans and a Polish Blue approached the cab. Were they deaf not to hear Mina's high pitched whimpering? Irena held her breath.

Before the German reached the wagon, Antoni tapped Shepsi's paw and she immediately began to bark and whine. Irena closed her eyes and said a small prayer. Shepsi continued to make all sorts of noises, loud enough so that Irena could not be sure anymore if she heard a whining dog or a fussy baby. Their papers were checked, and the Polish Blue briefly inspected the back, deterred by the bloody sheets and foul odor.

One of the two German gendarmes came up to Irena's side of the wagon and ordered Antoni to stop the dog's barking. Antoni shrugged his shoulders. The German, a young boy, fear written on his acne-scarred face, drew his Luger and pointed the barrel at the dog's head. "Shut this dog up!" he said. Antoni put his arms around Shepsi's neck and tried to hold her snout, efforts that looked like a good faith attempt to stop the dog's barking. But Shepsi struggled and squirmed and continued to make loud, high-pitched noises.

The German, his eyes wide with anger, pointed the pistol at Antoni. "Make him stop or I'll shoot you instead."

Irena gently touched the German's arm and looked sweetly into his eyes. "Please, your honor," she said with as much softness as possible. "She's just a young dog. We're trying to teach her, but she gets so nervous."

The other German said something funny to the young gendarme, who reluctantly holstered his pistol and waved the Hygiene Wagon through.

When they were safely on the Aryan side, Antoni tapped Shepsi's paw twice, and the big dog was immediately silent. Irena couldn't stop herself from hugging Shepsi, who lapped her face. She must have liked the taste of her tears.

CHAPTER 16

A Silver Spoon
Warsaw, April – July 18, 1942

By the spring of 1942, there were almost 50 different underground newspapers publishing in Poland. Every political, religious, and ethnic organization risked death to publish its own partisan opinion. The risk was finally realized on what came to be known as the "Night of Blood," Friday night, April 17, 1942, a major German *Aktion* in Warsaw, during which the Germans seized 60 prominent Jews and executed them in the street. In one way or another, they were all associated with the underground press – printers, writers, distributors, and financiers. Most disturbing was the report by an eyewitness that the SS worked from a list provided by the Jewish Police – the SP.

Jews escaping from the Lublin ghetto reached Warsaw in April and May with horrifying tales of Jews packed into cattle cars, more than a hundred in each, for deportation to Belzec. Reports of the liquidation of the Crakow ghetto and thirty thousand Jews deported from the Lwow ghetto spread like the Spanish Flu. One week later similar news from Mielec. *Biuletyn Informacyjny*, the newspaper of the underground government-in-exile, reported on the opening of a strange new camp, Treblinka, a camp without prisoners' barracks, sixty miles northeast of Warsaw, on the rail line.

The underground press also reported deportations and murder. Irena read a few of the illegal newspapers, especially the *Biuletyn Informacyjny*, which reported on "well substantiated rumors of death camps" – Chelmno, Belzec, Sobibor. Refugees from the Riga ghetto reported mass killings in the nearby woods. The Jews of the Lublin ghetto were deported to Belzec; nobody ever returned from Belzec, what the newspaper referred to as a "killing factory." The Germans continued to insist that all deportations were to labor camps.

Just recently, Irena heard more rumors about the new camp being built just northeast of Warsaw – Treblinka. Stefan's underground contacts suggested that it, too, could be a killing factory. There were no barracks for prisoners, only brick smokestacks. Others, most notably the *Judenrat* and the SP, insisted it was nothing more sinister than a transfer station for Jews en route to "work" camps or "resettlement" camps in the East. Where was the East? Some said as far away as Arabia, others said the Ukraine. Every bit of hearsay, no matter how outlandish, was repeated and refined into certainty.

On her way to work on Monday after the "Night of Blood," Irena read new German wall posters describing the crimes and the executions of the 60 Jews and a warning:

"AS LONG AS THE SECRET PRESS CONTINUES TO APPEAR, THERE WILL BE EXECUTIONS. THE JEWS MUST PUT A STOP TO THIS TREASON."

Every underground activist or sympathizer was put on notice, and Irena wondered if her name was on the Gestapo's list of suspects. But the underground press was not cowed; the next weekly issue of *Yediot* not only came out exactly on time, but in an expanded edition.

In the spring of 1942 a new word entered every Jew's vocabulary – *deportation*. More than rumors, official German publications discussed "mandatory relocations of Jews to work camps." Jews were forcibly removed from ghettos throughout Poland – "transported by train," the Germans said – "crammed into cattle cars," the underground press reported – and taken where? They just disappeared.

Ewa, a persistent optimist, accepted Schmuel's conclusions, very much those of the SP and Judenrat, that the camps were for labor. The Jews were far too valuable to the German war effort. And besides, the Germans have all the power. Best to acquiesce to their demands rather than inflame a violent reaction. Ewa's brother Adam came to exactly the opposite conclusion and was convinced the Germans meant to kill every Jew in Poland and that deportation meant death.

A week after the "Night of Blood," Irena was at CENTOS with money for Ewa, who looked as if she hadn't slept for many nights. Over the 18 months since the ghetto had been closed, Irena thought her friend had aged ten years. "The day after the *Aktion*," Ewa said, "thousands of new refugees arrived from Theresienstadt. We had almost no food for them, and no place to put them except in the main synagogue. The strangest thing was that we could do almost nothing for them except put a roof over their heads, and they were grateful."

"I wish there was more I could do to help."

Ewa's smile, albeit sad, returned. How Irena missed its authenticity from a better time. "My dear, dear friend, you must never think that. What you do... you restore my faith in humanity."

Irena felt self-conscious with Ewa's praise and asked about her Youth Circle.

"I try not to let them see my despair. I would only say this to you because you are such a dear and trusted friend, but I fear my optimism is slipping; more and more I expect tragedy and failure." Ewa looked down as if shamed by the words that leaked in an unguarded moment. "It's remarkable what can seem like a miracle these days. I've given up on deliverance. Now, just to be alive another day is miracle enough."

Irena gave Ewa an envelope filled with zloty for black market food. "I have to go. I'm on my way to see the Pinkus family."

"Be careful at the Leszno Gate, Irena. There's a new German guard. They are calling him *Frankenstein*. He shoots people for the slightest provocation and sometimes at random."

Irena hoped this was not true. "There are so many rumors."

"No, Irena. I saw this with my own eyes. Yesterday, I was walking down Leszno and heard pistol shots. Then a stampede came running towards me: 'Frankenstein is coming!' 'Frankenstein is coming!' I watched from a doorway as this ordinary-looking German soldier walked alone down the center of Leszno Street shooting at Jews who cowered in doorways. It could have been me. He stopped to reload his pistol then continued on his way, shooting. I don't know how many he killed."

★ ★ ★ ★ ★ ★ ★ ★ ★ ★

An hour later Irena stood in the doorway of the Pinkus flat, one they shared with 15 other refugees. She searched the bottom of her nurse's bag and found the forged Aryan *Kennkarte* in the name of Tadeusz Marzec, the new identity card for Aleksander Pinkus, a baby whose life was about to change. She had already written him onto her April list:

April 1942 – Aleksander Pinkus → Tadeusz Marzec – Szaserov #68

Irena saw Aleksander's mother right away, clutching him to her face. Saying goodbye – this was the worst moment for Irena. "After the war – you'll get him back," Irena explained again to Aleksander's parents as she dropped the amber Luminal into his mouth. "I keep a list," she said, showing them. "His Polish name, Tadeusz, it's only to save his life." Mrs. Pinkus sank to her knees, shaking and weeping in the doorway. She could not have understood Irena's words. The Luminal worked quickly, and Irena bundled tiny Aleksander in a blanket, then eased him into an "Infection Control" gunny sack with breathing holes. Irena left through the Gensia Street gate carrying Aleksander under her arm as if he were a medical parcel, timing her crossing with the evening return of forced laborers to the ghetto – a busy time for the guards, who counted slaves and checked them for contraband. They showed little concern for Aryans, like Irena, leaving the ghetto.

The first 500 yards past the wall, where Gestapo agents, informers, and *szmalcowniki* lurked, were the most hazardous. Sheltering Jews in Aryan Warsaw was now referred to as "keeping cats." If *szmalcowniki* picked up the scent of an escaping Jew, they came up from behind, "meowing" – signaling their intention to denounce unless they were paid. Of course, there was no guarantee they wouldn't betray the escapee anyway to be rewarded again by the Gestapo.

★　★　★　★　★　★　★　★　★

May 1942 – Avram Hofman → Ludwick Wirski – Praga, Chlodnicza #6

Mr. Leon Szeszko, a tram engineer and the husband of one of Irena's liaison agents, drove the first morning tram out of the Muranowski Square depot, which was still within the ghetto walls. In early May he agreed to help Irena test a new escape route by smuggling three-month-old Avram Hofman out of the ghetto on his tram. At 5 AM, in an apartment on Mila Street facing Muranowski Square, one of Irena's couriers, a teen-aged girl, code-named *Wika*, administered the Luminal, then sang Avram a sweet lullaby as he drifted into drugged sleep. She settled him into a cardboard box wrapped with brown paper and twine to resemble a mail parcel with discrete air holes. Curfew was still in effect when *Wika* left the tenement carrying the box. She kept to the shadows. Mr. Szeszko had left the side door of the tram depot unlocked the night before. She boarded Mr. Szeszko's tram on the first track, its door slightly ajar, and pushed the box under a seat. She checked again to see that the air holes were clear, then left. Nearly an hour later, a few minutes after 6 AM, when he normally arrived for work, Mr. Szeszko checked the box, disengaged the brake, and turned the lever to drive his tram out of the depot, out of the ghetto, to where it arrived empty at his first stop in Aryan Warsaw.

Irena was the first to get on and sat directly over the parcel. She felt every passenger's eyes on her. They must all have noticed that she wasn't carrying a parcel when she got on the tram. The box began to wriggle against her foot, and she thought she heard the complaints of a wak-ing baby. At the first stop she picked up the squirming parcel and heard whimpering; surely every passenger could hear it. She stepped off the tram and felt lightheaded, her vision darkening, desperate to keep from fainting. Just as her legs began to turn wobbly, she found a bench near the tram, sat and breathed deeply, letting her heart end its race. What, she wondered, must baby Avram be experiencing, rocking blind in a rough cradle – waking into pitch black?

The foster family that was to take Avram changed their mind when they learned he was a boy; circumcised boys easily exposed their foster families. Irena delivered him instead to Jaga's Lekarska #9, through the back alley and garden. Desperate, Irena visited with Sister Matylda Getter, who placed Avram with one of the Sisters of the Family of Mary convents.

★   ★   ★   ★   ★   ★   ★   ★   ★   ★

When they next met at CENTOS, Ewa seemed preoccupied and said in an off-handed, guilty way, "Schmuel wants to marry me." Her speech had slurred noticeably; her eyes heavy-lidded and bloodshot, as if by too much alcohol, or starvation.

Irena was disappointed, but said nothing.

"I could use some makeup," Ewa said, her cheeks emaciated hollows, her eyes unable to hold Irena's gaze. "Cosmetics," she imitated a laugh. "Who ever would have thought that cosmetics would become historical curiosities?"

"You look tired," Irena said. "And afraid."

"Schmuel reassures me that if there is a deportation many Jews will remain – the Judenrat, the SP, those who work in shops and factories, their wives and children. The worst is not knowing. Who can sleep anymore?"

"If you marry Schmuel, do you get your own Ausweis?"

"No, but I'm protected by his." She blushed. "People are marrying like crazy – it's another kind of epidemic – anybody with an Ausweis is desirable. Brothers and sisters are even marrying, just for the work permit. And the Rabbis are signing the contracts – to save a life, they say."

"What did you tell Schmuel?"

"I said I'd think about it. I've known Schmuel for a long time. He's not a bad sort. Mother and Father want me to say yes."

Irena had not told Ewa how brutal Schmuel had been at the gate with the child smuggler. "Ewa, it would be so easy for me to get you out of here."

Ewa closed her eyes and shook her head. "Please, Irena, don't ask again. My parents need me. My Youth Circle needs me. Out there, on the Aryan side, I would be a hunted animal."

"Then marry him, Ewa. Do it." There was an uncomfortable silence between them, then Irena said, "What does Adam think?"

"Adam? He's gone completely crazy," Ewa said. "He's moved to Mila Street. I went to visit him a few days ago and he showed me his pistol and petrol bombs. We had a terrible fight. He says the Germans mean to kill us all and he'd rather die fighting. Adam's crazy! He's crazy and he lives with crazy people. They put us all at risk."

★　★　★　★　★　★　★　★　★　★

DECREE: WARSAW – JULY 15, 1942

The curfew is reduced by one hour from 9 PM to 10 PM. Workshops and factories will stay open an extra hour, until 9 PM.

★　★　★　★　★　★　★　★　★　★

By July, every Jew in the ghetto finally accepted that deportation was a matter of when, not if. Desperate men lined up to secure a precious *Ausweis* – the work document that exempted them and their immediate family from deportation and permitted them to be chosen as slave laborers at workshops that made German uniforms and brushes.

Jozef the janitor had obtained the new key to the locked basement doors, and the Leszno Street courthouse was again available for smuggling children out of the ghetto. Irena had been working on the assumption that ten children taken out each week was the limit of her network's capacity. Mass deportation, she feared, would drastically alter the mathematics. Could they take 15? 20? Would it make a difference?

In mid-July Ewa telephoned Irena and asked her to come as quickly as possible – it was urgent. An hour later at CENTOS, Ewa greeted Irena without joy and closed the door to her office for privacy. "Schmuel says there is a new *Sturmbahnführer*. He overheard SP officers discussing deportations – they call them 'relocations' or 'shrinking the ghetto.' He said I should be sure to tell you. You see, he's one of us – he's a good person."

After leaving CENTOS, Irena immediately went to find Schmuel at his gate and asked him about the deportation rumors. Schmuel looked more uneasy, but still genuinely pleased to see Irena, or he put on a good show of it. Before he could answer, she reciprocated with her own generous gesture. "I hear that you and Ewa might be marrying."

He grinned the unctuous, gap-toothed smile that Irena hated, but maybe he could save Ewa. "I overheard SP officers planning in the ready room at Ogrodowa #15 – planning for relocations – the Germans say to work camps in the East. That's all I know."

"When, Schmuel? When?"

159

He squirmed. "I... I don't know. But it will be soon."

She smiled at him. "Ewa will be glad to hear how you have helped me."

Back at her office, Irena spoke urgently with Irena Schultz about how they might respond to a sudden deportation. "I know exactly what we need to do," Irena said. "We can double our capacity just by shortening each child's emergency care unit stay from 5-6 days to 2-3 days. We can put several children at once in a care unit. Sister Getter is willing to take more, we have couriers in the ghetto, and the courthouse escape route is usable again. We can take two or three times as many children – maybe ten times."

"Doesn't this make you nervous?" Irena Schultz said. "A few orphans every week is one thing – ten times that many – and not orphans – that's quite another. It's hard to keep that secret. You'll be denounced. It's a capital crime."

This business of risk felt bewildering to Irena. Of course she was afraid; everyone in Warsaw was afraid. She fought the Germans the only way she could; she worked in the spirit of her father's mission, something that kept his essence alive inside her. Irena had no doubt that her well-organized network could do more. All they lacked was money, and she felt certain they could get more from the Home Army, the government-in-exile, and the Joint. "You are my most trusted ally," Irena said to Irena Schultz. "The deportation will begin soon. I need your support and your intelligence to do this."

Irena Schultz shrugged. "Irena, I have complete faith in you. Just say the word."

They hugged briefly. "I'll speak with Jaga and Dobraczynski," Irena said. "We've no time to lose."

★   ★   ★   ★   ★   ★   ★   ★   ★   ★

Irena knocked a second time – much louder. The dark hallway reeked of urine and garbage.

"What do you want?" A muffled voice through the door.

"My name is *Jolanta*," said Irena. The door did not open until she added, "Ewa Rechtman's friend."

Israel Koppel, his eyes red and moist, opened the door to a baking hot apartment, dark and noiseless but for the buzz of obese flies. The silence was all the more noticeable for the thin and pale strangers who filled the three-room flat – according to Mr. Koppel, three families, 23 people. Koppel's stained clothing, like that of every other Jew in Warsaw, purchased during better times, hung on his skeletal frame. In the crook of his elbow an infant swaddled in a soiled cloth wriggled and fussed.

The July sun roasted the tenement, and Irena thought it a pity that all the sun's heat, but little of its light penetrated the Koppels' flat with its small windows. Irena sweated profusely in her nurse's uniform.

Mr. Koppel stepped back from the door to let Irena in. "Ewa said you could save our baby." He held up the tiny bundle in his arms. "Her name is Elzbieta Koppel – 'Bieta.' She was born 6 months ago in a snow-storm. Stanislawa – the midwife – she came through the storm and never charged us even a zloty." The baby sucked greedily on her father's little finger. Israel Koppel parted the folds of cloth for Irena to see his daughter's face, her glistening, eager eyes. "Is she not the most perfect baby you have ever seen?" he said. "She is thin, but she nurses well, so she cheats the ration system. It's her mother, Henia, who suffers." Koppel's wife Henia came up behind him, her emerald green eyes luminous and over-large in her gaunt face, her blond hair dulled by starvation. She said she was 31 years old, only a year younger than Irena, and Irena could see that Henia Koppel was once beautiful.

"Your baby will be with a loving family – just until the war is over. The same midwife who delivered her, Stanislawa Bussoldowa, will keep her for a few days. Then she'll go to Otwock, to the Rumkowskis."

Bieta began to fuss, and Mr. Koppel rocked her in his arms, gently hushing her. After a long pause, he asked, "What guarantees?"

Of course, Irena could give none. No one bothered to ask this impossible question of orphans. Now they all wanted guarantees and she literally talked parents out of their children. Irena had repeated the same answer a hundred times, her words no less searing now than the first time. "If Bieta is taken to Treblinka she will die. If she stays here in the ghetto she will likely die of infection or starvation." Each time Irena spoke these words, despite knowing their truth, she felt a lingering doubt about her own role as the persuader. How could she, who had no children of her own, possibly comprehend what Henia felt giving up her baby? How could she ever feel Israel Koppel's impotence?

The parents had more questions: "Will she be baptized? Will she grow up Catholic? Will she know her name? Will we ever see her again? When the war is over will we get her back?"

"I keep a record," Irena said and showed them the week's accounting, Bieta's name at the bottom of the tissue paper list.

July 18, 1942 – Elzbieta Koppel → Stefja Rumkowska – Otwock – Radosna #5

"You must decide right away," she said to the Koppels. "Arrangements must be made, papers must be..."

She thought Mr. Koppel was about to agree when Henia gripped his forearm and turned her lustrous eyes on Irena. "Tomorrow," she said. "I need one more night. Please, just one more night."

Irena hoped tomorrow would not be too late. She thought about the Koppels each time she woke from her agitated sleep, and, the next morning went straight away to their flat. Before she knocked at the door, she clearly heard Henia weeping, and was awestruck contemplating what the night must have been like for Henia and Israel, a night whose pain and despair made a mockery of Irena's mere waking and wondering. Israel Koppel opened the door holding Bieta. He tried to speak, but was unable. The grandfather, Aron Rohman, a wiry old man with crooked spectacles, stood beside his son and spoke for him. "We don't know you, but Ewa says you are trustworthy, and we have complete faith in Ewa. Take Bieta. Take her today before we change our minds again."

"Two hours," Irena said. "Have her ready by ten o'clock."

Irena returned at the appointed time carrying an empty carpenter's box. The ghostly refugees who shared the Koppels' flat watched Henia nurse her baby for the last time. Bieta smiled for her mother and burped easily. Henia took a deep breath and pursed her lips. Now the last embrace, then the last kiss – moments Irena dreaded – and finally the last desperate act of love when Henia gently settled her in the carpenter's box lined with the clean blanket Irena had provided. She shooed away flies and folded the blanket to get it just right. Once Bieta was content, Irena dropped the Luminal into her mouth, and she cooed and smiled again as Irena moved to close the lid. Henia stopped her and bent over to kiss her baby – to stroke her sweet face one last time. She took something from her pocket and put it in the box, something that shimmered in the dull light and sparkled beside Bieta's head – a silver spoon inscribed:

Elzbieta
5 January 1942

Henia looked away. Bieta's eyes began to flutter, the combined effect of warm breast milk and Luminal. Israel Koppel cleared his throat. "You must make certain, Pani Sendler, that Bieta's new parents keep this spoon." Tears welled up, and he wiped his eyes coarsely with his sleeve. "She must know it was a gift – from her Momma and Poppa." Henia was at his side, weeping into his chest.

Irena could not speak. The Koppels' nightmare was almost over – maybe in a week or a month or two months they would be deported to Treblinka where Irena believed certain death awaited them.

Irena trifled with the air holes to make certain they were clear, then closed the box and left the apartment. The box was heavier than she had anticipated, but she dared not stop to put it down. Every baby reacted differently to Luminal; there were no guarantees that Bieta would stay asleep for long.

A Polish bricklayer, Henryk, waited in the shadow of the tenement's courtyard and took the carpenter's box from Irena. Polish laborers frequently trucked loads of bricks, the rubble of bombed buildings, out of the ghetto. His flatbed truck, piled with salvaged bricks, idled unevenly in the street. Irena watched for SS or SP patrols as he gently inserted the box into a void in the stacked bricks on his truck, piling loose ones around the opening.

Irena directed Henryk to drive through the Nalewki Gate that opened onto the Krasinski Gardens, but there was an unusually long queue. She was hoping to see Schmuel for expedited passage, but today there were no SP at the gate. In rapid succession, three pistol shots exploded nearby.

Irena gasped and jumped in her seat. Henryk held her arm.

There was no choice but to face the Polish Blues and the Germans, one of whom beckoned the truck forward. Was it in her mind, or did she hear a faint moaning or fussing from the pile of bricks in the truck? Maybe the dose of Luminal was too small, or Bieta had spit some out. Irena's sweat turned cold. The German guard ordered Henryk and Irena from the cab and studied their papers carefully while a Polish Blue examined the flatbed load. A Ukrainian felt for weapons in Henryk's clothing. Henryk spoke more loudly than usual, acting as if he was somewhat limited in his mind, and continued to ramble on after the Polish Blue's questions had been answered.

The German guard became angry with him and threw his papers on the ground, then made him grovel for them. He grabbed Henryk by the collar of his overalls and pushed him back to his truck. Two Germans conferred for a moment. Just then another slave battalion arrived at the now crowded gate for processing and searching. The iron bars across the gate finally lifted and Henryk's truck was waved through. Irena thought she would vomit.

Henryk parked the truck on the other side of the gardens, jumped from the cab and recovered the carpenter's box. He put it down hard on the street, clearly anxious to be done with this. She gave him a roll of zloty, which he did not bother to count. He jumped into the cab of his truck and roared away, leaving a cloud of exhaust.

Irena carried the box off the main square into the gardens to an out-of-the-way path. She set it carefully on a bench and opened it. Suddenly bathed in dappled sunlight, Bieta stopped crying. She had wriggled her arms free of their swaddling, and somehow she had managed to grasp the silver spoon that glinted in the sun.

Irena left the box under the bench and carried Bieta across the Vistula to the Praga district, to Kaluszynska #5, the home of her temporary foster mother, Stanislawa Bussoldowa, the midwife who had delivered her. As one of the emergency placement units, Stanislawa had taken in several orphans already that week, passed one along to a foster family, two to Mother Superior Matylda Getter, and two others to the Carmelite nuns.

Though the baby's forged *Kennkarte* named her Stefja, Irena explained to Stanislawa, "Her name is Bieta. When you love her and hold her, call her Bieta."

CHAPTER 17

Liquidation
Warsaw, July – August 1942

Irena visited Stanislawa on July 19th, the day after Bieta's rescue, with bad news. "There were complications with Bieta," Irena explained. "Mrs. Rumkowski has been diagnosed with tuberculosis. She can't take her. Is it possible for her to stay a little longer with you?"

Stanislawa beamed. "Irena, after only one day I have fallen in love with this baby, but I can't keep her here. I'm a forty-year-old widow with grown children; my neighbors are already suspicious. I've had veiled threats from a blackmailer. But I know a woman, a nanny, her name is Olga. She lives in Michalin. I've known her for ten years. She has no children of her own. Let me talk with her."

Later that day, Stefan visited Irena. He was agitated and out of breath from running up the stairs. Deportation was imminent, he said. "I've heard it several times from reliable Home Army contacts. Couriers in the woods near Treblinka say the camp started receiving trainloads of people from other camps and ghettos. Thousands go in, no one leaves. There are no prisoners' barracks, no factories, no prisoners working. They just disappear. It's a killing factory."

The next day, July 20th, Judenrat Chairman Czerniakow announced that rumors of deportation or relocation were treasonous lies. Gestapo wall posters announced the death penalty for anyone spreading such rumors.

Ewa telephoned the next night, and Irena heard terror in her voice. "Schmuel said the relocations would start tomorrow."

"Is he sure?"

"Just today, soldiers surrounded the Judenrat building – Ukrainians, Latvians. Rumor has it that the SS have already arrested some of the

Judenrat; some were shot in their homes, some on the street."

There was nothing Irena could do – curfew was about to begin. "Marry Schmuel," she said.

★ ★ ★ ★ ★ ★ ★ ★ ★ ★

DECREE: WARSAW – JULY 22, 1942

By order of the German authorities, all Jews living in Warsaw, irrespective of sex and age, will be evacuated. Exemptions include:

Jews employed by the authorities or in German enterprises;

Jews working in German-owned factories;

Jewish members of the Judenrat or those who work for the Judenrat;

Jewish Police, the staffs of Jewish hospitals, and the sanitation squads;

Jews fit for work who have not yet been integrated into the labor process, to be concentrated in barracks within the shrunken Jewish District and put to work;

Jews hospitalized in a Jewish hospital on the first day of the evacuation and not in a condition to be moved.

This exemption includes the immediate families (i.e. wives and children) of those in the above categories.

Jews slated for evacuation may take along up to 33 pounds of personal belongings, including valuables such as gold, jewelry, cash and so forth.

Responsibility for the orderly conduct of the evacuation rests with the Judenrat, said decree to be executed by the Jewish Police (SP) under the direction of specified SS units.

To add indignity to cruelty, the Germans often chose Jewish holy days to initiate their most murderous *Aktions*. July 22, 1942 was the 9th day of the Hebrew month of Av – the date of the destruction of the first and second temples and the date on which the Spanish Inquisition expelled the Jews.

*   *   *   *   *   *   *   *   *   *

Irena knew this day was coming; she had worried about it for months. The morning of Wednesday, July 22nd, after seeing the posted decree, she told Irena Schultz to remain in the office that entire day – to be available on the telephone. Irena Schultz was to locate their network's ten liaisons and tell them to set in motion their worst-case scenario. Each liaison had his own couriers on both sides of the wall, mostly young women, prepared to smuggle children to emergency care units. In sum about 25 people were to be alerted, most of them on the Aryan side of the wall.

Irena strode as quickly as she could toward the ghetto. The streets felt electric with danger. Poles gathered about the wall posters exchanging gossip, opinion, and anxiety. To get to the Leszno Gate and present her papers, she had to cross a new cordon of auxiliary troops – Ukrainian, Latvian, and Lithuanian – deployed by the Germans in a ring around the ghetto. A lorry packed with SS soldiers drove through the gate. As soon as she entered the ghetto, Irena felt the magnitude of disruption. Leszno Street, usually one of the busiest, was deserted except for those beggars too weak to move. A few Jews in a great hurry scuttled across the street. Overhead, people leaned out of windows, craning for the Germans or the Polish Blues. Irena walked faster. In the distance a police whistle shrilled over and over. Automatic rifles fired.

And there were the feathers. White flakes floating through the air like snow flurries. Feathers everywhere, stirred up by summer winds into little squalls. Irena looked up in time to see a man hanging out a third-story window, shaking a down-filled comforter, loosing a tiny blizzard of white goose or eider down. Without knowing which streets were targeted for this first day of the deportations, Irena had decided long ago that she would just begin in whichever building she found herself, seeking parents willing to give up their children. Deportees were permitted only one bundle weighing no more than 33 pounds. Bulky comforters were emptied, then the cotton or silk covers folded flat into the bundle. Those who would not give Irena their children explained that upon "resettlement at a labor camp in the East," conditions could only be better and they anticipated re-stuffing their comforters before winter set in.

168

Mid-morning Irena happened to turn onto Zelazna Street where she saw a column of apprehended Jews in a forced march. They were four abreast including children and beggars, marching toward the north end of the ghetto to the train-loading platform, *Umschlagplatz*. Irena was horrified to see that the Jews were kept in line by a unit of SP who urged them on, occasionally employing whips and truncheons to spur on stragglers.

Unlike the deserted ghetto streets, CENTOS was chaotic. An unruly and desperate crowd filled every empty space, and more lined up outside. Hands clawed at Irena; people begged for food, for money, for an *Ausweis*, for sanctuary. Irena looked in vain for Ewa and was about to leave when she saw her trying to maneuver her way up the stairs carrying two heavy packages.

Irena called to her over the chaos and, miraculously, got her attention. They moved toward each other with difficulty. "Ewa, thank God I've found you." Irena was sweating and breathing hard. "You must contact all your couriers. The telephones still work, but it may not be long before they're disconnected. Irena Schultz is on the telephone at my office if you need her. The couriers must be prepared to lead children to escape points. I'm trying to find out which blocks will be targeted so we can get the children out in advance, but it will be difficult."

Only after Irena had finished her excited instructions did she notice that Ewa's face had lost its color. "Are you feeling ill?" Irena said.

"I've just come back from *Umschlagplatz*." She seemed to be staring into a vision over Irena's shoulder. "They were forced into cattle cars – more than 100 in a car. The children were crying. I saw someone try to object and he was shot by a Ukrainian." Ewa closed her eyes and massaged her temples. "I watched from Stawki Street as the last cattle car was filled. There must have still been 1,000 people crammed into the field beside the tracks. That train left *Umschlagplatz* with nine cattle cars. I didn't dare stay longer. People on the street were being picked up and brought to *Umschlagplatz* by our own SP."

"Ewa. Time is critical. Alert your couriers. I'll call you at CENTOS or I'll come to you. Do not leave CENTOS today!" Irena saw her tears starting to gather, and Ewa had to lean against the wall to stay on her feet. Irena took her arms. "My dear, dear friend. Now is not the time to mourn, or to be afraid. Please, Ewa. Do as I say. Time is of the essence."

Irena gave her another envelope of several thousand zloty. "I'll call you later – either at CENTOS or at your house. Be mindful of the telephone – it may be tapped, especially here at CENTOS. We'll speak later."

Irena walked as fast as she could across the ghetto – her mind racing, afraid, and overwhelmed. She felt no fatigue, though she had been on her feet for more than seven hours already and it was only the middle of the afternoon. Rumors spread quickly that the last train of the day had left – it was safe to be on the street again – a reprieve for one more day's struggle for food, a factory job, an *Ausweis*. Leszno Street filled again, more frantic than ever.

Late that afternoon, at the hottest time of day, Irena found Schmuel at his Leszno Gate post, standing apart from the recently arrived Ukrainian and Lithuanian troops. No one lined up to get into the ghetto. Schmuel looked worried, unsure, or maybe just overheated. He recognized Irena and went to meet her. There was less strut in his stride.

"How many?" Irena asked.

"Today? I heard six thousand." He looked down, guilty or ashamed, or both. "The worst of it was that I had to march them to *Umschlagplatz*."

"Six thousand!" Irena coughed to conceal her shock at his words. She tried to recover her poise. A tempest of thoughts and feelings stormed in her head. "Schmuel! I need to know which blocks are slated for the next *Aktion*."

"Do I look like a German?" he sneered.

"Then don't act like one."

His lip curled. "Pani Sendler – don't tempt me. All it takes is one word from me and you'll be in Pawiak, or worse."

Irena took a deep breath and softened her voice. "Please, I only want to help the children. I was just surprised by the number – 6,000 – in one day? How could that be?" Irena gave him a roll of 100 zloty notes, which he quickly jammed into his pockets. "I'm sure Ewa will be glad to hear of your cooperation. Which blocks? What time?"

Schmuel looked at Irena for what seemed like a long silence, then glanced up and down the street, to be sure they were alone. "Every day the roundups will be in the early morning; the trains leave *Umschlagplatz* in the early to mid-afternoon. After that, no other arrests for deportation will be made until the next day. Those who cannot be put on a train will remain overnight at Umschlagplatz and be on the first morning train."

"Where are the trains going?" She dreaded the answer.

"I don't know."

Irena moved up very close to Schmuel. "Now is not the time to be coy."

"Treblinka," he said. He looked down at his dusty boots. "Don't think too badly of me, Irena. We SP are in an impossible situation – a horrible bind. Not only must we assist in the deportations, but we each have a personal quota – five Jews delivered each day to Umschlagplatz, or we and our families will be deported."

Was it not enough to murder Warsaw's Jews, Irena thought? Why did the Germans feel compelled to compound their barbarity by dictating this gratuitous humiliation of pitting Jew against Jew? But Irena would not go soft now, just because she understood Schmuel's "horrible bind"; everyone was in a "horrible bind" these days. "And tomorrow?" she pressed him.

"I must impose a condition," he said.

She closed her eyes and nodded, anticipating the banality of his personal needs.

"You must swear not to alert tenants to the next day's Aktion – it would cause riots and the Germans would know their security had been breached."

Irena nodded again. "You have my word."

"They're targeting the Small Ghetto first. Tomorrow – Gensia Street jail, the refugee center, the old age homes, and Ciepla Street."

Irena understood that the Germans must have chosen all the easy targets – children in prison, weak and confused refugees, the old and the infirm, and one block of tenements – probably to train the auxiliaries in techniques of rounding up large numbers of people. She immediately became aware of everything that she needed to do. Imperatives jostled each other for attention. Activate the network. Find Ewa. Find Sister Getter. Call Irena Schultz. If she acted quickly, she and some couriers could still take a few children from Ciepla Street, though it was already late in the day. She ran down Leszno Street, through a panicked crowd.

Out of breath, sweating in July's extreme heat, Irena reached CENTOS headquarters at the other end of Leszno.

There was a loud and crushing horde in the lobby that Irena had to squeeze through to find Ewa at her desk, hovered over by five agitated men in threadbare suits shouting at her about "*Ausweis... Kennkarte...* ration books... Treblinka."

Ewa looked up and met her eyes.

The man nearest Ewa turned on Irena. "Wait your turn!"

Irena motioned that she needed the telephone, and Ewa pushed it toward her. Irena's finger shook as she dialed Irena Schultz.

"It's *Jolanta*," Irena said into the telephone. "I wanted to remind you of the Naming Day party today on Ciepla Street. Invite as many of our friends as possible to come."

She ended the call and motioned for Ewa to meet her in the women's lavatory.

When they were alone, Ewa began, "Irena! Thanks be..."

Irena whispered urgently, "Tomorrow's roundup – Ciepla Street. Alert the couriers today." Irena left quickly.

Through the hot afternoon and into the early evening, Irena knocked on doors along with several young women couriers, begging parents to give them their children, explaining, cajoling, answering the same questions, looking into the same desperate eyes. If the parents agreed, the children had to be prepared to leave that very moment – no time for deliberation – there would be no return visits. Families that refused hung on to the belief that "relocation" was for the best – at least they would be out of the ghetto. In the face of refusal or ambivalence, Irena discouraged long conversations and instructed her couriers to move on; the luxury of time had expired.

Irena felt the burden of her deadly knowledge – the devil's bargain she had made with Schmuel – save a few children, but don't alarm their parents. Doing wrong to do right. She tried to banish such thoughts, but they pricked at her.

Word spread quickly down Ciepla Street that a woman and her helpers (some said she was crazy) were asking people for their children. A few children came out that day through every leak in the ghetto wall:

basement holes, garbage bags, the courthouse, loosened bricks behind the Church of the Annunciation, sedated in cardboard boxes tucked among bloody dressings in Danbrowski's Hygiene Wagon, and sedated in the morgue wagon among the dead. At dawn, Leon Szeszko's tram left Muranowska Terminal, with a sedated baby in a box pushed under a seat. At that very moment, the Ciepla Street roundup began.

That day the children were dispersed to eleven emergency care units, where they were to stay only a few days, until they received forged papers and a more permanent arrangement at a convent, orphanage, or foster home.

Very quickly Irena's lists grew to almost 250 children placed as far away as Turkowice, a convent beyond Lublin. Those she could not save weighed heavily on her heart, like souls on a scale. When she rescued orphans only, Irena thought her network saved as many as died; there was a semblance of offset, of symmetry. But with the start of the deportations the imbalance became suddenly staggering. More troubling still, Irena realized that if, by some miracle, they could get more children out, there was not enough money to support even those already in hiding. Without a doubt, she would fail the vast majority of these children.

CHAPTER 18

Deportation
Warsaw, July 22 – August 1942

July 23, 1942 – Guta Etinger → Zofia Wacek – Praga, Markowska #21

When the door opened to Irena at Apartment 32, Ciepla #12, eight-year-old Guta was waiting. She stood very still behind a small battered valise, her legs so thin that her socks would not stay up. Her dark hair, though obviously just washed and braided, was dirty still. Guta's mother tied a small red bow on one braid then straightened Guta's soiled dress.

Irena turned away – she could not watch these last few moments.

Mr. Etinger's voice hoarsened and cracked. "Take her, quickly. Don't make us think about it any longer."

Irena lingered for a moment and repeated the pretense that made this desperate act possible. "After the war you'll be reunited."

"I don't think so," he whispered. "But thank you for that, young lady."

Irena took the child's hand and walked her onto Ciepla Street, across the wooden footbridge over Chlodna, then up Zelazna Street, toward the courthouse. As they neared the ghetto center, the crowds became thicker, noisier, more impatient and gruff. Irena gave Guta morsels of bread as they walked. The girl gripped Irena's hand so tightly that it hurt.

Red posters announced executions from the day before, some of them *Judenrat* members – the longest list Irena had ever seen. In the turmoil and confusion, someone pushed hard between them and broke their hands apart. Guta screamed as she was carried downstream like driftwood in a flood. Irena plunged through the mêlée and just managed to catch her coat. They forced their way through the throngs into the darkened courthouse lobby, just as crowded as the street, but acoustically augmented by the dark space overhead.

Jozef was expecting them and the escape through the basement tunnels went smoothly. They emerged on Ogrodowa St., in the Aryan world of relative calm. When the #25 tram came to a stop, Irena easily picked tiny Guta up in her arms, half as heavy as an 8-year-old should be, and boarded. A gallant young Pole seated across from the tram operator surrendered his seat for Irena and the child. Guta sat on her lap, her face buried in Irena's shoulder. In all the confusion Irena had said nothing to Guta, who spoke only Yiddish. The rocking of the tram calmed Irena enough for her to feel Guta quivering on her lap and sobbing. Other tram riders began to stare.

Irena whispered in her ear in practiced Yiddish, "Be calm, little girl. Your name is Zofia. Don't forget – Zofia."

Guta lifted her head and looked at Irena, her eyes brimming with tears, her weeping no longer muffled by Irena's coat, drawing ever more attention

"Haks Rakhmunes!" Guta cried.

This plaintiff Yiddish plea had become so ordinary in the ghetto as to go unnoticed. But on this tram, it was a confession punishable by death. Passengers whispered. Guta's sobbing grew louder; she stiffened, as if in a seizure.

Without warning, the tram operator applied the brake in the middle of the street, throwing passengers off balance. He looked at Guta, then began to shout. "Everybody out! Everybody out! There's something terribly wrong with the tram. It's not safe. Please leave now. Leave as quickly as you can!" He walked up and down the car, shooing people out the front and back doors. Irena was about to take Guta off the tram when he came near and whispered, "Not you. Please stay."

After the last of the passengers had fled, he closed the doors. "Kneel down on the floor," he said. Guta continued to cry loudly in Yiddish.

The tram started up again, screeched around corners, rocking Irena and Guta on the floor. After a long and jostled ride, it stopped on a quiet street.

The driver turned to Irena. "This is a quiet neighborhood. You're safe now. God be with you."

Irena looked into his eyes, those of an ordinary Pole. "Why?" she asked. "Why did you do it?"

"I don't know. I just did it without thinking. You'd better go."

Guta held Irena's hand, and they walked through Aryan Warsaw, across the bridge over the Vistula, to the Praga district, where she would be hidden. Guta's eyes widened with wonder, as if she had never seen clean streets, automobiles, and finely dressed women. In this part of Warsaw there was some food in the shops, and Irena bought Guta a pastry with sugar frosting, which finally quenched her tears.

★ ★ ★ ★ ★ ★ ★ ★ ★ ★

Irena met with Schmuel every day, exchanging civility and sweetness for his report of which blocks were targeted for roundup and deportation. He was usually able to give her two, sometimes three days' notice.

"I worry about Ewa," Schmuel said after the first few days of *Aktions*. "They're targeting the Small Ghetto first. It's just a matter of time before..." His voice hoarsened and he turned his eyes upward to drain any tear that dared to form. "Two days from now – Ceglana Street. Irena, you must make Ewa understand that if she marries me she'll be safe. I have an extra half pound of butter – for her – for her parents. I'll bring it to her. Please, Irena. Tell her."

Irena did tell her; she too wanted Ewa to survive.

The next morning, just after curfew ended, the two Irenas, in their customary nurse's uniforms, showed their infection control passes and went straight to Ceglana Street where they met five couriers. The stagnant air reeked of sewage and garbage. After almost a week of daily roundups and thousands of deportations, Irena's network took any child, any way they could. Time had run out on niceties or planning. Social Welfare lists were hopelessly out of date and inaccurate, tens of thousands of recent refugees unregistered, others moving from flat to flat.

The couriers spread out, going door-to-door. The two Irenas stood together for a moment in the central courtyard of Ceglana #8, looking up at a bright square of sky inscribed by the four tenements around them.

Wash hung from dirty windows.

"How many yesterday?" Irena Schultz asked.

"We took out 15. The Germans took 6,000. Sad to think that for us that was a good day. If there were more of us, more time, more money... It's the money – we need the money. If we'd had more time, we could have recruited more..."

Irena Schultz touched Irena's shoulder. "Irena, stop. We can't go through our lives suffering over those we couldn't save."

Irena stood in the middle of the courtyard and looked from wall to wall, the tenement teeming with life about to be extinguished, and she but a tiny lifeboat. She knew that if she survived the war, she *would* suffer for those she could not save, and this regret would shroud the rest of her life. Already her nightmares incorporated the tortured farewells of the mothers and fathers, the grandparents, but most painfully, the mothers.

★ ★ ★ ★ ★ ★ ★ ★ ★ ★

By the end of the first week, after more than 50,000 had already been deported from *Umschlagplatz*, Irena visited Ewa's ghetto apartment, Sienna #40, early in the morning. She carried treasures: four tins of sardines and a half pound of butter.

Ewa could not have weighed more than 100 pounds, her eyes sunken, the whites a muddy yellow, her once thin ankles swollen with fluid. Ewa's mother and father, both skin and bone, embraced Irena. "Adam is rarely home," Ewa said, "but when I told him you might come today he wanted to speak with you – so maybe we'll see him." The Rechtman flat had been stripped of most furniture – some of it burned for heat during the winter. Eighteen people lived there now, instead of four.

"This is for you, Ewa," Irena whispered, "and your family. Please don't give it away to your Youth Circle. I depend on your strength."

Ewa slipped the four tins into the pocket of her housedress, looking to see that none of the new residents watched. Just a few moments later, Adam, his curly hair and beard grown out since she'd last seen him, thundered in, breathing hard from running up three flights.

"Idiots and cowards!" He slammed the door behind him and dropped his knapsack. Then he noticed Irena and said, "Ah. The lovely Pani Sendler. Ewa said you might visit." He gave her a folded note. "For Stefan. Very important. See that he gets it – preferably today."

"What makes you think I know how to get something to Stefan?"

"Word has it that you can do anything you put your mind to. We need every possible PPS and Home Army contact. I know you see him in Praga."

Ewa interrupted. "Adam, you seem more angry than usual, if that's possible."

"The day after the *Aktion* began there was a meeting – the Public Council or Worker's Committee, something like that. Every activist in the ghetto, Zionists left to right, Communists, Bund, the Orthodox – the whole bloody mess of them. Our Bund leaders demanded active resistance, weapons, sabotage. We were scorned – *He-Halutz* and *Ha-Shomer ha-Za'ir*, the only groups to call for active resistance."

Ewa shook her head as if she had already lost her brother. "Schmuel says…"

Adam slammed his fist on the wall. "I don't give a damn what Schmuel says. He's a collaborator. He can go piss on himself."

"Adam!" Everyone in the flat watched the confrontation.

"Your boyfriend –" he flung it in her face – "his extra rations, his privileges – his reward for herding us like sheep to the slaughter. Have you seen the parade of the condemned? You should watch. There's one every day. Your pathetic boyfriend was whipping women and children who couldn't keep up. It's disgusting! His cheeks are fat because ours are not. And your CENTOS does little better. Aren't you ashamed?"

Ewa stiffened. "No, I am not ashamed! I feed people. I work with my Youth Circle. We care for children, orphans. I do something." Her mouth twitched. "Besides ranting, what have you done?"

"I'm going to kill some fucking Germans," he spit at her. "Those of us who are not sheep are getting guns, building grenades and bombs."

"You can't do that, Adam. Every German you kill, they kill 100 of us."

Ewa's mother stepped between her children. "Ewa – Adam, please. Can't we be civil?"

Adam turned from his mother. "Civil? Here? Those days are long gone." He stuffed a pair of trousers and a shirt into his knapsack. "I won't be troubling you anymore. I'm living with my *Ha-Shomer ha-Za'ir* group. Anielewicz is our leader – a magnificent and courageous Jew. We should all strive to be like him." He slung his knapsack over his shoulder. "I'll be in touch. Good-bye, Mother." He kissed her cheek quickly. She tried to hold his face, but he jerked away. His father waited helplessly by the door. Irena saw tears in his eyes as they embraced briefly, tentatively. Adam looked back at his sister. "I forgive you, Ewa. I hope you can do the same for me someday."

She turned her back on him.

Adam pulled a floppy beret almost to his eyes, and was gone.

★ ★ ★ ★ ★ ★ ★ ★ ★ ★

On the first Sunday in August, a hazy blue sky and hot sun, the kind of day Irena would have enjoyed four years earlier, Schmuel called her apartment at 6 AM from the SP station, obviously agitated. "Tuesday. It's Ewa's block. She won't listen to me. Talk sense into her. There's still time. Please." His voice cracked. "I love her."

Irena went straight to Sienna #40, where Ewa met her at the door to her flat, her finger to her lips. She stepped out into the privacy of the hallway and closed the door behind her. "Schmuel called me. Don't upset Mother and Father. I haven't seen Adam since our argument. He's hiding somewhere – in the Large Ghetto, I think." Ewa's eyes filled and she bit her lip. "I can't believe this is happening."

Irena pulled her into her arms, and all she could think was that this might be the last time she would ever hold her dear friend.

Ewa dried her eyes. "I'm so tired of being afraid. I'm tired of all the suffering. I try to remember when Warsaw was a city, when you and I went to concerts. It gets harder. I can't remember the smell of lilacs or even the Sabbath *Cholent*."

Irena held Ewa's shoulders and looked hard into her eyes. "Schmuel's desperate for you to escape – as am I. Marry him or come with me today. Please – I'm begging you."

Ewa looked away and shook her head. "Take a baby instead, or a child. For me there is only my family and my Youth Circle. They're my children;

they're my brothers, my sisters."

"But you could do so much." Irena couldn't stop her tears. "And you're my friend." How many times had Irena beseeched her? It seemed that pleading was all she did anymore: pleading with mothers for their babies, with grandfathers for their grandchildren, with Ewa to escape the ghetto. "There isn't much time, Ewa," Irena wept. "Maybe I can take some of your young people... maybe..."

"Irena," Ewa said, and now it was she who held Irena. "They won't leave. They'll care for the children, as they do every day. And besides, you or one of your helpers could be caught and that would be my greatest sadness." Ewa held Irena's face in her hands and looked into her eyes. "Listen to me. Knock on that door and the next one further down and the next one. Find a baby who will have no memory of this. And above all – bear witness."

Weak-kneed and trembling, Irena sank to the floor and cried, as much for herself as for Ewa. She wandered down the dark tenement hallway, asking herself what she would have done in Ewa's place. She honored Ewa's request and found two more children to take out, a baby of nine months and her older sister, a four-year-old named Alicja. They escaped through the courthouse.

★　★　★　★　★　★　★　★　★　★

By the second week of the Aktion, the SP no longer participated in the roundups. Schmuel confirmed that it was now exclusively SS officers directing German gendarmes, Ukrainian, Latvian, and Lithuanian soldiers in systematic, swift, and brutal sieges of blocks of buildings and streets. After everyone was out on the street, gangs of soldiers scoured the buildings, shooting those found hiding.

True to Schmuel's word, on Tuesday, August 4th, everyone in Ewa's building, her Youth Circle, her parents, and half of Sienna Street were rounded up and deported to Treblinka. Though she knew full well that no one was rescued from Umschlagplatz, that it was done, that Ewa would soon be dead, Irena went straight to Jan Dobraczynski's office. She begged him to intervene, to inquire of the Germans, to do something.

Jaga stood beside her, gently rubbing her shoulders, and when Irena had exhausted her tears, she brought her home and gave her a Luminal tablet so she would sleep.

The next day Irena arrived at the office an hour early, then made four trips to the ghetto, carrying more money than she had ever brought across and too much lard in each sack, as if daring the Germans to apprehend her.

★ ★ ★ ★ ★ ★ ★ ★ ★ ★

Schmuel had already informed Irena of the German decision to deport the pediatrician, Dr. Janusz Korczak, and the children in his orphanage. "There's nothing you can do for Korczak or his orphans," Schmuel warned. "It was a very high-level decision. Don't waste your time."

Two days after Ewa's deportation, Irena was one of the first to cross into the ghetto at the Twarda Street gate. She hurried up Sliska Street toward Korczak's orphanage to honor Ewa's request to 'bear witness.' In sight of the wall, across a rubble filled lot, Irena heard a faint cry – a strange mournful sound, like a mewling cat, muffled and hitching. A shadow moved along the wall – a woman wrapped in brown and gray rags like condensed smoke – holding a swaddled infant in the crook of her elbow. The woman stooped to pick up a small rock and heaved it over the wall, then retreated to crouch in the shadows. A moment later the same rock arched back over the wall from the Aryan side, and the woman stood up with intent, holding her bundle close to her chest and face. Even at this distance, Irena heard the woman suck two deep breaths, bend forward, swing her baby in both her arms, three times, and then with blazing purpose hurl it up in an arc that barely cleared the jagged glass atop the wall. No sound came back from the other side. The woman collapsed against the wall, her hands stroking the bricks, the two inches that separated her from her baby. She slunk away in the shadow of the wall.

Irena had seen many desperate acts of love – they were the core of every rescue – but what she had just witnessed was the most searing of all. In her mind she could not help but see the swaddled bundle rise in the air over the glass shards. Who beside Irena would know this had happened?

Who would remember?

She ran the last few blocks to Korczak's orphanage on Sienna Street, where, to her amazement, the roundup was already complete – a predawn raid. Irena could only imagine the children's terror as they woke to the dreaded whistles and the three German words every Jew knew too well – "*Alle Juden raus!*" (All Jews Out!). They would have looked out their windows and seen gray-uniformed SS commanders ordering yellow-uniformed Ukrainians to roust every living person inside.

By the time Irena arrived, Korczak's children were lined up in rows of four, all dressed in their blue denim holiday uniforms. Irena moved right up to the SS cordon by showing her Epidemic Control Pass to a German gendarme, a Ukrainian soldier, and two Jewish policemen. She stood next to Schmuel, among the SP who formed a second perimeter behind the SS. An officer called the roll, almost 200 names. Each child clutched a little flask of water, something one might carry for a picnic, and some carried books. Korczak, looking pale and sickly, walked up and down the line, reassuring the children. Irena was close enough to hear him say they were going to a place that had pine and birch trees like the ones in their summer camp and there would be birds and squirrels and rabbits. One of the older boys carried the green flag of King Matt, the symbol of children's freedom from Dr. Korczak's most famous novel for children, *King Matt the First*, the story of a child hero who succeeds against great odds.

At Dr. Korczak's signal they began their two-mile march to *Umschlagplatz* accompanied by their teachers. Word spread quickly, and thousands of ghetto residents lined the route to witness Korczak's last parade. He carried five-year-old Romcia in one arm and led ten-year-old Szymonek by the hand. The three of them led a line of children singing a marching song:

"Though the storm howls around us, let us keep our heads high."

Schmuel stood completely still, his face waxen stiff, a single tear coursing down his cheek.

Irena watched with grim resignation, Ewa's charge still ringing in her ears: "Bear witness." She followed Korczak's little army past the Children's Hospital, where Korczak had worked as a pediatrician, down

Sliska Street, over the wooden footbridge connecting the Small Ghetto with the Large Ghetto. Below the bridge, on Chlodna Street, an Aryan thoroughfare, Irena heard a Pole jeering, "Good riddance, Jews!"

Every other forced march of deportees to *Umschlagplatz* had been prodded along by the Jewish police shoving and beating their own people under the watchful eye of the SS. Not so the Korczak parade. No German, no Pole, no Jewish policeman injured a single child, as if the orphans were surrounded by an invisible force. No onlooker was detained. The orphans crossed Leszno Street, the crowd silent, reverential.

As the sun rose and the day turned from warm to hot, the younger children began to falter. Irena heard them ask to rest, to relieve themselves; they were hot, they were thirsty, but though weakened, they continued to sing. The Jewish Police formed a protective cordon about them. Irena heard Korczak shout encouragement, still holding Romcia in his arms.

They arrived at *Umschlagplatz* three hours later, face to face with an SS unit and Ukrainian soldiers holding whips, guns, and leashes against which dogs strained and snarled. They were herded through the iron gate directly to the large dirt field by the railway siding. It was almost noon, and already several thousand Jews waited in the relentless sun, crammed together, some crying, some praying, most mute, their eyes glazed. Some, still hopeful of rescue, passed urgent pleas through the fence, tried to save themselves by producing a useless document, an identity card, an *Ausweis* that was now irrelevant, a fistful of zloty.

Most onlookers dispersed before they reached the dreaded *Umschlagplatz*, and Irena stood a prudent distance away. If the day's quota was not met, anyone nearby was liable to be seized and forced onto the train. There was no food or water, and not enough breeze to stir hair. The deportees' meager belongings were bundled up in sheets or sacks, or stuffed into battered valises, many tied with twine. They relieved themselves where they stood on the dusty field for fear of becoming separated from children, a husband, a wife. SS and Ukrainian soldiers strutted through the pathetic crowd, cursing and whipping; the sadists laughed.

Just after noon the loading of red-brown cattle cars began. The doors growled open on rusted runners, and Irena smelled chlorine disinfectant. Soldiers urged, beat, and whipped the crowd, drove them toward the line of rail wagons, more than 100 people forced through the maw of each car. Jewish Police commander Schmerling, the SP officer most favored by the Germans, ordered the orphanage loaded. Korczak signaled his children to rise. The older ones helped the younger.

At that moment a German SS officer called for everything to halt. He strode through the crowd like a ship cutting a wake and approached Korczak. The yard stilled. Even those about to enter a cattle car stopped and turned to watch. The SS man handed Korczak a document that the old pediatrician unfolded and read. He took off his spectacles and squinted up into the blazing sun. Korczak shook his head, then let the document fall to the ground. He waved the SS man off with a contemptuous flick of his hand. "I will stay with the children," he said in measured tones, first in Polish, then German.

In the strange silence that the SS officer had rendered, Korczak signaled his orphans, and they formed up again into rows of four. The Jewish policemen spontaneously formed an honor guard on either side of the children. They stood at attention and saluted as Korczak led his orphans into the waiting cattle car, every child straight and true.

*   *   *   *   *   *   *   *   *   *

As the daily deportations continued, the prospect of death was acknowledged by all but the most deluded. Now almost everyone Irena asked eagerly surrendered their children, overwhelming Irena's network. Then something totally unexpected occurred. On August 15th new ghetto boundaries were decreed, and the ghetto entrance to the courthouse, Irena's safest and most reliable escape route, was sealed.

She met with Adam on Mila Street #18, where his ZOB fighters lived in a basement compound. Adam said nothing of Ewa and his parents, already ten days gone, but behind his stoic façade she could see both his wound and his wrath. He showed her his FN pistol – had her hold it – and bragged about the elaborate smuggling network of contraband through the sewers.

"I will not be sent to Treblinka," he said.

Irena too had lost a loved one, and she could understand Adam's murderous rage, but she was far too busy for revolutionary speculation. They had smuggled fifteen children that day, about the average. Irena gently pushed the pistol back into Adam's hands and said, "We need to use the sewers. I need a map – I need couriers."

Adam looked at her sideways, a little distrustful. He whispered to another young man who returned a minute later with the folded map. "For Ewa," Adam said and opened a large map of Warsaw with the sewer system drawn over in ink. "Three main lines, secondary tributaries, and every manhole in the city. It's hand-drawn but accurate. Still, there are minor errors. I'll arrange for couriers. We can't be too careful – the sewer is our ZOB unit's lifeblood. Your rescues must not interfere or compromise our traffic in any way. Do you understand? Much of our traffic goes through during the day. You can have the night."

After Ewa's deportation, Schmuel looked ashamed whenever he saw Irena. His cheeks lost their fat, and his eyes, once shifty and swaggering, were listless and glazed. He neither bantered nor smiled, but every day he gave Irena the addresses targeted for roundup. Irena's tissue paper lists grew quickly, and instead of monthly burials, she and Jaga now dug up the jars every week.

There was a serious backlog of rescued children – not enough emergency care homes. On Lekarska Street, Jaga enlisted some of her neighbors to take children just for a few days. One of the busiest emergency care homes was the midwife Stanislawa Bussoldowa's apartment, where she regularly hid four or five children at a time. Even the Warsaw Zoo, partially destroyed in the bombing, "The House Under a Crazy Star," was a reliable, though bizarre and unique hiding place.

Stanislawa Bussoldowa arranged a baptism for Bieta so she could obtain official identity papers. Irena inquired of Schmuel about Bieta's parents, Henia and Israel Koppel, and he confirmed that they had survived the first deportation sweep. Bieta's grandfather, Aron Rohman, was a slave laborer with an *Ausweis* who left the ghetto each morning to work all day in Aryan Warsaw. With Irena's help, Stanislawa arranged for the grandfather to see Bieta. It took only one bribe each for the two Polish Blues guarding the laborers.

After two brief visits, Olga, the nanny caring for Bieta, told Irena about the strange reunions. "When Pan Rohman first met me and Bieta, I explained to him that his granddaughter would have to be baptized, for documents, for safety. I thought it would be painful for him, but he only asked what Bieta would need for baptism. I was confused. How could anything be expected of Bieta's family? I told him a white dress and a crucifix – she needs a white dress, but that he shouldn't worry, I would find one.

"When he came the second time he dropped a small package wrapped with newspaper and twine into Bieta's perambulator and stroked his granddaughter's face, then walked away. I opened the package and there was a white dress, white shoes and a gold cross on a chain." Olga sat down on the park bench and cried. "How much food had that cost them? Then, about two weeks later I received a telephone call from Bieta's mother, Henia Koppel. She said she wanted to hear her baby's voice. I held the telephone near Bieta's ear, and almost immediately she cooed and gurgled as if she recognized her mother's voice. She tried to suck on the receiver. She held her hands out in front of her mouth reaching for Henia's voice."

★　★　★　★　★　★　★　★　★　★

In early September, at their daily meeting, Schmuel told Irena that the Koppels had been deported. "The father is dead," he reported. "Shot at *Umschlagplatz* two days ago. He refused to get on the train. The mother was deported to Poniatowa, near Lublin – a work camp. I suppose she's lucky – but not for long."

CHAPTER 19

Resistance

Warsaw, August – December 1942

Jaga closed the door to Irena's office and pulled a chair up close to her desk. Her eyes were red and tear-stained.

"What happened?" Irena demanded.

Jaga lit a cigarette and stared at its glowing tip. "We need money. I had to pay 200 zloty at the Chlodna gate today. *Szmalcowniki* routinely get 500, and I heard of someone having to pay 1,000."

"That shouldn't make you cry."

Smoke curled up and disappeared. Jaga sighed. "Another courier was shot yesterday. Marta – and Stefja Pyjek was arrested and taken to Pawiak."

Irena sat up sharply. Marta's death was tragic, but Stefja, one of her couriers, would surely be interrogated and tortured. Her betrayal would threaten her entire network. "What happened?"

"She was arrested with a few thousand zloty and 25 blank *Kennkarte*."

"What does she know? Who does she know?"

"The money was from Irena Schultz. She knows some of the emergency care units; she knows my house. Hanna is staying with my cousin for now."

"How old is Stefja?"

"Sixteen – maybe seventeen."

"I can't bear to think what she's enduring."

In the air between them hung the unbearable question – would Stefja break under torture? Letters smuggled out of Pawiak by sympathetic Polish guards told horrifying tales of what happened to those incarcerated in this walled-in medieval torture castle, sequestered in the middle of the Large Ghetto, a prison within a prison.

Many in her network carried *Cjank*, cyanide capsules. Irena was one of the few who didn't, but at times like this she reconsidered and found herself hoping Stefja did.

"How much is Stefja's life worth?" she asked Jaga. "I know – it's an indecent question. How much do you think it would cost to bribe Stefja out?"

"I asked Jan the same question," Jaga said, "and he just laughed and said even God doesn't have that kind of money. And if we did, our new accountant, that rodent Herr Meissen, questions every discrepancy." Meissen had been appointed by Kommissar Auerswald to audit and oversee the Social Welfare office books. Someone had finally detected irregularities, and any pretense of accounting cover-up was abandoned.

She crushed out the cigarette and was about to leave when she changed her mind and closed the door again. "I have a bad feeling, Irena. I wonder if we've been betrayed. I envy you that you have no children. It's Hanna I worry about the most – I mean if something should happen to her I'd never forgive myself."

After an uncomfortable silence, Irena said, "Jaga, you must be honest with me. Can you still do this? We all know the risks."

She gave Irena a slighted look. "Don't be stupid. Of course I can. I just need to weep now and again. Who else could bury the jars with you?" She seemed to regain her confidence. "And besides, it's my apple tree."

Jaga left, and Irena sat at her desk looking through the open door at the secretaries and assistants working at their desks. Which one would betray her? She contemplated her vulnerability – one betrayal leading to another – her entire network falling like dominoes. How fragile everything was – and thousands of lives here in Warsaw hung in the balance. An experience just a few weeks earlier gave her a larger perspective, that perhaps millions of lives hung in the balance.

It was a humid August morning during the deportations, just after the curfew ended. Irena had answered a soft knocking at her door and recognized one of the two men, Leon Feiner, a socialist lawyer and leading party member of the Jewish Bund. He introduced himself by his code name *Mikolaj*. With him was a thin, unshaven man wearing an ill-fitting wool suit, whom he introduced as Jan Karski, a diplomat for the Polish government-in-exile and a liaison to the Home Army. Irena shook Karski's hand and noticed the deep scars on the underside of his wrists. He had tried to kill himself. Mikolaj explained that Karski had been smuggled into Poland by the government-in-exile to gather evidence of the mass murder of Jews – he thought the number could be in the millions – to be an eye witness, to bring his account to Roosevelt and Churchill. Allied bombing of the rail lines leading to the camps could save hundreds of thousands. Leon Feiner asked Irena to give Karski a tour of the ghetto, which she did immediately. She was impressed by his courage and uncanny, photographic memory. He was clearly shaken by what he witnessed

Another knocking on her office door brought Irena back to the moment. It was one of her secretaries, who gave her a typed form and a peculiar look. Irena closed the door and couldn't help but wonder: What was the reward for betraying Irena Sendler?

★ ★ ★ ★ ★ ★ ★ ★ ★ ★

The deportations ended on the Jewish holy day of Yom Kippur, Monday, September 21st, the decimated ghetto now a ghost town suspended between life and death. Of the maximum ghetto population – more than 450,000 – only 30,000 legally remained, in four islands of factories and workshops surrounded by designated tenements for the laborers, their spouses and children. According to Stefan and the Underground, an equal number remained in hiding – the "wild ones" – illegals who occupied a secret city of abandoned tenements, surrounded by barbed wire and cut off from electricity and gas.

Irena had seen Adam only once since Ewa's death; no one wanted to be found during those two months. But now, more than a month after the last train to Treblinka, through Underground contacts in the Többens clothing factory, she set up a meeting with him in the ghetto, on Mila Street.

Her most urgent need was for annotated maps of the "wild area," where the wild ones lived in subterranean bunkers. They were the most at risk; they were the most eager to give up their children. Travel in the wild area was extremely hazardous – anything that moved was shot – and couriers needed precise directions.

It was a cool fall day, the threat of winter in the air, when Irena arrived at "*Landau's Shop*," a cellar on Mila Street. She was met in the shadowy entryway by *Zosia*, who looked to be no more than fifteen, her beret tilted defiantly on her head, old baggy slacks cinched tight with rope, a moth-eaten blazer over a man's shirt three sizes too large. Her dark hair had been cut short by someone who must have had a pair of shears but no experience. She carried a small bell in case she needed to sound the warning of an *Aktion*.

Zosia led Irena up four flights of stairs to a dark attic apartment with easy access to the roof for escape. Lathing showed through the rotting plaster. Adam sat on an old office desk oiling and polishing his ancient but luminous Polish FN revolver. He did not look up when Irena came in.

"Adam," Irena said. "I need your help." She kept her coat buttoned in the unheated attic, each word floating in steam.

His beard masked his emaciation, but his wrists were only bones. After an awkward silence he said, "I couldn't even help my own sister." Then he looked up. "We put up handbills everywhere. We told everybody *Umschlagplatz* means death."

Three other young ZOB fighters, gaunt-eyed and unshaven, sat on the floor propped against the wall under blankets.

Just above a whisper, Irena said, "Ewa knew." She let the words hang in the frosted air. "At first I thought she was fooling herself – you know, rose-colored glasses. But in the end she knew; she wouldn't leave her Youth Circle."

"Do you know what bothers me the most, Irena?" He stopped shining the revolver and looked at her. "When I think of Ewa, it's never a sweet memory – I only see her angry with me – arguing about my guns and bombs." He resumed polishing his 15 round pistol as if he were a boy with his first hunting rifle. "There is no cleaner, better-oiled pistol in all of Poland," he said.

"How did you get it?" Irena asked.

"The Home Army. You know, Irena, we Jews, we're officially a fighting force now – the ZOB – *Zydowska Organizacja Bojowa*. October 20th. A date for school children to memorize. I'm the commander, so I get a pistol and ten bullets."

Adam tucked the gun into his pants. He unfolded a 1935 Warsaw city map and drew penciled circles to pinpoint hiding places of wild ones – parents eager to give up their children. "Don't even bother about the legitimate ghetto," he warned. "Mostly they think that their *Ausweis* will protect them and their children forever. And they have their own flats again – no more ten people to a room. They're deluded, but relieved. They trust the Germans." Adam produced another map. "You'll have to use the sewers." He held a carbide lamp over a hand-drawn schematic of the Warsaw sewer system. The luminous blue flame hissed. "I'll introduce you to Sewer Man. His usual charge is 50 zloty per person. Very reasonable, all things considered. And reliable. We've used him for months to move weapons, ammunition, food, fighters, and agents in and out of the ghetto."

Yes, Irena thought, 50 zloty was cheap, but she couldn't imagine where it would come from. There were too many circles on the map, and Adam admitted that many more were uncounted and unknown. She would be lucky to save one in twenty. Irena folded the map into the false bottom of her nurse's bag.

She left the ghetto realizing that the occupation was over and the war had begun.

★ ★ ★ ★ ★ ★ ★ ★ ★ ★

PROCLAMATION: OCTOBER 30, 1942

The Jewish Fighting Force, ZOB, hereby informs the population that the following have been convicted of crimes against the Jewish People:

The Judenrat in Warsaw and its presidium, on the grounds of having collaborated with the conqueror in signing the deportation order.

The managers of the "shops" and the Jewish Police, due to their cruel treatment of the workers and the "illegal" Jewish population.

Retaliatory measures will be adopted in all their severity.

The day before the ZOB's proclamation was posted and circulated in the ghetto, the Jewish Deputy Police Commander, Jakob Lejkin, was shot to death as he walked from the police station to his home on Gensia Street. Lejkin, one of the few Jewish Policemen spared deportation by the Germans, had been an enthusiastic commander during the liquidation. Irena wondered if the last thing Lejkin saw in this life had been the flash of Adam's pistol.

Irena obsessed about how they could continue smuggling children to the Aryan side without funds to support them. In early November, a coworker at the Welfare Office, Stefania Dybczynska, not one of Irena's network, left a note on her desk.

I know what you are doing. I can help.

Stefania was an old acquaintance from university days, a fellow student of Professor Radynska. They had shared some classes but were never close, and even now she kept to herself. Irena lingered near Stefania's desk as she prepared to leave for the day. They exchanged knowing glances and walked out together.

When they were alone on the street, Stefania said, "I know you're helping Jews. I hear that 'keeping cats' is very expensive and that you need a lot of money. Someone, I can't say who, instructed me to tell you of a new organization – ZEGOTA. ZEGOTA has money. In a few days a courier will contact you. The code word is *Trojan*."

Irena watched Stefania walk off alone and wondered at the secrets Warsovians kept.

Irena's network no longer knocked on tenement doors. The "wild children," some called them "wild cats," who had neither papers nor ration cards, subsisted solely on smuggled food. Most lived in a secret labyrinth, a warren of attics and cellars, tunnels and crude bunkers without heat. Hatchways opened into sewer lines for smuggling. Irena and her liaisons scrambled over rubble and debris, were led through black tunnels, many reeking of sewage, and climbed through ceiling panels into concealed attics behind armoires and false walls in deserted apartments. The wild ones remained underground for weeks at a time without daylight, without a toilet, sometimes in spaces so cramped they couldn't stand. They were filthy and lice-infested.

With Adam's help Irena made final arrangements for five children to escape together through the sewers to the care of Sister Wanda Garczynska, Mother Superior at the Order of the Immaculate Conception. In preparation, Irena had visited the convent and spoken with one of the Sisters, Maria Ena, about receiving the children. They would pop out from a nearby manhole at five the next morning. The courier would take them to the convent, knock with a prearranged signal, and Sister would be waiting to let them in.

"Just out of curiosity," Irena asked Sister Maria Ena, "who made the decision?"

She seemed surprised by the question. "We all did," she said. "Mother Superior read to us in the chapel from John 15:13

> 'Greater love hath no man than this, that he lay down his life for a friend… these things I command you, that you love one another.'

"She asked for our unanimous agreement. We bowed our heads and prayed – and it was agreed. How could it be otherwise?"

★ ★ ★ ★ ★ ★ ★ ★ ★ ★

Irena smelled Sewer Man before she saw the glow of his carbide lamp in the basement of Muranowska #41. He seemed more shadow than substance, and except for the fact that he was an Aryan, no one knew anything about him. Some said he lived in the sewers. He wasn't happy to be taking five children – they made too much noise, they were inconvenient, a bother – but Adam had convinced him. When it came time for payment, he asked for only 50 zloty for all five. "They're small." He smiled, his teeth glowing.

After a nervous night Irena received a call from Sister Maria Ena. "Thank you, dear. We received the clothing."

CHAPTER 20

Zegota

Warsaw, November 1942 – February 1943

Historic cold invaded Warsaw in November 1942. Smugglers and black market operators took advantage of a life or death free market, and prices for coal, food, and medicine skyrocketed. To stay warm, to extract the most advantage from every precious lump of coal, legal workers in the ghetto and their families cohabited again in overcrowded flats.

Late in November, an hour before curfew, Irena was startled by bold but awkward knocking. She took a deep breath to calm herself and opened the door on a waifish teenager with a smudged face and cheek bones chiseled by hunger.

"I'm *Wanda*, and I have something for you." Irena pulled her into her flat, hoping she hadn't roused the suspicion of neighbors. The girl dragged a foppish beret from her head, disturbing dark hair, stiff and greasy, cut short like a boy's. "I have money." She trembled from the cold, her rabbit eyes darting about the room.

Irena was on her guard; Gestapo informers came in many disguises. "I'm confused," she said.

"The *Delegatura* – the Free Poles in London. For those hiding Jewish children."

"Who told you I hide Jewish children?"

"*Trojan.*"

Irena let down her guard. "Hush!" she whispered. "My mother is sleeping in the next room. She's ill. How about a cup of tea? You look cold."

"Yes," she said quickly. "But I have to leave soon." The young courier unknotted the rope that held up her pants and reached into her undergarments. "Five thousand zloty." She spoke as if reciting by rote from a training manual. "I'm your new contact for money, medicine, documents, and 'other items' that need to be smuggled into the ghetto."

Irena counted the bills and put the envelope in the pocket of her housedress. "This is an unexpected surprise. It couldn't be more timely." She poured a cup of tea and put out a slice of bread and jam, which *Wanda* ate quickly. "How old are you?" Irena asked.

"Seventeen," she said, chewing.

"How did you become…" Irena wasn't sure how to frame her question.

"I know my way around Warsaw better than any girl, and most men. Before the war I was a Scout. I have medals for climbing, running, and orienteering. My mother says it's impossible to be lost when I am with her."

"That's not a reason for risking your life."

She looked up from the plate. "I hate the Germans. They killed my family. Do you have any more bread?"

Far from doubting her credentials, Irena could only marvel at the way anger and grief could fuel such courage. Since the liquidation, the danger to couriers, mostly young Jewish women operating on both sides of the wall, had increased; many were captured, tortured, and executed.

Irena opened her pantry and brought out a half loaf of peasant bread. She pushed the bread and preserves across the table and nodded for her to eat. "Do you know what happened to Marta?"

She stuffed her mouth, her words muffled. "Shot – a few nights ago – outside the city. Too bad. I liked Marta. I heard she had 20,000 zloty – from an air drop." She pulled a magazine from her rucksack and slit the tape holding two pages together. "I almost forgot – these are for you." She gave Irena two forged *Kennkarte*.

Irena recalculated the cost of rescue. Before the liquidation, 500 zloty could sustain five Jews hiding outside the ghetto for three weeks, if they rationed food and didn't expend too much energy. Now that same 500 zloty would barely keep five Jews alive for a week. An encounter with a *szmalcownik* could cost 2,000 zloty.

Wanda slumped back in the chair and let her head drop on her chest. Irena worried she would fall asleep. "You said you had a message."

She jerked awake. "Yes. From ZEGOTA. There will be an important meeting with the writer Zofia Kossak. I'm to take you there." Her eyes softened and she smiled. "I've read all her novels."

"Zofia Kossak?"

Irena, too, had recently read Kossak's work – but it wasn't fiction. Two months earlier, in September, Stefan had given Irena a well-read and soiled copy of a manifesto, **PROTEST**, written by Kossak. She was a complex literary figure before the war – one of Poland's most popular and talented historical novelists, who was also infamous for her pre-war anti-Semitic essays and opinions. Now she pleaded with Poles to come to the aid of the Jews. The greatest enemies of true Poles and Catholics, she wrote, were hypocrisy and treason. In graphic prose, she described the liquidation of the ghetto, the trains, and Treblinka, and concluded her declaration:

> *All will perish. Poor and rich, old and young, women, men, young-sters, infants... Their only guilt is that they were born into the Jewish nation condemned to extermination by Hitler.*
>
> *England is silent, so is America, even the influential international Jewry, so sensitive in its reaction to any transgression against its people, is silent. Poland is silent. Dying Jews are surrounded by a host of Pilates washing their hands in innocence.*
>
> *Whoever remains silent in the face of murder becomes an accomplice of the murder. He who does not condemn, condones.*
>
> *We are required by God to protest. God who forbids us to kill. We are required by our Christian consciousness. Every human being has the right to be loved by his fellow men. The blood of the defenseless cries to heaven for revenge. Those who oppose our protest are not Catholics.*

The German administration reacted angrily to the appearance of **PROTEST** and again posted on every Warsaw street stern reminders of their year-old decree:

NOTICE
DEATH PENALTY!
FOR ASSISTING JEWS WHO LEAVE THE
JEWISH RESIDENCE DISTRICTS WITHOUT AUTHORIZATION

DEATH PENALTY!
FOR THOSE WHO PROVIDE REFUGE, FOOD OR AID TO SUCH JEWS

Two days later, though unnerved by the anticipation of sitting in the same room with such a celebrated writer and prominent intellectual as Zofia Kossak, Irena followed *Wanda* to 24 Zurawia Street, near Nowy Swiat, where she knocked in a coded rhythm and whispered a password. They were let in by a short, gray-haired woman with the kindest eyes Irena had ever seen. "My dear Pani Sendler, I am Halina," she said, her voice as sweet as her eyes. "Let me take your coat, dear. My husband, Julian, and I have heard so much about you. It is a great pleasure to meet you. Please, this way."

She followed Halina up to a third-floor apartment where she knocked with another particular rhythm. The door opened a crack, then a chain unfastened. Inside, Irena immediately recognized Zofia Kossak seated at a card table under a bare bulb. There were no pictures on the walls, one broken-down sofa, bare wooden floors. She had once attended a university reading by Kossak, and remembered her prominent, rounded cheekbones, gray-streaked hair in a serious bun, strong forehead and shoulders.

Standing behind Zofia Kossak, a man shrunken by malnutrition and disease, cleaned his glasses with a blood-stained handkerchief. His double breasted jacket was several sizes too large. Irena thought he looked tubercular.

He smiled, and his handshake felt small and bony. "I'm Halina's husband – Julian Grobelny – *Trojan*." His bloodshot eyes, like his wife's, radiated kindness and humor. He indicated Zofia Kossak. "This is *Weronika*. Everybody knows her; nobody knows me. In this business, that's a good thing." His voice was delicate. "We all have code names – for the outside. But here we can be ourselves." He introduced Irena to the other woman in the room. "Janina Raabe, or *Ewa*, a journalist." He motioned for Irena to sit in the one empty chair. "Just today I learned that your father was Dr. Stanislaw Krzyzanowski. A great man. I knew him from the PPS. I'm not surprised to see his daughter here. How many have you taken out?"

Irena felt a natural state of suspicion. "More than 650."

"How do you know?"

"I keep lists."

"Why?"

"So they will know their real names." Irena didn't like to be the center of attention or scrutiny. "And so we know where to send money to support the children."

"Please," Grobelny said, "be at ease. You know Zofia Kossak?"

"Of course." Irena bowed slightly. "Everybody knows Zofia Kossak. Your courage is well known."

Zofia's smile accentuated the rounded thrust of her cheekbones. "My dear Pani Sendler, I was born without fear, and without fear one cannot truly be said to be courageous. My mother, God rest her soul, said I had a congenital absence of good sense."

Irena felt uncomfortable sitting so close to her. "You take great risks."

"As do you and your network. It is the great sorrow of our time that one cannot be humane without risking one's life."

Irena wondered how much they knew.

Julian turned away from the table and coughed spasmodically. When he recovered he wiped the bloody handkerchief across his lips and said, "Pani Sendler, I should advise you not to engage in argument with Zofia about courage, or anything else for that matter. You will surely lose."

Zofia laughed. "Julian is a hopeless romantic. I don't know why we selected him to be chairman."

"Because no one else wanted the job." He turned back to Irena. "We asked you here, Pani Sendler, because we need your help, and we think you need ours. You remember Jan Karski – you showed him the ghetto in August. Every indication is that his pleas fell on deaf ears. So our leaders in exile have set in motion our own effort – a collaboration of the underground and civilians, such as you. Last month we created the Council for Aid to Jews, a conspiracy we now call ZEGOTA. As far as I know there is nothing quite like ZEGOTA anywhere. We are a partnership, Aryan and Jewish, representing charitable organizations, political parties of the right, left, and center – though not the Communists – Zionists, youth groups, professional, political, and social organizations – groups incapable of working together before the war, now forged into common cause."

"What does ZEGOTA mean?" Irena asked.

Zofia smiled again, and her cheekbones softly shone under the bare bulb's harshness. "ZEGOTA? Nothing – and everything."

"A nonsense word," Julian said. "We are named for Konrad Zegota, a man who never existed."

Zofia leaned forward to look Julian in the eye. "Not exactly, Julian."

"Do you see what I mean, Pani Sendler? She lives to disagree."

"Hush, Julian. Just the other day a university colleague of mine from before the war, a connoisseur of words, told me that there is an archaic root, *zegot* meaning 'to burn.' I suppose we are the keepers of a flame of sorts."

"As always," Halina said, "Zofia will find the flower growing out of the cement."

"I'll take that as a compliment."

"Be that as it may," Julian continued, "ZEGOTA and your network, Pani Sendler, are in the same business of saving Jews in general, children in particular. I know you're overwhelmed, as are we. There are precious few we can save." A paroxysm of coughing seized him again, and Halina brought him a glass of water.

Zofia continued for Julian. "ZEGOTA is nationwide – Crakow, Lwow, Radom, Kielce, and Piotrków. We work with the Home Army, and we've been endorsed by the *Delegatura* in London; they are sending us money – a lot of money."

"Two of our great urgencies," Julian said, "are no different than yours – smuggling as many children as possible out of the ghetto and providing for those in hiding on the Aryan side. We've had limited success and some tragic failures. Everywhere I go people say, 'See the two Irenas. They'll get you whatever you need.' What we need, Pani Sendler, is you."

"And your network," Zofia added. "You seem to be almost miraculously successful." Zofia leaned closer to Irena and put her hand on her shoulder. "We would like you to coordinate the Children's Division of ZEGOTA."

Irena thought she must not have heard correctly. How could they trust her with such a heavy responsibility, someone they didn't know except from anecdotes and rumors? That part of her that feared betrayal and failure told her that ZEGOTA was trouble. More people, more opportunity for betrayal. And always her dilemma, was it fair to risk her mother's life as well?

"You have the network," Zofia said. "We have the money – more than 100,000 zloty a month from London for you to use. No questions asked. Time is short. I have ties with Catholic clergy and wealthy estate owners. We can help place children in convents and on estates. Your network, your medical workers, sewer men, plumbers, morticians – God knows who else – you seem to know every which way in and out of the ghetto."

Irena felt that these people were genuine. And she needed the money.

"Think it over," Julian said. "But don't take too long."

Irena squared her shoulders. "I don't need to think it over. But I must have total autonomy. It must be done my way. I know exactly how to do this." She looked from Julian to Zofia. Had she spoken intemperately? Would they think her haughty?

Julian smiled and dabbed his lips again. "Excellent." He reached out a skeletal hand to seal the appointment. There were smiles all around the table, and Irena appreciated how rare it was these days to feel success.

"You'll need a code name," Zofia said. "Choose a name, or we can choose one for you."

"I already have one," Irena said. "*Jolanta*."

$$\star \quad \star \quad \star \quad \star \quad \star \quad \star \quad \star \quad \star \quad \star \quad \star$$

For a few months, Adam's ZOB fighting organization committed spectacular assassinations of blackmailers, collaborators, and Jewish SP officers. On a crisp Monday morning, January 18th, the Germans responded with a surprise *Aktion* to round up the wild ones. SS troops poured into the ghetto, and by midday another somber parade of Jews, four abreast, was prodded with whips and truncheons up Zamenhofa Street towards *Umschlagplatz*. But this death march was different. ZOB fighters had infiltrated the orderly march of the condemned, and as they approached the intersection of Mila and Zamenhofa, each fighter chose his target. At a pre-arranged signal, the fighters leapt from the line firing pistols and throwing hand grenades. Several SS troops were wounded or killed immediately. Panic ensued – soldiers fired indiscriminately into the chaotic, fleeing mob. ZOB fighters captured German weapons and bullets and disappeared, as did the day's quota of Jews. Over the next four days, the intrepid ZOB fighters used guerilla tactics and their meager cache of weapons – pistols, petrol bombs, homemade grenades, clubs, steel pipes, knives, their bare hands – to kill as many Germans as they could. Many of the ZOB fighters were killed. But, for the first time since the occupation, the Germans were afraid to pursue Jews into their attics and basements, many of which were now fortified bunkers.

The ghetto was sealed for four days, and Irena was denied entry. She read in the *Biuletyn Informacyjny* of January 28th a detailed account of the fighting, a celebration of "heavy German casualties," and the comment:

> *The valor of those who have not lost their sense of honor during the saddest moments of Jewish history inspires admiration, and it is a glorious chapter in the history of Polish Jewry.*

The ZOB's armed resistance, quickly dubbed the "January Uprising," inspired a new level of respect and admiration among partisans for the ghetto Jews. Writing in Underground newspapers, Polish Home Army agents – who before the January Uprising were either unsympathetic to the plight of the Jews or simply apathetic – now hailed the ZOB as a staunch ally and admirable fighting force. The flow of weapons, mostly through the sewers, increased.

But the ZOB was also convinced, as were most of the remaining Jews in the ghetto, that their time was running out. After four days of fighting, the gates reopened to Irena with her infection control pass. It was bitter cold again, and the ghetto seemed inhabited only by the dead, the once-crowded streets deserted, her shoes echoing on the cobblestones. Irena's network was in great demand as thousands tried to get their children out. Every emergency care unit was overcrowded, and the two Irenas sought as many new ones as possible. Irena pleaded with convents and orphanages. Mother Superior Matylda Getter of the Franciscan Sisters of the Family of Mary, who administered more than 20 orphanages in the Warsaw province, was especially courageous and willing in this regard.

Children came to Irena's network through the ZOB, now generally accepted as the operational government of the ghetto. Only four gates remained to the ghetto, and they were heavily manned by Germans who could not be bribed. Their inspections were too rigorous to risk smuggling children, and Irena's liaisons had to rely on holes through the wall and the sewers. All over Warsaw, the symbol of the resistance, of the Home Army, began to appear hastily scribbled on walls – an icon that resembled an anchor – the letter "P" superimposed on a "W," standing for Polska Walczy – Poland is Fighting.

After the January Uprising, the word "relocation" again inflamed disagreement in the ghetto. German wall posters and Aryan owners of ghetto factories and shops, especially Többens and Schultz, urged workers to volunteer for relocation to the Poniatow and Trawniki labor camps near Lublin, but their claims were aggressively refuted by ZOB posters and word of mouth entreaties:

**VOLUNTARY RELOCATION MEANS NOTHING
MORE THAN THE COMPLETE ANNIHILATION
OF THE GHETTO.**

Few Jews working in the shops and factories volunteered and forcible relocations began on February 16th. The ZOB responded by setting fire to factories before they could be moved. Gunfire from the ghetto was now a routine sound, and German units only entered in formations and with great care. The most dangerous areas were the bunkers of the wild ones. ZOB fighters hid throughout the ghetto in fighting units collecting guns and ammunition through the sewers and constructing homemade Sten-guns, petrol bombs, grenades, and land mines in secret weapons factories.

★　★　★　★　★　★　★　★　★　★

Twice a week at 24 Zurawia Street, an officer of ZEGOTA conducted "office hours," a time when couriers came and went with documents, money, clothing, and orders from ZEGOTA's leadership. Irena was summoned and met with Zofia Kossak, who greeted her as an old friend, but then looked at Irena with motherly concern.

"You look exhausted," she said. "You should get more sleep."

Of course Zofia was correct, but even as a little girl, Irena hadn't seemed to need as much sleep as others. She always felt a little motor ticking inside that kept her awake and thinking, a little dynamo that kept her legs swinging, her fingers tapping, her tongue flicking over her lips. "There's so much to do, Zofia. So many..."

"Don't explain," Zofia said. "I'm being completely selfish. The more tired you are, the more likely you are to blunder, which would cost us dearly. Believe me, Irena. I understand. People like us hardly sleep. Do what you need to, Irena Sendler. I understand, and I'm sorry for both of us."

Irena felt as if Zofia had looked into her heart and seen it writhing against a world so out of balance, so cruel that it threatened to break her apart – and she would sooner die than allow that to happen. Irena's greatest fear was that if she stopped plucking children from the ghetto, the full weight of this tragedy would sweep over her like a tidal wave and she would never get up again, something she could admit to no one, certainly not to Zofia Kossak.

Zofia's hand rested gently on Irena's shoulder. "You and I, we'll always be rescuing someone from the ghetto – however it may manifest itself in twenty or forty years."

Irena took a deep breath and sighed. She could hear her father telling her that people are basically good. She had to believe that when the good people in the world learned what was happening here, they'd put an end to it. What she said to Zofia was, "All our emergency care units are full. I need a home for a baby and an eight-year-old right away. Do you know anyone?"

Zofia looked long and hard at Irena, seeming to weigh conflicting judgments, then she scribbled an address onto a scrap of paper. "Try Dr. Wos. He's sympathetic."

Irena fell asleep on the tram then jerked awake, angry that she had missed her stop. It was half an hour before the return tram came; she could have walked back to Dr. Wos's apartment in less time. There was no excuse for such a waste. She was breathing hard from walking so rapidly from the tram to the well-appointed Wos family address. They lived in a spacious second-floor apartment in a grand old building constructed just after the Great War, what people now began to call the First War. Nowy Swiat #13 had survived the September 1939 bombing unscathed. The building next door was reduced to a shell. Irena knocked, and a man queried her through the locked door.

"Dr. Wos? I have something very important to discuss with you."

"Who are you?"

"My name is *Jolanta*." She lowered her voice. "ZEGOTA."

The door opened, and he pulled her inside. "Keep your voice down, young lady!"

"You were recommended by Zofia Kossak and Julian Grobelny. I understand you're sympathetic with the plight of Jews."

He took her measure. "You're here about hiding someone, aren't you?"

"Two children – sisters – a baby and an eight-year-old. Only for a few days. I'm begging you, Dr. Wos. Zofia Kossak thought…"

"I don't give a damn what Zofia Kossak thinks," he whispered. "She doesn't know me – she doesn't understand. I can't. We can't. We have two children of our own. If the Gestapo… Go away! Don't ask me to do something like this."

"Dr. Wos, Zofia said you are courageous and honorable. I know that you and your wife have already hidden others. These children will die tomorrow if they are not hidden."

Mrs. Wos, who had been standing at the dining room door, said, "Henryk. We have an extra bedroom. Maybe these children are cousins visiting from the countryside."

Dr. Wos looked from his wife to Irena and back. He sighed. "Bring them." He wiped sweat from his forehead. "*Jolanta.* You are either very courageous or very foolish – most likely both. Be careful. They will get you. Some day, they will get you. I will pray for you."

★　★　★　★　★　★　★　★　★

The winter was hard on Janina's heart condition. One morning as

205

Irena dispensed her mother's heart medicine, she said, "I worry about you, Irena. You've been very irritable lately. And I hear rumors – from the neighbors. People are asking about you; there are Gestapo lists with your name."

"Don't lecture me, Mother. During the First War you taught at an underground school. Father was the only doctor to treat poor Jews. The acorn didn't land far from the tree."

"I can't help it. I'm your mother. You've done so much already. Can't someone else do it?"

Irena grudgingly acknowledged to herself that her mother was right. She *was* more short-tempered with people, less hardened to frustration, and, worst of all, she felt her confidence waning. Each time she crossed into the ghetto she feared it would be her last. At the end of each day she suffered headaches severe enough to require a headache powder, though she told no one. And she was tired to her core; she could not eat more than a few mouthfuls of anything. If she sat for too long she fell asleep, and her legs ached from walking all day. Some days she thought she could not endure another moment.

"I don't want to hear this from you, Mother." Irena pushed back from her mother's bed. "I bought more coal yesterday. Gupta's prices are up again. He's a goddam extortionist."

Tears welled up in her mother's eyes, and Irena had to look away. "What you are doing is God's work," Janina said, catching her breath after each phrase. "What your father did was God's work. I bless you both for being so decent, so courageous. But I lost my husband. You lost your father. I can't bear to lose you."

Janina wheezed and bubbled, slowly drowning from heart failure, and there was little anyone could do to save her. "You sound terrible today," Irena said as she prepared to leave for the day. "Here. Take another water pill." There weren't many left.

As she waited for the tram, Irena suffered to think that she had put the welfare of strangers' children ahead of her own mother. She explained it to her mother as "the right thing to do." But Irena knew that what kept her going in and out of the ghetto was something more powerful and primal, a force that she could neither explain nor deny – something beyond rationality.

January 1943 Isek Rosner → Aleksander Boroski – Chlodna #89

There were heartbreaking failures. Irena had convinced the Rosners to allow her to smuggle their baby Isek out of the ghetto in the morgue wagon. But they could not bear the loss of both of their children on the same day, so they kept Mirjam for one more day.

Mr. Stachowiak drove the morgue wagon through the ghetto every day to pick up those who had died overnight. It had snowed, and the wagon left distinct tracks in the empty street. He stopped in front of Wolynska #10, where he could wait for no more than ten minutes. Irena made last-minute arrangements with Isek's father. "Quickly," she said, "before he pulls away."

Mr. Rosner motioned for Mirjam to come to him and whispered into her ear. She looked much younger than eight. Irena could not distinguish his words, but watched Mirjam's face blanch and her eyes widen. She buried her face in her father's chest. Like every ghetto child, she had learned how to cry silently. Irena noticed the hairpin holding back her dark hair, the same curled wooden design that Irena had used as a girl.

Isek slept at the breast. Mrs. Rosner rocked, her eyes closed, singing a dreamy lullaby. Mr. Rosner touched her shoulder, lightly, as if he might ask her to dance. Her lips pursed, and she sighed a deep hitching breath. Careful not to wake Isek, she gave him to her husband. Irena reached into her coat pocket for the Luminal and let a few drops fall into Isek's mouth. His little nose and lips complained, but he swallowed. "It will help him sleep," Irena said. "It's very safe."

Mrs. Rosner sank back into her chair, her face in her hands. Mirjam stared into the empty cradle. Out the dirty window Irena saw that Mr. Stachowiak had already opened the back door of the wagon and was wrapping a frozen body in canvas, and loading it in the wagon like a broken tree limb. He looked up at the Rosners' window, then at his watch.

Irena said, "It's time, Pan Rosner. Another chance may not come. I'll return tomorrow for Mirjam."

Mrs. Rosner crossed the room, and, wailing from a deep and primitive root in her heart, she seized baby Isek from his father's arms. She held his limp body close, kissing his face and head. Gently, Mr. Rosner took hold of baby Isek and left with Irena down the stairs.

Irena stayed close – she had seen men stumble at this moment, debilitated by grief. At the tenement door Mr. Rosner looked one last time into his son's face. His trembling finger touched Isek's sunken cheek, circled his forehead, around sleeping eyes, onto his cheek again, over soft lips which made automatic smacking motions, back to his warm cheek. He held Isek out to Irena and turned away so she would not see his tears.

There was no time to lose; Irena could ill afford sentiment. Mr. Stachowiak saw her at the doorway with the baby and left the lorry's cab. He looked up and down the street and jerked his head. Irena nestled Isek under her coat and sprinted through the slush to the back of the wagon, where Mr. Stachowiak had already opened the last shroud. Irena placed sedated Isek between the dead man's legs. Though the body was frozen, the interior of the van was warm enough for the short trip out of the ghetto through Gensia Gate, to the Jewish Cemetery.

Irena gave Mr. Stachowiak 200 zloty should a bribe be necessary, but the fear of typhus was such a powerful disincentive to German curiosity that the guards rarely searched the morgue wagon. Irena Schultz waited in the Jewish Cemetery with Isek's papers. She would carry him though a secret path into the adjoining Christian cemetery and then onto a tram.

The morgue wagon drove off, and Irena returned to the vestibule, where Mr. Rosner watched, tears disappearing into his beard.

Irena touched his arm. "I'll come for Mirjam tomorrow." She left before he could change his mind.

★   ★   ★   ★   ★   ★   ★   ★   ★   ★

The next morning, Irena entered the ghetto at the Leszno Gate. The Ukrainian soldier who put on a show of rudeness for the benefit of the SS officer in charge scrutinized her papers. As soon as she turned onto Wolynska Street her heart sank. The pavement was littered with personal effects – a child's shoe, a handkerchief, a cane, a Hebrew bible, smashed furniture thrown from an upper floor – and she knew that there had been an *Aktion*.

As she climbed the three stories to apartment 3B, the tenement sounded hollow. Doors stood ajar; no one answered her call. On the Rosners' doorpost the wood had been gouged, the *mezuzah* gone. A window had been smashed; Isek's cradle hung motionless in the middle of the empty room. Broken glass crunched under her boots. Near the cradle she stooped to pick up a hairpin – the one Mirjam had worn just yesterday.

CHAPTER 21

A Warm Bath

Warsaw, January 1943 – October 1943

After the January Uprising, the last telephone lines to the ghetto were severed, leaving as means of communication only letters (unreliable), couriers (dangerous), and word of mouth (confused, transposed, and rationalized). A new industry sprang up in the ghetto – construction and fortification of underground bunkers. Even in the legitimate areas Irena talked with mothers carrying black-market bricks, lime, and sandbags for bunker construction, or baking noodles and toasting bread into rusk that would keep for months. There was industry, but not optimism.

Irena's network was inundated, and from day to day escape grew more hazardous. More and more Irena relied on teenaged ZOB fighters for information and escape routes. She was asked frequently about cyanide capsules.

★ ★ ★ ★ ★ ★ ★ ★ ★

January 1943

Estera Strossberg → Zofia Bodys– Family of Mary Convent, Pludy
Rachela Aptaker → Jadwiga Szyszko – Family of Mary Convent, Pludy
Piotr Zettinger → Henryk Zmuda – Family of Mary Convent, Pludy
Izak Koperman → Witold Goerner – Family of Mary Convent, Pludy

At 3 AM Irena woke to faint knocking at her flat. She opened the door right away to avoid waking her mother or the neighbors. As the door swung wide, sewer stench gusted into her apartment. A teenaged girl with a small face, short dark hair, tiny in a black storm coat, stood shivering, her lips purple, several fingertips protruding from torn gloves. Behind her, four children huddled, a shivering dark mass of rags, arms, and legs, each breath a tiny puff of steam.

"I'm... I'm *Teresa*." Her voice trembled. "You're *Jolanta*, aren't you? We were separated from the others. The sewer worker – the one who led us – he was drunk. Someone yelled about poison gas and we ran. I'm sorry to disturb... I didn't know anybody..." She couldn't stop shaking and started to cry.

"Stop it!" Irena hissed, and pulled her into the apartment. The whimpering children followed like soiled ducklings.

As she was about to close her door, Irena saw her neighbor, Mrs. Marzec, looking through a slit in her doorway. Their eyes met for a moment, and the neighbor quickly closed her door. She was a generally cordial middle-aged woman who lived alone, but she was a *Volksdeutsche*, a Pole of German origin, many of whom were eager collaborators with the Germans. She and Irena had only exchanged polite greetings and never spoke about politics. If she didn't suspect Irena before, surely now she would know that she was "hiding cats."

Every Pole knew what happened to families that were denounced by informers or *szmalcowniki*. According to eyewitnesses, the family would be lined up in the street, in full view of their neighbors. First the father was shot, then the mother was made to watch as her children were killed one at a time – first the Jewish children the family had been hiding, then her own. Finally, the mother herself was executed. Their bodies were left in the street as a warning to other Poles until the morgue wagon came for them the next day.

Irena whispered. "Quickly, all of you, into the bathroom. Take off all your clothing. Everything!"

Irena shoveled coal into the small stove and opened every window despite the night's chill. She and *Teresa* undressed the four children, who, without their sewage-soaked rags, were little more than pale skeletons, four to seven years old, so shrunken that they could stand in the bathtub at the same time with plenty of room to spare, their eyes white spots in fouled faces. *Teresa* gave her a list of the children's names and ages; one stood out, the youngest. Irena directed them to sit down and began to fill the tub with warm water. She began to wash the septic sludge from their faces. She asked the smallest boy, "Are you Piotr?"

He looked at her through eyes of famine. "Yes. Piotr Zettinger."

"I know your father." She poured warm water over his head. He closed his eyes and smiled, as if this were an absolute pleasure. To *Teresa* she said, "Piotr's father is a lawyer. He worked with me at the Social Welfare Department before the war."

The bathroom door suddenly opened, and a cold draft blew in. Irena's mother stood in the doorway, steadying herself on the door jam, her eyes squinting to accommodate the light, her face contorted from the smell. "Irena, what's this?"

Irena returned to washing a girl's back. "Jews from the sewer, Mother. But don't worry. They'll be out of here by the time Pani Worczyska comes." Mrs. Worczyska came to the house each morning to care for Janina while Irena was out. She was an older woman, the widow of an engineer who had been murdered by the SS. Though Irena could make no assumptions, she seemed trustworthy.

After three and a half years of occupation, this was the first time Irena had brought the risk of hiding Jews to her mother's doorstep. No doubt her mother knew she was involved in Underground activities, but she had never asked Irena for specifics. It was understood that one did not share details, especially with close family members, spouses, children, or parents, in case of Gestapo interrogation.

Her mother stared from the doorway. "Don't just stand there, Mother. Get more soap!" She turned to the courier. "*Teresa*. Where are the children to go?"

"Across the Vistula – to Sister Getter's – The Family of Mary Convent in Pludy."

Janina returned with a small soap cake – not nearly enough to wash the four children, *Teresa*, and their clothing. "Here, let me help." She knelt next to the tub, side by side with Irena, and washed Piotr's back.

"I'm sorry, Mother. I didn't mean for this to happen."

"We'll need more soap," Janina said.

How ironic for the shit of Warsaw to betray her. There was nothing else to do but knock on Mrs. Marzec's door. All these years and now something stupid – not enough soap. Her neighbor opened right away to Irena's gentle knocking, as if she had been waiting on the other side. She was in her nightgown, a frightened expression on her face.

"I need some soap, Pani Marzec. I couldn't sleep, so I'm doing my wash, but I ran out of soap." A lame explanation was better than none at all.

"Yes, of course." Mrs. Marzec looked askance. She gave Irena a block of soap, then quickly locked her door. Irena was left standing in the hallway wondering what she was thinking. Maybe she was on the telephone to the Gestapo right now and the SS would come pounding on her door any moment. Just to be safe, Irena laid out the current list and a few counterfeit *Kennkarte* near the stove for rapid disposal.

Irena counted it a miracle that by 7 AM *Teresa* and four clean children left her flat with 1200 zloty and reasonably forged *Kennkarte*, the sewer odor mostly dissipated. But all day, as she worked in the ghetto, Irena worried about coming home, imagining the black sedan parked in front of their building, the destructive search of their apartment, the rough handling, the trip to Szucha #25 for interrogation. She had to banish the thoughts or it would be impossible to get anything done.

When she returned later that afternoon her feet trembled as she climbed the stairs, though everything seemed normal. The door was intact. Her mother met her as she let herself in, the odd trace of a smile on her face. "I met Pani Marzec in the hallway today. She said it was so odd that you would be waking her up to borrow soap at 3 AM. She felt sorry for you, that you must be off your head. I said that with your husband in prison you think of him and cry all the time, especially at night. I said you do the wash in order to forget."

* * * * * * * * *

When Irena walked the streets of Warsaw she imagined the sewer tributaries below, a fetid river now a highway of life. She had memorized the maps Adam had given her. Drain A under Towarowa and Okapowa

Streets. Drain B below Marshalkowska Street and Drain C under Nowy Swiat. All three main arteries came together beneath the Gdansk Station. The manhole at Prosta and Wronia Streets, "K-74," was one of the busiest.

Children often escaped together in groups of five or ten with one or two couriers. Her couriers, mostly Jewish girls who led children through the sewers, described finding more "sausages" (corpses) floating in shin-deep sewage that flowed through the four and a half foot main drains. Worse still was to have to crawl through a two and a half foot cross drain. Extricating Jews often required parking a truck over the escape manhole at the precise time they emerged, a maneuver that demanded expert coordination. Irena learned how to tap on sewer pipes and listen for the return signal over the rushing water.

As determined by the moon, the first Passover Seder of 1943, April 18th, coincided with Palm Sunday. Irena went into the ghetto as usual to arrange a rescue from a wild house. As she exited through the Nalewki gate she noticed more than the usual number of German gendarmes, Polish Blues, Lithuanian, and Ukrainian troops.

The next day, Irena arrived at Krasinski Square, just outside the ghetto, intent on entering through Nalewki Gate. There had been gunfire and explosions overnight, cordite laced the air, and smoke hung like a shroud over the Large Ghetto. A unit of SS troops was forming up. The pop! pop! pop! of small arms fire and the rattle of heavy machine guns reverberated from over the wall. A Howitzer cannon had been wheeled onto the square and without warning began firing every minute into the ghetto, each thumping round shaking the sidewalk. A crowd of Poles had already gathered in the square, curious but unconcerned about the crackle of gunfire from within the ghetto. Some held handkerchiefs over their faces, crude gas masks against the acrid air. Irena heard snippets of conversation.

"The Jews won't last three days."

"There must be Poles and Communists inside helping the Jews."

"I give the Jews credit. Who would think they would fight with guns?"

"Today the Jews, tomorrow us."

Suddenly, Nalewki Gate swung open, and an undisciplined unit of SS storm troopers fled the ghetto, dragging wounded comrades, some clearly dead.

Irena found it indecent to stand among Poles commenting and speculating – eavesdropping on catastrophe with impunity, while a few feet away, on the other side of the wall Jews were being slaughtered.

As the Uprising escalated, tanks and armored cars rattled through the Nalewki Gate. Fighter planes dropped incendiary bombs. It was three days before Irena heard an eyewitness account, from a courier – she couldn't have been more than 15 years old – who had escaped through the sewers. She told Irena about pitched battles between ZOB fighters and SS storm troopers. Ghetto workers abandoned their workshops and factories and disappeared underground into the vast bunker system developed in anticipation of a final *Aktion*.

Despite being vastly outnumbered and outgunned, the Jews proved to be persistent and elusive fighters, hiding in the elaborate underground city they had constructed. After a week of what Poles now referred to as the Ghetto Uprising, couriers reported that the Germans had begun burning whole blocks. The sky glowed red under smoke that billowed over the wall. The cannon on Krasinski Square fired with sickening regularity. Irena's network continued to place those who escaped during the fighting, mostly through the sewers, and to provide for those in hiding.

On Easter Sunday, black smoke still hung over the ghetto as Irena approached Krasinski Square on her way to Praga with support payments. As she neared the wall she heard music, a startling curiosity, and then beheld the most remarkable sight of a world gone mad. Through the early spring foliage she saw a giant child's swing and a merry-go-round. Irena had to pinch herself to make sure she was awake. An Easter fair had been erected next to the wall, the merry-go-round's organ playing *The Merry Widow Waltz*, horses gamboling up and down carrying squealing children and young lovers. It was hard to discern from which side of the wall the screams came. Little car swings carried Polish children high up into the air where, at the top of their arc, for a moment they could see into the ghetto. Hastily erected carnival booths surrounded the merry-go-round – shooting galleries, food vendors with onions and sausage, circus music from the hurdy-gurdy accompanied by the *pop! pop! pop!* of air rifles. Barkers tried to create a festive atmosphere, but the rattle of heavy machine guns, tank artillery, small arms fire, and police whistles overwhelmed any pretense.

Children swung up, down, and around, while their parents stopped to exchange greetings, some still dressed in their Easter Sunday best.

★　★　★　★　★　★　★　★　★　★

DECREE: WARSAW – APRIL 26, 1943

By order of the Warsaw Chief of Police. Any Pole who knowingly assists, in any way, a Jew escaping from the Jewish District will be executed immediately and without trial. Any Pole with knowledge of Jews outside the Jewish District will be sent to concentration camp.

★　★　★　★　★　★　★　★　★　★

Despite the decree, and because the Uprising was a fight to the death, caution was cast aside. Children unexpectedly popped out of manholes, covered with sewage, accompanied by teenage couriers. The Germans pumped poison gas into the sewers, which were now choked with bloated bodies. Yet children continued to escape, and Poles continued to shelter Jews. Every emergency care unit on Lekarska Street was full.

Money for ZEGOTA literally fell from the sky – parachuted into Poland tied about the waists of couriers from the Polish Government-in-exile in London. American Jews contributed significantly through the Joint Distribution Committee. But even with these funds – millions of zloty – Irena could not keep up with the demand to place children. Were it not for the convents and orphanages there would have been no place for them all. Of 2,000 already in hiding, at least half required 500 zloty each month – half a million zloty – for support. When the *szmalcowniki* "burned" a hiding place, urgent placement had to be found that same day. Sometimes the only option was for the children to escape to the forest – the most dangerous place of all to hide – where they were the targets of German troops and anti-Semitic partisan fighters alike. Irena needed twice as many liaisons, twice as many emergency units and permanent homes.

★　★　★　★　★　★　★　★　★　★

February 27, 1943 – Natan Gross → Aleksander Rakocz – Palanta #5
February 27, 1943 – Dawid Gross → Jozef Rakocz – Palanta #5

The Tuesday after Easter Sunday was a warm spring day, clear but for the burning ghetto's smoke. Irena delivered an overdue payment to Palanta #5 for the support of Natan and Dawid Gross, now Aleksander and Jozef Rakocz, in a foster home in Warsaw's Mokotowa district. As Irena prepared to leave the Rakocz flat, the older of the two boys, Natan, ran into the kitchen holding up a basket of eggs.

"Jolanta!" he said. "Want to see my eggs? Yesterday, me and Dawid," he began, then bowed his head in shame. "I mean Jozef. We went to church to bless our eggs. We waited in a long line. I thought that everybody looked at us in a funny way, so I sent Jozef up ahead to learn what we should do. Jozef returned and said it was not a big thing. The priest just blessed our eggs. Mother – she wants us to call her Mother – said it was important for us to do this."

Irena admired his eggs and said, "You're a very brave boy."

"Did you see Momma and Poppa? Will we go back home soon?"

From their flat they could see the smoke and smell the burning ghetto.

"I don't know," Irena said. "It's like eggs waiting to hatch. You just have to trust that they will."

"But these eggs – they won't ever hatch – even if the mother hen came back and sat on them. They've been boiled."

★ ★ ★ ★ ★ ★ ★ ★ ★ ★

What was to have been a five-day *Aktion*, the final elimination of Warsaw's Jews, had become a three-week "battle of the bunkers." Before the Ghetto Uprising the wall had become a wall of numbing, a psychological barrier of denial for Poles that only leaked its terrible truth at the four remaining gates. Now, every Pole's conscience was jarred awake.

During the Uprising, so many new names were added to Irena's list that once again she and Jaga dug up and reburied the jars every week. Following one burial, after putting away the carbide lamp and shovel, Jaga unfolded a soiled stack of handwritten pages that she had hidden in a cabinet. "A courier gave me this. It's the diary of her friend, a ZOB fighter. She smuggled it out. I don't know his name, but listen to this:

> I can't think of anything but breathing air. The heat in the bunker is unbearable. The air is mildewed. There is no air. A candle goes out for lack of air. I sit here open-mouthed. Too many people. One can't talk. All the food is spoiled. We haven't eaten in over a day. Nothing but dry bread. Our water has all gone bad.

"I suppose he's dead," Jaga said, smoothing the pages.

"These words, this document," Irena said wistfully, "it reminds me of dead stars whose light we see long after they're gone."

★   ★   ★   ★   ★   ★   ★   ★   ★   ★

On the evening of the final day of the Ghetto Uprising, Irena and most other Warsovians heard a huge explosion at 8:15. The next day Irena walked by Tlomackie Square and saw the still smoldering ruins of the Great Synagogue of Warsaw, the huge neo-Renaissance symbol of Polish Jewry that had been excluded from the ghetto a year earlier. A twisted candelabra jutted out of the rubble. Broken sections of the great dome, like a shattered bowl, lay over the debris.

The ghetto was no more. Smoke still billowed up to smudge low-hanging clouds. No bombs, no gunfire, no ambulance sirens, no more sounds of life or death. No more children appeared for ZEGOTA to hide. It was as if the spigot to the sewers had been turned off, the holes in the wall suddenly plastered over. Irena found herself at a loss. What was there for her to do? The one mission that had given meaning to her life, that had given meaning to the suffering around her, was suddenly over. When the ghetto was finally destroyed, and the children stopped coming, Irena knew that for every Jewish child her network had rescued, 50 or 100 were deported and murdered, each a nameless rebuke. She felt like a runner collapsing before the end of the race.

Irena returned to the Social Welfare office and stared at papers and files. There was still much to do for those in hiding, and her mother required more care, but there was no one left to rescue, and she realized it was rescue that had given meaning to chaos and cruelty.

"Weren't you afraid?" others would ask.

Her simple answer was, "Yes, I was afraid, but my anger was stronger than my fear." Her more enigmatic answer, closer to the truth was, "It was a need of my heart."

Five months later, Irena Sendler would be arrested and sentenced to death.

CHAPTER 22

Pawiak Prison

Warsaw, October 1943 – January 1944

Smoke drifted across the ten-foot ghetto wall for days after the Uprising was finally put down – most buildings demolished by fire or explosives. For the next five months Irena's mission as head of ZEGOTA's Children's Division was to support the 2,500 escaped children, most of them hidden in foster homes, convents, and orphanages in and around Warsaw – some sent as far away as Turkowice. Irena made home visits, carrying illegal documents and thousands of zloty sewn into the lining of her coat. The average support payment of 500 zloty a month made hiding Jews a business for some; others did it for nothing.

The night of Irena's Naming Day, St. Irene's Day, October 20th, her friend Janina Grabowska visited in the evening and brought a small Naming Day present for Irena. Traditionally, children in Poland anticipate their Naming Day, the saint's day for whom they were named, more than Christmas, Easter, or their birthday. But after five years of occupation and deprivation, Irena didn't think about her Naming Day; it had become a painful reminder of everything she and her country had lost.

Janina, a slender single woman with dark hair that she kept in a fashionable bob, was once a fellow social worker, and now her apartment at Ludwiki #1 served as one of Irena's emergency care units. Presently she harbored a Jewish boy and two young men. Before the war she was one of the brave ones to complain about the Nazis and the Polish fascists. The day they met, Janina held a Hitlerian black comb under her nose and strutted and stammered in bad German to everyone's delight. Tonight she brought a glass jar of illegal home-brewed vodka to toast to a better year.

They were old friends, and they reminisced late into the night – well past curfew. Irena set up a cot for Janina. They talked about how times had changed, how their lives had unfolded in unimaginable ways. Janina said, "If I would have made this up in 1936 you would have said I was crazy and you would have been right." Before getting into bed, Irena laid out two tissue paper lists next to the window. "Just a precaution," she explained to Janina. "The garbage bin is just below my window."

Two hours later, Irena was jolted awake from a deep sleep by rough knocking at the door.

"*Macht auf!*"

Irena flew out of bed in an instant, stumbled across the room, bumped her shin against Janina's cot, and snatched the lists from the table. She crumpled the tissue papers to look like trash, jerked open the window, and was about to throw them out when she saw two SS soldiers looking up at her from below in the courtyard.

"Give it here," Janina hissed from behind her. She grabbed the crushed lists from Irena's hand and stuffed them into her brassiere. "They came to your house. They're looking for you, not me."

Irena's chest ached; she had been careless – under her bed was a large cache of zloty, which she was to deliver the next day to the convent in Pludy along with an illicit birth certificate, two *Kennkarte*, and a baptismal certificate. It was too late to hide them.

"Stay with Mother," she said to Janina. Irena finger-combed her hair. "Say everything is all right."

Irena took a deep breath and opened the door before it was smashed. Ten SS troopers poured into the apartment.

"Be gentle with Mother," Irena pleaded with the leader. "She has a bad heart."

Every drawer was pulled out, the mirror and pictures pulled down, carpet turned over. After the apartment was ransacked and secured, a Gestapo agent strode in – tall, stocky in a black leather coat, black gloves, and peaked military cap. Irena saw no pity in his steely eyes. He walked through their two-room flat and signaled Irena's mother off the bed. He motioned to one of the SS men, who used the bayonet on his rifle to disembowel the mattress and lacerate the pillows. Feathers hemorrhaged onto the floor. He gestured for Irena's mother to return to her bed, clicked his heels and finally spoke. "You will be good enough to sit very still. I am not here for you."

One soldier held his pistol on Irena and Janina in the next room. The others resumed their search of the flat. Feathers swirled, dispersed by the mayhem, floor boards pried loose, bureau drawers emptied, closets eviscerated, mattresses slashed open, bed frames disturbed, Irena's own bed partially collapsed. They still hadn't found the money or documents, but she knew they would. This would be her death. Surprisingly, she was more sad for her mother than afraid for herself. What could be worse than watching your only child treated so cruelly – executed for having been decent – kindness a capital crime?

"Get dressed," the Gestapo officer ordered.

Though Irena's bed had collapsed it had not been turned over, so miraculously, they never found the zloty and the *kennkarte*. She remembered the advice she had received a hundred times, even as a child from Grandfather Ksawery: don't show them that you're afraid. "Where are you taking me?" she demanded.

"Szucha #25."

Irena felt the ache in her chest become sharp as an ice pick. Szucha #25 – the dreaded address where the Gestapo interrogated, tortured, and executed. Few prisoners returned home.

Knowing that Janina had the lists on her person and that incriminating evidence was under her bed, Irena was eager to leave quickly. Still wearing her bedroom slippers, she threw on her jacket and let the SS officers escort her out. As she was led to the paddy wagon she heard Janina behind her. "Irena! Irena! Your shoes." The Gestapo agent allowed Irena to sit on the cobblestone street to take off her slippers. While she changed shoes, Irena watched her mother in her white nightgown leaning against the building's door-frame watching, and her fear and anger turned to heartbreak.

A soldier lifted Irena roughly to her feet and pushed her into the back of the police wagon. She stared out the back through a small window covered with wire mesh. There was her mother, supported by Janina. Maybe this was the last time she would ever see either; the only question was how much torture would she endure before death's relief?

Two soldiers sat in the back with Irena. As the Gestapo wagon drove through the empty streets, cold night air flooded inside. Irena put her hands in her coat pockets, where she made a horrifying discovery – one of the tissue paper lists of names had become separated from the others.

One of the soldiers, a boy of maybe 18, dozed; the other was distracted, looking through another small window. Irena turned her back and feigned sobbing, leaning her forehead against the metal frame around the window's mesh. The list was so fragile that it easily tore into scraps, and Irena let the wind rip them out of her fingertips. When the last bit blew out, she sat back exhausted with a fierce headache. There was nothing simulated now about her sobs.

★ ★ ★ ★ ★ ★ ★ ★ ★ ★

At Szucha #25 she was placed in the *Tramway* – a holding cell for prisoners awaiting interrogation with several other women and men. It smelled of vomit and urine. Speaking was forbidden. People had carved messages into the stone wall with their fingernails.

"I told nothing!"
"Mother, I love you. Zofia W."

Her name was called. As she left the cell she was grabbed by the arm and pushed into the interrogation office, an austere windowless room with a dark wooden desk and chair and a bench for the prisoner. A moment later a tall and fit middle-aged officer in a freshly pressed SS uniform walked into the room and sat at the desk. He picked up Irena's file and read it as she remained standing.

"Please, sit down," he said in accented but fluent Polish. His inflection suggested a degree of sympathy. "Neither of us wants to be here, Pani Sendler," he said, "but it is necessary." He looked back through her file. "We'll find out sooner or later," he said softly. "Just tell us what you know about ZEGOTA, about the terrorists, and you're free to go. Believe me, it's much better for you – and your ailing mother."

Irena told her prepared story. "I'm just a social worker, maybe guilty of being a bit too zealous for my clients, but certainly not subversive. I would never..."

"Pani Sendler, let's dispense with this charade, shall we? ZEGOTA. Names and addresses. That's all we want." He gave Irena her file, which contained several signed denunciations and confessions about rescued children; each account mentioned Irena Sendler, underlined in black. On the very first page she learned how she had been betrayed. One of Irena's meeting places, code named "boxes," was a laundry on Brackiej Street. The proprietress had been arrested for some other reason. According to the file she "broke under torture"; she had divulged Irena's name, among others, and confessed about "a secret organization," without mentioning ZEGOTA. The report was appended with the date of her execution.

"Who are they, Pani Sendler? Where does the money come from?"

Irena feigned reading each page to quell her panic, to give herself time to think.

She and Jaga were the only two people who knew where the lists were buried – a secret that, if revealed, would betray thousands of children and the brave Poles who hid them. What was her life worth, weighed against the thousands of others who risked theirs? Nowhere did she see herself referred to as the head of the children's division of ZEGOTA, leaving her to hope that this German didn't really know whom he was interrogating. She forced herself to ignore his polite and reassuring façade – to see that he was no different than a *szmalcownik* – blackmailing her by suggested threats and unknowable consequences, nothing specific, only the threat of threat.

"I'll tell you everything I know." Irena tried to sound airy, blithely stupid. "But I don't know much. I'm just a social worker with a very sick mother, who takes up all my life. Who has time for mischief?"

"We know you're only an intermediary; maybe you're being taken advantage of by criminal elements. It will go easier on you if you tell us right away. You'll go home to your mother. She needs you." He handed her a typewritten list. "Look at this list of people. Anyone you know?"

Irena was distressed to read how much inside knowledge the Gestapo possessed about ZEGOTA meetings and meeting places. Beside her name it said "Conspirator," without further details. Her beloved Stefan's name was on the list, as well as others from her network. ZEGOTA's leadership, Julian Grobelny and Zofia Kossak were at the top.

"After our conversation, you will be questioned more vigorously at Pawiak. Your next inquisitor may not be so kind as I."

"I can tell you only the truth," she said.

"Pani Sendler, I am the most reasonable man you will speak with. *Après moi, le déluge.*"

After their unproductive interview, SS guards pushed Irena into a Gestapo wagon with ten other prisoners for transport to Pawiak Prison. Conversation was forbidden. One man lay unconscious on the floor, blood oozing from his battered scalp, his eyes bruised and swollen shut. It was already dark when they were driven through what was once the Leszno Street gate. The Germans had destroyed virtually every building except Pawiak Prison, the formidable castle in the northern end. The wagon bumped over bricks and debris that littered this once main ghetto boulevard. Even in the dark she recognized the burned out shells of tenements she had visited, the Femina Theater, the hospital at the corner of Leszno and Zelazna. As they drove up to the gates of Pawiak, Irena thought, how ironic and thoroughly crushing, returning to the dead ghetto not as a rescuer but as a prisoner. Her efforts had been so inadequate, a disappointment that haunted her every day, and now she would pay the ultimate price. The truck stopped at the flood-lit barbed wire gate to Pawiak, a pool of light in the dark rubble. The men's prison, a long four-story brick behemoth, with a slate roof like dinosaur plates, abutted the laundry and warder barracks. A central courtyard, where many prisoners were executed, separated the men's prison from Serbia, the women's prison.

In exchange for the nightgown she still wore from her arrest, Irena was issued a striped grey and black prisoner's uniform. She would begin her work assignment the next day – the prison laundry. A matron led her down a dimly lit corridor into a cell block where the stench churned her stomach. She was assigned to #23, an 8 x 12 foot windowless cell with two bunks and seven other women. In the semi-darkness the other women were no more than shadows that grudgingly made room for her. They took turns lying on the bunks, two on each, head to foot, while the other four sat folded up on the floor. Irena had been awake for almost two days – on adrenaline – afraid and uncertain. She fell into fitful sleep, reawakened every hour by a church bell in the distance, waking to the nightmare that was too real.

She met her cellmates in the morning when the lights came on. The oldest of the seven, Basia, a sweet and soft-spoken grandmotherly woman, about the same age as Irena's mother, seemed to take a keen interest in her. They talked long into the next night about their lives before the war. "I have heard about you," Basia said. "You rescued Jewish children."

Irena's first reaction was fear. Basia or any one of her cellmates could be an informer. According to ZEGOTA every cell in Pawiak had one. On her second day at Pawiak, she was taken to the interrogation room where she met her tormentor, a stout German with round black-framed spectacles. Unlike the suave Gestapo officer at Szucha #25, who spoke Polish, this one relied on a translator. His SS tunic was only partially closed; he had two or three days' growth of beard and smelled of alcohol and tobacco. The matron pushed Irena onto a hard bench and left.

"I am Herr Bach, like the composer – a distant cousin I like to believe." He locked the door then lowered his face to just inches from hers. "Irena Sendler, I want names, addresses, code names, drop-off points. If you help me, I'll help you. If you don't..." He showed her a black whip. "I don't ordinarily beat women, but my life depends on your confession. If I fail to get information out of you, I will be sent to the Eastern Front. My life or yours."

Confession was unthinkable, and Irena held firmly to her story that she was a simple social worker with a sick mother – a nobody. He did not beat her that first day, but promised he would the next.

Anxiety and hunger kept Irena awake her second night in Pawiak. Basia sat up with her, and they shared memories of favorite foods. With a wry smile, Basia said, "It's amazing what you can accommodate. You get used to the hunger pains." She had been a Kindergarten teacher for 20 years, but most recently she directed the Jordanowskiego Garden, a popular botanical garden and playground in Warsaw. That was where she ran afoul of the law and she had already been incarcerated for a few weeks. Most everyone in Pawiak actually had committed a crime – a crime of survival, compassion, or decency.

Four of the women in Irena's cell had had their heads shaved, a humiliation reserved for prostitutes. There was excitement in the cell that evening – subdued, but animated nevertheless. One of the prostitutes, Helena, had obtained two cigarettes from a guard, along with a smuggled letter from her mother. She had stolen a few matches from the kitchen where she worked.

In the middle of Irena's second night in Pawiak, they shared Helena's two forbidden cigarettes. After the second cigarette was smoked down to nothing they were startled by the rattle of a key unlocking the door. A German prison matron barged in, demanding to know who was responsible for the tobacco. Silence. They were lined up outside the cell in the damp stone hallway. The matron went from one woman to the next, searching their eyes for guilt.

"I could have you all shot for this, and no one would care." She motioned for each of the head-shorn women to step forward, then slapped each prostitute across the face. "You're all animals. Get back inside!"

The matron's boot steps echoed down the long hallway, and one of the prostitutes said to Irena, "Frau Beelzebub. The Polish warders are not as bad. They'll slip *grypys* – smuggled notes – for us."

Basia asked Irena if she liked to sing. "I don't know," Irena said. "Except for school, I never did."

"Perhaps you'll join our little choir. Most nights we try to sing – even just a little bit." Basia had perfect pitch and a soft alto voice. They sang a Polish lullaby for her, one that Irena knew well, in three-part harmony. Irena felt the possibility of beauty and hope struggling to stay alive. When they were together in their cramped cell, they talked about their lives before the war, about food – always food – recipes, meals, celebrations. Two of the women had children whom they missed terribly and worried about. They talked about their husbands, and Irena mentioned Mietek in prison but said nothing about their estrangement or about Stefan. Her first priority was to get a message to Stefan.

Daily interrogations with Bach took her from the laundry room, where she stood at a sink for twelve hours scrubbing underwear with a wire brush. Twice a day Irena lined up with the others to be marched to the "toilet" – a cement room with four holes where each woman was allowed a short time over the hole to relieve herself. German matrons watched, and, for Irena, the humiliation exceeded the stench.

At the start of Irena's second week in Pawiak she awakened to commotion in the hallway and the commandant's boots slapping the floor outside the cell. "Don't be afraid," Basia whispered. "They're not coming for you."

The commandant called out twelve names; cell doors clanked open and shut. Irena heard a woman cry out, "No! No! Please, no!" Another whimpered as she was dragged past Irena's cell.

Basia's arm was around Irena. "The firing squad. They say it's quick. They always come first thing in the morning. After that you're safe. It's horrible to live like this, but this is the way it is."

Later that morning Irena was strapped, arms and legs, to Herr Bach's interrogation chair. Every day he asked the same questions. His beatings began lightly at first, striking her legs and feet with a truncheon; then he moved on to the whip, standing back, lashing at her feet and thighs, each strand cutting like a steel wire. After an hour he signaled for the straps to be undone, and the matron led her back to the laundry, where she had to stand for ten more hours on her swollen throbbing legs, blood clotting her prison pinafore to her skin.

Each day was unpredictable, depending on Bach's mood, a spectrum that ranged from subdued to enraged. He made a point of using the previous day's welts on her thighs and feet as targets. She tried to fortify herself by envisioning the faces of Stefan, her father, her mother, Ewa. Sometimes she conjured up Stefan as an avenging angel breaking into the room and shooting, stabbing, choking, or clubbing Herr Bach. (The whip came down across her thighs, and she heard herself screaming.) She answered his questions automatically while in her mind she was in Otwock, walking along the Vistula holding her father's hand on a Sunday morning. She played with her cat behind her father's sanatorium. (Again the whip across both thighs. Was it her wailing? The sound seemed farther away.) Her mother's maiden name was Grzybowski. Her father's father was Ksawery Krzyzanowski, and he lived in Tarczyna. Her great-grandfather, also named Ksawery, was a hero of the 1863 Uprising. He was tortured by the Russians. (Bach's foul breath up close.) "We know you're involved with ZEGOTA." She answered the same as always. (Whip lashes cut her feet.) Her father was the only doctor in Otwock who would treat the Jews. He said people are all the same, regardless of nationality or ethnicity. (He beat the sensitive tops of her feet with a baton.) There are only good people and bad people. Most people are good. Most people are good. Most people are good.

Every day before entering the interrogation room, Irena decided which childhood memories she would cling to and admonished herself to be strong; so much was at stake.

Every day she made another scratch in the wall, her personal calendar among those of so many other inmates; few calendars lasted longer than 30 days. On Irena's 35th day she endured a particularly vicious beating. Herr Bach was drunk and staggered about the small room, his speech thick and filthy, swinging his whip with abandon. Her mother had often told Irena how she had almost died when she was two years old, from Whooping Cough, and then again when she was eight from a brain abscess that complicated her recovery from the 1918 Spanish Flu. Why had she survived, only to die this way? Irena lost consciousness and regained awareness on the cement floor of the toilet room, lying in her own dried blood.

⋆ ⋆ ⋆ ⋆ ⋆ ⋆ ⋆ ⋆ ⋆ ⋆

By the middle of her second month in the laundry, the pain in her legs was unbearable. She was so weak that in order to stand unaided she had to lean against the sinks or ironing racks. Her nose bled every day; since childhood, Irena had been sensitive to strong detergents. She worked with a score of other women, washing the black and gray underwear of prisoners and the white of prison warders. More than a few German undershorts were smeared with feces, and the women joked that the Germans were so afraid that they soiled themselves.

Some incarcerated Jewish women were allowed to have their children with them if there was no one to care for them at home. Twice each day the children were allowed to run free in the courtyard, which amused the

SS guards. One day while using a stiff wire brush to scrape German shit from a pair of undershorts, Irena watched a Jewish boy, maybe three or four years old, through the laundry window playing with two sticks. An SS officer knelt and held out some candy for the child; he beckoned for him to take it. The boy took one sweet in each hand and smiled. The guard patted him on the head, and the toddler turned and walked away across the yard. The SS man removed his Luger from its holster, casually aimed at the boy's back, and shot him dead. Irena covered her mouth with a soapy hand.

Scrubbing the Gestapo underwear tore holes in some, especially the pieces that were the most stained. One day four Gestapo prison officials came into the laundry and ordered all 20 women to the courtyard reserved for executions, where they were lined up in a row. One of the officers held up a particularly ragged pair of shorts, like a flag that had been blasted with a shotgun.

Walking down the line holding the underwear aloft, his aide read off the names of ten women, not Irena, and ordered them to step one pace backward. Irena shook uncontrollably, her heart banging against her chest wall. The first pistol shot exploded behind her in the courtyard, and a woman fell dead. In rapid succession nine more. She heard each woman crumple and fall. Irena's tears blurred the spectacle of the bodies dragged to one corner of the courtyard like so many sacks of soiled clothes. When they returned to the laundry room, one of the survivors, Dr. Hanna Czuperska said, "Girls! Are you breaking down? This is a normal day at Pawiak. Nothing unusual."

* * * * * * * * * *

Dr. Czuperska was right. By Christmastime, after 70 days in Pawiak, Irena's daily terror had become almost ordinary – at least predictable. It was miraculous that she had survived for so long. She had also begun to accommodate the inescapable conclusion that she would die in Pawiak. Everything before Pawiak was eclipsed, numbed, even the acute grief she had felt after her arrest. She thought, this must be what it feels like to disappear.

On Christmas Eve, a sanitary team of prisoners entered her cell to disinfect it. Among them was someone she knew, Jadwiga Jedrzejowska, who instructed Irena to go to the dentist.

"But I don't have any problem with my teeth." Irena didn't understand.

"Go to the dentist."

While she drilled a perfectly healthy tooth, the dentist, Hania Sipowicz, was able to talk quietly with Irena. "I'm putting a *grypsy* in your cheek – it's from ZEGOTA."

In her cell that evening, just before the corridor lights went out, Irena read the note, careful not to be noticed.

"Don't worry. We are doing everything we can to save you. ZEGOTA."

It was like lighting a candle in cavernous darkness. For the first time in 70 days, Irena dared to feel hopeful. She tore out the word ZEGOTA and swallowed it, then sent her own return note by the same dental route, a note jammed inside her cheek:

"The lists are safe!"

Nobody escaped Pawiak, so Irena wondered what ZEGOTA could possibly do for her. The *grypsy* was but an ounce of hope to counter a hundred pounds of certainty that she would soon be executed.

Several evenings after Christmas, Basia seemed distressed and said she couldn't sing that night. "I'm worried about my children. I will be shot tomorrow."

"Don't be foolish," Irena said. "How could you know?"

"I just know it. I feel it."

The next morning the Gestapo agent stopped in front of their cell. "Basia Dietrich, sentenced to death. Step out!" Half an hour later Irena heard a volley of gunfire from the courtyard. Later that evening, when she returned from the laundry she noticed a small square of color amongst her gray bedding on the cell floor. Basia's last gift – a small religious portrait of Jesus, one that many Poles carried. On the back were three words, *Jezu ufam tobie* (In Jesus we trust). Irena hid it next to her heart.

The only cause to celebrate New Year's Day was having survived into 1944. More prisoners arrived; another twelve were executed. But it was

231

not an ordinary day. In the laundry one of the Polish guards passed Irena a *grypys* from Irena Schultz, code-named Janka:

> Dear Jolanta,
>
> I had the doctor come to see your mother. She is not doing well. Her digitalis is unavailable. He suggested increasing her water pills from four to five times a day. Your mother didn't want me to tell you about this — she worries so about you and doesn't want to sadden you. But I thought you should know.
>
> > Be strong, we love you,
> > Janka

Irena was grateful for the note, for the infinitesimal reminder that she was Irena Sendler, that her mother was Janina Krzyzanowski, who was dying of a failing heart. With her own imperfect heart, Irena prayed that her mother would die before she was executed.

Sustained, restful sleep was impossible. Irena's legs throbbed, and each time her cellmates moved and jostled, the pain woke her. Day by day she increasingly saw death as her only relief, but worried that her death would certainly hasten her mother's demise. When she looked at the picture of Jesus, she thought of Basia and the power of love, even in Pawiak, and it gave her a small measure of peace – and courage.

During interrogations and beatings she said to herself over and over, "There is nothing more they can do to me. I'm already dead."

On January 20th Irena lined up in the morning, as she had for 100 days. The SS-*Hauptsturmführer* strode down the corridor and stopped. In a booming voice he read out the names of the condemned.

"Irena Sendlerowa!"

Though every day she was prepared to hear her name, the actual moment felt like falling over a precipice. In the moment before the guard dragged her out of line, Irena pressed the picture of Jesus into the hand of the newest inmate in her cell, a young mother arrested for smuggling. The woman had been crying continuously for two days, desolate that she would never see her children again. As she was led away with the others selected to die that day, Irena told her, "For the sake of your children, be brave and strong."

There must have been 20 women with her. The German guards swore at them and pushed them toward the Pawiak truck, where a Polish guard with gentle hands helped them climb up. "Be careful," he whispered to Irena. "Don't hit your head. God bless you."

Irena felt reassured to know that her countrymen still cared about her.

When they arrived at Szucha #25, Irena was pushed from the lorry into the entryway. The pain in her legs was constant; she could barely walk. She prayed only for a quick and painless end. Other women were crying; some called out for their children, their husbands or parents. Some prayed. One by one, each woman was called and led through a door on the left.

"Irena Sendlerowa!"

PART THREE

Kansas and Warsaw, February 2000 – May 2008

CHAPTER 23

National History Day

Kansas, Feb – May 2000

At the end of February, Liz e-mailed the Jewish Foundation for the Righteous (JFR) asking about Irena's burial place. The next morning, she turned on the computer and was surprised to find a prompt response from David Weinstein:

> Dear Elizabeth,
>
> I was surprised to get your e-mail inquiring about Irena Sendler's final resting place. In our previous correspondence we neglected to tell you that Irena Sendler is still alive. She's 90 years old and lives in Warsaw. Here's her address: Irena Sendler, Plac na Rozdrozu 3, Apt. 22, 00-584, Warsaw, Poland. Since she is one of the Righteous Among the Nations, JFR has been sending her a monthly stipend for her support. I'm not sure she'll write back, but you might want to try.

She reread it several times, thought it was a joke or a prank, then decided it was real. Her eyes grew large; she was afraid to exhale, as if she might blow the message away. Very quietly, almost to herself, she said, "Mr. C."

The bell rang, and 1st period students spilled into the classroom as if a spigot had been turned on, dropping backpacks, laughing, gossiping, flirting.

Liz stared at the screen, hardly breathing, and said again, more forcefully, "Mr. C.!" She kept repeating herself; each time her voice pitched higher and louder, until she was shouting and the classroom was suddenly silent.

Mr. C. crouched down to read the screen. "Well, I'll be," he said. "Well, I'll be. This changes everything."

Liz bolted from the classroom in search of Megan and Sabrina, whom she found in neighboring classrooms. They burst back into Room 104, where Mr. C. interrupted his lesson only to point them to the video room in back. "Start writing the letter," he said.

> February, 2000
> Dear Irena,
>
> *We are three students from Kansas. Our names are: Sabrina, Megan, and Liz. We are 17, 15, and 15 years of age. Our group has written a short dramatic performance about your life and the Holocaust. Liz plays you in the drama. We are entering this drama in a local history competition.*
>
> *We saw your name in a magazine and have done a great deal of research over the past school year. We have received information from the Jewish Foundation for the Righteous and from Yad Vashem of Israel.*
>
> *Your story is one of great inspiration to our classmates. We so admire your courage. We tried in our performance to show the events of the Warsaw ghetto. You are one of the great women of the past century, as far as we're concerned.*
>
> *We have several questions. Do you speak English or German? Do you have family still alive? Do you keep in touch with any of the children you saved? If so, do you have the address or telephone number of any of the children, that we might contact them? Were there any books written about you? How are you doing?*
>
> *May we send you money for postage? Here are pictures of Megan (blue sweater, with glasses), Sabrina (white blouse, with glasses) and Liz (saxophone, sunglasses).*
>
> Thank you so much. You inspire us.
> > Sabrina Coons, Megan Stewart, and Liz Cambers
> > P. S. – Our teacher, who is working with us on this project,
> > is Mr. Norman Conard.

They enclosed $3 for postage so she could write back.

What the girls didn't know was the reason that Irena's son, Adam, had never responded to their letters. Adam suffered from the same premature heart disease that had afflicted his father, Stefan, and his grandmother, Janina. On September 23, 1999, at the age of 49, he suddenly died of a heart attack. That very same day, in Uniontown, Kansas, Liz had selected the article about Irena Sendler from the National History Day file, and *The Irena Sendler Project* began.

★　★　★　★　★　★　★　★　★　★

The girls checked e-mail and snail mail every day anticipating some response from Poland, but unspoken superstition kept them from saying anything about it. Weeks, then a month passed, and still nothing. They distracted themselves from their disappointment by focusing on the approaching Kansas History Day competition at the end of April, refining the play's script, rehearsing too much, adjusting their costumes, fussing with props.

Late in March, six weeks after their letter to Irena, at an after-school rehearsal, they studied a newly found photograph of Warsaw's Jews lining up to enter the ghetto in November 1940. Megan put down the magnifying glass and sighed. "You think she'll ever write back?"

"She just has to," Liz said. "I gotta know how she escaped from Pawiak Prison."

Sabrina's shoulders slumped. "She's really old. Like, ninety. Maybe she's just too tired or feeble."

Liz said, "Or maybe she doesn't want to be reminded of that horrible time."

Megan picked up the glass again and hovered over the photograph, studying each enlarged face, each person about to enter the ghetto. "I wonder if they knew they were going to die. Mom says Irena is probably thinking more about the next world than this one."

Sabrina was often the last one to speak. "She stared down the Nazis. Why should she care about us?"

★　★　★　★　★　★　★　★　★　★

It was one of those soaking April rains that releases a musty, though pleasant fragrance of decay and turns the prairie green overnight. Sabrina stopped at the front office to pick up Xerox copies for 4th period Social Studies and the mail. The secretary handed her a thick Air Mail envelope to bring back as well. She saw the return address – Warsaw, Poland – and let out a 'whoop!' She left the Xerox copies and the other mail on the counter and ran down the hall where Liz was just turning into Room 104.

She held up the envelope. "Liz! Poland! Irena Sendler!"

Liz grabbed the hefty envelope from Sabrina and turned it over – *Irena Sendlerowa*. "Oh, my God! It's her! I can't believe it! It's really her." Holding the envelope in both hands, staring at the return address, she made for the door. "We'll have to get Megan…" and they were gone.

They returned out of breath, Megan's cheeks flushed like a painted china doll.

Once again the girls gathered in the privacy of the sound-proofed video room. They cleared the table of videos and notebooks, papers, a single mitten, a bag of potato chips.

"Open it, Liz," Megan begged. "What are you waiting for?"

Liz used a scissor as carefully as a surgeon to cut open the thick envelope, her hands trembling. She unstuffed and flattened a handwritten letter and copies of official documents and photographs. Her brow furrowed, and then she began to laugh.

Megan grabbed the letter and said, "Oh, no!" After a moment she, too, was giggling and passed it on to Sabrina.

"Polish," Sabrina said. "I mean, I guess it's Polish. A lot of z's and no vowels."

Liz studied the photographs and passed them one by one to Megan. "This must be her, like, a long time ago – maybe during the war. She was beautiful. She's not much older than we are. Here she is dressed like a nurse. This is her too, but it must be years later, talking with children. And here she is as an old lady. Man, she looks really sad."

"What else is in there, Liz?" Megan asked.

"A certificate that's in … like, not English."

Liz motioned for Mr. C. to come into the video room and gave him the papers. "That's Hebrew and that's French," he said. "It's from *Yad Vashem*.

I think the French says something like, 'Remembering is the secret of redemption,' then it says 'Attestation for Irena Sendler. She put her life in peril to save Jews during the Holocaust. A tree has been planted on the Avenue of the Just on April 5th, 1983.' This next page is another document from Yad Vashem that says on October 19, 1965, Irena Sendler was named Righteous Among the Nations and is presented with a medal. On the medal it says, 'Who saves one life, saves the universe whole.' This next one is in English. It says that she was made an honorary citizen of Israel in 1985. It says at the bottom: 'This recognition is an expression of the esteem and thanks harbored by the People of Israel for those Righteous Among the Nations who, through their noble deeds, rekindled the light of humanity during the darkness of the Nazi era in Europe.'"

Megan puzzled over the certificates. "Gee, all these awards and honors from Israel and nothing from Poland?"

"It's weird," said Liz. "In Poland Irena Sendler has been like a secret for 60 years."

"I'm guessing everybody knows," Sabrina said.

"I guess you'd have to call it something else," Megan said, "not a secret."

Liz turned over the last document. "Polish. Looks like some kind of receipt."

Mr. C. told them how he had met a Polish student at Emporia State and was telling her about Irena Sendler. She told him about another Polish student at the University of Kansas, and he thought one of them would be able to translate. He flipped through a Rolodex file. "Here they are. Anna Karasinska – Emporia State University, and Krzysztof Zyskowski – University of Kansas." He looked at his watch. "Girls, back to class."

*   *   *   *   *   *   *   *   *   *

Two weeks later the translation came back from Krzysztof Zyskowski. The girls and Mr. C. met in the video room, huddled together over Irena's documents and photos:

Dear Mr. Conard, Sabrina, Megan, and Liz:

Below is the translation of the correspondence from Irena Sendler. It was a pleasure to learn about this hero of Poland.

Why don't I know her?

Kristof
Krzysztof Zyskowski
Natural History Museum – Ornithology
University of Kansas, Dyche Hall
Lawrence, KS 66045

THE LETTER:

My dear and beloved girls, very close to my heart!

I was greatly moved/touched by your letter. Most of all, I was interested in what influenced your choice of the subject.

I am curious if you are an exception or more young people in your country are interested in the Holocaust.

I think that your work is unique and worth disseminating. I am very anxious to receive and read your play.

Despite the fact that in the world history there have been cases of oppression of Jews, there has not been a country whose agenda would be the extermination of the entire nation.

For that reason your work has a great value for the world. These monstrous crimes/atrocities cannot be repeated!

My parents have taught me that if someone is drowning one always needs to/should give a helping hand/rescue them. During the war the entire Polish nation was drowning but the most tragically drowning were Jews. For that reason, helping those who were most oppressed was the need of my heart.

I do not write here about my entire activity. I am sending you some documents that describe my activity.

I talked to some people who survived the Holocaust because they were saved by "ZEGOTA." Some of these people live in Poland. Others are scattered around the world. Typically, they do not want to talk about those horrible times, they do not want to think about it, they want to forget. For me it is enough to say that I was saved from Pawiak Prison after 100 days. It was a miracle.

I have been ill for the last 10 years. I am 90. I almost cannot walk. Many of my illnesses are the result of war experiences, Gestapo imprisonment. I am a veteran of war.

I live with my daughter-in-law and granddaughter and my daughter lives nearby. Unfortunately my other close relatives are no longer alive.

The $3 postage money I donated to the public institution that helps poor children (receipt enclosed). You do not need to send me more money because I receive my social security. I will always find money for correspondence with friends.

I am sending you my best thoughts, the most cordial greetings for your parents, and for Professor Norman Conard my deepest thanks for his guidance and help with your initiative.

Devoted/loving,
Irena Sendlerowa

THE ATTACHMENTS:

PHOTOGRAPHS:
Photograph 1: Hospital of the Warsaw Uprising. My "war daughter," Irenka, sister of the writer Bogdan Woydowski.
Photograph 2: Irena Sendlerowa speaks to school children in Israel.
Photograph 3: Me with Wanda Rottenberg, representative of Poalej Syjon.
Photograph 4: Irena Sendlerowa in August 1999.

DOCUMENTS:
Diploma of Righteous Among the Nations
Diploma of planting of the honorary tree in the Avenue of Justice
Honorary address to Irena Sendlerowa from Montville Township, New Jersey
Diploma of Honorary Israeli Citizenship
Receipt for the donation of $3 from the Board of the Circle of Children's Friends certifies that Mrs. Irena Sendler donated to our institution the amount of $3 (three American dollars) for charitable use. Sincerely, Jan Leckowski, President

"It's strange," Megan said. "One of the first things she asks is if other young people in America are interested in the Holocaust. Seems like tons of people are interested in the Holocaust. I mean, there are thousands of books, web sites, plays, movies. But maybe that's not true in Poland."

Megan held two photographs of Irena side by side, one young and beautiful with dark hair and determined eyes, dressed as a nurse, her disguise for entering the Warsaw ghetto, the other a white-haired elder with a black hairband. She looked from one photo to the other. How mysterious that this could be the same person. What was life like for each of these Irena Sendlers? What kind of life separated these two images?

Sabrina's brow furrowed. "Who are we to tell the Polish people about their history?"

"It's a question historians face every day," Mr. C. said. "Who gets to write history? Whose stories get told and, just as important, whose don't? Which memories get disturbed, and which are forgotten? What is saved and what is lost forever? History is not only facts, it's interpretation – it's written by the people who tell it. You guys are making history – telling Irena's story when no one else would, not even Irena herself. It's an interesting problem."

"She rescued children," Megan said. "The Polish people should be proud of this amazing woman. Why wouldn't they want to remember someone who rescued children?"

Mr. C. leaned forward earnestly. "Don't forget, after the war Poland was a Communist state for 45 years – Poles who were anti-Fascist, like Irena, were mostly anti-Communist, too. Those who would fight one authoritarian government would fight another. Maybe after 45 years it fades from memory. Sabrina's question is important. Is it right for us to make them remember? Liz, what do you think?"

"I just think it's, like, a normal human thing to do. When something awful happens, you don't want to think about it or remember it. I can sure understand that."

Megan said, "I can see why it's weird for us – a bunch of American teenagers – to do this. But why hasn't Irena told her story? What about her family? You think she's just too humble – like a saint or something?"

"Maybe she wanted to," Mr. C. said, "but under Communism you didn't tell your story. And maybe Poles couldn't hear it from her directly. She says in her letter that what you girls are doing has great value for the world. I think she wants you to do this."

Megan picked up the $3 receipt for the orphanage. "After all these years, and everything she's been through, she's still taking care of children. I do want to tell her story to the world."

*   *   *   *   *   *   *   *   *   *

Debra Stewart recovered from chemotherapy, and the Stewart family returned to apparent normalcy, what Megan called "BC," *before cancer.*

Now that the girls knew Irena was alive – now that they had "heard" her voice in a letter – Liz felt more awkward at rehearsals, or more self-conscious, she wasn't sure which. After one particularly trying afternoon, Liz told Megan that she felt silly pretending to be Irena – a living woman who could just as well speak for herself.

On Kansas History Day – the first Saturday in May – they loaded up the school's Suburban with props and costumes, their anxiety as penetrating and invisible as a winter wind. Megan and Liz argued about how to pack the metal **WARSAW GHETTO** sign, then Liz dropped her end of the painted stage flat and tore a corner. Megan noticed Sabrina closing her eyes and counting each deep breath through flaring nostrils. It was a long drive to Abilene, to the Eisenhower Center which hosted Kansas History Day, and, once again, there were frequent bathroom stops.

"What if we lose?" Liz asked from her back seat.

Megan had already considered that possibility and said, "We already won. No matter what, we rescued her story. I don't know what we'll do with it, but it won't be buried again for 60 years. It's like when God pushes you in ways you don't understand."

*   *   *   *   *   *   *   *   *   *

The National History Day motto hung over the stage at the Eisenhower Center:

HISTORY DAY, A FUN WAY TO LEARN

It was an unruly theater – each project a short scene, presented on stage, while in the auditorium a hushed, but feverish cacophony of continuous comings and goings of other teams, finalizing makeup and adjusting their costumes. In their assigned classroom Megan made up her face to look like a dying Jew from the ghetto – dirty and starving – and Liz fussed with her nurse's pinafore and cap. A parent from another school came into their room and asked, "Are you three doing the woman who saved children? I've heard it's amazing. Good luck!"

At that moment *The Irena Sendler Project* was called to the stage. The restive audience quieted to watch them perform flawlessly and applauded energetically at the end. During the question period after their performance, one of the three judges commented on their correspondence with Irena. Another judge said, "You've brought tears to my eyes, and that doesn't happen very often."

For the first time, Sabrina's father watched them perform. He came into the auditorium carrying a large plastic bag and sat in the row behind the girls.

They won First Place. As they went onstage to receive their medals to a standing ovation, Sabrina's father opened the plastic bag and placed a bouquet of roses on each of their seats. When she returned, Sabrina picked up her bouquet and turned around to see tears streaming down her father's face as he stood, wildly applauding.

★　★　★　★　★　★　★　★　★　★

On the long car ride home, all they talked about was the letter they were already composing to tell Irena of their victory. They would ask her more questions to perfect the script, to correct any mistakes before the National competition, less than 6 weeks away. Their script now included her escape from Pawiak Prison, but they couldn't imagine how that miracle had occurred. They compiled a list of questions: How had she made that first decision to take an orphan off the street, knowing she put herself and her family at risk of death? What were all the ways she smuggled Jewish children out of the ghetto? What about ZEGOTA? What about the lists? But most perplexing of all, why did no one in Poland know her story? Why was Irena Sendler forgotten?

As they drove into Uniontown, Liz asked, "How do you think people go about making these huge decisions, like Irena deciding to rescue children? Like parents giving away their kids?"

She couldn't help but wonder about her own mother's decision. She wanted to believe it had been hard for her to leave, but her Mom was a mess – a drug addict, a prostitute – and Liz was pretty sure she hadn't thought about it long or hard. As she remembered it, her Mom just got pissed off and left – bang! Didn't even say goodbye. And the reason? Maybe she was so messed up that she had no reason, and that hurt the most.

"Irena was doing God's work," Megan said with conviction.

Liz responded with a hard edge. "I want to know why she did it."

Sabrina said, "I've read that people do things like this on the spur of a moment – without thinking too much – you know – like, impulsively. Maybe if they thought too much they wouldn't do it."

"She called it a need of her heart," Megan said. "My pastor says that's how God speaks to us – through our heart."

Sabrina shrugged. "The thing that really bothers me is this. If I was in Irena's shoes, would I do what she did?"

★ ★ ★ ★ ★ ★ ★ ★ ★ ★

Irena's reply came a few weeks later:

June 6, 2000

My beloved, very close to my heart girls!

Thank you for your letter and for sending me your play "Life in a Jar," and also for the second letter in which you inform me that you performed the play and won the first place (at State). I congratulate you from the bottom of my heart! I wrote an incredibly long letter after receiving your play, but I was not able to finish it because I became very ill. I am going to hospital for a few weeks. I will finish that very long letter after I get back home. Meanwhile I am sending you my most affectionate and most tender greetings and clasp/nestle/hug you to my heart.

Your very devoted/loving
Irena (Jolanta)

★ ★ ★ ★ ★ ★ ★ ★ ★ ★

The trip to Washington, D.C. for National History Day, the farthest Megan and Liz had ever gone from home, didn't turn out the way they had expected. The University of Maryland College Park Campus, a few subway stops from D.C., hosted over 5,000 students, parents, and teachers who gathered on June 12th to hear National History Day director Cathy Gorn welcome them: "You now join almost 800,000 students in this great adventure. National History Day is like the song 'Hotel California.' Once you check in, you never get out."

They had a free afternoon to be tourists in D.C. and decided to visit the Holocaust Memorial Museum. They had free passes, and Megan and Liz were eager to go. Sabrina shrugged her shoulders and said, "I guess."

From the National Mall they turned onto Raoul Wallenberg Street, named after the Swedish diplomat who rescued thousands of Jews, up to the entrance of the U. S. Holocaust Memorial Museum.

Mr. C. handed Megan and Liz each a pass to the museum. "It's a powerful exhibit – it can be difficult," he said as they walked through the curved entryway. "Do you all have tissues?" He held another pass out to Sabrina. "You don't have to do this."

Sabrina tightened her lips into a line and took the ticket.

As they entered the exhibit hall, they passed seven larger-than-life photographs of rescuers and right away recognized the photograph of young Irena – the same photo she had sent them. "Holy smokes!" said Megan. "It's her! Maybe there's more about her inside."

They stopped before a black-and-white photograph of the Auschwitz gate, reminiscent of their **WARSAW GHETTO** gate prop, this one inscribed, "*Arbeit Macht Frei*," (Work Makes You Free) – the lie that greeted Jews on their way to extermination.

Once inside, each girl drifted off alone, captured by the gravity of a photograph, a video story, a cattle car with white letters and numbers scrawled on red-brown wooden slats. Megan dabbed at her eyes and felt herself displaced outside the safe boundaries of books, computer images, and stories from disembodied voices over phone lines. In this hall she moved a giant step closer to the Holocaust.

Sabrina, her eyes glistening, stood alone before a video monitor, before a woman, a survivor who explained matter of factly how her mother had died at Auschwitz. "She was selected," the woman said. Sabrina's lips began to tremble; she crossed her arms tightly around her chest. In the next moment she could not stop herself from sobbing.

Megan was at Sabrina's side and gently led her to a seat outside the room.

"I'm OK," she said. "Really, I'm OK. I just got to thinking about this woman telling her story over and over, sometimes to no one at all, day after day in a dark room."

"Maybe let's just sit here for a moment. Take a break. It's not easy."

"I'm just surprised, is all. I mean, I don't usually do this."

"You wouldn't be normal if you didn't do this."

An hour later Liz returned, her eyes red.

Megan said, "I wonder what else the Museum knows about her."

They asked an administrative assistant, who was eager to do a search for them, but he found nothing more than a paragraph summary of Irena, which had the wrong year of her birth and said it was unknown if she was still alive. He was glad to hear what they knew and suggested they e-mail their information to the Research Director of the Museum and send Xerox copies of Irena's letters and attestations.

As they left Megan said, "We know more about Irena than this great museum. We need to tell this story – to them – to everybody."

★   ★   ★   ★   ★   ★   ★   ★   ★   ★

Their performance in the National competition did not go well. Overwhelmed by their visit to the Holocaust Museum the day before, they bungled critical lines and left others out entirely. In spite of the errors, *Life in a Jar* received high scores, but failed to win a national award. Cathy Gorn found the Kansas girls afterwards to congratulate them on their work. "This is way beyond National History Day," she said. "This is my wildest dream of National History Day. You started out as students of history and you've become agents of history."

A National History Day volunteer gave Mr. C. a message from Stanlee Stahl, executive director of the Jewish Foundation for the Righteous, inviting them to New York City to present *Life in a Jar* at the JFR office for some board members, staff, and several Holocaust survivors. The girls had been looking forward to a day of leisure, of shopping, more sightseeing. Would they sacrifice their day off to take a long drive to New York City to perform the play? Mr. C. reminded them that it had been the JFR that had helped them connect to Irena.

"They're like experts about the Holocaust, right?" Liz asked. "Maybe they could answer some of our questions – you know, about Poland and Polish people and stuff."

"We may never get good enough answers to those questions," he said. "I think it's more important to look forward, to build bridges – like sharing *Life in a Jar*."

They drove in one car without costumes or props – crept up Seventh Avenue in Manhattan traffic, then shot up 19 floors, higher than the girls had ever been. They were met by a trim, middle-aged woman with short hair wearing a conservative but fashionable suit. "I'm Stanlee Stahl, executive director. Welcome." They followed her into the board room and each girl's eyes widened when they beheld the Manhattan skyline through a wall of glass.

Ms. Stahl introduced their Kansas guests and asked those sitting around the boardroom table to introduce themselves.

"Mrs. Rachel Simkowitz – survivor of Auschwitz."

"Mrs. Tova Cohn – survivor Bergen-Belsen."

"Mr. Bernard Myer – survivor Dachau."

Though they had met Holocaust survivors at the Midwest Center for Holocaust Education in Kansas City, they had never performed their play in such an intimate setting for survivors. Megan felt uneasy – troubled that they were about to pretend, to play-act in ordinary street clothes, the experiences of these real people who had lived this nightmare – survivors for whom this was much more than a schoolgirl's history project. They might be critical or dismissive; they might be insulted or hurt all over again. The performance space between the board table and the panoramic window was narrow – too close to their unusual audience. No lights, no props, no makeup. Though the boardroom was air-conditioned, Megan wiped sweat from her forehead and upper lip. So many ways for this to go badly, she thought.

The boardroom was silent as Mr. C. introduced the play. Sabrina began as the Narrator, her voice hypnotic, compelling attention. A survivor sitting at the table suddenly put her hand to her mouth.

Irena: *Mrs. Rosner?*

Mrs. Rosner: *I've talked with my husband. You must take our children. It breaks our hearts, but you must take them. We will all die. (long hesitation) There are no set rules you can live by. You say to yourself, if I live by this set of rules I'll be OK. But yesterday I saw a German soldier shoot a woman passing by. I saw him walk out on the steps and he drew his gun and shot the woman. I couldn't figure out what she'd done. (Hangs head in sorrow)*

A young intern came in to deliver a message and remained standing at the door, unable to leave.

Marie: *Irena, what are you doing?*

Irena: (Liz pretending to write) *I'm putting the names of the latest children on my lists, and putting all the lists in jars.*

Marie: *Are you mad? You can't leave any evidence for the Nazis to find. You will get caught. You know to conceal Jews is punishable by death. How do you find families to adopt these children?*

Irena: *The Underground helps. Families are willing to*

249

sacrifice. Orphanages help, convents, everyone can make a difference. Everyone can show courage.

Marie: *And what will you do with the jars?*

Irena: (Liz makes a digging motion.) *Today I bury these jars in the ground. When this is over I will dig them up and find the children and tell them who they are.*

The play ended with Megan's last line:

Marie: *This is life in a jar; Irena has inspired the entire world.*

At the end there was no applause. It seemed to Megan as if time had frozen. Sabrina pulled out her chair at the board table and quickly sat down, her face hot and flushed. In the street the city had been loud and busy, crowded and dirty, but from 19 stories up the city was as quiet and clean as a postcard, the only sound, a few Holocaust survivors clearing their throats.

Ms. Stahl began to clap, and very quickly everyone in the room joined her. One survivor slowly pushed back and stood with arthritic effort. He steadied himself with both hands on the table, and the room quieted. "There are many ways to tell the truth," he said. "When I heard about you and what you are doing, I thought, 'What can these children from Kansas possibly teach me – a Holocaust survivor?' Your play is a reminder of what happened to me – to my family. For this I am very sad. I suppose it is good to weep and remember what happened to us. But we all have different reasons for weeping and not all of our tears are the same. You tell a simple story – a dramatic story – that tells a simple and dramatic truth. Sometimes simple stories are the most powerful – like fairy tales – except this one is true."

CHAPTER 24

Benefactors

Kansas, July 2000 – May 2001

When they returned to Kansas from Maryland, three e-mail requests to perform *Life in a Jar* awaited them, two from synagogues in Kansas City and one from a Jewish congregation in St. Louis, Missouri. Throughout the summer they received more invitations, from Jewish, Protestant, and Catholic congregations and churches, civic clubs, schools, and service organizations. There was a local buzz about *Life in a Jar*, generated by word of mouth, the internet, and regional television news interviews.

In the 12 years Mr. C. had been overseeing National History Day projects at Uniontown High School, *Life in a Jar* was the first to generate so much attention beyond the competition. Requests for performances continued to pile up. With the euphoria of grand beginnings, the girls met and decided to take this project on the road; they were prepared to make the necessary sacrifices.

At the same meeting, Megan laughed and said, "I know this sounds crazy, but let's perform the play for Irena in Poland."

"Sure," Liz said, "right after we win the lottery."

The Uniontown school district was one of the smallest and lowest-income districts in Kansas – a rural district where more than half the students received free or reduced-cost lunches.

Taking *Life in a Jar* on the road promised to be complex and time-consuming. There were so many details for each performance – lodging, food, performance space, sound, lights. They enlisted a road manager – Jessica Shelton, a freshman, who was confident that she could handle this challenge. After all, she had managerial experience; she was the supervisor of her Taco Bell shift in Fort Scott.

Soon after, Nick Caton joined the project (they needed a man to play the German Soldier), and they produced a short video showing two scenes from the play and footage from television news interviews. As they began to perform, especially for Kansas City's large Jewish congregations, they met survivors and children of survivors who shared stories of witnessing parents murdered, of enduring hunger for years, of hiding in filthy barns.

After one performance, as they drove back to Uniontown, Megan said, "I think there's something wrong with me. When I first heard these awful stories I thought I would vomit. Now, they don't seem so crazy. It's like I'm getting used to it. It's not right."

Liz had a theory that each performance of *Life in a Jar* detonated a bomb in the memory of people who didn't know they were still mourning, guilty, mad, or ashamed. "Strong stuff gets riled up." When Liz shared her bomb theory with Sabrina and Megan, Sabrina noted that no matter how sad the play made people feel, no matter how awful the memories, no matter how many tears, everyone thanked them for the performance.

The girls began putting out a glass jar before each performance to represent the jar in which Irena had hidden the children's names. A sign explained that audience donations would be sent to Poland to help with Irena's living and medical expenses.

But the money never stayed with Irena. Every check they sent was acknowledged with a receipt from the charitable organization or orphanage to which she immediately donated the funds. Megan wondered why a hero such as Irena wouldn't feel worthy of accepting these small contributions. More than once Irena wrote that her only regret was that she hadn't done enough and that so many children had perished. They could only conclude that her mission had never ended.

Invitations to perform *Life in a Jar* increased dramatically after July 2000 when award-winning journalist Stan Finger published an article about *The Irena Sendler Project* in the Wichita Eagle, one of the first major newspaper accounts:

> *Three students from Uniontown High School have catapulted Sendler's name and her amazing life story into national prominence as a result of a play they performed for National History Day in Washington, D.C.*

Yet almost from the day they began working on their project, the students discovered few people had heard of Irena Sendler. When she was in Washington for National History Day, Megan Stewart was telling a student from New Jersey about their skit. He said, "Oh, Oskar Schindler! I've heard of him!" And Megan said, "No, it's a woman and her name is Sendler." After their performances, their teacher, Norm Conard, said, "People keep asking about why we haven't heard of this woman." The students hope to continue raising money for Sendler, who is in frail health, and they hope to visit her in Poland. The project has taught them many things, they said, but none more valuable than what they call 'the power of one.' "One person," Sabrina Coons said, "can make a difference."

★　★　★　★　★　★　★　★　★　★

In early September another letter in Polish came from Irena with receipts from two orphanages for exactly the amount of money they had raised from their most recent performances. A week later they had their translation and Megan read it out loud:

My dear beloved girls close to my heart,

I thank you immensely for the letter, the play, the photographs, and the emblem of your school. I read everything very carefully. Part of it was translated by my granddaughter and part by my friend who is a professional interpreter. I can not read on my own for three years now. I have to use a magnifying glass because diabetes has destroyed my eyesight. Before I go to the main content of your play about me titled "Life in a Jar," I need to tell you or mention that you are uniquely wise, interesting, and thinking girls full of sensitivity to troubling wars. Being interested in problems of the Holocaust. It is so very difficult to understand for everyone who was not only directly an object of the criminal exhibition of the Nazis, but also for those who were not eyewitness of their exhibiting. It is almost impossible to understand everything that the Nazis have done to the several million people, including the six million Jews.

Despite many books written that were published world-wide and in the United States regarding the Second World War, the whole criminal activity of the Nazis cannot be comprehended by any sane, mentally healthy or normal thinking human being. Your sensitive hearts subconsciously sent you to look for something more, something that went beyond these atrocities and this search for the truth and some faint tiny trace led you to me.

I think it is important for you to know that on 23rd September, 1999, a few months before your first letter to me, my son Adam suddenly died. He was only 49. There can be nothing more sorrowing than to lose your child, something I understand in a new way now. My heart is broken and this has worsened my health. Unfortunately, it is necessary for me to go to the hospital.

Also I cannot communicate with you because of the serious illness of one of the employees of the Jewish Institute, Mrs. Holena Goboska who used to type all my correspondence on the typewriter. This has made it impossible to finish the material that I meant for you. The other people are not able to type up my letters because my bad eyesight makes my handwriting not very legible.

I am writing this because I want you to understand my long silence. I'm sorry.

Analyzing our contact so far, one needs to mention that your whole activity is quite unusual and unique. My perspective is, this I must add, that your integrity, fortitude and rare perseverance in obtaining the goal that you set for yourselves, are admirable.

I predict or expect that you will get to reach whatever success you seek. After all I have 55 years of experience working with young people, especially those 14-16 years old such as yourselves.

For that reason I was active with young people of your age which makes me believe that all of you, despite the many difficulties that complicate life, will get very far. I wish you "from my whole heart" my immense congratulations and most tender affectionate greetings for you, for your family/close ones, for Professor Norman and for the Pole who translates my letters.

> Yours truly and loving very much,
> Irena "Jolanta" from ZEGOTA

News of Adam's death chilled their joy in receiving Irena's letter.

Megan looked back in their NHD logbook and found that *The Irena Sendler Project* began on September 23, 1999, the exact day Adam died. "Is that spooky, or what?" Megan said, and realized in that same moment that if she looked at this coincidence from a spiritual perspective, it was the unseen hand of God.

Liz turned back to Megan and said, "It makes sense that Irena didn't have kids until after the war. I mean, if she had kids of her own, how could she take away other people's kids?"

Sabrina studied Irena's letter. "I read somewhere that most women in the ZEGOTA network didn't have kids."

★   ★   ★   ★   ★   ★   ★   ★   ★   ★

With the start of the new school year, the girls experienced their first harassment, mostly from certain boys. Notices about *Life in a Jar* were defaced or ripped off bulletin boards. One student seemed inordinately proud of himself as he proclaimed in the hallway, "I hate niggers, Jews, and fags!" Most of the taunting was aimed at Megan, who they called "Jew-girl" or "Jew lover" in the hallways and lunchroom. Though they made her nervous, Megan showed no emotion and thought to herself, Hate the sin, not the sinner.

"They're idiots," Liz said to Megan after rehearsal. "And jealous of the attention we're getting."

Mr. C. reacted to each incident; he spoke with the principal and school board members about racial and ethnic intolerance. After their 25th performance of *Life in a Jar*, a local school board member confronted Mr. C. with his own "serious concerns about the project." He demanded to know how much money the girls made from each performance, if there were other secret funds, and about the use of the Suburban for non-school activities. Didn't he even care that collecting money would ruin the girls' sports status?

"Have you seen the production?" Mr. C. replied.

"I don't need to see it to know what's going on," he retorted. "It's a political project that has nothing to do with the American History you're supposed to be teaching."

Soon thereafter, Howard Jacobson, a prominent businessman, and his wife Ro, both influential and active members of the Kansas City Jewish community, fell in love with The Irena Sendler Project and the girls. When they learned of the school board member's objections, Howard Jacobson wrote a letter to the school superintendent and the chair of the school board praising the impact this play was having on local communities, and emphasizing how important it was that students, as well as their parents, indeed Americans in general, be inspired by what one person can do to save lives. "These students represent the best image that a small town could project and Life in a Jar is changing stereotypes and caricatures of students from small towns. I've enclosed several newspaper articles from the Kansas City Star as well as several church bulletins and the Jewish Chronicle. The students have been interviewed by several local TV stations in and around the Kansas City area. What wonderful publicity for your school district." He enclosed a check for $1,000 to help defray expenses for Life in a Jar and pledged to give at least that amount for five years or more.

School board concerns ceased.

* * * * * * * * * *

Mr. C. watched every performance of Life in a Jar with a burgeoning sense of wonder that these teenagers, not especially good actors, routinely brought audiences to their feet, many in tears. He asked people who had seen the play why they thought it had this profound effect.

"Protestant girls from rural Kansas, rescuing the story of a Catholic social worker from Poland who rescued Jewish children from the Nazis. It gives me hope."

"These girls are goodwill ambassadors for America."

"Why doesn't anybody know about this lady? There's something poignant about learning such important history from children."

"I don't know. It just got to me – opened up a whole reservoir of sadness I didn't know was inside me."

"Sometimes it takes a simple story to tell a complicated truth."

"I was in Poland and I'm very old. Not many of us are left. It's up to people like you to keep our memories alive – to tell our terrible stories so they never happen again."

"I can't even talk about it."

The girls never tired of answering the same questions over and over, mindful of the powerful impact they had on people. Some questions they couldn't answer, the most frequent of which was, "Will you visit Irena Sendler in Poland?"

Throughout the fall, though Mr. C. was occupied with the next crop of National History Day students and those involved in other diversity projects, he continued to accompany the cast members almost every weekend for performances of *Life in a Jar* in the Kansas – Missouri area. The students involved gave up their wages from weekend jobs to travel for hours, set up and perform in emotional venues, followed by questions and powerful, often elemental, discussions. They met survivors and children of survivors, most of whom were eager to share their astounding stories with the students, as if *Life in a Jar* was an altar upon which to enshrine their own memories and heartbreaks.

They had the technical aspects down to a science – even special packing cases for props and the stage flat. Although everyone knew exactly what to do, setup and preparation still required at least two hours. They ate a lot of pizza.

Appeals for performances exceeded time available, travel restrictions, and final exams, and they had to graciously decline many requests. In January 2001, six months after National History Day, Bart Altenbernd, assistant principal of the Westridge Middle School in the Shawnee Mission school district, a suburb of Kansas City, called Mr. C. and pleaded with him to present *Life in a Jar* twice for the eighth graders on a day they were already scheduled to perform twice at another school. Ordinarily, Mr. C. would have declined, but Bart Altenbernd was someone special. He had been the principal at Uniontown High School from 1988-1991 when Mr. C. was just starting tolerance and diversity projects, and he had been best man at Mr. C.'s wedding. They stayed in touch. That year, 2001, Bart was charged with developing five projects for his school's "Diversity Day." He called Mr. C. to ask what he was doing regarding diversity, and he told him about *The Irena Sendler Project*.

Bart Altenbernd would not take no for an answer, and, against his better judgment, Mr. C. finally acceded and they performed four times in one day. The performance for Bart Altenbernd's eighth graders was not remarkable in and of itself. But one of the teachers watching the final performance was John Shuchart, a successful businessman who had taken a year's sabbatical from his company to volunteer as a teacher – "to give back to the community." He was so moved by the story and the performance that afterwards he invited the students, their parents, and Mr. C. to lunch at an upscale Chinese restaurant in Kansas City.

They sat at a great circular table, and before they ordered, Shuchart asked them, "Where do you want to go with this?"

Megan immediately said, "To Poland! We want to meet Irena and bring more of her story back to the U.S. We're raising money for the trip – selling candy. That always seems to work."

Shuchart lifted one eyebrow. "How much have you raised?"

Megan blushed. "Well, we just started. I think $81."

"She's 90 years old," Shuchart said. "You said her health is not good. Time's a-wastin'. You have to go immediately. I'll see what I can do."

Two days later he called and announced, "I've raised the money. I'm sending you girls to Poland."

★ ★ ★ ★ ★ ★ ★ ★ ★ ★

Three parents accompanied the girls to Poland in May 2001 – Debra Stewart, who was in remission and feeling well, her hair regrowing, curly and luxuriant, Grandpa Bill, and Grandma Phyllis. They, and Mr. C.'s wife Karen, paid their own way. Because of health concerns, Sabrina's mother's doctor would not allow her to travel – something about her diabetes. By early March they had their airline tickets, and the girls wrote a newsy, excited letter to Irena about their opportunity to visit her in Poland.

Irena's response was a seven-page missive that again began, "My dear girls, very close to my heart." Their communication, she wrote, was the best medicine for her health and she was less "depressed in the spirit." She wrote about her co-conspirators, all social workers like herself, nine women and one man, about her liaisons in and out of the ghetto, "mostly young girls close to your own years," with detailed accounts of all the ways they had rescued children. But not a word about Pawiak Prison.

Liz was troubled by a paragraph on page three of Irena's letter:

> I also want to ask you to never do any harrowing thing because I will be grieved by that. What I was doing was only from the need of the heart and because of how I was raised. My parents taught me two rules that humans should follow, one — remember that the people can be divided only into good and bad; it doesn't matter what religion, what race, and what nation the person is descended.
>
> And the second rule — when somebody is drowning, this person needs to be rescued.

"Why do you think," Liz asked, "she'd tell us not to do what she did? It's like getting a letter from your mother, or something."

Megan said, "Yeah. Sort of 'do as I say, not as I do' but it's all backwards of how it usually goes."

"You know when those bullies at school called us Jew-girls?" Sabrina said. "What if they had said they were going to kill us if we didn't stop *Life in a Jar*? When you're scared you act different than you think you would — or should."

Megan closed up her backpack and said, "I'll bet that's how it began in Germany and Poland — just name calling. It's hard to know when to stand up to bullies. But Irena doesn't want us to take any risks, like she did. Liz is right — she wants to protect us, like a mother."

Megan was half out the door when she turned for a moment. "She says it was a need of her heart. But, protecting children — I mean, isn't that a need of everyone's heart?"

★　★　★　★　★　★　★　★　★

One of the first Polish-Americans to embrace *The Irena Sendler Project* was Bozenna Gilbride, living in New York on Long Island. She was well-connected in Warsaw, and an expert on ZEGOTA. After seeing the play, she sent the girls a book about the Polish resistance organization, which had more specifics about Irena and helped them learn about the Polish resistance and the partisans. Bozenna told them harrowing stories of the underground, but she had no idea how Irena had escaped from Pawiak Prison. After Irena was recognized in Israel in 1965, Bozenna had interviewed her, and, in the early 1990's she had helped produce two documentary films about ZEGOTA, one of them narrated by Eli Wallach. But they did not enjoy a large audience, and she had been frustrated that her endeavor had fallen on deaf ears. Just three weeks before *The Irena Sendler Project* began, Renata Zajdman, an orphan rescued from the ghetto by Irena's network, had interviewed Irena as well. But, against all logic or justice, Irena's story remained obscure. The Kansas girls' enterprise was the latest effort to "discover" Irena's story.

Bozenna helped them develop an itinerary for their visit to Poland with interviews, tours, and translators in Warsaw. She was in contact with Elzbieta (Bieta) Ficowska, the six-month-old baby who Irena had smuggled out of the ghetto in a carpenter's box. Bieta invited the students to perform at the Children of the Holocaust Association's annual meeting in Poland.

Renata and Bieta began overseeing Irena's care with the help of a coordinated fund-raising effort by Bozenna Gilbride, the *Life in a Jar* Project, and other child survivors. Bieta agreed to act as an executor and ensure that all contributions raised by the Kansas students went to Irena's care.

A few weeks before their departure, Bozenna called Mr. C. from Warsaw saying she had a friend, Marcin Fabjanski, a young reporter for the *Gazeta Wyborcza* – *The Warsaw Voice* – the largest-circulation daily in Eastern Europe. He was based in New York City, and his newspaper wanted to send him to Uniontown.

Mr. C. met Marcin at Kansas City International Airport and drove him to Uniontown High School, where he sat in the last row of the classroom, trying to be as invisible as possible. Marcin interviewed the girls and their parents, saw the *Life in a Jar* video, and walked around an ominously deserted Uniontown village square, past the post office, past shuttered businesses and empty storefronts. Marcin's last evening in Kansas was warm and starry skied. Sitting on the Conards' deck, he asked a few clarifying questions, then closed his reporter's notebook. "You know what troubles me the most?" he asked. "In my on-line search of the *Gazeta Wyborcza* archives I could find no story and only one reference to Irena Sendler. I'm still young and idealistic. I worry sometimes that seeing too much of the dark side will turn me into a cynical old reporter. But after spending time here, my faith is renewed. What you encourage in your students – this is good for the world."

"There's a Native American story," Mr. C. said, "about a boy who came to his grandfather angry at a friend who had done him an injustice. The grandfather said that he too had felt great anger for those who had taken so much from him and his people. But, he explained, hate wears you down and does not hurt your enemy. It's like taking poison and wishing your enemy would die.

"The boy didn't understand until his grandfather said it was as if there were two wolves that lived inside him who fought each other for his soul. One wolf was vengeful and angry, the other forgiving and kind. The boy asked, 'Which one wins, Grandfather?'

"The old man smiled and said, 'The one I feed.'"

★ ★ ★ ★ ★ ★ ★ ★ ★ ★

Unbeknownst to the Kansas students, their journey to Poland coincided with the 60th anniversary of the World War II massacre in Jedwabne, Poland of between 200 and 1,000 Jews, not by the Germans, but by their Polish Gentile neighbors. Jan Gross's provocative book about the massacre, *Neighbors: The Destruction of the Jewish Community in Jedwabne, Poland* (published in 2000 in Polish and 2001 in English), had opened a raw wound in the conscience of Poles. Under Communism, wartime resistance and rescue had been condemned, even criminalized; rescuing Jews was not something to celebrate. *Yad Vashem* medals, and the stories of heroism and decency they rewarded, had been hidden away – buried like shameful treasures. Consequent to Jan Gross's revelations (Jedwabne was the site of a forensic excavation), an official investigation sparked national controversy, outrage, and soul-searching. With the wounds of war re-opened, Poland was hungry for her wartime heroes.

Marcin's feature article appeared in the *Gazeta Wyborcza* two days before the American students from Kansas landed at Frederic Chopin Airport in Warsaw. After nearly 60 years of silence, Irena Sendler's story was front-page news.

CHAPTER 25

We're Not in Kansas Anymore

Warsaw, May 2001

T he arrivals terminal at Frederic Chopin International Airport bustled with the babel of international travel, public address announcements in Polish, English, and German, and the muted cacophony of anxious travelers. Uniformed guards and discrete barricades herded the Kansans, three teenage girls and five adults, toward customs.

"Lizzie!" Grandpa Bill called to her. "Slow down. You don't want to be getting lost here." He leaned toward Mr. C.'s ear and said, "How do you say *no comprende?*"

Mr. C. pulled a Polish phrase book from his back pocket. "*Nie rozumiem.*"

"Where are the toilets?" Big Bill Cambers's eyes darted nervously.

"*Gdzie sa toalety.*"

Liz yelled from up ahead. "Hey, Mr. C.! What if our rides don't show up?" She smiled as if she thought that might be fun.

"Relax, Liz," he said, though he felt anything but relaxed. Elzbieta Ficowska had e-mailed them that "young friends" would meet them at the airport. Another leap of faith, more uncertainty. How strange, even amusing, that Irena Sendler had organized an intricate network of rescuers during the war and saved thousands of young lives, yet trying to move eight Americans from Kansas to Warsaw was so complicated.

Polish customs was quick and efficient, these wide-eyed Americans with their virginal passports as innocent as any group the inspectors had ever seen. After clearing customs they waited for their luggage by the International Arrivals exit door, a two-way mirror the girls couldn't see out, but those waiting for passengers could see in. Every time the doors opened, they caught a glimpse of a boisterous crowd; cameras flashing – people waving and shouting.

Sabrina said, "Was there someone famous on our flight?"

"Maybe Britney Spears," Liz joked.

After recovering their luggage they started through the door. Immediately, they were engulfed by a pressing crowd, assaulted by microphones, camera lights and shutter clicks, men with video cameras, pushing and squirming. It was impossible to understand what anyone was saying.

A sign suddenly thrust up in the crowd: "*Sendlerowa Girls.*" Megan went up to the sign-bearer and said, "We're the Sendler girls."

A cameraman's lens closed in on them, a reporter shouldered through the crowd and pushed a bouquet of flowers into Liz's hands, then a microphone into her face. "How is it feeling," he asked, "to be the girls who are bringing a Polish hero story to the light?"

A fusillade of questions in various permutations of English bombarded them. Megan turned and found Mr. C.'s eyes. "What do we do?"

He shrugged, "Stay together and answer their questions!" His index finger painted a giant smile on his face. "And smile!"

The girls no longer held hands, each being interviewed by a different reporter. Lights flashed. Poles came forward to shake their hands. A young woman whose name badge said "*Wall Street Journal*" tried to get their attention. "I have limousines waiting for you at the curb. Please follow me."

A dark-haired young man intervened. "Please, I am Adam and this is my sister Maria. Our mother, Zophia, sent us to get you."

Two middle-aged women forced their way through the crowd. The shorter woman pointed at Adam and Maria and said in perfect English, "Those two – they're with us." She was breathing hard, but spoke with authority. She reached out an introductory hand. "Renata Zajdman – from Montreal. We've e-mailed. This is my friend, Elzbieta Ficowska. She doesn't speak English. Irena rescued her as a baby. Please come with us. We have cars waiting."

Elzbieta smiled and embraced each of the girls as if she knew them well. There were tears in her eyes. She gave Mr. C. an envelope. "A new itinerary," Renata explained. "From Irena."

The young *Wall Street Journal* reporter interrupted to repeat that she had limousines waiting. A brief argument ensued in Polish, and the reporter turned away in disgust. Adam and Maria led them through the throng of flashing cameras and shouting reporters.

They left the terminal into hot and humid air, the tumult suddenly stilled. Adam and Maria led them to four tiny cars, Polski Fiats double-parked at the terminal's curb. Photographers' lights suddenly flared anew, and a cameraman filmed them squeezing luggage, props, and finally themselves into the cars.

Liz turned around in the front seat and earnestly said to Mr. C., "This is a little scary. We're OK, aren't we?"

He nodded. "We're OK, Liz."

★　★　★　★　★　★　★　★　★　★

As they checked into Warsaw's Ibis Hotel, Mr. C. was given a stack of messages, the most urgent from the U.S. Embassy, from Ambassador Christopher Hill, who was extremely eager to meet them. Would they please call the embassy as soon as possible to confirm the interview arranged by Irena Sendler for Friday, May 25th at 2:30 in the afternoon? The other messages were mostly from news organizations, radio, and TV stations requesting interviews.

In their hotel room Sabrina and Liz checked out the bathroom. Liz examined the travel samples of lotion, soap and shampoo. "Sabrina, are you as nervous as I am?"

"Yeah – I guess. I mean, this is crazy. How did we get here? They're gonna find out that we don't know what we're doing."

★　★　★　★　★　★　★　★　★　★

Megan woke up to the telephone ringing and Liz groaning in the next bed. Bleary-eyed, she fumbled for the receiver and noticed the electric clock. 6:45.

An energetic man's voice greeted her, "Good morning. Hello? Polish

265

television here. We are wanting for you to make a small dramatic performance – just a small scene from your play, if you would be so kind. Please, we will make a film of you in front of Ghetto Fighter's Memorial."

Megan sat up and pushed her sleep-wild hair from her face. "Could you wait ... could you just wait a minute? Wait." She said it too loudly, as if the reporter was deaf.

"Liz! Liz! Wake up. This guy's from Polish TV. He wants us to do a scene from the play."

Liz disappeared under her blanket. "I'm sleeping," she mumbled.

Megan picked up the phone again. "Can you call our teacher? He's in room 534. Five ... three... four."

A few minutes later Mr. C. called their room. "Megan, we're going to do this – right now. The Mrs. Rosner scene," he said. "Five minutes."

A few minutes later he knocked on their door. "Are you ready? They're waiting in the lobby. Hurry up!" The entire group was scheduled to be at the Children of the Holocaust Association of Poland's meeting place at the Nozyk Synagogue at 10 AM. At best this unexpected TV event would give them a jump start – help them shake off jet lag. At worst it would disrupt their whole day. The desk clerk and two businessmen checking out of the hotel for an early flight gawked as Megan, in a frayed, distressed dress from the 1940's, her face scuffed and dirty, strode through the lobby as Mrs. Rosner, a soiled peasant's kerchief binding her luxuriant hair, her feet pinched into her grandmother's cracked black shoes with cubes for heels. She strutted in a proud way, wide awake despite jet lag and the early hour. Liz, not a morning person under the best of circumstances, was only half awake as she shuffled behind Megan, dressed as Irena in her white nurse's pinafore.

Though Sabrina wasn't in the scene, she came along. No, she wasn't upset not to be performing. "It's the best scene," she said. "Break a leg!"

The Polish TV van zig-zagged through Warsaw's rush-hour traffic and came to an abrupt halt at the sudden serenity of the massive Ghetto Fighter's Memorial, a 35-foot-high sculpted slab of granite, like an enormous gravestone at the head of several square blocks of well-kept grass and a copse of trees. "We are in the ghetto," the producer informed them. "Mila Street – the Jewish resistance headquarters, is just a block away."

266

Megan stepped out of the TV van, not into the Warsaw ghetto, but into a small urban park in the cool morning air, an expansive silence and calm of contoured green. Megan supposed there were bones under her feet and no doubt many spirits. Yet it was just a park, like a park in any city, everything around her too normal, too peaceful to be the site of the unbelievable suffering she now knew so much about. The extreme dissonance caused her to shiver. It was early enough that the sun, rising behind the monument, cast dramatic shadows from seven larger-than-life ghetto fighters surging out of the granite. The TV crew unfolded lights, ran cables, and unpacked their cameras. Following the Jewish tradition for graveside visits, people had left small stones at the base of the monument.

Their translator pointed to the monument and said, "Those massive blocks of granite in the monument – they're from Sweden. Ironically, they had been previously ordered by Hitler's own sculptor, Arno Breker, for a monument to Hitler in Berlin." He looked at his watch and consulted the film director. "We have a little time to kill until they're ready. I was instructed to tell you about this place.

"The monument was built in 1948, the same year I was born. Stalin, despite his well-known hatred of Jews, approved the monument. My parents tell me that when work began on it there was nothing but rubble as far as one could see. Imagine." He swept his arm around in a circle. "Imagine nothing here except this huge monument – like a tombstone. Everybody was suspicious as to why the Communists would allow it as the sole monument to the war."

"One of our questions," Liz said, "is why no one in Poland knows Irena Sendler."

"Maybe not so many Poles know Irena Sendler," the translator said. "But every Pole knows someone like her. The problem, as I see it, is that we Poles have become numb. We know the facts, the dates, the narrative. Some people say they don't want to have their faces pushed into that cesspool – it's over, we should move on. Under Communism you had to be very careful. There were two basic rules: Do not speak ill of the Soviet Union and do not speak well of the Polish partisans and their 1944 Uprising against the Germans. The dirty secret that every Pole knows is that the Russians betrayed the Polish freedom fighters. The Red Army waited across the Vistula while the Germans killed more than 200,000 men, women, and children and leveled Warsaw. Then Stalin re-wrote history, celebrating the saving of Poland by the Red Army and the Soviet Union. Polish partisans, our heroes, suddenly became outlaws. Ten years ago I would have gone to prison for saying this to you.

"And Stalin was successful; he reshaped memory. This memorial is – how do you say – a metaphor. When it was first erected there was nothing here except this monument. A person could not help but notice. Now, look." Again he gestured with his arm to the surrounding city. "Our new masters, the Russians, rebuilt Warsaw around this magnificent memorial. They built square block proletarian buildings and soon enough this monument, no longer a gravestone in a dead city, is but one more stone cube in a city of stone cubes."

"I still don't understand," Megan said. "If this is the only monument to partisans or resisters that the Communists allowed, why choose the Jewish revolt? Why build a monument at all?"

"Stalin approved the monument right after the war – a cynical gift to us Poles who saw this as yet another Russian betrayal – an insult to the memory of Polish underground heroes. And it helped keep anti-Jewish feelings alive. Every year the Communist government sponsored a commemoration at this monument despite state-authorized anti-Semitism.

"Ironically, now the monument is a symbol of resistance. Solidarity began holding rallies here in 1983, invoking the spirit of the Ghetto Uprising."

Mr. C. squinted at the sun-silhouetted monument. "I think our visit may be stirring up painful memories. I certainly hope not."

"Yes, of course," he said matter of factly. "But a hopeful sign as well – that Poland is changing. Under the Communists your visit could never have been allowed." He pointed across the green. "Do you see those scattered black marble stones? Symbolic gravestones. This is a cemetery. Many have died here."

They positioned themselves on the monument's shaded side, and while they waited, Megan studied the faces of the fighters erupting from the stone, especially the girl, maybe she was Megan's age, holding a rifle, maybe a courier for Irena's network. She looked out over the placid green space, empty except for a few Poles hurrying to work, a young mother and her baby, empty benches and chess tables, and tried to imagine a battlefield of Jews fighting Nazis not so very long ago. Once again Megan wondered if it was all right for them to be play-acting here.

A brisk wind caused Liz to hold tight to her kerchief as she took her place in front of the monument. The Polish cameraman signaled. The newsman tapped his watch, and they began the Mrs. Rosner scene on the monument's granite ledge.

Most of those who passed stopped, and some asked the film crew what was going on. Off to the left of the monument, between two linden trees, Sabrina noticed an elderly woman with a cane watching. The woman was certainly old enough to have been a girl during the war. She nodded knowingly as Irena took Mrs. Rosner's child. She was close enough for Sabrina to see her gold Star of David necklace and silent tears streaming down her cheeks. As the scene ended she limped away through the trees and disappeared.

When Megan and Liz rejoined the group, their translator shook their hands. "Very moving. I look forward to seeing the entire play."

Megan asked about an oddly shaped commemorative stone to the right of the monument that leaned out of the ground like a vandalized headstone.

"It's a monument to ZEGOTA," their translator said. "Do you know ZEGOTA?"

"We know about Irena Sendler's involvement with ZEGOTA."

The translator looked into his tour guide book. "Yes, here it is. September 1995. American Friends of ZEGOTA. There was a ceremonial dedication with the Chief Rabbi of Warsaw and a Polish Bishop."

They gathered around the stone, which was engraved in English and in Polish:

1942 – ZEGOTA – 1945

THE ORGANIZATION ESTABLISHED BY
THE POLISH UNDERGROUND STATE
TO RESCUE JEWS OF THE HOLOCAUST.

IT WAS THE ONLY SUCH ORGANIZATION
IN GERMAN-OCCUPIED EUROPE
WHICH WAS SPONSORED AND FUNDED
BY ITS GOVERNMENT-IN-EXILE.

Megan's face suddenly animated as she remembered the promise they had made before their trip. "Bozenna! We have to take a picture of us here at the monument, for Bozenna." Megan explained to their translator, "Bozenna is one of our Polish-American friends. She helped make this monument possible."

As they stood together over the ZEGOTA stone, Mr. C. thought how this simple engraved tablet told an immense history. He wondered what, if anything was different about their efforts to tell a Holocaust story; there were so many, each told in a particular way, as if the spirits of the dead demanded of the living at least an archive. Was it their persistence or their innocence, or both? Maybe it was just the right time. He knew that history was fickle in that way, reaching certain tipping points, and it was hard to know exactly why. One thing was certain – in the flow of history no one knew the future; one had to carry the torch when it was handed to you.

CHAPTER 26

Stories

Warsaw, May 2001

Media attention was incessant that day: American reporters from CNN and the Associated Press, a German TV crew, and Polish journalists. That same morning the Kansas visitors met the Polish TV documentary film crew that would be shadowing them, director Micha Dudziewicz, his daughter Marta, and a sound technician.

Their first full performance of *Life in a Jar* was for the aging survivors, rescuers and those rescued, the Children of the Holocaust Association of Poland. They met every month since the fall of Communism at the Nozyk Synagogue. Built in the grand style of the 1880's, it was the only Warsaw synagogue to survive the war – remarkable, given its location inside the ghetto. (They later learned that it only survived because the SS had used it for a horse stable.) To accommodate the eight Americans, their Polish friends, several translators, the press, and the documentary film crew, the Association moved their meeting to the large banquet hall. This dwindling community of witnesses, mostly women, sat around a long table and greeted their guests from Kansas with applause and warm smiles.

The chairperson of the Association, Zofia Zaks, asked the survivors to please stand or raise their hand. One by one they introduced themselves, first twenty men and women who had been rescued as children, then seven older rescuers. After a brief silence, Liz started clapping, but quickly stopped, self-conscious, as if she had violated a social norm. One old man, who stood with effort, started to clap his gnarly arthritic hands and applause quickly spread to the entire room.

Zofia Zaks explained that their gatherings, in addition to keeping memory alive, celebrated miracles: that this synagogue survived the war, that they survived the Communists and lived to reach this day. She explained to their American visitors that the Association was founded in 1991 after the fall of Communism. "Incredibly, until just recently there has not been a Polish textbook about the Holocaust. We in the Association try to disseminate knowledge about Nazi crimes. Many heroic Poles are still hesitant about revealing their histories – the long shadow of Communism. Others have no idea that they were Jewish children saved by Poles and brought up as Christians. Our purpose is to consolidate memory and continue to condemn expressions of intolerance, particularly anti-Semitism, in public life. We also give monetary support to our members, particularly those who are infirm. Many of us are still looking for our lost relatives or some remnant of our extinguished lives. We are the last eyewitnesses and survivors of the Holocaust.

"Under Communism, this meeting would never have occurred. You would not have been invited to Poland. During those dark years rescue was considered taboo, off limits. After the war Irena Sendler, the hero you celebrate, was interrogated by the security police. She was considered a danger to the state – one of the most dangerous. Her children were denied educational opportunities and she was threatened with prosecution and incarceration.

"But it is not so simple as to merely blame the Communists for Poland's state of denial. Curiously, it has been more than ten years since democracy has returned to Poland and rescuers are still not publicly celebrated, because of another kind of occupation – our own shame. Anti-Semitism still stalks Poland. Some Poles collaborated with the Germans, some aided and abetted their barbarity. It is never easy to look at oneself in the mirror of history and see cowardice or brutality. Those who were brave, those who acted with integrity and decency, hold up another mirror for all Poles to gaze into.

"Your visit and the innocence of your message have come at a time ripe for healing and remembrance. Others have tried to do what you are doing, to no avail. Now we are hopeful again."

They performed *Life in a Jar* in street clothes, without props or stage sets. The kitchen loaned them a milk jar. Mr. C. made introductory comments phrase by phrase, pausing for the Polish translation. It was awkward and threw off the ease with which he normally introduced the project. As they prepared themselves on an imaginary stage which would soon become a theater of searing memories, he instructed the girls to, "Speak slowly – do everything slowly. Like a slow motion movie."

Though at first they were clumsy and out of synch, very soon hand-kerchiefs and tissues came out of worn gabardines and shapeless house-dresses. Megan clutched a tissue and dabbed at her eyes throughout the entire play. At the end, those who still could, slowly stood up from their seats, while others clapped from their wheelchairs.

When it was quiet again, one woman raised her hand. "What hap-pened to Irena's lists?"

It was a frequently asked question following their performances and one of many to which they still had no answer. Megan explained that this was part of their mission to Warsaw, to learn the fate of Irena's precious lists. They would ask Irena and also Hanna Piotrowska, who was a twelve-year-old girl during the war when her mother and Irena had buried the lists in her backyard at Lekarska #9.

The girls presented gifts to the Association – a framed and auto-graphed picture of them, and a large sunflower wall-hanging from Kansas. While cake, tea, and juice were served, Megan explained that the sunflower was the state flower of Kansas. After their presentation, time was allowed for interviews with the elderly members of the Association, many of whom, in preparation for this, carried bags with old photographs and mementoes from the war. Each of the girls sat in a different corner of the hall speaking individually, taking notes and making audio recordings.

"I was a partisan during the war," a wiry man in a wheelchair explained to Sabrina's tape recorder. "It was the most intense experience of my life. Our hopes were so high after the war, but right away the Communists came. As soon as the Russians occupied us, they labeled partisans as trai-tors – even fascists. Can you imagine – fascists? Membership in the Home Army was a crime punishable by years in a Soviet prison. So many Jews were Bolsheviks before the war that people blamed the Jews for Poland's Communist takeover. I had to lead a double life and deny that of which I was most proud. When my children were older, I didn't dare tell them about ZEGOTA or what I did.

"I remember so well the ZEGOTA trials a few years after the war. Many of our most celebrated heroes were imprisoned, sent to Siberia, even executed. Cardinal Stefan Wyszynski, the leader of Poland's church, was put under house arrest in a monastery in the south; it seems one of the nuns who worked with him was an agent for the Soviet security police."

Megan talked to a thin gentleman without hair, who could still hardly believe that a ZEGOTA memorial had been built. "Irena was at the memorial dedication in 1995," he said, "though she didn't speak. She was very small and humble. Poles who were ZEGOTA became 'enemies of the people.' They were barred from jobs and education. Nobody helped the Jews more than ZEGOTA, but after the war, membership in ZEGOTA became a label of criminality. Once again decency became criminal!"

Megan wrote a reminder to herself to ask Irena about how she suffered after the war for her ZEGOTA membership.

Liz spoke with a short white-haired woman. "I was in the city of Tarnow a year after the war ended. Mind you, young lady, it was a year after Hitler's defeat. I was one of many thousands of Polish Jews who survived the war by fleeing to the east – to the Soviet Union. We weren't treated well there, but at least we weren't murdered. When we were repatriated after the war we were not greeted with open arms. Our Jewish community – those few survivors – acquired a building in the center of town; it was on Goldhammera Street. It was our synagogue, our ritual bath – the mikvah – and our Jewish school. One day, out of the blue, the Polish Communist army ordered us to vacate the building. They posted a guard at the door; he danced, screamed and sang offensive Polish songs during our last morning prayer service. He and others mocked us as we prayed. Once again, we were afraid for our lives."

An old man, who until now had been a mute observer, walked tentatively forward and put an ancient identity card in front of Liz. "Look at this. It's my labor certificate – from the Regional Labor Office in Dabrowa Gornicza – certificate no. 102466, July 5, 1945 – issued to me when I returned to Poland after the war. Look here." He pointed a wizened finger. "This round stamp with the letter 'J' for Jew."

A woman in a wheelchair told Sabrina, "My synagogue, in Wlodawa, was seized and converted into a movie house to show political propaganda films."

Megan heard, "I tried to get back some furniture I gave to a neighbor before I fled Poland at the start of the war. She said it was now hers and she refused to even speak with me."

Another said to Sabrina, "There was a family that took in a Jewish baby and after the war they refused to give him back. They said he was their child now."

Liz's next interview was with a child survivor, Piotr Zysman Zettinger, who had come especially from Sweden to greet the students. Piotr was a slight, balding man, who hadn't spoken except to introduce himself, until the students dispersed into small groups.

"I want to tell you about the best bath I ever had."

Liz scribbled notes furiously to keep up with his memory of the war.

"I was only four years old when Irena rescued me, so my memory of that time is not very strong. It seems more like a recurrent nightmare than a clear memory of walking through the Warsaw sewer on a cold night in 1942. There is a girl, one of Irena's couriers from the ghetto, no more than a teenager, who holds my hand all the time. If she lets go I start to cry and there can be no crying in the sewer – the sound echoes. I want my mother. This young woman says I will see her again, but I don't believe her. We have to stay in the sewer all day to prevent capture. It's very cold and I am wet and shivering. Now, whenever I smell even the faintest odor of a sewer, I am immediately transported back to that foul, dark tunnel and then to Irena's hallway, waiting for her to open the door to her flat in the middle of the night when everyone is asleep. There are three other children with me, though I am the youngest. Irena puts us all in a bathtub and washes us with warm water. This moment I remember exactly. It is a most delicious moment – like being born all over again, into a loving world."

"And your mother?" Liz asked.

"I didn't know it then, but she was saved as well, and a long time later we reunited."

Liz thought of Piotr's warm bath and wondered what it must have been like to remember so precisely that glorious moment. Not that everything was all right after that, Piotr explained. It was not. But there was that moment of grace in the bathtub, something Liz, in her own life, still awaited. Liz thought of her own rescue. After her mother had fled, she was taken into state's custody by social workers who took her to a court building where everybody was busy. She clung to her tattered Raggedy Ann as she moved from one emergency placement shelter to a foster home and then, finally, into Grandpa Bill's custody in Mapleton. Maybe there were a lot of warm baths in between, but she didn't remember any of them, not like Piotr.

"What happened to your mother?" Liz asked.

"She gave me up to Irena's network. She thought she would never see me again. Can you imagine that? She told me later, when I was old enough to understand, that it was the only thing she could do to save me. I try to remember what it was like to say good-bye, but everything happened so quickly – and I was only four – there was not a lot of time to think about these things."

Beyond the particular horrors of it, Piotr's story bothered Liz because it was too much her own. Sometimes she wondered why she chose this project. There were other stories – other heroes. Why Irena Sendler?

Piotr stopped his narrative and looked askance at Liz. "Young lady, are you feeling all right?"

Liz sat up and nodded. "Yes. Yes, of course. I'm fine. So what was your family like – I mean before the war?"

"My parents knew Irena from before the war. From family stories I know that during the 1930's, during the great unemployment time in Poland, my father Jozef Zysman, a lawyer, helped Irena's social welfare office and he had a great friendship with her. They worked with Jewish social committees helping poor people in Warsaw to avoid eviction from their flats.

"I don't like to speak too much about the time of the war, because it is a bleeding wound. Others have described the activities of Irena Sendler very well. I will only say that I remember that Irena took care of me after my escape from the Warsaw ghetto through the sewer. She found me a place to hide. According to her she did what anybody would do, but, of course, that is not true.

"There is something I remember from after the war, something which very well characterizes the personality of Irena. One day in the spring of 1968 Irena invited me to her apartment on Na Rozdrozu Square, where she still lives today. It was a shameful time of anti-Semitism in Poland. Our Communist leader, a dreadful man named Wladyslaw Gomulka had just given an infamous anti-Jewish speech. Irena said to me, 'Piotr. I am in touch with my other helpers from the war, and if the situation gets worse we are ready to be active again. You and your family can count on us.' Obviously, those words meant a lot to me. For me, Irena is like a good fairy.

"A few years ago Irena wrote to me that her life is sad, especially after her son tragically died. I wrote back in condolence and said I hoped that what she had done during the war brought her satisfaction and calmness during these moments."

After Piotr, a small, slight man asked to have his picture taken with Liz. He said, "I was only six or seven when my family hid three Jews in the barn." Liz took notes. "We lived outside of Warsaw on a farm and in our barn we had horses. In one of the stalls we dug a hole really only big enough for one person, but three lived in it. We covered the hole with straw and at night we fed the horses and brought scraps from our table for the hiding Jews. I wasn't ever really afraid because I was too young to understand it all, but I do remember going to the barn several times during the day to talk with them and give them comfort. The Jews we hid were very scared – all the time. They lived in our barn for over a year, until the war was over. Because they lived in that hole without any movement, they could not walk when they were finally free to leave. I don't know where they came from or where they went, but I think about them every day. I'm not really a rescuer. It was my parents. They never explained why. It was not something one talked about. But here I am today – to tell you my story."

Just before noon, the girls were given a tour of the Nozyk Synagogue and invited to share the lunch that was offered every day to impoverished Jewish senior citizens. On the menu that day was cabbage soup, shredded beets, barley groats, and a patty made of chicken that still had many bones. The girls ate very little, but they talked non-stop with those sitting near them. What began as a quiet gathering of shy and frail seniors became a noisy and raucous free-for-all, each girl surrounded by survivors in animated conversation. Their hands gestured the universal language of enthusiasm, of urgency, of the quickening of blood that had languished too long. Zofia Zaks, beaming, ended the program by thanking their Kansas visitors for their important work. "I haven't seen this much excitement in years. Your visit has been such an inspiration. Sometimes years go by and no one seems to care what happened to us, and then young people like you come along. It's a blessing."

Megan felt the sadness of this – that for so many years these real heroes, these real survivors were unable or unwilling to tell their stories. Maybe it was right after all – maybe even necessary – for the three of them to pretend to be the heroes, to play the roles that the real heroes, the survivors, couldn't play. These Poles had suffered the absurdity of senseless fate – the randomness of who survived and who perished. She began to comprehend the anguish of having been rescued – distress that remained throughout each survivor's life – a debt that could never be repaid. She only hoped their simple play was a balm and not an irritant.

In the afternoon, the girls returned to their room and sprawled across the beds to write in their trip journals. Sabrina put out the "Do Not Disturb" sign. The clock radio played a Polish rock station.

Megan sighed. "Each story was so sad. After a while I couldn't take notes anymore; I just listened. But now I feel terrible – maybe those stories will be lost because I didn't write them down."

"It's so weird," Liz said. "Two of the people I interviewed on tape didn't want me to share their story with the media – they didn't want any publicity at all. They couldn't say why, just that it would not be good for them."

"Still, they all wanted to talk," Megan said. "It must make a person crazy to hold memories like this inside for so many years."

Sabrina said, "Everyone I talked to said, in one way or another, 'Perhaps you won't tell my story, but you must tell Irena's story. The world must never forget.'"

Megan leaned back against the bed's headboard, closed her eyes, and said, "My first interview today was with this old guy who had kind eyes. The first thing he told me was that he saw his parents shot to death. I thought those same kind eyes I was looking into had seen such horror. After that, every person I interviewed, I looked into their eyes and thought the same thing. It was hard to concentrate on their stories because their eyes were so ... I don't know ... disturbing."

Sabrina looked up from her writing. "I interviewed a journalist. She told me such personal things, I felt like I shouldn't be writing all of it down – like I was intruding on her privacy. I even asked her if it was OK to write down what she told me. She said to write it all. She said memories are what live on after you're dead. She talked really slowly to make sure I got it all down; she made sure every name was spelled correctly." Sabrina turned the pages of her notebook. "She said Irena had saved her as a child – took her out of the ghetto when she was six and brought her to an orphanage run by the nuns in this town – she spelled it for me – Turkowice. Irena had given her an illegal birth certificate, one from a dead Polish girl of her age, a girl she tried to become. Once she was nearly found out. The Nazis came to the orphanage quite often, sometimes once a week, to search for hiding Jews. This particular day a soldier demanded that she say her prayers and cross herself. She knew the Polish prayers and crossed herself correctly, but almost gave herself away when she said they were going to evening Mass. At that time the church service was only conducted in the morning, something every Catholic should have known."

They wrote in silence for a few minutes before Sabrina observed, "All these stories, all these survivors. Sometimes it's too much, you know what I mean? And to be here in Warsaw, with these people, in a synagogue that was in the ghetto – it's big."

"You know what's starting to bug me?" Liz said. "Having so many cameras and microphones shoved in my face. I mean, Irena is the hero, not us."

"Yeah," Megan said. "I know. At first it was exciting, but it's getting real old."

Sabrina nodded. "Yeah, it makes me feel really icky, too."

"Come on, ladies." Liz jumped off the bed. "Let's go complain – right now."

In the adjacent room that Mr. C. shared with his wife, Liz repeated their gripe about the media. He turned a chair around and sat backward on it, his chin propped. "First of all, there's something really important that you should just accept as true even if you don't believe it. The press considers you heroes, even though you haven't done anything nearly as courageous as Irena. Do you know the expression, 'If it bleeds, it leads?' Newspapers love human drama, whether it's gang violence, or crashed cars, or missing children, or *Life in a Jar* – it sells newspapers and TV ratings. You're Protestant girls from a little town in Kansas with no Jews, no people of color. If you were Jewish girls from well-to-do families in Kansas City or New York City this story wouldn't be nearly so appealing to the media. It's just the way the media operates. For better or worse, you three are interesting young ladies. Get used to it. Make it work for you. And besides, what you're doing *should* be celebrated."

"But Irena's story is so much more amazing," Liz said.

He nodded vigorously. "Your mission is to tell Irena's story, right? Sometimes you tell it with the play and sometimes you tell it through all those reporters asking the same questions over and over. By telling *your* story, the media tells Irena's story to the world. We shouldn't be angry with them; we should bake them chocolate chip cookies!"

He searched through his briefcase and took out a folder bulging with letters and e-mails. "I brought these along just in case you had a crisis of confidence. Maybe you should read them again – or keep a few in your pocket. They're all about you and the impact you have on people. Remember where this started? One little paragraph. And now – look what you girls have made happen."

Megan took a handful of e-mails and whispered to herself, "God moves in mysterious ways."

"Mr. C.?" Liz asked. "Tell me again, why do we have to wait three more days before we meet Irena?"

"It was Irena's decision, Liz. The itinerary Bieta gave me at the airport was from Irena herself. I'm sure she has good reasons. She may be 91 years old, but she still calls the shots."

"I can't wait that long."

"You've waited 18 months. You can wait another three days."

★ ★ ★ ★ ★ ★ ★ ★ ★ ★

That evening the Kansas visitors were invited to a dinner party in their honor at the apartment of Elzbieta Ficowska. On their way there, Renata told them how baby Bieta, one of Irena's 2,500 rescued children, was hidden in a carpenter's box, smuggled out of the ghetto in the middle of a load of bricks on a Polish bricklayer's truck. Before closing the lid on her sedated baby, the last time she would ever see her, Bieta's mother placed a silver spoon in the box, a spoon engraved with her name on one side and her date of birth on the other. They listened in reverential silence.

Elzbieta's spacious and tastefully furnished apartment was already crowded when they arrived. "Welcome to Poland," she said through a translator. "Please, call me Bieta. My friends call me Bieta."

In her high-ceilinged apartment hung drawings and a framed letter from Marc Chagall, who'd been a friend of her husband, Jerzy Ficowski. Ficowski, a celebrated poet, also displayed three etchings by the Jewish writer and illustrator Bruno Schulz, killed in the war, as well as a large oil portrait of his beloved Bieta as a younger woman. In honor of the girls' visit, he composed a poem and read it aloud. The girls cried openly at the tenderness of Bieta and Jerzy's expressions of care for them.

The Chief Rabbi of Poland, Michael Schudrich, had left the forensic excavation at Jedwabne, the site of the massacre of Jews in July 1941, to attend this dinner.

Atop one bookshelf a stuffed hawk stared down. There were several *menorahs*, Jewish candelabras, in the parlor. A handsome young serving man in a black waistcoat tinkled a dinner bell, and the dinner guests were individually seated around a huge oval dining room table.

Debra Stewart sat between Bieta and one of the translators. After the first toast, Bieta turned to her and said, "I understand that you, too, are a survivor."

"Yes," Debra Stewart blushed. "I suppose I am."

"Then you understand the special burden it imposes. It is a special knowledge that we share."

Liz asked Bieta questions about Irena, many of which Bieta could not answer. Then Liz asked, "Why do we have to wait so long before meeting Irena?"

"This I do not know," Bieta said. "She's very humble and probably considers herself the least important part of your visit. She doesn't consider herself a hero, only a decent person. I was only six months old, yet Irena says that I was the hero – the hero of my mother's heart. Irena says it is the parents and grandparents who are the heroes." As Bieta spoke of her deliverance, other conversation hushed, leaving only the clearing of throats and the gentle tinkle of glasses and silverware around the table. Bieta's cheeks had flushed. "So many of those Irena saved, especially those saved as very young children and babies, don't know that she was the one to whom they owe their lives. Many don't even know that they are Jewish. During the war no one talked about it – such information could cost the lives of a rescuer's entire family. They simply became the Catholic children of their foster parents. After the war, under Communism one did not admit to saving Jews. I myself did not discover that I was a rescued Jewish child until I was 17, when students at my high school began to call me a Jew. I didn't understand, so I asked my adoptive mother, Stanislawa Bussoldowa, the midwife who delivered me. After the war, when I was three and a half, she adopted me from the care of my war-time nanny, Olga. She called Irena, who came right away and told me my story."

Like an honor guard, the four servers stood behind Bieta's chair in respectful silence. "Today I tell you this history without shame, without fear. But it was not always so. Too many Poles have left memory buried. But there is a new feeling rising in Poland, and what you three girls have done is part of this awakening – a springtime. One day all Poles will understand how much they owe to Irena and Poles like her. My daughter knows, because Irena is for her like a grandmother. My daughter's two little boys know Irena because she visits often. One day they, too, will understand how much they owe to her." She stopped to clear her throat and wipe her eyes.

After rich desserts were cleared away, Bieta asked her guests to retire to the parlor. Once all were gathered there, she tapped a shiny knife on a wineglass for attention. She motioned for Liz, Megan, and Sabrina to come close to her. "You see that I have many important artworks and books in my home, all wonderful and dear to me." From behind her on a shelf she picked up something small enough to fit in one hand. "But this is my greatest treasure." She opened her hand to show her guests a small rectangular wooden box, dark blue, very old, very plain. "This is all I have of my parents. I have not a single photograph of my mother or father."

She opened the box and there, nestled in purple velvet, was Bieta's silver spoon engraved in script:

Elzbieta

She took the spoon from its setting and gave it to Sabrina, whose hand trembled as she turned the spoon over to Bieta's birth date:

5 January 1942

Sabrina passed the spoon to Megan, who already had tears in her eyes. Debra Stewart stood behind Megan, holding her shoulders.

Liz held it the longest, puzzling over this profound relic, and she figured there were so many pieces to memory, large and small, visible and invisible. Some people chose to think about them, chose to keep them close in their minds and hearts. Others tried to forget. But as she knew only too well, when something dreadful happens, try as one might, there is no forgetting.

CHAPTER 27

It is Just Below Your Feet
Warsaw, May 2001

Irena's itinerary now directed them to Auschwitz. They rode the high speed train from Warsaw to Crakow, then a bus to the concentration camp, and finally walked under a warm sun into the camp, holding each others' hands as they passed under the infamous gate – *Arbeit Macht Frei* (Labor Will Set You Free). Liz felt the gravel under foot, ominous crunching, no surroundings, no atmosphere, no substance, only Auschwitz. They passed the double cordon of barbed wired, once electrified.

"It was just a year ago," Megan whispered, "at the Holocaust Museum – we saw that picture of this gate and now we're under it. Gives me the chills."

Inside the first structure, a dreary office building, they saw the entrance to the gas chambers on their left. The walls were an archive of maps and photographs of SS guards selecting new Jewish arrivals – those for work, those for death. There were machine guns, newspapers with war coverage headlines, aerial photographs of the concentration camp, each image captioned in Polish, English, and Hebrew.

Again the crunch of gravel as they walked toward the second burnt-red brick building. Inside, they were led to the right in a single file down a corridor lit by the faint glow of daylight from each room. In the first, behind a glass panel, piles upon piles of hair – blond, brunette, gray, black – in clumps and braids. In the next room a stack of mattresses piled unevenly upon each other. One mattress, lumpy and stained, doubled over against the others as if it had a sick stomach, had been cut open to reveal hair oozing from the inside. The sign explained that the German guards filled their mattresses with human hair so they could sleep more comfortably. In the next room piles of suitcases with names, addresses, and place of resettlement; another was piled with prosthetic limbs, another with eyeglasses, the next with cooking utensils, pots and pans, and one last room filled with toys.

Outside again, their guide had them stop in front of a small, nondescript structure built into the ground with a tall chimney. This, she explained in heavily accented English, was the crematory. Piles of fresh-cut flowers had been placed upon the remains of the ovens.

A minivan drove them to the "ramp" where Jews were unloaded from cattle cars for selection – women with children, the elderly and crippled to the left, to the gas chambers – men and women fit to work to the right. The brown brick arched entrance through which the train entered the camp, gaped like a pitiless maw.

They had read the books, seen the diagrams, the photographs, knew of the cruel selection that occurred at the unloading platforms, but here was three-dimensional reality, buildings, barbed wire, artifacts. The girls drifted apart, each on her private journey through this factory of death. Megan wrapped her shawl tightly around her shoulders. Liz walked with her arms crossed, her head bowed. Sabrina tried to read every caption, tried to understand every word – her expression hard and unchanged.

Later, they were taken inside a reconstructed barracks, built to house up to 800 prisoners in layered sleeping bunks – each inmate granted a space so narrow as to bring claustrophobic terror to the most disciplined.

It was the layered sleeping bunks – sleeping shelves – tier upon tier – that finally broke Sabrina. She imagined abused, skeletal prisoners squeezed into such small spaces – how scared and uncertain they must have been, how humiliated – wondering if they would survive the night – wondering if the next day would be their last.

Sabrina too had once slept on a shelf and, though she hated to think about that, or the poverty her parents' divorce brought upon her family, the memories came anyway. Awful memories were like that; they came at you when you least expected them, when you could least resist their bullying. She was in 2nd grade, and they had to move into a tiny shack, so small that she had to sleep on a shelf with her sister, Sarah. Her parents had separated a year earlier, and her father and oldest brother had moved to Oklahoma. She stayed with her mother, three sisters, and one brother in Boise, Idaho, still living in a real house, until her tottering world fell apart.

Before that awful morning, her mother was working three jobs to pay the bills, and Sabrina saw very little of her. Every night she crept into her mother's bed to snuggle until the alarm took her again, before sunrise. The scent of her White Musk perfume lingered after her mother tip-toed out the sliding glass door from the bedroom to the porch. It was barely dawn when her mother's car hit black ice, spun around three times and crashed into a brick wall.

During her long rehabilitation, she couldn't work, and her diabetes was not well controlled. They lost their home and had to move into the shed behind Aunt Kathy's house. They tried to give their tiny home some dignity by calling it their "cabin," but it was no more than a spacious, insulated shed, just big enough to divide in two – one half with a recliner, love seat and bean-bag all squeezed together for someplace to eat and watch a small TV that ran off an extension cord from Aunt Kathy's house. Her Mom hung a sheet, behind which were their sleeping shelves. On the rare occasions when Sabrina visited with other children, she marveled at their lush bedrooms, stuffed animals, dolls, and soft, spacious beds. She never spoke of the "cabin," or the craziness, or the shame.

At the end of 2nd grade, when she felt she couldn't endure the degradation of her life anymore, her parents reunited and she moved again. This time it was the Army that relocated them – to Virginia – and, though not a happy home, by comparison it felt like deliverance. Every year or two after that, the Army moved the Coons family again, and, when asked, Sabrina couldn't say where home was.

She felt a cool draft, a tremor, a weakness in her legs. The memories choked at her throat, and try as she might to stop them, the tears poured down her cheeks anyway. She couldn't control her sobbing, and the edges of the room grew dark. Her head swam dizzily, and she crouched down to keep from fainting, her arms hugging her knees. Liz and Megan squatted beside her, their arms around her. Each held the other like frightened children. Sabrina buried her face in Liz's shoulder and wept from a place so well protected that only Auschwitz could crack it open.

Mr. C. felt a pang of guilt for the pain brought to these girls, young women just reaching an age when the finality of death could no longer be denied, when they began their lifelong struggle with unanswerable questions about their own mortality, about the arbitrary and cruel wantonness of life and death. Yes, he thought, this moment comes to everyone, but not so suddenly, and rarely with such singular, heart-wrenching drama and cruelty.

At the end of the day, as they waited on the train platform in Crakow, Megan said to Mr. C., "You know how Irena wrote to us that she feels like she should have saved more? I never did understand what she meant. I mean, she did so much, how could she have regrets? But I think I understand a little better now. She was an angel from heaven, and for each one she saved there must have been a hundred, or a thousand, she couldn't save. Of course it broke her heart."

★ ★ ★ ★ ★ ★ ★ ★ ★ ★

Irena's itinerary sent them to Treblinka the next day, a very different experience, though profound and disturbing in its own right. Warsaw's Jews weren't murdered at Auschwitz, but at Treblinka, the death camp 60 miles to the northeast. Instead of a tour guide, they were led by Renata Zajdman and Bieta's daughter, Ania. If Auschwitz was a museum, an historic preservation, meant to attract and inform the world's conscience, then Treblinka was an abstract memorial, a shrine of commemoration in the secret recess of a pine forest. There was no crematorium, no barbed wire, no physical remnant of the camp, which the Nazis destroyed before retreating. The girls followed a cobblestone path, past six memorial stones, each inscribed in a different language. The English stone explained that the Treblinka death camp was in operation from July 1942 to August 1943. During those 13 months 800,000 Jews were killed.

Other stone markers delineated the camp's boundaries. The girls passed through a symbolic entry gate, two granite slabs leaning towards each other like petrified guards. In place of Auschwitz's eerie silence, birds sang in the pines. They walked along a symbolic train track, a line of granite slabs, lined up like railroad ties, an invocation of the rail line that brought victims to the camp. The stone track ended at a cement loading platform. Two hours after the Jews arrived, they were dead.

They continued on silently, each in her own thoughts, until they stopped at an imposing monument – a 26-foot-high granite memorial stone sculpted to resemble a giant tombstone with a crack down the middle in which votive candles and flowers had been placed. Behind the tombstone was a huge circle of grass, a cremation pit and mass grave surrounded by a ring of 17,000 stones of different sizes and colors.

"Why 17,000 stones?" Liz asked.

Renata said, "It is the number of Jewish communities destroyed in the Holocaust. On 130 of the stones is the name of a village or town from which Jews were deported."

Megan wandered among the engraved memorial stones and suddenly stopped. "Here's Otwock – where Irena lived as a child."

They didn't notice the only stone to bear the name of a person, Janusz Korczak, the pediatrician, who died here. A few days later, Irena would tell them how she had come to know him and how she had witnessed his final march through the ghetto with the children of his orphanage to the *Umschlagplatz*, the train loading platform in Warsaw where the cattle cars for Treblinka were filled.

As they retraced their steps out on the cobblestone path, Liz noticed that Ania and Renata lingered behind, Ania weeping in Renata's arms. Their family's ashes were here, somewhere.

★ ★ ★ ★ ★ ★ ★ ★ ★ ★

The next day, Irena scheduled them for a walking tour of the ghetto guided by the preeminent historian and scholar of the Warsaw ghetto, Professor Jacek Leociak. Renata accompanied them on the tour, which began at the Jewish Historical Institute, a museum and research institution for the study and documentation of Jewish life, history, and culture in Poland.

Professor Leociak, a slight sage with boyish good looks wearing an open sports shirt and a backpack, called them to attention in the main exhibit hall of the Institute. With the exception of a bit of gray streaking his auburn hair, one would never suspect his elite academic stature. He spoke English with a lilting British accent, his hands articulating, emphasizing, beseeching. "To give you a sense of scale – try to imagine. There were 1800 streets in Warsaw – only 73 of them were in the ghetto. Three hundred and eighty thousand Jews – thirty percent of the population of Warsaw – were squeezed into two and a half percent of the area of Warsaw. In the ghetto eight people lived in each room.

"These are cold numbers – something of the mind. Soon we are going out into the actual streets. The ghetto will be just below your feet. You will see no remnant, very few signs marking it. If you didn't know, there would be nothing to indicate that you were in the Warsaw ghetto. Incredibly, there is no complete written Polish history of the Warsaw ghetto. Think about what this means. How could something so important in a nation's history be ignored? It is not forgotten. Every Pole knows. It is ignored."

Before embarking on their walking tour, Professor Leociak wanted them to watch Nazi film footage taken in the ghetto. As the black and white film began, he warned the students of graphic images and reminded them of who made this movie. "It is a film made by Germans in May 1942. People always forget the context – that the photos and films are made by Nazis. I would like to stress, it is very important to understand and see that this is not neutral, not objective photos. It is perverted. There is a kind of mocking and persecution, like looking at exotic animals when a hunter goes to remote places in the world and he has a camera and makes photos of different species. It is the same attitude as the Germans towards the Jews. We shouldn't forget about the perpetrators."

From his backpack he produced three maps that he had painstakingly constructed, showing every house in the Warsaw ghetto at three successive times, each perimeter smaller as the Germans strangled the ghetto. He pointed out the rare building that survived the war and the few commemorative plaques. The first was at the very start of their tour next to the Historical Institute, a small plaque marking the Great Tlomackie Synagogue, demolished by the Germans in May 1943 at the end of the Ghetto Uprising. "If you want to understand the ghetto," he explained, walking backwards to face the students, "you must understand that the ghetto is a place of really big contrasts. The population of the ghetto is divided in different levels. There are rich people, nouveau rich people who became rich through smuggling, and the people dying on the streets from starvation. Every Jew is condemned to the same fate, but before the deportations began they are living very different levels of life.

"We are now passing through one of the 22 access gates into the ghetto. The ghetto wall is built from the bricks of buildings destroyed during the German invasion and bombing in 1939. The Jews are made to build their own prison; the bricks and labor are Jewish; all expenses are paid by Jews. Eleven miles of wall topped with glass embedded in cement.

"The Nazis completely destroy the ghetto after the 1943 Uprising, but you must realize that the roots of the ghetto still exist beneath the ground. We walk like on a glass surface painted black. Below us is the real city. The ruins of the ghetto were never removed from this place, only shaped. It was technically impossible to remove the rubble. The whole settlement was built up after the war on the ruins of the ghetto, the ruins shaped into picturesque hills. And the buildings were built from the bricks of the ghetto. They picked up the bricks, melted them in special mills, and made so-called ash brick.

"Across from where we stand now was Leszno #2, the place of CENTOS where Irena frequently conspired with Ewa Rechtman, a Jewish social worker. It is also where the most well known café and cabaret in the ghetto was located – The Sztuka – the arts café."

Leociak pulled a thin book of photos from his backpack. "Here is a photograph of this street during the war. Today's street sign says Solidarity but in 1940 it was Leszno Street and only half the width of this boulevard. We are walking on top of Leszno Street, on top of the ghetto. There is no sign to announce this startling fact. If you could dig into the layers, you would find broken dishes, tin ware, spoons, human bones.

"Now imagine you are on Leszno Street." They followed Leociak through a covered entrance into the courtyard of a shabby tenement. In the middle of the courtyard of Leszno #13 Professor Leociak extended his arms in a wide circle. "This is one of the few buildings to have survived intact. It was to a building like this that Irena Sendler would come 60 years ago. We are in the same building, in the same courtyard where Irena comes. What is different is the smell – it was awful, and the crowding – there were people everywhere.

"Here you can see the whole structure of the tenement from before the war – a closed court with a gate, a microworld. In the ghetto are approximately 2,000 such microworlds, and in each a 'house committee' is chosen to represent the tenants of the building."

Megan raised her hand tentatively, and Professor Leociak nodded in her direction. "Irena wrote to us that many Jews wouldn't give up their children because they didn't believe the Germans would kill them. When did the Jews know that they would die?"

"This is a profound question. The first message about the mass killings in Eastern Poland, like Ponary, around Vilna, comes to Warsaw almost a year before the liquidation of the ghetto. But this news only reaches a very small circle of people in the ghetto. The Ringelblum archives tell us that in the autumn of 1941 some people believed this, especially those active in the Underground. In March 1942, when *Aktion Reinhard*, the murder of the Jews in the General Gouvernement, began, a lot of common people from the east sent letters through the post to their relatives and friends in the Warsaw ghetto with the message: 'They are killing us. Be careful. Take refuge, because they are killing us.'

"The people living in the ghetto receive these letters and they don't believe them; they say it's impossible. Maybe Germans can extinguish one little town, but Warsaw is the biggest ghetto in Europe. This cannot happen here. It's a typical psychological mechanism – a self-defense – or you may call it denial. And then the deportations begin.

"Our experience of death is so that the people from outside die, but we believe that we are exempt. We won't die. It is also important to understand how difficult it is for people to realize that the whole ghetto, almost 400,000 will be sent to death. It is unbelievable. There is no precedent – this has never happened before. I think it is impossible for people to realize this story."

"Why didn't more Jews try to escape?" Sabrina seemed baffled. "I mean, Professor Leociak, you said at first it was pretty easy to sneak out of the ghetto."

Leociak nodded vigorously. "It may sound strange and peculiar, but for many Jews it is safer in the ghetto. People would escape to the Aryan side only to sneak back because they cannot survive outside the ghetto more than one or two months. Not only because they have no money, but because they cannot stand the tension, the daily fear."

Megan said, "So you had to be rich to hide outside of the ghetto?"

Leociak smiled. "This is the miracle with Irena. She gives the chance of escaping to the poorest ones who have no chance to escape because they have no money and no acquaintance. She is a light – a spiritual light in the darkness. She establishes the whole structure – the links of friends and hiding places for the people who can never establish this by themselves. Irena doesn't help rich people in the ghetto. Rich people can manage by themselves, but the orphans from the poor families would certainly perish. Irena starts with the street orphans, the ones with nothing. She starts from the lowest level, the real helpless ones."

They passed the old courthouse, one of the many escape routes Irena and her liaisons used, its façade still pockmarked with bullet holes from the 1944 Uprising. Further along Leociak stopped in front of the Femina Theater, now a cinema, but during the war it was the Carnegie Hall of the ghetto. They waited to cross Solidarity Street, now a busy thoroughfare with four lanes of heavy traffic. "You must understand the sound of the ghetto," he said as they waited for the light. "Let's call it Leszno Street again, to help us remember. Here we are surrounded by cars and trucks, but in the ghetto there are no motor vehicles. The sound of a motor is a thing of danger. Only the Gestapo has cars, and if you hear them prowling, someone will die."

Several blocks on, at the intersection of two ordinary streets, Renata stopped to point out a manhole cover. "That is where I entered the sewer to escape," she said. A little farther down she pointed to a street corner and said, "There I rifled the pockets of a dead man, looking for bread."

Megan tried to imagine Renata as a 14-year-old girl, only a year younger than herself, and what it must be like for her to still carry those memories. "What did you do every day?" Megan asked.

"Books. I found books and would read them by daylight in a warehouse, sitting with corpses. Until the sewer, reading was my only escape."

By mid-afternoon their feet ached from walking on the hot asphalt, and they began to complain. "You should feel a little uncomfortable," Leociak said. "This is what it feels like to walk the streets of the ghetto in the summer. Remember, it is just below your feet."

They were in the northern part of the ghetto now, on tree-shaded streets that could be in any city. "I grew up in Communist Poland," Professor Leociak continued, "quite close to where we are now standing. I was born in 1957 and went to the Femina Theater, the cinema we just passed. I used to walk behind this building to high school and grammar school. My kindergarten is behind this house. When I was very young, while I was digging in the dirt near my apartment I found a fork and a broken cup from the ghetto and that sparked my interest in history and the ghetto. It has been my life's work. Everything I know about the war and the ghetto I learned under Communist rule, which is another strangeness.

"I lived near to where the Ringelblum Archive was discovered. After the war there were only hills of rubble, the level of the street always lower than the buildings, because the buildings were erected on the rubble. Here you find the smoked bricks. On that little square across the street, Nowolipie #68, is where the Ringelblum ghetto archive was hidden in the ground. Look – there is no commemoration or plaque. Pardon me, I don't understand it.

"Two close members of Ringelblum's group survived the war, Hersh Wasser and Rachela Auerbach. Hersh Wasser is a secretary to Ringelblum who knows exactly when and where the archives are buried during the liquidation action – August 3, 1942. Two unknown teenagers are told to carry ten iron boxes filled with papers into the basement of Nowolipie #68 and bury them underground. They are in a hurry because the whole area is being liquidated. They have not enough time to protect well these containers. That's why the containers, when they were discovered, are filled with water. Jewish teenagers who are active in the underground are responsible for protecting the material – they are the ones to bury the containers. But before burying them they write a few sentences, a Last Will and Testament, on a sheet of paper and put it inside the container. We discovered this.

"It is written just a few minutes before the digging. What do they ask for? Not for rescue of their lives. They realize that their lives are over. They ask a future generation to read this archive and remember it. They address it to you and me and everyone. These teenage Jewish boys in August 1942 write something for us – a plea to preserve the archive and read it again in the future peaceful world. The question is always, have we listened to the message?"

It seemed to Megan that in Warsaw everything important was buried in the earth – Irena's lists, Ringelblum's archives, the ghetto.

"When I look at you girls from Kansas," Leociak continued, "I think the legacy has been passed on."

They walked up another block to a ruined wall topped with barbed wire. A leafless tree sheathed in bronze, with many plaques attached to its metallic trunk, stood next to it.

"This is the remnant of the notorious Pawiak Prison. Erected by Russians in 1835, it is a prison for Polish patriots fighting against Czarist Russia, partisans like Irena's great-grandfather. Under the German occupation Pawiak becomes one of the cruelest prisons in Poland. When the Nazis flee they destroy everything but this remnant of Pawiak and that tree. I remember from my youth it was a living elm tree with leaves – the only living remnant of that time. Now it is artificial – bronzed. The plaques commemorate some of the prisoners killed."

He paused for a moment, considering their exhaustion after a long hot day. "Do you want to know how Irena escaped from Pawiak?" he asked.

It was as if an approaching electrical storm crackled the air. Liz gasped. The girls each took a step closer.

CHAPTER 28

Escape From Pawiak

Warsaw, May 2001

The sign at the entrance to The Pawiak Prison Museum warned that this was a disturbing place; children under 14 years would not be admitted. In all her letters, Irena seemed unwilling to speak of Pawiak. Mr. C. suggested to the girls that "Irena may not want to be reminded about Pawiak."

Professor Leociak had them wait in the courtyard outside the prison while he descended a cement ramp leading ominously to the museum's underground entrance.

The girls were tired, their feet ached, and the sun had given Sabrina a headache. Glad for the respite, they sat on a bench in the courtyard, waiting for their guide to return. Liz slipped off her sandals and massaged her bare feet. She pointed out the grass growing through cracks in the courtyard. "It always blows me away how grass cracks concrete."

Megan wore her worried smile. "I don't know if I'm more excited or scared."

Just then Professor Leociak walked back up the ramp accompanied by a raven-haired woman in a long dark dress. The silver chain holding her dark glasses glinted in the sun. Leociak cleared his throat. "Girls, this is a difficult place. If any of you would rather not ..."

"I want to know what happened here," Liz said. "I want to know how she escaped."

"This is Maria Wierzbicka," he said, "your Pawiak guide. She can give you a tour now. She can answer your questions. I will be saying goodbye and meet you again tomorrow for a tour of *Umschlagplatz*. I know this has been a long day and I'm sorry, but there is so much to tell and you are only here for a short time."

They followed their new guide down the ramp underground into a dim, stone-walled silence – a chill and damp waiting area, empty but for one museum guard. Before beginning the tour, Maria explained the hundred-year history of Pawiak Prison and how in 1965 the Communist government created the Pawiak Museum. She led them through a dark tunnel-like corridor that prisoners had walked, their footsteps magnified, echoing like jackboots, and invited them to sit in a reconstructed cell. "This is exactly the kind of cell Irena would have sat in for three months. It was intended for two prisoners but the Germans filled it with eight or ten." She closed the heavy wooden door, and they immediately felt the claustrophobia of the space. She pointed to a small hole in the door at eye level. Maria held open the door for them to leave, and in the corridor outside the cell she showed them the hole again, a little round peep hole cut in the door. "The *Juden* hole – the Jew hole. The SS guards – they were so cruel – they would put their pistol to the peep hole and randomly shoot into a crowded cell.

"Irena was tortured, and she fully expected to die here with her fellow prisoners." Maria led them down the corridor to a large room, whose only light, a sickly jaundiced glow, radiated eerily from display cases set into the walls that contained instruments of torture. Silhouetted, Maria opened an envelope and unfolded a letter, several typewritten pages. "I have been told that you still have not met with Irena." She raised her glasses to her eyes. "That must be a great frustration. Professor Leociak tells me that Irena prefers not to talk about Pawiak. It is too painful. But she dictated her experience, and Professor Leociak asked me to read it to you here in Pawiak.

"Please sit on these benches. They are original. On these very benches prisoners were made to sit, all facing the same way. Interrogators came up behind them and demanded they betray comrades on the outside. As each refused they were shot in the back of the head.

"Here is Irena's letter:

> *My Dear and Beloved Girls,*
>
> *I find it very difficult to talk about my experiences in Pawiak, so I will relate them to you by these notes. The two most chilling words for*

anyone to hear in Warsaw during the war were 'Pawiak' and 'Szucha #25' the Gestapo interrogation center. Prisoners like me, suspected of Underground activity, were either executed or died during torture. It's a miracle I survived."

Liz felt Irena drawing closer – alluring, baffling – her words a tantalizing intimation of her presence – a compounding of excitement and anxiety that she found familiar, disturbing, yet curiously intoxicating. Maria read Irena's description of her arrest on her Naming Day, October 20, 1943, of Basia and the laundry, of the shooting of a boy in the courtyard, of the beatings, the despair, the depravity. But it was more than a letter. Hearing Irena's story while seated in the dark Pawiak basement – in the very structure where that depravity unfolded – infused Irena's words with a fierce need for Liz's attention. It was horrible, but she had to hear it all. Maria continued:

There must have been 10 or 15 women selected to die with me that day. The German guards were rough and pushed us into the Pawiak truck. I remember one unexpected tenderness. A Polish guard who helped me was gentle. "Be careful," he said. "Don't hit your head. I'll pray for you."

Many executions were carried out at Szucha #25, so there was nothing unusual about my transfer there. I had no doubt that I would be shot that morning. Death would be a relief – less to fear than one more beating. I had not divulged any names or any details about our network or the children's lists. If I broke down, the entire Children's Division of ZEGOTA was at risk.

We were pushed off the lorry into the Szucha #25 entryway which gave no hint that it was a portal to hell. Inside the lobby as each woman's name was called again she was led through a door on the left. Then we heard a pistol shot. Some of the women began to cry. One fainted. When my name was called I was taken through another door, on the right. Oh God no, I thought, no more beatings. I wished I had a cyanide capsule.

A German SS officer, an SS Untersturmführer pushed me into the room where I fell onto my knees, my legs still throbbing from previous beatings, swollen so tightly I thought my skin would burst. A German guard stood at the door, my suffering nothing to him.

The officer dismissed the guard. My heart sank. I could not endure another moment of pain. He lifted me from the floor and helped me across the room. He unlocked another door that led into an alleyway. I remember feeling the chill of a crisp January morning. I had not seen the sun for 100 days, and when it came out from behind a cloud it blinded me. I stumbled and the Untersturmführer gripped me hard under the arm, lifting me without regard for my pain. He led me across Aleja Ujazdowska, past Park Ujazdowska, where Mother and I once had a picnic by a pond. The German hurried me along, my legs burning with pain. I was confused. He turned me around a corner, onto quiet Wiejskiej Street, where he released his brutal grip on my arm and I almost fell. Then he said, in Polish, "You are free. Get out of here as fast as you can."

I must have been in shock because I leaned against a street lamp thinking I was dreaming or maybe already dead. The officer shook me by the shoulders. "Don't you understand? Get out of here."

I could only wonder if he was real. His breath came quickly, agitated. He turned and began to walk away. "I need my Kennkarte," I said as resolutely as I could.

He looked back, dumfounded. I felt my strength return and insisted. "Give me my Kennkarte!"

He marched up close to me and I saw his apprehension turn savage. He slapped me hard across the face with his black gloved hand and now I fell to the ground, tasting blood. He walked away.

I pulled myself up against the lamp post and looked around me at a deserted street. I limped into a pharmacy a few doors away. Fortunately, there were no patrons at the time, because I still wore the gray with black stripes of Pawiak Prison clothing. The pharmacist, a young woman, looked up from her counter. I will never forget her look of shock that made me realize how awful I must have looked. She led me to the back of the store without asking a question.

In the back room, behind a curtain, she said, "My name is Helena." She gave me a glass of water and some drops of medicine to calm me down.

Slowly, I felt myself waking from an interminable nightmare. "I'm Irena," I said automatically.

Helena combed my knotted, wild hair as best she could, then put generous dabs of cologne on my face and neck, on my arms and stomach. It stung too much for my legs. Helena never said anything about how badly I smelled. She gave me old clothing to change into, a cane to help me walk and money for the tram. I rested there for an hour, and then took the #5 home.

My heart still galloped in my chest. Luckily I found a seat on the tram, exhausted, my legs on fire, my mind confused. I stared out the window, the rocking tram relaxing me, the normality of life returning. Like a lost child, I thought of nothing but finding my way home.

At the next stop a boy selling newspapers suddenly jumped onto the tram. "Everybody, jump out! There's Gestapo arresting people at the next street." I had no papers, no Kennkarte, nothing to keep from being arrested again.

People began to jump off while the tram still moved. A gentleman helped me; he held my hand, but I fell anyway onto my hands and knees, which split open and bled.

Somehow I managed to get on another tram and finally dragged myself home. When Mother opened the door I couldn't say who was the happier; we fell into each other's arms crying and laughing.

I was so exhausted and confused that I fell asleep in my bed without noticing how sickly Mother had become while I was in Pawiak.

I later learned that it was ZEGOTA that had bribed the SS Untersturmführer for my release. I also learned that he was arrested a few weeks later and executed. It was one of the largest bribes ZEGOTA ever paid. I think my friends in ZEGOTA must have liked me very much to do this. The next day my name appeared on the red posters announcing those executed the day before.

My dearly beloved girls — we will meet in person very soon. I wanted you to know about Pawiak before we meet, so I would not have to speak with you about that part of my history and that of others who suffered a worse fate. Your efforts are the best hope for the world that these horrors should not happen again. I, of course, mean all this for your teacher, Professor Norman, as well and send my good wishes to your parents as well.

Devoted/loving,
Jolanta – Irena

★　★　★　★　★　★　★　★　★　★

The tour ended in a museum hall, dimly lit like the rest of Pawiak, each glowing display case of artifacts and photographs an island of light in a dark sea. There were final letters from prisoners to their loved ones before execution, secret notes – *grypys* – smuggled out of the prison, chess pieces made of moldy bread. An inmate painted watercolors of her cell signed by all 18 inmates who had shared the space, none of whom survived. Liz, Sabrina, and Megan stood together before one particular glass case that displayed a pair of blue embroidered booties made for an infant born in Pawiak.

In the belly of Pawiak, Liz felt incomprehensively small, crushed by its weight, entangled in the complexity of history, overwhelmed and discouraged. Comparisons paled: their simple play and Poland's tragic history, her own painful memories and those of survivors, American teenagers in the new millennium and Poles still mired in the last. How could she ever hope to understand, let alone encourage the Polish people to remember, their painful past? They'd already presented the play 40 times; they'd probably have to perform it 200 times, or 2,000 times before the whole world knew about Irena.

Liz felt in her pocket for the e-mails from people who had seen *Life in a Jar*. She resolved that Pawiak would not crush her, as it had not crushed Irena. Furthermore, she resolved that at each subsequent performance, when she played Irena, she would remember Pawiak; she would feel its cold heaviness, its cramped silence, she would think of those small blue booties. And she would transform this abomination into inspiration and strength.

CHAPTER 29

"You Rescued the Rescuer"

Warsaw, May 2001

The following day they completed their tour of the ghetto with Professor Leociak, visiting the *Umschlagplatz* memorial, a rectangular area smaller than a tennis court, enclosed by four marble walls on which are inscribed, in alphabetical order, the names of Jews murdered in Treblinka. *Anna, Aron, Avram,* and hundreds more. He showed them 60-year-old photographs taken by the Germans of the exact spot where they now stood, a massive holding area filled with Jews awaiting transport to Treblinka. Afterwards, Leociak took them to meet a prominent Polish writer, Michael Glowinski, who had been rescued by Irena as an 8-year-old boy. His memoir, *The Black Seasons,* had just been published.

Professor Glowinski greeted them warmly in Polish at the door, and Leociak, who would be their translator, introduced him to the girls as a distinguished professor of literature at the Polish Academy of Sciences and a well-known author. "Professor Glowinski's latest book, which I recommend heartily to you, is a wartime memoir, *The Black Seasons.* It was very well received in Poland and is to be translated into English soon."

Professor Glowinski's study had the musty scent of old books and scholarly journals, hundreds of which covered three walls from ceiling to floor. Professor Leociak gathered the girls at a round table on which he spread the same ghetto maps he had shown them the day before on their tour.

Glowinski, slightly hunched over and bookish, his silver hair thinning and disordered, began in Polish. "I thought I would explain about my rescue first, then we can share some sweet cakes and tea. I am one of many people who owe everything to Irena Sendler, having been rescued by her from the ghetto when I was eight. She also saved my mother and father and my cousin Piotr Zettinger, who fled through the sewer. I understand you've talked with him already. That is good.

"As a boy I looked very Jewish – what in those days we called having 'bad looks' – and so I was hidden in a convent, one of many which helped Irena and ZEGOTA place children."

Professor Glowinski recounted his hair-raising history of fleeing from one hiding place to another, of despair and betrayal, a bizarre chess game with a blackmailer (worthy of Fellini or Bergman), and other close escapes. As Professor Leociak translated, he moved his finger across a map of the ghetto following Glowinski's flight, first in the ghetto, then onto the bigger map of Warsaw to point out his hiding places, and finally a map of Poland to help them understand his journey to the convent at Turkowice, his ultimate sanctuary.

"I was nine years old and I assumed my mother was dead. One day the orphans of Turkowice are invited to visit with a wealthy patron – a compassionate gesture. I am sitting on the philanthropist's Persian carpet with the other orphans and we are served sweet cakes by his maids. In a shocking moment, I recognize one of the maids as my mother. At the same moment she recognizes me, but we cannot acknowledge each other. She serves me a sweet cake, then moves on to the next boy."

At the conclusion of their visit, as Professor Glowinski was saying good-bye, he abruptly stopped – then said something that would be repeated over and over. "Irena rescued me and many others." His voice sounded husky, teary. "That was a long time ago – and almost forgotten. Now you girls – you are the rescuers; you are rescuing Irena's story for the world." A profound silence hung in the room. "You rescued the rescuer."

★   ★   ★   ★   ★   ★   ★   ★   ★   ★

There was one more person to visit before Irena, one more pilgrimage, one more piece of the puzzle – Hanna, whose mother, Jaga Piotrowska, had helped Irena bury the lists of names under her apple tree. Surely she would know what became of the lists. Amazingly, Hanna still lived in the same house, and the girls approached Lekarska #9 full of anticipation.

Hanna Piotrowska-Rechowiczowa, a thin, stately woman, waited at the top of the concrete steps. She stood out against the gray building in her twilight blue gown, shoulder-length, straight brown hair, a bright red scarf over her shoulders, hands together, fingertip to fingertip. The façade of Lekarska #9 differed from the others – pockmarked with randomly distributed holes, each one accentuated by a dollop of cement.

"What's with the holes?" Megan whispered to Sabrina as they mounted the steps. She admired Hanna's sculptural necklace of three silver clamshells reflecting light onto her delicate features. Megan figured that if Hanna was twelve when the jars were buried, she'd be almost seventy.

Hanna smiled shyly and said in practiced but awkward English, "Irena's girls from Kansas." She noted their curiosity about her pocked wall and said, "Machine-gun bullets." She continued in Polish, "From the 1944 Uprising. Lekarska Street was one of the few blocks in all of Warsaw to be left standing. These bullet holes are memorials. My neighbors didn't want reminders – and I understand completely – they plastered over the holes. We did just the opposite. My husband is an artist."

She invited them and the documentary film crew to come inside to share apple cider and cookies from the dining-room table. In many ways #9 was an unusual house. A live tree grew in the stairwell, and the walls were covered with Hanna's husband's paintings including a startling *Trompe d'oeil* wall painting of a grand winding staircase under a jeweled chandelier, curving up the parlor wall and disappearing into the corner of the ceiling. Painted grape vines grew on the walls.

As she had in Pawiak, Megan felt the immensity of being in this very house where Irena and Jaga Piotrowska had regularly hidden children and buried the lists. "I was 12 years old," Hanna explained. "I was not supposed to see. But one night, very late, I woke up and went to the window. I saw the shadows of my mother and Irena cast by a small lamp, digging beside our apple tree, burying the jars."

Megan didn't want apple cider – she wanted the apple tree. Where was the tree? Why didn't Hanna take them to see it immediately? She wanted the lists. Surely Hanna knew all about the lists – how absolutely vital they were. Through the back window Megan saw thick shrubbery in an overgrown garden. Which was the apple tree?

Hanna revealed a startling new detail. "Across Lekarska Street, across from this very house, was an SS barracks. My job was to ring a small bell if any suspicious person came near the door or if SS soldiers from the barracks came too near. I remember Irena." She looked up into distant memory. "She was young and beautiful – always alone, unless she came with a child. Always she came through the back – through the alley. Irena was very determined and always in a hurry."

Hanna told them about her mother, Jaga, and lamented her death in 1988, just one year too soon to see Poland free at last. She excused herself and rummaged in the back of a closet in the next room. She returned with a leather-bound citation and a hinged wooden block in which was set a silver medal.

"*Yad Vashem*," she said. "And here is a picture of my mother from that time. She was quite avant-garde – quite beautiful."

"You must have been scared," Megan said. "How did you get through each day? Did you pray a lot?"

"After awhile, being afraid feels ordinary. One doesn't know anything else."

Liz couldn't restrain herself. "What happened to the lists?"

Hanna shook her head. "After the war Irena came and dug up the jars and put all the lists together."

"And... And ... what happened?"

"The Communists came and no one spoke of the lists again, at least not to me."

"What about the apple tree?" Sabrina asked.

Hanna's smile returned. "That I can show you. Follow me. We'll go the long way around – the way my mother and Irena did it in those days." She pointed across the street. "Because of the SS barracks they did all their secret work out back, from the alley."

At the end of Lekarska Street they turned left and then left again into a narrow passage that bisected the block, behind the houses, lined with tiny backyard gardens. As they walked down the alley, Hanna pointed to one house. "They hid three Jewish children," then pointed to the next house. "They hid four children."

She stopped at the gate marked with a faded #9 and invited them into the overgrown plot. "On Lekarska Street we hid 40 or 50 children." Her expression darkened with memory. "The little ones were the most difficult. Some would cry. The older ones knew to keep still." She smiled impishly. "It's amazing, but true – the Germans never arrested a single person on this street."

She led them through the dense foliage to the tree, overgrown, its trunk gnarled and leaning. "Every year it still produces a few apples," she said, stroking the wrinkled bark. She closed her eyes for a moment. "They were milk jars, usually two or three of them."

The girls knelt by the tree, their fingers raking the loose dirt. Liz traced a heart.

Mr. C. stood beside the tree, holding a low limb. "*Yad Vashem* is Hebrew for 'memory of a name.'" A warm wind blew up the alley and rustled the tree's leaves. "This is holy ground."

Liz thought he had a way of saying things that would sound pompous or weird if an ordinary person said them, but he had been a teacher for so long that it sounded natural and important.

No one spoke, no one moved for long moments, and then Liz asked, "What exactly did the jars look like?"

Hanna tried to explain in Polish then interrupted herself. "Come." She motioned for them to follow her. "Let's go back inside." In the room with the painted staircase to nowhere, Hanna opened an armoire and searched on a crowded shelf until she found an empty milk bottle; she held it up for the girls to see. "This is not an original. Those are all gone. But it is from that time period, very similar." She put it in Liz's hands. "A small gift for you. Use it in your play. Show the world what Irena and my mother did."

CHAPTER 30

Hearts and Sunflowers

Warsaw, May 2001

Irena shared a small apartment with her daughter-in-law, her grand-daughter Agnes, and a small dog in a modest building on a quiet street in Warsaw. Eight Kansans arrived in two Polski Fiats that had to double park beside the USA *Today* press van, the documentary film crew's panel truck, and several cars with press passes that allowed them to park illegally.

Sabrina had not fully recovered from her sleepless transatlantic flight, and every night since she had slept poorly. She was further agitated by Auschwitz and now worried about the strangeness of finally meeting Irena. Maybe Irena would be disappointed. It stirred up familiar anxieties of moving from town to town – suffering the antithetical fears of attachment and rejection. Yet, in those sleepless hours, Sabrina also tasted the sweetness of anticipation that kept her motivated and upbeat.

Megan held her mother's hand as they left the cars, and Debra Stewart confessed that she was as nervous as a jackrabbit. Megan's anxiety was buoyed by expectancy, her disquietude diminished in the sure knowledge that not only her mother, but Jesus walked beside her. Though still bewildered, she was grateful to have been chosen for this amazing experience, one that endowed her with a responsibility, an obligation she felt proud and willing to carry.

Liz felt excitement and terror, and wondered, how could two such discordant feelings inhabit her simultaneously?

The documentary film director, Micha Dudziewicz, asked the Kansans to wait while they replaced a blown light so they could film them again arriving for their first meeting with Irena. The girls readily agreed to this staging of reality, which caused Mr. C. to wonder: could something staged be as true – or truer – than what it was re-enacting? *Life in a Jar* was a simple, naïve, fictionalized account of Irena's true story. They fully expected to perform their play for Irena herself, and his persistent worry was that she would be disappointed; she had already written to them about errors in their script. His preeminent fear was that Irena would be dismayed with them for tampering with her story. And who could argue – it was, after all, her story. Yet, he knew that if history is not told in a manner that engages interest, particularly youngsters', then for most people it's as though it never happened. He had no doubt Irena would like the girls, but would she like their play?

A stern Social Welfare nurse stood sentry-like at the doorway to Irena's apartment, gesticulating stridently at the press to wait there in the hallway – no, they could not come in. She turned her steely eyes on the girls and rattled at them in Polish. Even their translator recoiled from her words. "The nurse is concerned," he explained. "She says Irena has been ill. Her blood pressure is high and her diabetes is not doing well. She tires easily. She may only be able to speak with you for 15 or 20 minutes, then you must leave. She's quite frail." The nurse motioned for them to follow her. She opened the door and pointed to the tiny bathroom at the end of a short hall in the apartment. "Wash your hands first. You must not stay long."

Irena's friends and family crowded the small apartment chattering as if at a reunion. When the girls walked in, conversation ceased; the attention of 20 people focused on them. Someone called out a question in Polish, and suddenly they were barraged with greetings, questions, and photographs. The nurse cut a narrow swath for them to follow through the room. Megan smiled nervously and repeated the one Polish greeting she knew. "Dzien dobry (Good morning). Dzien dobry." She coveted Mr. C.'s ability to remain relaxed yet proper with strangers, his smile generous and genuine. Another translator, Ludwik Stawowy introduced the girls to Irena's daughter, Janka, a dark-haired, middle-aged woman.

"You are how many years?" the nurse asked Megan.

She pulled back her shoulders and lifted her chin. "I'm 16."

"That's nice." The nurse's expression hard, impenetrable.

Megan followed Liz down a short hallway to the lavatory, past a not quite closed bedroom door. Sabrina was the first to see her; she called to Liz and Megan but hesitated, because of nerves. They bunched together, peeking through the doorway, and Liz gently pushed it open. There was Irena, less than five feet tall, standing behind her chrome walker, smiling, her coal-dark eyes surprised. She wore a black dress and a black headband across her pure white hair. Irena's smile turned puckish, the tip of her tongue flicking across her lips. Liz began to clap, then Megan and Sabrina, right behind her, and like pond ripples their applause spread into the living room. Was it for Irena? For the Kansas girls? For the moment? Irena motioned with one hand – come to me. And they did so, cautiously, for Megan thought her frail as crystal. Irena looped her arm around Megan and pulled her cheek down to her own. Liz and Sabrina stood by Irena's walker, Liz's hand covering her mouth, shocked to be there. Tears streaked Megan's cheeks. Abruptly, the applause stopped, as if only silence was suitable for this moment.

Janka broke the spell by coming into the room to help her mother sit again, with obvious discomfort, and smoothed a cotton blanket over her lap. A small excited dog of no particular breed suddenly appeared, licked Irena's hand, then scampered off again.

The girls sat on the carpet around Irena's feet in a semicircle.

Mr. C. stood behind the girls. Irena summoned him with the slow wave of her arm. There were tears in his eyes when he knelt beside Irena's chair.

"Professor Norman." Irena held his face in her hands and looked into his eyes. Her smile was completely radiant, and tears ran down the cracks in her cheeks. "Professor Norman," she said again, then thanked him in Polish. "Dzienkuje. Dzienkuje."

Debra Stewart came next. Irena looked from Debra to Megan and back. "Mamma-Megan. Mamma-Megan," she said, and they embraced. From that day on, Debra Stewart was known in Poland as "Mamma-Megan," a nickname of high honor that she proudly took home to Kansas.

Each in turn, Karen, then Liz's grandparents, Bill and Phyllis Cambers, warmly greeted Irena, whose face delighted anew with each introduction.

Liz burbled with child-like excitement, "We brought you presents."

Sabrina opened a package and unfolded a huge pink paper heart signed by the students of Uniontown High School. Megan presented Irena with a vase of flowers, and she and Liz held up a wall hanging of sunflowers. Irena instructed it be put where she could see it. On her bedstand she directed their attention to the photograph of her "Kansas Girls."

She pointed to the wall hanging. "You know the sunflower has great meaning for me and those of my age. The 1944 Uprising against the Germans began on the first day of August, 'Sunflower Day.' I have such sweet memories of pre-war days when many of the sunflowers were taller than me." She laughed, and each one in that small room heard the irrepressible joy of a younger woman's happiness.

"Thank you for your gifts – but most of all for your visit. I have so much to tell you." She put on a heavy pair of glasses and picked up handwritten papers from the table beside her chair. Irena looked up and smiled again at the girls; her restless eyes magnified by thick glass. The Social Welfare nurse leaned down and whispered in her ear, but Irena shooed her away with a smile and a flick of her hand, and began her prepared remarks. She had to slow down for the translator.

She wanted the girls to know the names of all the heroes; there were so many who should never be forgotten. During the 1944 Uprising, she acted as a nurse in a makeshift hospital while fighting raged around her and Warsaw was systematically destroyed by the Germans. She and Stefan worked side by side with courageous physicians like Dr. Henryk Palester and a woman, Dr. Skokowskiej-Rudolf, a pediatrician who specialized in children's tuberculosis. Neither had much experience with trauma, yet they performed surgery daily. Did the girls know that she was on the Gestapo's most wanted list? She told of how she was stabbed by a deranged German deserter and the wound became infected and she nearly died.

Her vigor only increased as she told her stories. Finally, she paused and removed her glasses. "Maybe I should stop now. And besides, I too, have gifts to give."

From a bag at her feet, she presented each girl with a necklace – a silver heart on a chain. Still smiling though her voice choked with emotion, she explained, "I give to each of you a piece of my heart."

Megan said, "You've already done that, for almost two years."

A camera flashed to capture each girl securing her heart around her neck.

"Before I give you more of my speech, I want to know if there is some important question that burns inside you."

Megan immediately asked, "Why did you do it? I mean, why did you risk your life to save Jewish children? And how hard was it for the mothers to give their kids to you? We want to know how you rescued the children. What happened to the lists? And how ever did you..."

Irena laughed and held up her hand to stop Megan. "I'm too old to keep up with you. But let me first say that I had many helpers, and I want you to know about all of them. The world should never forget them. First and foremost were my 'moi lacznicy' – my liaison officers, all Christian social workers – nine women and one man. You know about Jaga Piotrowska and you have met her daughter, Hanna. She hid more than a dozen children in her house at Lekarska #9. You also know of Irena Schultz – the 'other Irena' – whom you have called Marie in your play. She was a dear friend and one of the smartest people I have ever known. There was Izabella Kuczkowska, who helped me with the very first rescues through the courthouse. Janina Grabowska hid many children and partisans in her apartment. There was Wanda Drozdowska, Zofia Patecka, Lucyna Franciszkiewics, Roza Zawacka, Maria Roszkowska, and the only man, Wincenty Ferster. Let me not forget Jan Dobraczynski, my supervisor at the Social Welfare office, who used his connections to allow and assist our forgeries and larcenies. Some of these heroic Poles we lost, and I still grieve for them. Before the war, Jadwiga Deneka placed orphans with surrogate families. During the war her apartment, Obozowa #76, in the Kolo district, was an emergency care home and underground press distribution point. In 1943, just a month after I was arrested, she was apprehended by the Gestapo. They tortured her, but she gave up nothing before she was executed." Irena had to stop and wipe at her eyes with a small embroidered handkerchief.

She sighed deeply as she collected herself again. "Your first question – why have I done this – I have answered many times. It was a need of my heart. After the German invasion, Poland was drowning in a sea of tragedy and brutality. And of all the Poles, the Jews were the most in need of aid and the least able to care for themselves or their children."

"What about the lists? What happened to the lists?"

Irena smiled and closed her eyes, transported again to another time. "After the war ended, every day I am thinking about the jars waiting to be unearthed and their precious tissue paper lists. I had promised all those mothers and fathers and grandparents. It was the only guarantee I could give them.

"You've met Hanna, Jaga's daughter, and you've seen the apple tree. During the war we buried the jars late at night. That first spring after the war, Jaga and I got down on our knees in full daylight, and dug into the soil for the last time to retrieve the jars. We used large spoons and our hands to dig up the earth. I remember how the dirt smelled, so rich and full of the promise of peace. My shoes and dress became completely soiled. After three years of secretive nighttime burying and unearthing, I still instinctively worried that the neighbors would see. Jaga did not want Hanna to know about the jars, but I know that she did.

"That remarkable day in the spring of 1945, digging in the daytime, it felt strange and wonderful and different, though not altogether happy. During the war we added new names and buried the jars again. But this time was different. As long as the jars were buried we didn't have to admit to ourselves that all the children's parents were dead. I think memory is like that – we bury it to keep from hurting, but always it needs to be dug up. Jaga and I, we hoped nothing more would disturb the childrens' broken lives.

"One of the bottles had broken, those lists damaged beyond reading, but from the others we were able to make a crude accounting." Irena put on her thick spectacles and resumed reading from her notes.

"About 500 children placed in monasteries (Jan Dobraczynski and Jadwiga Piotrowska)

About 200 children placed in the house of Father Boduen (Maria Krasnodebska and Stanislawa Zybertowna)

About 500 children placed with RGO (Polish Council for Care), the main board of care (Aleksandra Dargielowa)

About 100 teenagers, youths of 15-16 years old, directed to the forest to join the partisans (Andrzej Klimowicz, Jadwiga Koszutska, Jadwiga Bilwin, and Julian Grobelny)

About 1200 children placed with foster families. (Helena Grobelna, wife of Julian Grobelny, Maria Palester and her daughter Malgorzata Palester, Stanislaw Papuzinski, Zofia Wedrychowska, Izabella Kuczkowska and her mother Kazimiera Trzaskalska, Maria Kukulska, Maria Drozdowska-Rogowiczowa, Wincenty Ferster, Janina Grabowska, Joanna Waldowa, Jadwiga Bilwin, Jadwiga Koszutska, Irena Schultz, Lucyna Franciszkiewicz and Helena Maluszynska.)

"Many children were already hiding outside the ghetto, and we aided them with food, money, and papers. With all our other worries after the war, the chaos, the displaced persons, the refugees returning home, I couldn't imagine how I would track down more than 2,500 children and their relatives. Warsaw had been destroyed. Ninety-five percent of Warsaw's population was displaced refugees. The addresses on the buried lists were useless – it was impossible, but I felt the obligation of my promise.

"Others of my network and I began trying to locate the children, but the chaos was extreme. Poland was full of orphans. Those hidden in convents or orphanages we could find, but because their parents were dead we needed to locate surviving relatives – an almost impossible task. I was not surprised that the Soviet government had no interest and offered no help. We now began to realize the unanticipated implications of finding living relatives. There would be more trauma, especially for the younger children. They would be taken from the only family they had ever known and returned to a surviving, often distant relative. But it had to be done. Otherwise, they would never know their real names, their parents, or even that they are Jewish.

"After more than a year of trying, I spoke with Adolf Berman, president of the Central Committee of Polish Jews about my frustration. The lists were written on very thin tissue paper, and my biggest fear was that they would deteriorate to the point of being unreadable.

"By this time my little Janka was born – March 31, 1947. I named her in honor of my mother Janina, who died during the war. With all the extra burdens of motherhood I knew I could never locate the children on my lists. With a heavy heart, I gave the lists to Berman, who promised to do his best to reunite families.

"Berman left Poland to go to Israel a few years later and took the lists with him – or copies of the lists. He lived on a Kibbutz with Polish survivors – the Ghetto Fighters' Kibbutz. I'm sorry to say that I don't know what happened after that."

Irena was quiet for a few moments. "I have many regrets, but my biggest failure is that I didn't do more – that I couldn't save more children, that I couldn't find them after the war. I often have nightmares of the children crying when I take them from their parents. And I remember those I left behind. I'm very old now. I can see very clearly my failures."

Irena stopped and drew a sighing breath. "Many remembrances trouble me, still weigh heavily on my heart all these years later. I will tell you now something that you cannot believe, but it is true. Once, in the ghetto, I saw a mother throw her baby over the wall. Can you imagine?"

Liz and Sabrina scribbled notes, but Megan put down her pen and met Irena's eyes. This old woman's honesty and humility pierced the armor of formality between the ages, and Megan felt juices of goodness rise inside her. Irena was so real, so normal, so one of us.

Irena took a sip of water, cleared her throat, and continued for almost an hour. She explained about the repressive post-war years under Communism, and her voice turned heavy with anger as well as sadness. She had to be discrete about her wartime activities. Her children knew very little until 1965 when she was awarded the *Yad Vashem* medal. Janka, who was 17, had just been admitted to Warsaw University and was suddenly informed that her acceptance had been revoked. Two years later, her son Adam faced the same discrimination. It broke her heart that her children should suffer for her decency.

Irena's vigor rebounded when she reached the end of her remarks – comments about the recurrence of hatred and intolerance and the numerous genocides since the Holocaust. She shook a warning finger at the tyrants of today, at the inequities and intolerances that persist. She ended by noting that, "Under German occupation I saw the Polish nation drowning, and those in the most difficult position were the Jews. And those who needed the most help were the children. So I had to help. It is not true that this was a heroic act, only a simple and natural need of the heart."

CHAPTER 31

Remembrances

Warsaw, May 2001

After Irena had lunch and a brief nap, the girls resumed their places at Irena's feet, fully expecting to perform *Life in a Jar* for their most eminent audience of one. All through lunch they had nervously tittered about how Irena would love their play, even if they only performed in her tiny bedroom – it was still only 15 minutes long, and they'd performed out of costume before.

Irena began by asking if they had more questions, and Megan raised her hand. "One of the survivors I interviewed at the synagogue said something that still bugs me a lot. He said, 'I had the feeling that for this to happen there could be no God.'"

Irena tapped her chin thoughtfully. "There *were* miracles, and there was good luck. Praying kept up some people's spirits, though the suffering was beyond understanding. At that time I did not have a strong belief in God, but there was one time when my good fortune was beyond chance, and, who knows, maybe God himself had intervened.

"My network of rescuers had been relatively fortunate after we joined with ZEGOTA; only a few dead, one in Pawiak. One evening I was at Jaga's house on Lekarska Street waiting for darkness so we could bury the newest lists. Suddenly, we heard the dreaded police whistles. Troops poured out from the SS barracks across the street and began a sweep from each end of Lekarska Street. It was Hanna's job to ring a small dinner bell if she saw strange people, the Polish Blue police, or soldiers near the house. It had never been necessary, but suddenly the whole block had become a military operation. Hanna must have been petrified, for she rang the bell insistently until Jaga took it from her and told her to go and read a book in the attic. I myself had a young girl, Sara, with me, who I had just taken from the ghetto. The lists we were to bury that night sat on the table. It is a terror I cannot describe well – whistles blared, soldiers screamed orders, their boots beat the cobblestones. Jaga grabbed the lists and stuffed them into her brassiere. She would hide behind a false wall in the upstairs closet. I had never seen her looking so grim. I took Sara to the basement behind another false wall, into a tiny space where we played a game of who could be the quietest, and we waited for the Germans.

"But they never came. Each column of troops, all very young, probably new recruits learning how to search, how to find hidden rooms and false walls, assumed the other had searched the middle building, #9. By chance, at that time no other children were hiding on Lekarska Street, and no one was arrested. Now I think that was a miracle."

Megan said, "My pastor is always saying, God's ways are mysterious to us."

Liz squirmed to find a comfortable position; she could not wait another moment. "What ... what about our play?" she asked.

"I read your play several times," Irena said. "There are one or two points that I have corrected, but on the whole it is very true to history. It is painful to go back in memory. But we must remember this terrible time. And you must tell this story."

Sabrina asked, "Were there any more mistakes? We want it to be perfect."

"It will never be perfect," Irena said. "Memory is fragile, and not many of us are left." She dabbed at her eyes, then cleared her throat again. "In your play, you act that I am telling the German guards at the gate that the child I am taking across has typhus and needs to go to hospital. This is not true. The Germans were more afraid of typhus than anything else. That officer would have immediately killed the child and likely myself as well.

"And, I believe I have told you this already, that you have the name of my helper wrong. You call her Marie, but she is another Irena – Irena Schultz. Maybe you did this because it will be too confusing to have two Irenas, but those who knew us were not confused; she was very tall and I am very small. They called us 'the two Irenas,' and we were very clever at fooling the Germans. Irena Schultz was a brilliant person. I miss her very much. She died in 1983."

Irena talked about other co-conspirators, how rescues were carried out, about the Hygiene Wagon and Danbrowski's barking dog Shepsi, how much it cost, forgery, bribery, threats. She drew the girls in closer, taking them into secret confidence, and said, "Sometimes ZEGOTA had to murder blackmailers."

For every question the girls asked, Irena had two about Kansas, *Life in a Jar*, their parents and brothers and sisters. For another hour she told them stories about her childhood, about defying anti-Semitic rules at Warsaw University and being suspended for her defiance.

"What about boys," Liz asked. "I mean you must have had boyfriends."

Irena's eyes glazed for a moment, then she smiled. "Yes, there was Mietek and Stefan."

Liz and Megan exchanged expectant glances.

Irena paused and contemplated the girls' faces, deciding how much to tell them, how much to keep private. She explained that her first husband – Mietek Sendler – was a childhood friend. Though they had a good friendship, the marriage was difficult and they separated. He was a prisoner of war. After he was repatriated, they divorced and she married Stefan, who was the father of her two children. That marriage also faltered, and Stefan suddenly died when Janka was 14 and Adam was 12. He was a good father, she said, then had to stop.

When she regained her composure, she motioned for Ludwik Stawowy, her friend and translator, to come close, and whispered something he translated for Mr. C.'s ears only.

"My dear and beloved girls," Irena said. "Now I am tired, but you will come again tomorrow in the morning before you fly back to Kansas."

Megan thought, What about the play? Irena was supposed to see the play. Why didn't Irena want to see the play as soon as they came? Maybe they would perform it tomorrow; it was short enough, and they could fix the script. Wasn't it the play that made all this happen?

They left the building and looked back at Irena, who waved a handkerchief to them from her window until they turned the corner.

As they drove back to the Ibis Hotel, squeezed into the Polski Fiats, Megan asked, "Mr. C.? Why didn't we do the play?"

"Irena said she doesn't want to see the play."

"What?" Megan was astounded.

"Why?" Liz asked.

"She said she was very sorry, but she didn't think she could watch the play – it would be too painful. She liked reading the play very much, but she was afraid to see you perform it. Isn't that peculiar? Irena Sendler was afraid."

★   ★   ★   ★   ★   ★   ★   ★   ★   ★

They returned the next morning under a brooding sky that sprinkled rain. Their journey was about to end, and, like the heavy air, the girls were subdued. They knew that there would be a lot of work when they returned to Kansas with more than 20 hours of audio recordings and almost 13 hours of video.

Irena's wish not to see *Life in a Jar* hung heavily with Megan. She understood Irena's reasons but still felt hurt and disappointed. Wasn't this all about the play, their most cherished gift to Irena?

Megan and Liz's Fiat arrived first, and they waited for the others at the curb. Liz slouched against the car door with a grieved expression. "Do you think this will be the last time we ever see her?"

"Could be," Megan said. "She's 91 and not well. I'm praying for her. I hope she lives to be 100, or more."

The sanitary nurse greeted them again at the door and dispensed the same stern expression she'd worn the day before. She issued the same injunction to "Wash your hands!" Fewer people crowded Irena's apartment, and the only media present were the documentary film crew.

"As I told you yesterday," the nurse said, "Irena's blood pressure has been very high and her diabetes very poorly controlled." Megan prepared herself for another lecture. "But after your visit yesterday, and today, I have never seen her blood pressure so low. Your visit is good medicine." She allowed herself a slight smile. "She can hardly wait to see you."

Irena greeted each one and again asked, "Do you have any burning questions?"

Sabrina said, "I still don't understand why your heroism wasn't better known."

Megan said, "Everybody we tell your story to asks why they don't know you. It's not fair."

"Yes, my dear girls, the world is not fair. It is for you to make it more fair. People like me, people with the *Yad Vashem* medal – I think many wish I would just quietly die without reminding them of our dark history. A life is full of wonderful things and terrible things. Still, I try to remember the good, but sometimes it's too difficult – too painful.

"Sometimes the unthinkable happens. During the war my mother was very sick with a heart condition. There was not enough medicine; she could not eat properly and ..." Irena stopped mid-sentence. "It's painful for me to remember this now, but I was not a very good daughter, and maybe I hastened my mother's death. I'll never know. I understand why it is painful for Poles to remember. We all have painful memories. To recall these events is most unpleasant, but necessary."

"We don't want to cause you any discomfort," Mr. C. said. "Tell us only as much as you feel you want to share."

"Professor Norman, you are a good man. There should be many more like you in the world. I am committed to the truth – so I will tell it to you.

"After I was arrested, Mother became quite depressed and her heart failure worsened. There was nothing I could do from Pawiak, and she became quite weak. One of the burdens I carry is the full knowledge that my illegal activities put my entire family at risk of execution. I had to choose between my mission and my mother, and, God forgive me, I chose my mission.

"The day after my escape from Pawiak, which you now know how this miracle occurred, I was escorted by a liaison girl to Henryk and Maria Palester's apartment at Lowicka #51. I required two canes to walk the few blocks from the tram, each painful step renewing my angry determination. I was glad to be angry. In the four years of the war I learned that if fear was a kind of starvation, then anger was bread and water, life-sustaining, if not nourishing. I hobbled up to a freshly applied red wall poster, the color that announced executions. The young liaison girl pointed out my name along with 17 others. My crime: 'Aiding and abetting Jews, consorting with Underground elements.' For the first time in over 100 days I laughed.

319

"But my laughter quickly turned cold. It had been almost four months since my arrest, and if Stefan was still alive he would read the poster and see that I had been executed. My mind raced, thinking of all my needs and responsibilities – Stefan, ZEGOTA, my mother.

"After it was discovered that I had escaped, the Gestapo came looking for me. They questioned Mother, barged into the Social Welfare office to search my desk, interrogated co-workers, and reminded them that aiding a fugitive carried the death penalty. ZEGOTA provided me with a new *Kennkarte*, birth certificate, and ration card in the name of Klara Dambrowska. I was no longer Irena, but Klara, and I was on the run with forged documents, like all the other people I had helped.

"Through my contacts with the Polish Socialist Party, the PPS, I learned that Stefan was a liaison between the PPS and the Home Army and he was hiding in Otwock. I was able to send a communication reassuring him that I was indeed alive. But I would not see him for many months since even with well-forged documents, travel was dangerous. And I was too weak to go to him.

"I recuperated with friends and liaisons, sleeping at a different house every night. For a few days I stayed at the strangest hiding place, the Warsaw Zoo, along with an armadillo and fox kits that had been nursed by a cat, as a guest of the zookeepers and rescuers, Jan and Antonina Zabinski.

"At every opportunity I visited Mother, though never alone. My companion waited in the stairwell to warn me should the Gestapo appear, in which case I would flee onto the roof, hobble across three buildings and down into a courtyard. The doctor said Mother's heart medicine was not effective anymore; it would be miraculous for her to live another year. The parish priest began to visit.

"One day Mother said something that still haunts me today. She said, 'Promise me, Irena, you won't come to my funeral. They'll be looking for you.'

"I tried to argue with her but she made me promise, and I did. I could have done more for my mother, a thought that gives me much guilt. My only consolation was that during the war she never once said, 'Don't do it.' I took that as encouragement.

"A few days after escaping Pawiak I went to see Zofia Kossak about my ZEGOTA work. I wanted – no, I needed – to resume my work. She discouraged me, said I should disappear for awhile, but I insisted. I asked Zofia about my escape and she told me that ZEGOTA paid a large bribe – the largest bribe they ever paid. Then she asked me a disturbing question. Did I want to know what happened to the SS guard who took the bribe? I could only remember how roughly he handled me and how he slapped my face. I said, 'Why should I care?'

"Zofia told me anyway. She was like that. He was denounced, arrested, and executed.

"By February 1944, the ghetto was long gone, bombed and burned to rubble after the Ghetto Uprising was crushed. There were no more children to rescue, but thousands of children to support in hiding. Zofia and Julian Grobelny agreed that I could assist with distributing money and forged papers and securing new hiding places for those who were 'burnt' – exposed by blackmailers. I could not return to my office, where Gestapo surveillance was constant. But, with my new identity and my high quality forged papers, I was able to travel by train to outlying districts and towns.

"On one such journey, while returning from Skierniewicach, my train was unexpectedly stopped and pulled onto a siding. An SS officer slid open the compartment door. He examined each of our papers, coats, and luggage. I was on my way back to Warsaw, having already distributed forged documents and money sewn into a secret lining in my coat. Except for my forged *Kennkarte*, I carried nothing incriminating.

"He showed me a list of names, then asked in very bad Polish, 'Know any of them?'

"My own name stood out as if the letters were on fire, and a little further down, *Stefan Zgrzebski*.

"I shook my head and handed the paper back. I said, 'No. No one.' He returned my papers and left the compartment.

"Mother died in her sleep on March 30, 1944. Just as she had feared, the Gestapo came to the church and the graveside, wearing dark leather coats and swastika lapel pins. It served their purposes to be easily recognized. They were asking about me."

Irena paused; she looked from one girl to another and said, "I don't mean to be difficult, but I want to speak with only Megan. Not for very long."

When they were alone, Irena leaned in close. "You know, my dear Megan, during the war we intended to defeat Hitler and the Nazis. And we did. Anything is possible. You just have to do the right thing – one footstep after another and ..." She paused and took Megan's face in her hands. Irena studied her for a moment. "How is Mamma-Megan doing with this cancer? It's a terrible thing, is it not? More and more people seem to get cancer these days. I don't understand. But Megan, look at me." She held her with firm, trembling hands. "Your mother is a strong person. I have been told that she intends to defeat this cancer."

Megan melted into Irena's arms. She wept freely, and Irena stroked her head, whispering reassurances that needed no translation.

*   *   *   *   *   *   *   *   *   *

In her wheelchair, Irena led the girls out of the bedroom into the living room, smiling and waving. There were light snacks on a table, and it felt to Megan like a birthday party. Somebody proposed a toast, and glasses of blackberry and apple juice were raised to Irena, and then Irena toasted "Professor Norman and my dearly beloved girls."

Mr. C. responded with his own accolade. "Our deep thanks go to Irena," he said. "Compared to what you and the Jewish and Polish people lived through, our difficulties are trivial. Compared to your courage, we are, all of us, only children. But you are our hero – our role model. We will carry on your mission – your deep commitment to respect for all people. I want to offer a toast in Hebrew – one we all know well – an aspiration to which you, Irena have contributed so much. L'Chaim – To Life." Even the documentary cameraman put down his video-cam and picked up a glass.

"L'Chaim – To Life."

After a respectful silence, Karen said, "In doing their research, the students learned that in tribute to your wartime courage you receive a small monthly stipend from the Jewish Foundation for the Righteous in New York."

"Yes," Irena said, "they are very generous. But I have not needed for much. I receive letters and cards from some I rescued, occasional phone calls. They keep me from despair. But old friends and co-conspirators are dying. My greatest fear is that after the last survivor is gone, memory of the Holocaust will disappear. This pain is greater than the pain in my legs. It has been my great sorrow to live a long life knowing that when I am gone remembrance might be extinguished."

She turned her eyes to the three girls and spoke more quickly, impatiently. "I think it is time for us to say good-bye. But before you go, I must tell you something very important. I want you each to be very careful. Don't do what I did. It would break my heart if anything happened to you."

Megan felt certain they would never see Irena again, at least not on this Earth, and her tears welled up. She stood up and hugged Irena, who said, over and over, "*Kocham was*." (I love you.) She held each girl's face closely after they embraced – memorizing them for eternity.

"*Kocham was*," each girl responded.

Their flight was leaving in a few hours. Irena's daughter, Janka, led them out of the apartment into the dark of the hallway, where she stopped, her face in shadow. Ludwik translated for her. "I don't like to speak in front of people, but thank you for telling my mother's story."

A fine misting rain had begun as they left the building. They looked back at Irena leaning out of her window, waving. They stood in the rain and waved back to their hero, her sad face radiant, raindrops like tears streaming down her window pane.

CHAPTER 32

9/11 and a Prairie Full of Pain

Kansas and Warsaw, September 2001 – Spring 2002

Megan was Mark Stewart's firstborn, and he raised her to be a good Christian, a good student, to do her chores, and to speak her mind. To his satisfaction and dismay, she was too much like her Dad to do any less, and sometimes, when she "got a bee in her bonnet," Mark Stewart cringed at her determination and stubbornness. Like her mother, she was book-smart, earning high honors, and in an argument she was usually right.

During moments of quiet and reflection, often at church, Megan contemplated what an awful lot of life had intervened in the two years since her first day as a freshman, before *The Irena Sendler Project*, before her mother's cancer, when she had confidently predicted, "I'm going to be valedictorian." Now she was a junior, her Mom was in remission, her Dad's hips and back hurt so bad he couldn't get on his tractor anymore, and she wasn't so sure about her prediction. After traveling half way around the world to meet Irena, she saw her life on the Stewart farm through transformed eyes; she bridled when her father ordered her to help Travis feed and water the cattle and haul hay.

"I've got a Spanish quiz and a history paper due," she said. "Mom always said school work comes first."

"When I was your age ...," Mark Stewart began.

"I know, Daddy," Megan sighed. "You carried mail, some days you walked 14 miles, and the only thing that mattered was the farm. Daddy, I'm going to be a pharmacist, not a farmer."

Mark Stewart sighed. He turned to Travis, two years younger and two inches taller than Megan, who shrugged and went out to do as he was told. Already broad-shouldered and strong from putting up hay and playing football, Travis was easygoing and shy to a fault. Everybody loved dependable, "go with the flow," Travis. He was so good with a football that as a freshman he was chosen for Varsity and State Football competition – something almost inconceivable. He loved nothing better than to drive his Dad's tractor, and when Mark Stewart finally needed a hip replacement in September 2001, Travis did most of the farm work, and got to drive the tractor.

As much as she felt disoriented, even a little depressed after their visit to Warsaw, Megan also felt renewed enthusiasm for their mission, as though she had been personally chosen by Irena to carry her torch. Her mother was feeling well again, which gave Megan every reason to be hopeful, and she and Kenny were very much in love after almost two years together. Performances of *Life in a Jar* were scheduled through the summer of 2001 at churches, civic centers, and synagogues in Kansas and Missouri, and as far away as Chicago.

Liz, also in somewhat of a funk, brooded over their Warsaw visit, haunted by the stories of mothers and fathers giving up their children. Most disturbing of all was the recurring image of the mother throwing her baby over the wall. Irena had it right – there were no guarantees and maybe everybody's world falls apart in one way or another, some more spectacularly than others. Since returning from Poland, Liz couldn't stop ruminating over her own mother leaving her on that West Kansas farm and she wondered again if she was still alive.

✶ ✶ ✶ ✶ ✶ ✶ ✶ ✶ ✶ ✶

Sabrina had graduated from Uniontown High the previous May and enrolled at Fort Scott Community College late in August. It was all her family could afford. She continued to attend most rehearsals and performances, and she joined Megan and Liz on September 10th for an interview on Kansas Public Radio, KPRS in Pittsburg, Kansas. Their interview was broadcast the next day, September 11, 2001 at 7:45 AM CST during National Public Radio's (NPR) *Morning Edition*.

Emily Rusinko:	But the girls say the most emotional part of the trip was meeting Sendler face to face for the first time.
Mr. C.:	It's a beautiful story. A story for all seasons, a story for all peoples and a story of tolerance and love and understanding that our world needs now maybe as much as it did in 1942-1943. Our goal is to tell Irena Sendler's story. But these young women are doing more than that. They have become agents of history. They are repairing the world.

★　★　★　★　★　★　★　★　★　★

One minute later, at 7:46 AM CST, American Airlines Flight #11 pierced the North tower of the World Trade Center in New York City. A few minutes later NPR news interrupted *Morning Edition* with news of the first attack. For most people 9/11 is a newsreel, perfectly preserved, always available; they will remember exactly where they were and what they were doing, when they heard the news. For Public Radio listeners in eastern Kansas, they had just listened to the founders of *The Irena Sendler Project*.

The next day, September 12th, the girls were scheduled to perform at Synagogue B'nai Jehudah in Kansas City, a performance that Mr. C. assumed would be canceled, like most every other discretionary entertainment in America.

Before first period Jessica Shelton, the newest member and road manager of *The Irena Sendler Project*, poked her head into Mr. C.'s classroom, where he was talking with two students about the attacks. "Oh, sorry. I'm confused. Are we still on for tonight? Everything's ready."

At first glance, he thought she looked remarkably composed and unemotional, as if she were the only person in America not to hear the news. But something was not quite right; he wondered if she would say anything about the attacks.

She continued unperturbed. "I've got the Suburban van, made all the contacts in Kansas City, emergency contacts and phone numbers, a map, food."

"Maybe you'd better call Rabbi Taub at B'nai Jehudah."

"Yeah. I was kind of wondering the same thing. I'll call him right away." Jessica turned to leave the classroom, but abruptly stopped, as if she'd suddenly remembered something important. She turned, and now her eyes were red. "Yesterday was my birthday, Mr. C. I don't want to share my birthday with ... with this... this thing."

He stood up from his desk and put his hand on her shoulder. "I didn't know. Happy Birthday, Jess." He felt ridiculous that he could find no other words to say except "Happy Birthday." But then truer, more meaningful words came to him. "I'll never, ever forget your birthday."

After first period, Jessica returned to the classroom, upbeat again and smiling. "Rabbi Taub said he was about to call us and yes, of course, he'd love to have us perform, if we would. He said they need *Life in a Jar* now more than ever."

Uniontown High School's secretary, on the verge of retirement, stuck her head into the classroom and monotoned, "Mr. C., phone call."

He followed her to the front office feeling numb, as if the air was cotton, as if he moved through a dream world. He picked up the blinking phone line in the deserted teachers' lounge.

"Hello? This is Emily Rusinko – from KPRS? It's been a horrible two days here. It must be for you, too. I just wanted to tell you that we have had a lot of phone calls and e-mails today about my interview with all of you yesterday. Do you have time for this?"

"Of course," he said.

"This one's typical. E-mail from a man who said, 'I could not have made it through the day, a day of great sorrow, without the story of Irena Sendler and the girls.'" Her voice sounded close. "Your interview helped a lot of folks yesterday. They all said the same thing – thanks for bringing us some hope in the midst of this tragedy." Her voice husked up, and she was obviously close to tears herself. "Yesterday, you and the girls, you did that for me, too. I wanted to thank you for starting to fix the world at the very moment it was breaking. Thank you. I... I have to go." And the phone line went dead.

Through these horrible two days, Mr. C. had tethered his emotions so he could counsel and reassure students, interpret the unfathomable, listen to the halting voices of teens who didn't know what to ask. Now, alone in the teachers' lounge, holding a telephone, staring unfocused into a funereal silence, he broke down. He sat alone in the lounge still holding the phone to his ear before he realized that he should put it down.

★   ★   ★   ★   ★   ★   ★   ★   ★   ★

With props, costumes, and sound equipment, the girls and Nick Caton rode in the school's Suburban up a deserted Route 69 to Kansas City. Mr. C. turned off the radio. "It's going to be all right," he said.

"You don't need to keep saying that," Liz said, slumped down in the back seat.

"Actually, I *do* need to keep saying that."

Megan leaned against the window staring out unfocused, her lips praying silently. Sabrina's eyes were closed, but Liz knew she was awake. The world had tipped over – everything was different. The excitement she usually felt before a performance had turned to dread.

At the entrance to Temple B'nai Jehudah they were stopped by a security guard who searched the van, asked about the weird props in the back, and finally motioned them forward into the parking area. A gray-bearded gentleman in a three-piece suit met them in a banquet hall filled with folding chairs. "I'm Rabbi Taub." He shook Mr. C.'s hand, then took off his wire-rimmed spectacles and apologized. "I'm sorry we have to meet under these circumstances. It may be that only a few people will come tonight, but my wife and I, we are so looking forward to your presentation."

Howard and Ro Jacobson, who were to become great friends and benefactors, were also scheduled to attend the performance on September 12th. Prominent and generous members of the Kansas City Jewish community, they had heard about The Irena Sendler Project and Life in a Jar for more than a year, and they were eager to finally see the play and meet the students. But on September 12th, Ro wasn't sure they should go. She needed to stay home, to listen to the news, which for so many in those first days after the attack exerted a magnetic compulsion – a lifeline against a dreadful reality. But Howard had a strong feeling, he wasn't sure why, that it was necessary for them to attend. This was an inspirational story, he told Ro.

328

It would be good for both of them.

The *Life in a Jar* cast set up for the performance without the usual good-natured joking and bantering, each in their own thoughts. The stage was set, lights and audio check complete, and the girls and Nick waited in a classroom down the hall that had Hebrew letters on each wall. Every few minutes Mr. C. returned with an update.

"Just a couple of people ... a few more ... half full ... seats full ... one row of people standing... two rows of people lining the back wall... people sitting on the floor. It's time. Break a leg!"

The banquet hall lights dimmed, and a spotlight illuminated the lectern – their cue to go on stage. Conversation ceased. Mr. C. stood at the lectern and allowed a deep stillness to go on – a long moment of reverence, an eerie quietude that the audience understood and shared.

"I suppose we will remember September 11th the way the Polish people remember September 1, 1939, the day the German army invaded Poland. Overnight everything changed. No one could possibly imagine what was to follow, but everyone feared it."

The play took longer to perform – each girl instinctively speaking more slowly, each line given its full weight. Liz read the last line of the play through tears. "Now frail and in her 90's, Irena Sendler lives in Warsaw, Poland and still shows the courage and commitment that changed the world."

A spotlight shone on the empty lectern, the stage otherwise dark and deserted. One person began to clap – timidly – ready to stop if she was alone, but like a match to gasoline, an ovation filled the hall. Then someone cheered, others hooted, some stamped their feet on the wooden floor, and many openly and shamelessly wept. The applause continued for more than 15 minutes – their longest ever. The cast returned to the stage and bowed and bowed again, but there was no end. It was clearly not about them. The lights came up and still the applause, the girls and Nick clapping along with the audience, standing together shoulder to shoulder.

The audience resumed their seats and Megan explained how *Life in a Jar* came to be, about National History Day. She also mentioned the economic plight of Bourbon County, the seventh poorest in the state of Kansas. Most high school graduates wanted to attend college, but for many it was a dream deferred; they could ill afford it.

Howard and Ro Jacobson turned to look at each other and silently mouthed the same word. "Scholarships!" Ro, chairwoman of the scholarship committee for the Kansas City chapter of the National Council of Jewish Women, and Howard, a trustee for several private foundations always seeking new worthwhile projects to support, went to their respective boards and received strong support for a scholarship program for the students. Many of the board members had already seen *Life in a Jar*, and within a few days they had created a significant scholarship fund with pledges of more. The scholarship money was not only for *The Irena Sendler Project*; some was earmarked for students from Southeast Kansas who won State or National History Day competitions with other tolerance and diversity projects. Over the next three years, eight scholarships were awarded to students who participated in *The Irena Sendler Project*. To date that number has grown to fifteen.

Howard now looks back on eight years of their association with *The Irena Sendler Project* and says of the students: "I know their association with *Life in a Jar* has been a life-changing experience. None of them started this project with the idea of winning scholarships, or being interviewed for TV or newspapers, or having the opportunity of traveling to Poland to meet Irena Sendler. They were moved by the intensity of this very powerful story and wanted to share it with as many people as they could. Little did they realize how many millions around the world would see them on television throughout Europe and the U.S. or read about them in national magazines. None of us understood how powerful their website would become."

CHAPTER 33

Where Are You Going Now?

Warsaw, 2002-2005

In March 2002, the Uniontown High School newspaper announced:

> "The Irena Sendler Project is the winner of the first Tikkun Olam
> Award, to be presented in Kansas City on March 10th, a day proclaimed
> by the mayor to be Irena Sendler Day. Tikkun Olam is Hebrew for 'To
> Repair the World.'"

Several Kansas City Jewish congregations sponsored the award. Art
Garfunkel performed a benefit concert in Irena's honor, and Irena sent
a brief video greeting from Warsaw. Bieta and her daughter Ania came
from Poland to represent Irena. The project's dear friend Renata Zajdman
flew in from Montreal. The World Federation of Jewish Child Survivors
of the Holocaust was represented by its President Stefanie Seltzer and
Vice President Rene Lichtman, who was so impressed with the students
that he asked them to perform in Michigan where he taught history at
the University of Michigan. The governor of Missouri was there as well to
honor Irena Sendler, as was Mr. C.'s former principal and best man, Bart
Altenbernd.

Bieta and Ania stayed for a week, taking part in several performances.
Bieta brought her silver spoon to America, and each time she showed it,
an immeasurable silence filled the room. To touch and hold this icon, her
mother's final gift, this tiny monument, brought tears to everyone's eyes.

Renata Zajdman had previously shared her story of escape from the
Warsaw ghetto with the girls, and they surprised her by adding to the play

the role of an orphan representing Renata.

[Since then, Irena Sendler Day has been declared in other towns, cities and states, including Warsaw (June 2005), the State of Vermont (October 2008), and most recently, Scranton and Lackawanna County, Pennsylvania (November 2009)].

By 2002 *The Irena Sendler Project* was well known to Kansas City where they had performed several times for Jewish congregations. Each time they were welcomed into the homes of generous philanthropists – Howard and Ro Jacobson, Gayle and Bruce Krigel, John and Jenny Isenberg, and John and Stevie Shuchart.

★   ★   ★   ★   ★   ★   ★   ★   ★   ★

Their second visit to Poland was the gift of John Shuchart (assisted by 11 other sponsors), the same Kansas City businessman and philanthropist who had helped finance their first trip to Poland. All he asked was that he accompany them.

A few weeks before their trip they received an e-mail saying that Irena had been sick, but she was, nonetheless, very excited to be seeing them so soon. She wanted to thank them again for their efforts on her behalf.

★   ★   ★   ★   ★   ★   ★   ★   ★   ★

A week before the second trip, Mr. C.'s phone rang at 11 PM on Sunday night. He had just fallen asleep and was confused (the alarm clock already?) then reached for the telephone with dread. His first thought, Irena is dead.

It was Sabrina, her voice hoarse and unsteady. "I don't think... I can't ... I can't go to Poland. It's Mom. She ... yesterday ... she ... she died. Nobody knows why. She just died. I thought I should tell you. I can't talk anymore now."

It took him a moment to register her words. It could not be; he didn't hear correctly. Sabrina's mother, Lorinda Coons, was a vital woman, mother of six, and a booster of *The Irena Sendler Project*. She was not yet fifty. How could she have died?

A few days later he called Sabrina "just to check in and see how you're doing. Anything we can do for you?"

She thanked him and said, no, she was OK, or at least as good as could be – and besides, she had a large family. But he could hear in her voice that she was not OK.

The next day a letter came from Irena thanking them for their part in helping to move her to the Franciscan senior care facility.

> I am 92, but I have my new life; it's just begun. I have my own room and bathroom, with radio and telephone near my bed. On my wall are the sunflowers from Kansas and the pictures of my five hearts (the Uniontown students). I am so looking forward to your visit.

Mr. C. e-mailed Sabrina a translation of Irena's letter, and she called him as soon as she received it. "I want to go, Mr. C. Can I still go?"

"I never gave your place away, Sabrina. I was hoping you'd reconsider. Your Mom was such a champion of this project – she was so proud of you for doing this. I think she would have wanted you to go. And Irena would have missed you terribly."

*　*　*　*　*　*　*　*　*　*

Their second visit with Irena, like their first, was busy with performances, interviews, and tours. Sabrina put on a brave face and shed no tears, at least none that anybody saw. Liz loved being in Warsaw again – this time knowing her way around at least somewhat, and knowing a few Polish phrases. Her anxiety from the first trip was replaced in equal measure by curiosity and excitement.

At the end of one long day, when they reviewed their journal entries with each other, Liz told Megan and Sabrina about interviewing one of Irena's assistants in the Social Welfare Department. "She didn't save any Jews; she said she was too afraid – everybody was afraid. But she knew what Irena was doing. She said no one talked about it. It was all very hush-hush and frightening, because the Gestapo gave people rewards for such information. She said she felt afraid for Irena because everyone in the office knew what she was doing, and anyone could be arrested at any moment." Liz paused. "I can't imagine being afraid for your life day after day, month after month, for years."

Liz and Megan interviewed Wladyslaw Bartoszewski, a founder of ZEGOTA and now Poland's Foreign Minister. "He was only 19 when he formed ZEGOTA," Megan explained to Mr. C. "He was in Auschwitz for almost a year – and miraculously survived that, too. He told us about the courier program – mostly young women. A lot of them were arrested, tortured, and killed. That's what Irena told us, too – most of her helpers were young women who didn't have children. They were no older than us girls."

"There are so many amazing stories in Poland," Megan continued. "But no one knows them. I'll bet some are as amazing as Irena's story."

"That's what's so important about what you're doing," Mr. C. said. "Everybody has a story. But these people will take their remarkable stories to their graves if we don't uncover them, write them down. That's immortality. We humans – we're storytellers, not that different than when we lived in caves and sat around a fire telling tales. It's the way we make sense of the world. It's what history is."

"Weird to think of it that way," Megan said.

"It's crazy," Sabrina said, "how everything can change so quickly. You're never ready for it. It just clobbers you." After an awkward silence, Sabrina said quietly, almost as an aside. "Yeah, that's it. Out of nowhere. I think Mom knew there was something wrong with her heart. Makes me mad that she didn't say anything. She could have prepared us." Megan put her arm around Sabrina, but she stiffened. "I got really mad at my sister during the funeral and all, seeing her kids there. Mom won't get to see my wedding, she won't meet my kids, and they'll never know their Grandma Lorinda."

Liz understood Sabrina's anger all too well. She wished she had words of comfort or advice, but none came to her.

When they finally met with Irena, they were delighted to see her in the tranquil Franciscan care home, a paragon of serenity and comfort, the elderly residents attended by monks and nuns who, as if in a medieval cloister, floated silently in timeless robes.

Irena welcomed them warmly to her tidy room. She motioned for Sabrina to sit on the carpet beside her and lay her head on Irena's lap.

She rocked slowly back and forth. "I will never understand," Irena said sadly, "why things happen the way they do. Why I am 92 and your mother died so young. Why so many died and we could only save a few. We are like little children when it comes to these matters. We feel everything, but understand little."

Irena held Sabrina's face in her hands, looking steadily into her eyes. Tears streaked down both their faces, and Irena stroked her head. "Sabrina, Sabrina, weep with me for all those who died too soon."

They remained that way for many moments, a respectful silence in the room until Sabrina sat back dragging her sleeve across her eyes. Still sobbing, she said to Irena, "My Mom – she always said this is the finest thing I've ever done."

* * * * * * * * * *

During this second visit, Irena told the girls the remarkable story of Jan Karski, a representative of the Polish government-in-exile – a spy sent to Poland in August of 1942, during the liquidation of the ghetto, to bring eyewitness evidence of the Holocaust to Allied leaders. Since Irena knew the ghetto so well, the underground had asked her to give Karski a tour, after which he was taken to a partisan unit in the forests near Lwow. They disguised him in a Ukrainian uniform so he could witness firsthand the murders at transit stations en route to the Belzec extermination camp. He then returned to Warsaw where a dentist removed several of his teeth so the resultant swelling would disguise his Polish-accented German. He escaped from Poland to Berlin, then through Vichy France to Marseilles where the French underground smuggled him across the Pyrenees into Spain. Karski carried evidence – a key whose hollow shaft contained microfilm of hundreds of documents. Several weeks later he was in London telling his story, begging the Allies to at least bomb the rail lines to the camps. Newspapers declined to print his accounts; no one could believe his allegations. Neither did Churchill nor Roosevelt.

* * * * * * * * * *

When they returned home, the girls researched Karski's remarkable mission to report the Holocaust to a doubting world. On the web they learned of the annual *Jan Karski Award for Valor and Compassion*, presented by the American Center of Polish Culture. Liz and Megan nominated Irena for the award. Bieta Ficowska and Stefanie Seltzer, President of the World Federation of Jewish Child Survivors of the Holocaust, also nominated Irena. Three months later the American Center of Polish Culture awarded the 2003 Jan Karski medal to Irena Sendler.

Irena was too frail to travel to the U.S. to accept the honor and requested "Professor Norman and my dear girls to receive the award in my name. It would make me so happy." Megan, Sabrina, Mr. C., and Kathleen Meara, a new cast member, flew from Kansas City to Washington, D.C., where the *Karski Award* was presented.

At the start of the ceremony a large photograph of Irena as a beautiful dark-haired young woman in a nurse's uniform, her disguise for entering the ghetto, was projected onto a screen, while the First Lady of Poland, Jolanta Kwasniewska, read a letter from Irena:

> *This award is not for me only. I accept it on behalf of all those who helped me. I am the only one left. There were so many Jewish resistance fighters, not only the ones with guns and Molotov cocktails, but those who ran the House Committees and Youth Circles and kept hope and civility alive, especially for the young people. So many agreed to take in the children — at risk of death.*
>
> *You award me because I am one of the few remaining to bear witness. But I tell you, I only did what any decent person would do in such horrible times.*
>
> *I do not consider myself a hero. The true heroes were the mothers and fathers who gave me their children. I only did what my heart commanded. A hero is someone doing extraordinary things. What I did was not extraordinary. It was a normal thing to do. I was just being decent.*

A week after the *Karski Award* the President of Poland, Aleksander Kwasniewski, bestowed Poland's highest honor, The Order of the White Eagle, on Irena.

Pope John Paul II wrote a personal letter to congratulate her:

Honorable and dear Madam,

I have learned you were awarded the Jan Karski Prize for Valor and Courage. Please accept my hearty congratulations and respect for your extraordinarily brave activities in the years of occupation, when – disregarding your own security – you were saving many children from extermination, and rendering humanitarian assistance to human beings who needed spiritual and material aid. Having been yourself afflicted with physical tortures and spiritual sufferings you did not break down, but still unsparingly served others, co-creating homes for children and adults. For those deeds of goodness for others, let the Lord God in His goodness reward you with special graces and blessing.

Remaining with respect and gratitude I give the Apostolic Benediction to you.

Pope John Paul II

Irena was honored in ceremonies from Buenos Aires to Montreal. Hidden Children groups, the World Federation of Jewish Child Survivors of the Holocaust, the Canadian Foundation of Polish-Jewish Heritage, the International Raoul Wallenberg Foundation, the Milken Family Foundation, and many more organizations recognized her accomplishments.

★　★　★　★　★　★　★　★　★　★

In the wake of their second trip to Poland, over 1,000 newspapers carried stories about Irena and the students. They received letters and e-mails from teachers and students in Poland, the U.S., and Canada; others called seeking performances or suggestions about how they might emulate The Irena Sendler Project – finding Righteous Gentiles in their own communities and telling their stories, or performing their own version of Life in a Jar.

The Today Show in New York came to Kansas and featured the girls' story. A school in Japan performed Life in a Jar. Polityka, one of the most prominent Polish magazines, announced a poll to choose "the ten women who had exerted the biggest influence on the fate of Poland." To facilitate the task of choosing candidates, *Polityka* published a list of 100 prominent Polish women and what they had accomplished, including Irena Sendler.

If *The Irena Sendler Project* was to continue, they would need a new generation of students. Sabrina was in college, and Megan and Liz were due to graduate from Uniontown High that year. Jessica Shelton and Nick Caton had signed on, and Liz suggested that Megan's younger brother Travis would be a good addition to the cast. Megan was skeptical. Except on the football field, Travis was painfully shy; he could not speak in crowds and eye contact was difficult.

Her concerns were ill-founded; Travis played the role with uncanny authority, and Megan thought it was scary how much he sounded like their Dad when he was angry.

$$\star \quad \star \quad \star \quad \star \quad \star \quad \star \quad \star \quad \star \quad \star \quad \star$$

In June 2003 *The Irena Sendler Project* began a "summer tour" during which they visited West Virginia, Michigan, New York City, and Connecticut. During this tour they initiated a new tradition. They publicly presented one of Irena's heart necklaces for someone special in the audience to hold during the performance – to honor a family member, a survivor, a dignitary, a friend, or a teacher.

Some of Megan's prayers were answered; others were not. Her father recovered from his hip replacement and he was back full-time to farming as well as driving the school bus for extra income.

But just before the summer tour Debra Stewart's cancer recurred. Telling no one, she volunteered to drive the Kansas students and their props on the first leg of their tour, to Beckley, West Virginia on a hot June day in 2003. Mr. C. drove to Beckley from the opposite direction, from the National History Day competition in College Park, Maryland where Jessica Shelton and Lacey George had just placed 5th in the nation with their exhibit *If Not for Miss Nutter*. Their project honored Corinthian Nutter, an African-American teacher and civil rights pioneer who stood up for equality in education in 1948. She was now 97 years old, and they had visited her in the course of their research.

Jessica's little brother Jamie and their mother came along as well.

Jessica's mother had broken her foot just before History Day but wouldn't let a cast and crutches stop her from going along. At National History Day Jessica was sick with a sore throat, fever, and headache that was later diagnosed as mononucleosis. "Just give me more Advil, Mom. After everything I've done, I am not missing this." National History Day ended, they packed the Suburban, and Mr. C. drove all night to get to West Virginia in time for the performance. With Mr. C. it was always packed schedules and close calls, but this time he thought he had cut it too close.

Somehow, they all met in Beckley, and were only an hour late arriving at the beautiful Tamarack Center in the hill country of West Virginia. Debra Stewart declared it a miracle. Kathleen Meara, the first student in the play not from Uniontown High School, was nervous as a barn cat. This was her first performance, and in the fall, when Liz was set to leave for college in Missouri, she would assume the role of Irena. The kids were in a frenzy trying to do in one hour what normally took two – props, the sound system, lights, costumes, makeup, another run-through of new script lines. The huge auditorium dwarfed the sounds of setup.

Debra Stewart intercepted Mr. C. at the back of the auditorium where he listened to last-minute practice of new lines, his arms folded on his chest. She asked to speak with him outside.

When they were alone she said, "I've had more tests – at the hospital. They found something."

His brow wrinkled.

"It's the cancer. It's back." She held her tears. "I haven't told Travis or Megan. Promise me you won't say anything until the tour is over. I'll be starting chemo again, as soon as we come back. But I don't want them to worry."

He took her hand. "I'm so sorry, Debra."

"I just worry about my kids," she said, and a tear fell. "Guess I'm just a mother."

"You know," he said, "since you've been ill Megan has changed so much. A year ago I thought she might drop out of the project. I wondered what it was that kept her interested. I thought for sure she would be off on a million other things. And with Kenny and all. But after you were sick, something changed. She became the leader of the group. She's matured in an incredibly short time."

"Promise me you won't say anything," she said.

"How bad is it?"

Tears welled up again. "It's pretty bad," she said. "It's in my liver."

He thought of his own mother, stricken with cancer before the age of 60, and he couldn't stop his own tears. It was her illness and death in 1985, the untimely rupture of mother and child, that had brought him back to Kansas and to Uniontown. He opened his arms to Debra Stewart, and they cried in each other's embrace.

★ ★ ★ ★ ★ ★ ★ ★ ★ ★

"Over 2,000 people saw you perform," Mr. C. said after the tour as they finally drove into Uniontown on a hot Kansas afternoon. "You touched over 2,000 people in a profound way. You should be proud of yourselves."

There were hugs and tears in the parking lot as they said good-bye. Someone asked for a photograph, and they leaned against the Suburban, the sun glinting off their heart necklaces. As Sabrina took suitcases and props out of the Suburban, she told Megan and Liz that they might not be seeing as much of her for awhile; she was transferring to Kansas State in the fall, thanks to a scholarship from Howard and Ro Jacobson. "I didn't want to say anything until after the tour. I didn't want to upset you, or ruin the tour."

She was about to walk away, when she stopped and added, "I just wanted to say that even though I'm leaving, I don't want to lose any of you and I don't want to lose *Life in a Jar*." Her voice was husky with emotion. "What with all the moving around I kind of keep to myself. I kind of live in my head a lot. I always thought that it's better to be strong and independent. But I guess we really need each other. Irena couldn't have done what she did without the people who helped her. And they all risked their lives to do it. I guess I'm lucky – I only had to risk you thinking me stupid or pathetic – or both. I wanted you guys to think I was OK – you know, normal. I don't know. And then my Mom... It's all confused. But, you held me up. Irena held me up. You're my friends and I wouldn't have missed that for the world." She kissed Liz and Megan and turned to go.

She was almost at her father's idling car when she turned back and called across the parking lot, "And Mr. C., I'm for sure gonna be a teacher – a teacher like you."

Debra Stewart stood back, watching first Sabrina's farewell and then Liz's departure with Grandpa Bill. Megan was exhausted and fell into her mother's arms, then suddenly gasped and pulled away when she saw her arms were covered with bruises.

"Mom, what's going on?"

"Wait until your Dad comes home."

"No! Tell me now!"

She signaled for Travis to join them, then said very matter of factly, "It's the cancer. The cancer is back. I beat it once; we can do it again. I'll tell you more tonight with Daddy."

The moment her father walked through the door, his face ashen, Megan felt his heavy heart. No one spoke as her mother sat the family down at the dinner table.

"The cancer has moved to my liver – five spots. My blood test shows higher cancer markers. I'll need more chemotherapy."

Megan felt herself tearing up again and said, wistfully, "Why can't it be like it was before? I pray all the time for you to be just like before."

"There's always suffering, darling," Debra said to her. "You don't pray to Jesus to make everything better or to get what you want. That's what children do – it's a magical way of thinking. Every time you walk into church, the first thing you see is a man on a cross. He died to save us – not to give us everything we want – to save us. That's what's so hard to understand. It's not about Him answering your prayers – it's about you being like Him no matter what happens on this Earth. 'Thy will be done.' There will always be sadness and pain."

Megan had heard these words before, many times, and she accepted their truth and wisdom, but now these same words surged deep inside and became an ache in her heart. She would have to make room for this disturbing realization.

Debra served the dinner and Mark nodded for her to say grace.

* * * * * * * * * *

The next evening, as the Stewarts watched the local news and weather, a commercial came on for The Cancer Treatment Centers of America, "where the most up-to-date medical care, complementary medicine, and spirituality are the cornerstones of healing." Megan exchanged glances with her mother and father – they all felt at that moment that God was telling them that this was where Debra needed to go. Her first appointment was less than a week later, and the oncologist immediately admitted her to begin chemotherapy – every three weeks for three days – every three weeks for a year.

Megan kept one phrase in her consciousness and whispered it to herself at trying times each day, "Thy will be done," and over time, she found solace in surrendering. Her pastor often said that "When God moves in your life, a light shines in the dark. And nothing is ever the same again." That was what Professor Leociak had said about Irena on their tour of the ghetto – that Irena was a light – a spiritual light in the darkness. She was that for Megan as well – a light in the darkness. The world was full of pain and miracles, and Megan needed to understand how both could fit into her world.

Debra Stewart's cancer went into remission again, which allowed Megan and Travis to be part of The Irena Sendler Project's third trip to Warsaw, in the summer of 2005 to celebrate Irena's 95th birthday and to perform the play at several venues. Meagan Easter and Melissa Query, two new cast members, came on this trip as did Liz and Jessica Shelton. Their itinerary for this visit was no less crowded than the previous two.

They reunited with Irena at her care home for her birthday celebration. On the third floor of her otherwise tranquil care facility, the conference room blazed with fluorescent light, whirled with the noise of media crews and conversation. Irena's friends and relatives crowded the room. A long table down the middle had been set with flowers, white paper plates, yellow napkins, white plastic cups, cookies, and colorful juice boxes. Irena sat in her wheelchair at one end of the room, a small presence, wearing her customary plain black dress and black headband across her white hair, waving as people came in, greeting them one by one. When Mr. C., the girls, and Travis came into the room, Irena's smile animated and she held out her arms for them to come. Irena embraced each student and expressed her special joy at finally meeting Travis who knelt beside her wheelchair.

The Kansas students brought Irena a birthday cake with a "95" candle in the middle. There were toasts to celebrate Irena's long life. Then, as she had on each of their previous visits, Irena sat forward in her wheelchair, put on thick spectacles, and proceeded to read from several handwritten pages, admonishing world leaders about contemporary wars and genocides, pointing her finger, in emphatic Polish.

She returned to the subject of the Warsaw ghetto. "Less than one percent. That's how many we saved. But the arithmetic, though severe, is important. During the liquidation of the ghetto, 5,000 to 8,000 Jews were taken every day to Treblinka and murdered. During the entire war – more than five years – we saved only 2,500 children. The mathematics of rescue was also severe. To save one Jewish child, ten Poles and two Jews had to risk death. To betray that same child and the family that hid him required only one informer or, worse still, one blackmailer. The risk of being caught by the SS was not prison, but death – death for the entire family.

"We all have to ask ourselves, 'What would I have done?' But understanding does not erase the regret I feel for my own insufficient efforts. Less than one percent. I agree with Wladyslaw Bartoszewski, one of the organizers of ZEGOTA, who said, 'Only the dead have done enough.'"

⋆　⋆　⋆　⋆　⋆　⋆　⋆　⋆　⋆　⋆

Their first performance was in the auditorium of Poland's largest daily newspaper, *Gazeta Wyborcza*, with a readership of over one million. The capacity audience included Polish high school students.

Afterwards, several of the Polish teenagers stood on the stage, shoulder to shoulder with the cast of *Life in a Jar*, and answered questions from the audience. A young man, a student who spoke beautiful English, said, "There are almost 60 student groups doing this kind of work in Poland – inspired by Irena Sendler and the Kansas students."

As they left the stage, Liz noticed an elderly gentleman, pale and fragile in the second row, hunched over, with scant white hair, wearing a wool suit, though it was June. Except for a mild tremor, he sat completely still, cradling something in his lap that he completely enclosed with his hands – a secret or a treasure.

One of the Polish students knelt beside the man's seat, and the old man recognized him and smiled. The Polish teen motioned for Megan and Liz to come meet him. "He's a rescuer," the Polish boy explained. "Our school adopted him as our hero. Just a few months ago we renamed our school in his honor. It was your efforts with Irena Sendler – that's what inspired us."

"Can you show me what you have there?" Megan asked.

The man looked up at her, his bloodshot eyes brimming with tears, and slowly opened his hands to display his silver *Yad Vashem* medal. He offered his treasure for Megan to hold. A blush rose in his pallid cheeks. He explained how he had hidden Jews, then said, "After the war I put this in a very good hiding place – a metal box that I buried in my basement. I was afraid to tell anyone except my wife. I did not think I would bring to view this medal again in my life. Thank you."

Megan gave the round medal to Liz. After all these years, Liz thought, and his heroism is only now recognized.

Liz knelt beside the old man's chair and put the *Yad Vashem* medal back in his hands. "Thank you," she said. "For what you did – thank you."

Liz thought again of the Jewish mother who threw her baby over the ghetto wall – a desperate act of love; she thought of this man's courage, of Irena's courage – all desperate acts of love. She remembered her mother's Buick and the cloud of dust she left behind fleeing Liz and that West Kansas farm, and for the first time, Liz was prepared to believe that maybe, just maybe, for her mother, fleeing was a desperate act of love.

★   ★   ★   ★   ★   ★   ★   ★   ★   ★

Their next day's performance was at the State Jewish Theater. It was June 1st, the International Day of the Child, and the mayor of Warsaw had declared it Irena Sendler Day as well, noting the appropriate connection. When the Kansans arrived at the theater on Grzybowski Square, German television was setting up alongside the Polish documentary crew. This 350-seat auditorium had become home to Jewish and Yiddish theater in

Poland since 1950. It was housed in a building constructed over what was once the main Jewish market square in the ghetto.

The Chief Rabbi of Poland, American-born Michael Schudrich, greeted Mr. C. and the students. "You know," the rabbi said to them. "This moment is the ultimate revenge on Hitler. Protestant kids, celebrating a Catholic rescuer of Jewish children from the Warsaw ghetto, performing in a Jewish theater in Warsaw. And they are being filmed by German television."

★ ★ ★ ★ ★ ★ ★ ★ ★ ★

Before catching their flight home, they had enough time for one more short visit with Irena. Though Irena had never seen the play, she said she would like to hear Meagan Easter, who now played Mrs. Rosner, say her lines. She took Meagan's hands and held them tightly. They both closed their eyes, and Irena looked pained as she heard words that echoed from 60 years past.

Mrs. Rosner: *Take them now, for we cannot bear to think about this any longer. We have them ready to go. Hannah, the nice lady will take you and Baby Isek to someplace where you will feel much better. We will see you sometime soon.*

CHAPTER 34

The Last Visit
Kansas and Warsaw, May 2008

Debra Stewart died of her cancer on June 12, 2006, just nine days after she witnessed Megan and Kenny's wedding. That same year, inspired by her Christian faith and the Hebrew phrase *Tikkun Olam* – to repair the world – Megan became the Program Director for the Lowell Milken Center. A new non-profit organization developed and directed by Mr. C., the Lowell Milken Center's mission is to inspire project-based learning celebrating unsung heroes like Irena Sendler and her philosophy of respect and understanding for all people. Megan was instrumental in promoting Irena Sendler's nomination for the 2007 Nobel Peace Prize by the President of Poland and the Prime Minister of Israel.

Beginning in 2007, the annual Irena Sendler Award "For Repairing the World" has been presented to a Polish and American educator for their innovative and inspirational teaching of the Holocaust that also reflects Irena Sendler's respect for all people, regardless of background. Metuka Benjamin, from the Stephen S. Wise Temple in Los Angeles, has been the organizer and benefactor for this award, which is now also supported by the Goldrich Family Foundation.

The first recipients of the Irena Sendler Award were Robert Szuchta, of Warsaw and Norm Conard of the U.S. In April 2008, Megan and Mr. C. traveled to Warsaw again, with two other student participants, Jaime Walker and Jessica Shelton-Ripper, to join Metuka Benjamin in presenting the second annual Irena Sendler Award. The Polish recipient was Anna Janina Kloza, a Polish history teacher at High School No. 6 in Bialystok. The American honoree, Andrew Beiter, an 8th grade social studies teacher from Springville, New York, accompanied the students with his six-year-old daughter.

Following the ceremony, Mr. C. and the three girls visited with Irena, who had just been discharged from the hospital after another illness that had weakened her considerably. Since their first visit in 2001, they thought each would be their last. This time, because she was 98, the specter of Irena's passing hung heavily, particularly with Megan, who missed her mother terribly.

This was Jaime Walker's first visit to Poland, her first meeting with Irena, and she could hardly sit still through the award presentation. A strong young woman with broad shoulders and shoulder-length brown hair, Jaime's smile radiated warmth and trust. Each summer she grew a bumper crop of freckles. During her junior year at Pittsburg State University in Kansas, Jaime met Megan Stewart in a huge lecture hall. On campus there was a buzz about Megan and her project, and she had heard Megan's guest lecture about *The Irena Sendler Project* to her psychology class. They started talking, found they had much in common, and quickly became friends. After a few months Megan asked if Jaime would help out with *Life in a Jar*, and she gasped, "Oh, my God! Yes!" Within a year Jaime was a regular cast member, playing the roles of The Blackmailer, Mrs. Rosner, and Sister Matylda Getter.

After graduating with a degree in financial administration, she became the Development Director of the Lowell Milken Center – Repair the World Foundation. It never occurred to her that she would ever be so fortunate as to meet Irena Sendler, but now here she was, walking down a Warsaw sidewalk, oblivious to the sun-drenched street, anticipation overwhelming her senses, completely aware only of her heartbeat.

After a long hospitalization, Irena had been back in her care home for three days when they visited with her, accompanied by Metuka Benjamin, Bieta Ficowska, Renata Zajdman, Andrew Beiter and his daughter, and the rabbi of the Stephen Wise Congregation of Los Angeles. Because of Irena's weakened condition, the three girls were allowed only two minutes as a group with her. Her daughter Janka was with her, as was Andreas Wolff, a filmmaker and friend of Janka, who filmed the reunion. Kinga Krzeminska, Irena's friend and translator for the past two years, sat at

Irena's bedside holding her hand. Kinga, a tall, trim young woman with curly brown hair and an alert expressive face, had recently completed a Master's thesis on representations of the Holocaust in popular culture.

The three girls were allowed in, Jessica first, followed by Jaime, and then Megan. Irena lay in a twin bed by the window of her small room. Megan was shocked by how she had aged, how weak she seemed, lying on her back, her head propped up. But she smiled broadly when they came into her room, and tried to raise her head. She wore the same black head-band across her white hair that was in all her photos. Jaime thought how tiny she was under the blankets, like a child with an old woman's face.

Sunflowers were everywhere. On the wall next to Irena was the sun-flower quilt they had presented to her on their first visit. Right beside her bed were all of the gifts they had given her over the years – decorative items adorned with sunflowers, sunflower pillows, sunflower picture frames.

Each wall was covered with her most precious photos including one of her "dearly beloved girls." They brought a bouquet of flowers, a time-honored Polish custom. Jessica hugged Irena gently, and Irena asked through Kinga about her family.

Jessica proudly presented a photograph of her baby. "This is my daughter, Lilly."

Jessica stepped back from the bed, and Irena saw Jaime for the first time. She smiled as if happy to see an old friend. Jaime's mind went blank, and all she could do was kneel by Irena's bed. Irena spread her arms, and Jaime fell into them. She wanted to tell her that she played Mrs. Rosner, the Jewish mother who gave up her children to Irena in the ghetto – that Mrs. Rosner had looked into Irena's eyes 60 years ago and it was the greatest sorrow and the greatest good either of them would ever know. She wanted to tell her that she loved her and how much she had looked forward to this meeting, and that she was her hero and that she, Jaime, was not worthy to represent her life, and that she pledged to honor Irena with a life of tolerance and kindness. But all she could do was cry.

Irena soothed her with Polish words a grandmother might say to her favorite grandchild, and Kinga, herself deeply moved by their meeting, translated some of them. "You are such a beautiful girl," and "tell me all about yourself."

"I'm the newest member of *Life in a Jar*," Jaime managed to say, then remembered the gift she carried. She unwrapped a small wind chime with a basket of sunflowers and a little bird on top, chimes that tinkled celestial in Irena's room.

"Someone with great taste must have picked this out," Irena said with a twinkle, and they both smiled.

Megan took Jaime's place, and Irena's expression electrified – she licked her lips excitedly. "We love you so much," Megan said. "You are our hero. We are so grateful for what you teach us." It was almost time for them to go and Irena was very weak, but she rallied to tell them how beautiful they were and how they were growing up so wonderfully.

Jaime could not hide her tears as they left. Andrew Beiter's daughter looked up at Jaime and patted her hand. "It'll be all right," she said with wistful surety.

They stood together in the dim hallway outside Irena's room, and Mr. C. said to Megan, "Momma Megan is smiling down on us."

★　★　★　★　★　★　★　★　★

Their visit was so brief that there was precious little time to sit and speak with Irena as they always had before. Though their disappointment was deep, they were consumed by their ambitious schedule of presentations and meetings with educational and Holocaust groups, just as on previous visits. Three days later, Kinga called them with an urgent request – would they please see Irena again. Irena was very clear about needing to see them again, and Kinga was on her way to their hotel to pick them up. She met them with a bouquet of flowers, and they made their way back to Irena's care home.

The girls and Kinga, all about the same age, quickly became friends. Kinga was effervescent, good-natured, and forceful in making things happen. She talked about Poland, about her life and her studies, and they told her about the U.S., and Kansas, and their hopes and dreams. They invited her to come to the U.S., and she said she was planning an internship at the U.S. Holocaust Memorial Museum and she'd visit them in

Kansas. (Later that night, Kinga was surprised to learn that she had been awarded an educational grant from Metuka Benjamin, who had helped establish the Irena Sendler Award.)

With Irena they saw another aspect of Kinga – patient and delicate, her voice soft and understanding. To see them together was a powerful thing in itself, the two of them so comfortable, so happy to be with each other.

Back at the care home, they found Irena sitting in her chair once more. She looked stronger, and this time they stayed for almost an hour.

They talked more about their families, the Irena Sendler Award, what they had done in Poland this time, about *Life in a Jar* and their presentations, and described their powerful meetings with child survivors.

Megan lifted the heart necklace from inside her blouse and held up the pendant. "We're all wearing our hearts." Jaime and Jessica held up theirs.

Irena looked from one girl to the next and said, "You carry a piece of my heart with you every day."

This visit was intimate – a true measure of their close and enduring friendship. Irena talked a little more about her life but had no prepared remarks, and she repeated stories they had heard before. Irena evinced a special fondness for Megan, who had been so central to the program from the beginning and whose joys and sorrows Irena had shared. She told her how sorry she was about the death of her mother, then asked about her brother Travis. She asked Jessica about her baby, she asked what each of the girls was doing, and she asked about the Lowell Milken Education Center. She was curious about them and their world in the same way her letters had always been, like letters a friend would write, or questions a close relative would ask. Her special regard for Mr. C. – for "Professor Norman" – had revealed itself most poignantly during their previous visit when she said, "You've taken the place of my son."

A large yellow candle burned in Irena's room, and they took photographs of her with it – a symbol of the light she had brought to the darkness. Over and over, often with tears in her eyes, Irena said they, too, were a light in her life, and she loved them very much.

Her last comment before they left echoed in their hearts. "You have changed my country, you have changed your country, and you are changing the world."

And Jaime thought, no, Irena, we only tell your story. People don't come to hear about us; they want to know about you and what you did, how you changed the world. She wanted to say, "All the people you saved – that's your legacy, a legacy that lives on in all those people and everyone who is touched by your story." What Jaime said was, "Oh, no Irena. We've done nothing."

Kinga laughed. "Don't argue with Irena. It won't work."

When it was time to go, Irena held each girl and Mr. C. for a long time. Before releasing them from her fragile embrace, she made the sign of the cross with her thumb on their foreheads, her final blessing before saying good-bye.

Kinga later told them that after they left, Irena said how much she had enjoyed their time together and that it was necessary for her to have seen them one more time.

        *   *   *   *   *   *   *   *   *   *

A week later, on May 12th, Megan's birthday, Bieta was visiting with Irena while she ate breakfast. Irena was in good spirits. Without a sound, her head slumped forward, and Irena Sendler died in peace.

Irena Sendler, 98 years old, a week before her death, during the students' last visit with her in 2008. *(Photo courtesy of Kenny Felt, www.kennyfelt.com)*

Irena Sendler in 1939 at the age of 29.

Irena Sendler at age 95.

#9 Lekarska Street, with bullet holes in the façade from the August 1944 Warsaw Uprising. Irena's lists of hidden children were buried under an apple tree in the backyard.

Irena's co-conspirator and dear friend, Jadwiga (Jaga) Piotrowska. Beside her photograph is the *Yad Vashem* medal awarded to her as a Righteous Gentile.

Megan (Stewart) Felt

Elizabeth (Liz)
Cambers-Hutton

The Four Founders
of *Life in a Jar*

Jessica Shelton-Ripper

Sabrina Coons-Murphy

First visit with Irena, 2001. From left to right, Megan Stewart, Liz Cambers, Sabrina Coons.

Mr. Conard and Irena visiting on the 3rd trip to Poland, 2005. (*Photo courtesy of Megan Felt*)

Megan Stewart as Irena Sendler in a performance of **Life in a Jar**. *(Photo courtesy of Kenny Felt.)*

Jaime Walker as Mrs. Rosner, saying goodbye to her baby before Irena smuggles her out of the ghetto, in a performance of **Life in a Jar**. *(Photo courtesy of Kenny Felt.)*

Jaime Walker holding the jar and Megan Stewart with a replica of Bieta's silver spoon, during a performance of **Life in a Jar**.

Liz Cambers and ghetto gate in a performance of **Life in a Jar**.

Megan Stewart and Liz Cambers performing at National History Day Competition. University of Maryland, 2000.

Jaime Walker as Mrs. Rosner and Travis Stewart as a Nazi guard in a performance of **Life in a Jar**. *(Photo courtesy of Kenny Felt.)*

Hanna Piotrowska-Rechowiczowa (center), who was 12 years old when she watched Irena and her mother, Jadwiga (Jaga) Piotrowska bury the jars in her back yard. She is pictured here with her husband and the **Life in a Jar** students visiting Poland in 2005. They are, from left to right, Meagan Whitehead, Liz Cambers, Travis Stewart, Melissa Query, Megan Stewart and Jessica Shelton.

Mr. Conard, Megan Felt and Kinga Krzeminska receive an award at the Polish Consulate in Chicago. Organizations around the world have awarded **Life in a Jar/The Irena Sendler Project** with honors on behalf of Irena Sendler.

Jaime Walker, who plays Mrs. Rosner, the black-mailer and the Catholic sister. (*Photo courtesy of Kenny Felt.*)

Liz Cambers and Elzbieta (Bieta) Ficowska with the engraved silver spoon Bieta's mother placed in the carpenter's box in which she was rescued from the ghetto.

Maegan Easter, who played Mrs. Rosner, meeting Irena on their third trip to Poland, 2005.

Chicago Public Library, 2008. Kinga Krzeminska, Irena's translator and friend, participating in a panel discussion about Irena and the new Musuem of the History of Polish Jews in Warsaw.

"The Warsaw ghetto is just below your feet." Professor Jacek Leociak, Warsaw ghetto scholar, on Chlodna Street during a tour he gave the students in 2005. From Left to right. Last row: Meagan Whitehead, Jessica Shelton, Professor Leociak and Liz Cambers. Middle row - Melissa Query and Megan Stewart. Front - Travis Stewart.

Zakopane, Poland. 2005. **Life in a Jar** performance for the 14th Annual Conference of the Holocaust Children's Association – the Polish Child Survivors. From left to right: Elzbieta Ficowska, Jessica Shelton, Liz Cambers, Megan Stewart, Melissa Query, Travis Stewart, and Meagan Whitehead.

Liz Cambers with a rescuer she interviewed during the first visit to Poland in May 2001. He was 7 years old when his family hid three Jews in their barn.

Rabbi Michael Schudrich, chief rabbi of Poland, with Sabrina, Liz, and Megan at a performance of **Life in a Jar.** (*Photo courtesy of Kenny Felt.*)

Irena's translator and friend, Kinga Krzeminska (center), Renata Zajdman (right), saved by Irena's network, and her daughter, Sharon, during the Vermont tour of **Life in a Jar**, 2008

Elzbieta Ficowska, right, (saved by Irena) and Stefanie Seltzer, left, President of the World Federation of Jewish Child Survivors of the Holocaust. This appearance was at the national conference, honoring Irena Sendler.

Israeli stamp commemorating Irena Sendler after her death in 2008.

Child survivor Renata Zajdman and Megan (Stewart) Felt with **The Courageous Heart of Irena Sendler** movie poster—2009. *(Photo courtesy of Kenny Felt.)*

Irena with a translator, Megan Stewart, Travis Stewart, and Liz Cambers at Irena's 95th birthday party in Warsaw, 2005.

Megan Stewart, Jessica Shelton and Jaime Walker at the ZEGOTA monument in Warsaw, adjacent to the Ghetto Fighters Monument—2008.

The Warsaw Ghetto Fighters Monument, where the girls performed a scene from **Life in a Jar** for Polish television on their first visit to Poland in 2001.

EPILOGUE

What began as a National History Day project by two 14-year-olds and one 16-year-old in 1999, mushroomed into a worldwide educational enterprise to carry on Irena Sendler's legacy – to teach tolerance, respect, and understanding of all people. In their 1999 research on Irena Sendler, the Kansas students found only one internet reference to Irena Sendler – from *Yad Vashem*. Now there are thousands. There have been over 25 million hits on the **www.irenasendler.org** web site.

In 2009, Hallmark Hall of Fame produced a film, *The Courageous Heart of Irena Sendler* and presented the world première in Fort Scott, Kansas, at the Liberty Theater, as a way of honoring the *Life in a Jar* project. Mercy Hospital donated a red carpet and the local McDonald's loaned the Liberty Theater klieg lights. A local business provided limousines for the students. For the first time in the history of Hallmark productions, CEO Don Hall and his wife, Adele, attended the première, underscoring the importance of the project and the movie. Also attending were Writer-Director John Kent Harrison, Executive Producers Brent Shields and Jeff Most, and other Hallmark representatives as well as current and past cast members. The four founders, Megan, Liz, Sabrina, and Jessica were introduced. Special guest, Renata Zajdman, rescued by Irena as a child and now living in Montreal, spoke and said that Irena would have liked the film. Mr. C. received a standing ovation and shared these thoughts: "All teachers aspire to make a difference in the lives of their students and see their students make a difference in the lives of others, but this is unusual. It is to the credit of the great story of Irena Sendler. It is to the credit of these young people."

Four days later, on April 19th, the movie was broadcast across the United States on the CBS television network. *The Courageous Heart of Irena Sendler* has been honored with the 2010 Annual Christopher Award, a prestigious prize saluting producers, directors, writers, and illustrators whose work exemplifies the highest values of the human spirit.

Founders Liz Cambers-Hutton, Jessica Shelton-Ripper, and Sabrina Coons-Murphy still participate when possible in this project, and Megan (Stewart) Felt works full-time as the Program Director for the Lowell Milken Education Center – Repair the World Foundation, a new non-profit organization whose mission is to galvanize a movement for teaching respect and understanding among all people regardless of race, religion, or creed. In 2007 Norm Conard was chosen to be the Director of the Lowell Milken Center, which is currently working on 16 educational projects in the United States and 6 internationally, modeled on *The Irena Sendler Project*. Each one aims to help young people seek out and explore the histories of unsung heroes, understand their lives and aspirations, and become inspired by their deeds and their words. The students' presentations are based on high-quality research, often primary source references, to tell their vital stories.

To date, 38 students have become involved with more than 290 presentations of *Life in a Jar* in the U.S., Canada, and Poland. More than 60 schools in Poland have developed Holocaust/*Life in a Jar* projects modeled on *The Irena Sendler Project*. Several hundred U.S. schools have completed similar projects. As of February 2010 over 2,000 schools have viewed the *Life in a Jar* DVD (produced by the Milken Family Foundation) and the teacher study guide, and more than 200,000 people have seen either the play or the DVD of the play.

Kansas City friends of *The Irena Sendler Project* still play a large role. After eight years, Howard and Rosalyn (Ro) Jacobson continue to offer scholarships to deserving students in and around the Uniontown area who work on tolerance projects. Bruce and Gayle Krigel continue to host the cast of *Life in a Jar* each year and encourage them. John and Jenny Isenberg will never forget their trip to see Irena and their yearly visits with the cast. Irv Robinson cherishes his time on the journey.

Stefanie Seltzer, President of the World Federation of Jewish Child Survivors of the Holocaust, continues to support and encourage the project. Survivor Renata Zajdman, who inspired the role of the orphan in the play *Life in a Jar*, travels with the students for some presentations. Friends and neighbors from Bourbon County, Kansas take great pride in this local project which has reached around the world to such powerful effect.

Many articles have been published in newspapers and magazines in the U.S., Israel, Poland, and internationally about the "rescuers of the rescuer" – the students from Kansas. Irena Sendler has become a national hero in Poland, and there is open discussion of Poland's difficult and tragic history during WW II. Poland's national trauma is being healed by the cleansing effect of illumination and the anodyne of stories like Irena Sendler's.

Irena Sendler was nominated for the 2007 Nobel Peace Prize by the Prime Minister of Israel and the President of Poland. Jakub Jaskolowski, from the Chancellery of the President of the Republic of Poland, wrote to Norm Conard and the Kansas students:

> I would like to mention that our common efforts to nominate Irena Sendler to the Nobel Peace Prize are means to larger idea. This would be wide educational project set on against racism, anti-Semitism, and xenophobia. You and your pupils already started doing this, time for the others, and we are glad that you are with us.

In December 2009, the National Bank of Poland minted a 20 zloty coin with the images of three courageous women who saved Jews during the Holocaust: Irena Sendler, Sister Matylda Getter (who helped Irena and is a character in the play *Life in a Jar*), and ZEGOTA founder and underground leader, Zofia Kossak.

Holocaust education in the U.S. and Poland has always been a prominent aspect of *The Irena Sendler Project* in all its manifestations. A new Holocaust education DVD/study guide has been published and distributed to educators in more than 2,000 schools in the U.S. Every year the *Irena Sendler Award*, generously funded by Metuka Benjamin and the Goldrich Family Foundation, presents $10,000 to the teacher in Poland and in the U.S. who best present Holocaust education in their schools in the spirit of Irena Sendler, developing and enlisting unique and creative methodologies.

THE IRENA SENDLER AWARD RECIPIENTS

2007

Poland: Robert Szuchta – Warsaw, Poland
United States: Norman Conard – Fort Scott, Kansas

2008

Poland: Anna Kloza – Bialystok, Poland
United States: Andrew Beiter – Springville, New York

2009

Poland: Beata Maliszkiewicz – Opole, Poland
United States: Sarah Powley – West Lafayette, Indiana

POSTSCRIPT

What is the legacy of Irena Sendler? What is so engaging about *Life in a Jar* and these young people from Kansas? Most fundamentally and obviously, the *Life in a Jar* students care about this history. *The Irena Sendler Project* is a tribute to the powerful benevolence and curiosity of our young. Yet, something deeper is revealed.

History is the past, but there must be some present accounting, a critical balancing of justice and compassion, if for no other reason than for the traces that remain of that merciless history.

After the *Life in a Jar* performance at the Jewish Theater in 2005, someone in the auditorium found a fossilized remnant of WW II's brutality – a glove made of human skin. How many other grim artifacts will be uncovered? There may be many, because Poland has had to endure first fascist, then Communist, oppression – two generations of Poles deprived of discourse, expression, or reconciliation. In many other victimized nations, a successful model for preserving and healing the past – Commissions of Truth and Reconciliation – are valiant, if imperfect, efforts to shine the light of history on the travesties citizens have visited upon each other and to discover avenues of redress and forgiveness. They seek to archive and confer permanent legitimacy to the historical record so none may dispute or deny; they seek to restore civic trust and healing – to honor history. But every perpetrator cannot be tried; every hero will not be recognized. And where in our ethical regard do we hold the terrified bystander? More disturbing yet, what would each of us do in similar circumstances?

The *Life in a Jar* project, a Truth and Reconciliation Commission, a children's crusade, impossibly frail in the tempest and cacophony of the world, has been unusually successful – widening the circles of appreciation for Irena's heroism and her philosophy. The response to *Life in a Jar* in Poland has been immense, elevating Irena Sendler from an unknown to a national hero and Nobel Peace Prize nominee.

At a *Life in a Jar* presentation, Howard Cohen, the Chancellor of Purdue University-Calumet, said, "History is not history until it is written or told." This has become another motto of the *Life in a Jar* project along with *Tikkun Olam* and Michael Glowinski's tribute to the Kansas students, "You are the rescuers of the rescuer."

Life in a Jar appeals to our best instincts – our most noble intelligence – offered with simple elegance by a handful of kids from Kansas.

WHERE ARE THEY NOW?

FEBRUARY, 2010

Wednesday, September 23, 2009 marked the 10th anniversary of the beginning of *Life in a Jar* and *The Irena Sendler Project*. The legacy of Irena Sendler's story, rescued and championed by the students from Kansas, continues today. Where are they now? Here are brief bios of some of the principal participants. Over the last decade, 38 students have been involved in the project.

Megan (Stewart) Felt, founder, is a graduate of Pittsburg State University in Pittsburg, Kansas, and is program director of the Lowell Milken Education Center. In high school Megan was named a National Coca-Cola Scholar for her community service. She was also selected to the 2nd team USA Today All-American Academic Team for 2003. She was recently nominated for the BRICK award, as one of the ten outstanding young adults from the United States who is "changing the world." Megan continues to work on the project and performs in *Life in a Jar*. She travels to each presentation, works on the *Life in a Jar* DVD, does individual presentations, and stays heavily involved. She has participated in over 200 *Life in a Jar* presentations. Megan is married to Kenny Felt, a professional photographer, who has contributed his photographic skills to the project and this book. Megan played the role of Irena for many years. Irena passed away on May 12, 2008, Megan's birthday.

Elizabeth Cambers-Hutton, founder, graduated with a history degree from the College of the Ozarks in Branson, Missouri. Living four hours away from her hometown has not stopped her from continuing to spend a great deal of time working on the project she started in 1999. Liz visited Irena in Poland three times and is adamant about telling Irena's story of hope and courage. Her goal is to teach inner city high school students what she has learned, that one person can change the world. In high school she received a number of awards, including the Presidential Service award. Liz married Graham Hutton in 2007 and is currently teaching history in Lebanon, Missouri.

Sabrina Coons-Murphy, founder, visited Irena twice in Poland. She graduated from Uniontown High School and Kansas State University with a degree in elementary education and middle school mathematics, after which she taught kindergarten for two years and preschool for half a year. Sabrina and her husband Jeff have two children, Owen Warren and Aubree Lorinda. She is currently raising her children, and plans to return to teaching in the next few years.

Jessica Shelton-Ripper, founder, is from Fort Scott, Kansas and graduated from Pittsburg State University in Pittsburg, Kansas with a degree in psychology. She was born on September 11, 1984. She has participated in over 150 *Life in a Jar* presentations, has been the road manager of *The Irena Sendler Project*, and has played the role of Irena's friend and co-conspirator, Marie, in the play. Jessica placed 5th nationwide at the National History Day for her project about Corinthian Nutter, an African-American civil rights pioneer. Jessica and her husband Dallas have two children, Lillian Marie and Logan Christopher.

Travis Stewart is a graduate of Uniontown High School and Pittsburg State University in Pittsburg, Kansas, where he majored in plastics engineering. In *Life in a Jar*, Travis portrays the rescuer Dr. Wos, and a German soldier. He visited Irena in Poland during the summer of 2005 and still spends considerable time working on the project. Travis married Karlee Daylong in June, 2009.

Jaime Walker joined *The Irena Sendler Project* in November 2005 after meeting Megan Stewart in college. She visited Irena in Poland in 2008. Jaime graduated from Pittsburg State University in Pittsburg, Kansas as a business finance major in 2007 and helped establish the Lowell Milken Education Center, where she worked for two years. Jaime received her M.A. in 2009 and now works at the Federal Reserve in Kansas City. She married Mike Berndt in May, 2010.

Kinga Krzeminska, Irena Sendler's translator and friend over the last few years of her life, has been a great help to *The Irena Sendler Project* and assists the Child Survivors of the Holocaust Association in Poland. Kinga completed her Master's thesis on representations of the Holocaust in popular culture. During the summer of 2008 Kinga served an internship at the U.S. Holocaust Memorial Museum and traveled with the *Life in a Jar* cast for numerous presentations. She is now earning her doctorate from the Polish Academy of Science.

Maegan Whitehead-Easter, *Life in a Jar* cast member for four years, visited with Irena and performed in Poland in 2005. She won national awards in chemistry and Spanish and was named to the Kansas All-Academic Team. Maegan graduated as a pharmacy major from the University of Kansas and works as a pharmacist in Kansas City. She and her husband Kale have one child.

Melissa Query joined *The Irena Sendler Project* in 8th grade. She visited Irena and performed in the play in Poland in 2005. Melissa is now a university student and is married to Josh Sammons.

Kathleen Meara, a University of Kansas graduate, works at the Research and Graduate Department at the University.

Nick Thomas attends Wichita State University.

Nick Caton graduated from college, is married, and works as a Project Engineer in Kansas City.

Theresa Schafer at 15, is the youngest and newest member of the cast. She plays the orphan and has enchanted audiences with her singing of the orphan's Hebrew song.

Norm Conard taught social studies at Uniontown High School in Uniontown, Kansas for more than 20 years. A third-generation educator, his teaching style exceeds traditional classroom boundaries by encouraging his students to develop projects of tolerance and diversity. His dream and the dream of his students has been to establish a foundation to promote project based learning about unsung heroes, modeled on *The Irena Sendler Project*. Toward that end, he retired from the classroom in 2007 to found and direct the Lowell Milken

Education Center in Fort Scott, Kansas. One of his great sources of pride is having seen over 170 of his students win state history championships and 60 of his students achieve national recognition in the National History Day Competition. He has received many local, state, and national awards. "Irena Sendler has changed my life," Conard says, "and the lives of my students. She continues to make a huge difference in our world." He and his wife Karen still work with the original student founders of the project, all of whom are in their mid- to late-twenties.

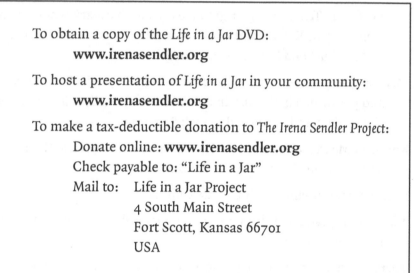

To obtain a copy of the *Life in a Jar* DVD:
   www.irenasendler.org

To host a presentation of *Life in a Jar* in your community:
   www.irenasendler.org

To make a tax-deductible donation to *The Irena Sendler Project*:
   Donate online: **www.irenasendler.org**
   Check payable to: "Life in a Jar"
   Mail to: Life in a Jar Project
               4 South Main Street
               Fort Scott, Kansas 66701
               USA

ACKNOWLEDGMENTS FROM THE IRENA SENDLER PROJECT

All the Polish heroes who helped rescue Warsaw's ghetto children could not be named in this book. They should all be honored.

These Poles, mostly poor themselves and crowded into small flats, often with children of their own, risked their lives to provide hiding places for Jews. They also gave their warm hearts to the children whose fate it was to live through hell on earth. Here is a partial listing:

Irena Sendler's "moi lacznicy" – her Social Welfare network of rescuers: Jadwiga Piotrowska, Irena Schultz, Izabela Kuczkowska, Janina Grabowska, Wanda Drozdowska, Zofia Patecka, Lucyna Franciszkiewicz, Mr. Wincenty Ferster, Roza Zawacka, and Maria Roszkowska.

Emergency Care Network: Jadwiga Bilwin, Jadwiga Deneka, Maria Kukulska, Maria Palester, Zofia Papuzinska-Wedrychowska and her husband Stanislaw Papuzinski, Janina Waldowa, Halina Nowak, Sonia Szeszko, M. Felinska, A. Adamski, and Aleksandra Dargiel, who ran the children's section of the Central Relief Agency (RGO).

The flats were often small, the children had to remain hidden during the day, and they could only be out of hiding in the darkness of night or twilight. When the children became ill, which they often did, they were cared for by physicians and nurses, including Professor A. Trojanowski (1905–1964 – a well-known surgeon), Professor Michalowicz (Professor of Pediatrics, University of Warsaw – he was in concentration camps from 1942–1945) and his daughter-in-law Dziatka Michalowicz, Dr. Zofia Franio (born 1899, who also hid Jews in her apartment), Dr. Hanka, and Dr. A. Meyer from the Old Town area. Helen Szeszko ("Sonia") served as a nurse for the hidden children.

ZEGOTA, the Council for Aid to Jews in Occupied Poland, a resistance organization (the largest in Europe) of Christian Poles who helped Jews, was the organizing model and agent of resistance in Poland – a vast conspiracy of goodness. The Poles of ZEGOTA deserve special honor. It was ZEGOTA that hid and fed Jews, gave them false identities and documents, money, food, and hope. One of ZEGOTA's heroes, not mentioned in this book, but remembered by Irena Sendler, was Emilia Hizowa, an architect, who was fascinated by secret hiding places, a fascination she put to good use as head of ZEGOTA's Housing Section, arranging for hiding places. She survived the war and employed her architectural talents to restore Old Warsaw.

★   ★   ★   ★   ★   ★   ★   ★   ★   ★

It was Irena's idea to add students (cast members) from other schools as a way of reaching out to more young people. She suggested this on the students' second trip to Poland, and it gave her great joy to see this model incorporated into *Life in a Jar*.

Life in a Jar and *The Irena Sendler Project* are the result of thousands of hours of meticulous research and time invested in telling Irena Sendler's story to the world. What follows is only a partial accounting of the commitment and tenacity of these young people from Kansas.

Present Cast Members
Project involvement hours – as of February 10, 2010

1. Megan Stewart - 4,014
2. Jessica Shelton-Ripper - 2,790
3. Liz Cambers - 2,196
4. Travis Stewart - 2,023
5. Jaime Walker - 1,768
6. Sabrina Coons - 1,230
7. Kenny Felt - 441
8. Beth Perrey - 438
9. Kinga Krzeminska (Poland)- 418
10. Theresa Schafer - 365

11. Patricia Schafer - 297
12. Nathan Davolt - 133

All-time cast members
On the basis of hours involved as of February 10, 2010

1. Megan Stewart (Present cast member)
2. Jessica Shelton (Present cast member)
3. Liz Cambers (Present cast member)
4. Travis Stewart (Present cast member)
5. Jaime Walker (Present cast member)
6. Melissa Query
7. Sabrina Coons (Present cast member)
8. Maegan Easter
9. Kathleen Meara
10. Nicholas Thomas
11. Jaime Shelton
12. Janice Underwood
13. Lacey George
14. Ellie Perrey
15. Kenny Felt (Present cast member)
16. Beth Perrey (Present cast member)
17. Kinga Krzeminska (Poland – Present cast member)
18. Theresa Schafer (Present cast member)
19. Gage McKinnis
20. Gabe Bradbury
21. Patricia Schafer (Present cast member)
22. Lacy Ermel
23. Kayla Wagner
24. Andrea Wynn
25. Nick Caton
26. Candice Lowry
27. Jessie Shadden
28. Nathan Davolt (Present cast member)

29. Rebekah DeMoss
30. Dallas Ripper
31. Kayla Burress
32. Kalisa Erny
33. Katja Baar (international exchange student)
34. Robert Ellis
35. Kate Spainhoward
36. Conor Stephens
37. Kale Easter
38. Chase Ermel

Many other students in Bourbon County and Eastern Kansas have participated in this project, and they should all be recognized for spreading Irena Sendler's legacy. They built an archive of thousands of pages of research, written and compiled, about Irena Sendler. Listed here are the top eighteen:

Megan Stewart, Jessica Shelton, Liz Cambers, Travis Stewart, Jaime Walker, Melissa Query, Sabrina Coons, Maegan Easter, Kathleen Meara, Nicholas Thomas, Jaime Shelton, Janice Underwood, Lacey George, Kenny Felt, Kinga Krzeminska (Poland), Ellie Perrey, Gage McKinnis, Theresa Schafer.

Parents and family of the *Life in a Jar* cast gave their time, encouragement, and generosity to further this project. They have been vital to its success and we thank them. We also acknowledge and honor the people of the Uniontown and Fort Scott communities who supported the project in so many ways, among them Danny and Willa Ellis and Jim and Paulette Smith.

National History Day has had a long and fruitful presence in Uniontown High School's social studies classroom, producing over 100 diversity projects.

Deep appreciation and thanks to Andrea Smith, who has volunteered uncounted hours as *The Irena Sendler Project* webmaster (**www.irenasendler.org**). We are so grateful for her expertise and dedication.

From the very beginning, *Life in a Jar* has been honored to receive the friendship and generous financial support of benefactors such as Howard and Rosalyn (Ro) Jacobson, Gayle and Bruce Krigel (Gayle organized the *Tikkun Olam* banquet on March 10, 2002, which honored Irena Sendler and the Kansas students), John and Jenny Isenberg, John Shuchart, Irv Robinson and many others. They have funded the students' trips to Poland, created scholarships for those involved with diversity and tolerance projects, and befriended and hosted the students and their families.

Lowell Milken has been an enthusiastic supporter of the work of *Life in a Jar* and The Irena Sendler Foundation. He has funded the creation of the Lowell Milken Center (**www.lowellmilkencenter.org**) in Fort Scott, Kansas to further project-based learning about unsung heroes in the fashion of *The Irena Sendler Project*. We are especially indebted to the efforts of Dr. Jane Foley in creating the Lowell Milken Center and Stephanie Bishop for her theatrical assistance in producing the *Life in a Jar* DVD that has been distributed to over 2,000 schools. The *Life in a Jar* DVD can be obtained from **www.irenasendler.org**

Megan Stewart's husband, Kenny Felt (**www.kennyfelt.com**) has given generously of his professional photographic talents to document *Life in a Jar* and *The Irena Sendler Project*. Some of his photographs are in this book.

Scott and Amy Karlen and their girls from Florida have been active supporters of the project, and their assistance is deeply appreciated.

Life in a Jar: The Irena Sendler Project could not have been possible without the devotion, hard work, and hospitality of all the wonderful people who volunteer their time, share their homes, and continue to spread Irena Sendler's legacy. Though they are too numerous to mention, the project honors them and treasures their contributions always.

★　★　★　★　★　★　★　★　★　★

The *Life in a Jar* students have visited Poland six times through 2009, and we are indebted to our Polish friends, many of whom were rescued by Irena or have become her friends over the years. Some appear in this book. Elzbieta Ficowska and her late husband, Jerzy Ficowski, Renata Zajdman, Jacek Leociak, Michael Glowinski, Hanna Piotrowska-Rechowiczowa, Janka Zgrzembska (Irena's daughter), Agnieszka Zgrzembska (Irena's granddaughter), Piotr Zettinger, Yale Reisner, Wladyslaw Bartoszewski, Ludwik and Barbara Stawowy (translators in Poland), Tomasz and Tosia Kasprzak (translators in Poland and welcome to their two new daughters, Helena and Marianna), Kinga Krzeminska (Irena's translator), Anna Maria Karasinska Cook (translator in the U.S.), Thomasz Szarota, Anna Trojanowska (translator in Cracow), Michael Traison, Andrzej and Ania Ficowska-Teodorowicz (Bieta's daughter and son-in-law), Ewa Wierzynska, and Jadwiga Zynek.

Elzbieta Ficowska, rescued by Irena as a six-month-old, now the president of the Children of the Holocaust Organization in Poland, was active in Irena's care. She has been a gracious host and generous supporter of *Life in a Jar* in Poland and helped Irena plan for the students' visits. Bieta works to bring tolerance studies to schools throughout Poland, where she speaks out for remembering the Holocaust, caring for the survivors, and preserving the stories of rescuers and survivors. She is a powerful voice for "repairing the world." Her daughter, Ania Ficowska-Teodorowicz and Ania's husband Andrzej, who hosted the *Life in a Jar* group several times in Poland, are valued friends of the *Life in a Jar* students. Ania has visited Uniontown, and the entire family plans a future trip. Their two sons, Carl and Phillip, are favorites of the students.

Renata Zajdman survived the war in the streets of Warsaw until she was rescued by Irena and the underground ZEGOTA. She has visited Kansas and participated in *Life in a Jar* presentations in the U.S. and Canada, where she lives. Renata is the inspiration for the part of the orphan in the play.

Stefanie Seltzer and René Lichtman, President and Vice President respectively of the World Federation of Jewish Child Survivors of the Holocaust, have been generous hosts for *Life in a Jar* at various venues in Poland and the United States. Stefanie and René care deeply that the world learns the stories of child survivors. Stefanie has been with the *Life in a Jar* students on a number of occasions, spent time with Irena, is a close friend of Elzbieta Ficowska and Renata Zajdman, and has great energy for telling the story of Irena Sendler and other rescuers. Her and René's work with the World Federation and their dynamic publication is an inspiration.

We also thank the Polish chapter of the World Federation of Jewish Child Survivors of the Holocaust for its generous support and for inviting *Life in a Jar* to its 2005 conference in Zakopane, Poland.

Rabbi Michael Schudrich, Chief Rabbi of Poland, has been a good friend of Irena and the *Life in a Jar* students. He has been to several presentations, both in the U.S. and in Poland, and always meets with the *Life in a Jar* cast when they visit Poland. Rabbi Schudrich is an active participant in the Irena Sendler Award and promotes Holocaust education in Polish schools.

Agnieszka Zgrzembska, Irena Sendler's lovely granddaughter, is the same age as the girls who founded *Life in a Jar*. She was present at several events during *Life in a Jar* trips to Poland. She was very special to her grandmother and is always a part of the Irena Sendler Award to Teachers ceremony.

Stanlee Stahl and the Jewish Foundation for the Righteous that she directs connected the students with Irena at the very start of the project and continued supporting her, as they do other Righteous Gentiles, until she died.

Bozenna Gilbride, who wrote and produced two films about ZEGOTA, has been a consistent friend and supporter of the project. Marcel Fremder, a child survivor, has also been a dear friend and supporter in the United States.

AUTHOR'S ACKNOWLEDGEMENTS

Here is a ghost story.

On a cold night in February, 2004, I came into my pediatric office to see a patient. On my desk was a copy of the December 2003 *Ladies' Home Journal*, opened to the article "The Woman Who Loved Children" by Marti Attoun about Irena Sendler and the Kansas teens. I don't keep the *Ladies' Home Journal* in my waiting room. To this day I don't know who left that article for me to find, but it launched me on the journey that led to *Life in a Jar: The Irena Sendler Project*.

Who are you?

★　★　★　★　★　★　★　★　★　★

I could not have written this book without Norm Conard and his students from Kansas, Megan (Stewart) Felt, Liz Cambers-Hutton, Sabrina Coons-Murphy, and Jessica Shelton-Ripper, who are agents of this history. They gave me hours of interviews, provided photographs, answered my questions with patience and grace, and contributed constructive feedback.

Thanks to Karen Conard, a warm and gracious host, who made me feel welcome during my visits to Kansas, and to Bill Cambers, Liz's grandfather, who gave me an unforgettable tour of Fort Scott.

I am deeply indebted to Professor Jacek Leociak, who has demonstrated a profound interest in *The Irena Sendler Project*. He is a leading Polish voice for historical integrity – for remembrance, for truth, and for reconciliation. On one unforgettable day with Professor Leociak in 2005, walking the Warsaw streets where the ghetto once stood, he noted, "Incredibly, except for a few scholarly exceptions, there is no complete Polish history of the Warsaw ghetto." That has now been corrected by the publication of his book *The Warsaw Ghetto: A Guide to the Perished City*, written with co-author Barbara Engelking (Yale University Press, July 2009). Professor Leociak mentions two other important books: one by Israeli historian Yisrael Gutman, *The Jews of Warsaw. 1939-1943: Ghetto, Underground, Revolt*, translated from Hebrew by Ina Friedman (Bloomington, Indiana University Press, 1982); and another by Polish historian Ruta Sakowska, *Ludzie z Dzielnicy Zamkni te [The People From the Closed District]*, I ed. 1975, II ed. 1993.

There are no words to describe how important my wife, Chip, has been to this book. She has been my 1st, 2nd, 3rd, ... and last reader, and I esteem her eagle eye, her ear for language, and her editorial judgment. My gratitude and love is deep and wide.

Chip and I extend special thanks to Ludwik Stawowy for his friendship and assistance to us during our 2005 visit to Poland.

I owe abundant thanks to Eva Garcelon, faithful friend and Polish translator, who spent hours translating Polish texts and articles, including the most authoritative text, written with Irena Sendler, by Anna Mieszkowska and Janina Zgrzembska, and published by MUZA. Not only did Eva help me understand Polish culture, holidays, idiomatic expressions, etc., she has also been a valued reader of several drafts of the manuscript. Eva assisted with the Vermont tour of *Life in a Jar* in October 2008, during which she assembled and curated an exquisite collection of Warsaw ghetto paintings by Wladyslaw Brzosko, an eyewitness to the Ghetto Uprising and its annihilation.

A heartfelt thank you to my dear friend Jean Shappee, who drove the students all over Vermont during their 2008 tour, showering them with her faithful assistance and loving presence.

I have been privileged to benefit from the editorial talents of novelist Michael Lowenthal. His grandfather was born in Poland, and Michael understands this history from the heart.

I am blessed with a community of insightful readers and friends, willing to review and comment on drafts of the manuscript. These include Priscilla Baker, Margie Beckoff, Carol Crawford, Susan DeWind, David Gusakov, Mary Kellington, Margaret Olson, David Rosenberg, Jean Shappee, Eva Simon, Ron Slabaugh, Anne Wallace, Adam Woods, and Alex Wylie.

My long time friend Win Colwell, a book designer in Middlebury, gave of his heart, imagination, and technical expertise to fashion this book with care.

Thank you, Amy Graham, my trusty copyeditor. You fixed an awful lot of commas.

And appreciation to Stacey Rheaume and Hannah Minton, my Xerox angels.

BIBLIOGRAPHY

AUTHOR INTERVIEWS:

Interviews with Irena Sendler
Interview with Irena's daughter, Janina Grzybowska
Interview with Hanna Piotrowska-Rechowiczowa, daughter of Irena's co-conspirator Jadwiga Piotrowska. Hanna was 12 years old when she watched Irena and her mother bury the jars with the children's names under the apple tree in her back yard at Lekarska #9, where she still lives today.

Interviews with the Founders from Kansas:
Norm Conard
Elizabeth Cambers (and her grandparents, Bill and Phyllis Cambers)
Megan Stewart (and her parents, Mark and Debra Stewart)
Sabrina Coons
Jessica Shelton

Interviews with other participating Kansas students:
Jaime Walker
Travis Stewart
Melissa Query (and her parents)

Interviews with child survivors rescued from the Warsaw ghetto:
Elzbieta Ficowska
Michael Glowinski
Renata Zajdman
Leah Balint

Interviews with Polish academics:
Michael Glowinski – rescued by Irena Sendler, professor of literature at the Polish Academy of Sciences and a well known writer.
Jan Jagielski – Director, Jewish Historical Institute, Warsaw
Jacek Leociak – Professor, noted authority on the history of the Warsaw ghetto.

Interviews with Poles:
Ada (Szymanska) Boddy – Child survivor
Rena Szymanska – Child survivor
Michael Schudrich – Chief Rabbi of Poland
Ludwik Stawowy – friend of Irena and her family

Michael Traison – attorney in Warsaw
Jadwiga Zynek – Friend of Irena

United States interviews:
Randy Rockhold – Superintendent of Schools, Uniontown Kansas District
Howard and Rosalyn Jacobson – Kansas City Philanthropists
Bruce and Gayle Kriegel – Kansas City Philanthropists
Bart Altenbernd – Former Principal, Uniontown High School

OTHER INTERVIEWS WITH IRENA SENDLER:

Mieszkowska, Anna and Zgrzembska, Janina. *Matka Dzieci Holocaustu: Historia Ireny Sendlerowej*. Warsaw, Poland: Warszawskie Wydawnictwo Literackie MUZA SA, 2004.

Zajdman, Renata. *Interview with Irena Sendler – Warsaw, 1999*. World Federation of Jewish Child Survivors of the Holocaust. 1999.

Documentary Film: Dudziewicz, Michael. *Sendler's List*. 2002. Special Jury Prize, Stockholm International Documentary Film Festival. 2003.

Documentary Film: Nockowoska, Maria. *The Visit*. Polish State Television documentary about the *Life in a Jar* students during their 2005 visit to Poland. 2005.

PRINCIPAL SOURCES:

Ackerman, Diane. *The Zookeeper's Wife*. W.W. Norton & Co., New York, 2007.

Attoun, Marti. The Woman Who Loved Children. *Ladies' Home Journal*. December 2003, p. 94-105.

Bartoszewski, Wladyslaw and Lewin, Zofia. *Righteous Among Nations: How Poles Helped the Jews – 1939-1945*. Earlscourt Publications LTD, London, 1969.

Chesnoff, Richard. "The Other Schindlers." *U.S. News & World Report*. March 21, 1994, p. 56-64.

Czerniakow, Adam. *The Warsaw Diary of Adam Czerniakow*. Ed. Hilberg, R, Staron, S, Kermisz, J. Yad Vashem, Jerusalem, 1968.

Davies, Norman. *Rising '44: The Battle for Warsaw*. Viking, Penguin Group, New York, 2003.

Gross, Jan T. *FEAR: Anti-Semitism in Poland After Auschwitz*. Random House, New York, 2006.

Gross, Jan T. *Neighbors: The Destruction of the Jewish community in Jedwabne, Poland*. Princeton Univ. Press, New Jersey, 2001.

Grupinska, A., Jagielski, J., and Szapiro, P. *Warsaw Ghetto*. Parma Press, Warsaw, Poland, 2004.

Grynberg, M, ed. *Words To Outlive Us: Voices from the Warsaw Ghetto.* Translated by Philip Boehm, Henry Holt and Co., New York, 2002.

Gutman, Yisrael. *The Jews of Warsaw, 1939-1943: Ghetto, Underground, Revolt.* Indiana University Press, Bloomington, 1982.

Jagielski, Jan. *Jewish Sites in Warsaw.* Jewish Historical Institute, Warsaw, 2002.

Kacyzne, Alter. *Polyn: Jewish Life in the Old Country.* Edited by Marek Web. Henry Holt & Co., New York, 1999.

Kaplan, Chaim A. *Scroll of Agony: The Warsaw Diary of Chaim A. Kaplan.* Translated by Abraham I. Katrsch, Simon & Schuster Inc., New York, 1965.

Kassow, Samuel. "A Stone Under History's Wheel: The Story of Emanuel Ringelblum and the *Oneg Shabes* Archive." *Pakn Treger, Magazine of the National Yiddish Book Center.* p. 14-23, Amherst, MA, 2003.

Keneally, Thomas. *Schindler's List.* Simon & Schuster, New York, 1982.

Korczak, Janusz. *Ghetto Diary.* Yale University Press, New Haven, 2003.

Leociak, Jacek. *Text in the Face of Destruction: Accounts from the Warsaw Ghetto Reconsidered.* Translated by Emma Harris. Zydowski Instytut Historyczny, Warsaw, 2004.

Lifton, Betty Jean. *The King of Children: A Biography of Janusz Korczak.* Schocken books, New York, 1988.

Ringelblum, Emmanuel. *Notes from the Warsaw Ghetto: The Journal of Emmanuel Ringelblum.* Translated by Jacob Sloan. McGraw-Hill, New York, 1958.

Roland, Charles. *Courage Under Siege: Starvation, Disease, and Death in the Warsaw Ghetto.* Oxford University Press, New York, 1992.

Sendler, Irena. "The Valor of the Young." *Dimensions: A Journal of Holocaust Studies.* 1993; vol. 7, no. 2, p. 20-25.

Sendler, Irena. "Actions of Youth in the House Committees of Warsaw Ghetto." *Bulletin of the Jewish Historical Institute.* Vol. 118, no. 2, 1981.

Szpilman, Wladyslaw. *The Pianist: The Extraordinary True Story of One Man's Survival in Warsaw, 1939-1945.* Translated by Anthea Bell, Picador, New York, 1999.

Tomaszewski, Irene and Werbowski, Tecia. *Zegota: The Council for Aid to Jews in Occupied Poland, 1942-1945.* Price-Patterson LTD., Montreal, 1994.

Yitzhak, Arad. *Belzec, Sobibor, Treblinka: The Operation Reinhard Death Camps.* Indiana Univ. Press, Bloomington, 1987.

ADDITIONAL SOURCES:

Berg, Mary (pseudonym). *Warsaw Ghetto: A Diary.* S. L. Shneiderman, ed. Prepared by Norbert Guterman and Sylvia Glass. New York: L. B. Fischer Publishing Corporation, 1945.

Davies, Norman. *God's Playground: A History of Poland.* Columbia Univ. Press, New York 1982.

Davies, Norman. *Heart of Europe: A Short History of Poland* Clarendon Press, Oxford, 1984.

Dwork, Deborah, ed. *Voices & Views: A History of the Holocaust*. The Jewish Foundation for the Righteous, New York, 2002.

Dwork, Deborah. *Children With a Star: Jewish Youth in Nazi Europe*. Yale University Press, New Haven, 1991

Dwork, Deborah and van Pelt, Robert. *Holocaust: A History*. W.W. Norton & Co., New York, 2002.

Frank, Anne. *Anne Frank: The Diary of a Young Girl*. Doubleday & Co., New York, 1952.

Gilbert, Martin. *The Righteous: The Unsung Heroes of the Holocaust*. Henry Holt and Co., New York. 2003.

Gilbert, Martin. *A History of the Twentieth Century: Vol. 2: 1933-1951*. Avon Books, New York, 1998.

Gilbert, Martin. *The Holocaust: A History of the Jews of Europe During the Second World War*. Henry Holt and Co., New York, 1985.

Hersey, John. *The Wall*. Alfred A. Knopf., New York, 1950.

Jerzy, L. and Sawadzki H. *A Concise History of Poland*. Cambridge Univ. Press, Cambridge, UK 2001.

Kazik (Rotem, Simha). *Kazik: Memoirs of a Warsaw Ghetto Fighter*. Yale University Press, New Haven, 1994.

Korbonski, Stefan. *Fighting Warsaw: The Story of the Polish Underground State 1939-1945*. Macmillan, New York, 1956.

Krall, Hanna. *Shielding The Flame: An Intimate Conversation with Dr. Marek Edelman, the Last Surviving Leader of the Warsaw Ghetto Uprising*. Translated by Joanna Stasinska and Lawrence Weschler, Henry Holt & Co., New York, 1986.

Kumove, Shirley. *Words Like Arrows: A Collection of Yiddish Folk Sayings*. University of Toronto Press, 1984.

Kurek, Ewa. *Your Life is Worth Mine: How Polish Nuns Saved Hundreds of Jewish Children in German-Occupied Poland, 1939-1945*. Hippocrene Books, New York, 1997

Kurzman, Dan. *The Bravest Battle: The Twenty-eight Days of the Warsaw Ghetto Uprising*. Putnam, New York, 1976.

Michener, James A. *Poland*. Ballantine Publishing Group, New York, 1984.

Shirer, William L. *The Rise and Fall of the Third Reich – Vol. I and II*. Simon & Schuster, New York, 1959, 1960.

Shirer, William L. *Berlin Diary*. Alfred A. Knopf, Inc., New York, 1941.

Spiegelman, Art. *MAUS: A Survivor's Tale*. Pantheon Books, New York, 1973.

Stewart, Gale. *Life in the Warsaw Ghetto*. Lucent Books, San Diego, 1995.

Uris, Leon. *Mila 18*. Doubleday, New York, 1961.

CPSIA information can be obtained
at www.ICGtesting.com
Printed in the USA
BVHW030533180223
658665BV00001B/68